LIVING WITH A 98-YEAR-OLD ROCKET SCIENTIST:

M*ISTER* B.

LYNN BYK

WITH JOSEPH BYK

~

Large Print Edition
10 9 8 7 6 5 4 3 2
Names: Byk, Lynn.
Title: Mister b: Living with a 98-year-old rocket scientist/ Lynn Byk. Joseph John Byk
   Description: Littleton, Colorado : Capture Books,[2018] | Includes index.
   Identifiers: LCCN: 016901273 | ISBN 0997162503 (CS)
   978-0-9971625-6-1 (hard cover) | ISBN 13: 9780997162509 (large print) |
   ISBN 978-0-9971625-1-6 (ebook)
   Subjects: LCSH: Byk, Joseph John. | Aging parents-Family relationships. |
   Engineers-Family relationships. | Older men-Family relationships. |
   Intergenerational relations.
   Classification: LCC HQ1063.6 .B95 2018 (print) |
   LCC HQ1063.6 (ebook) | DDC 306.8740846-dc23

HUMOR/RELATIONSHIPS
BIOGRAPHY/MEMOIR/GREATEST GENERATION/AEROSPACE
NONFICTION > PHILOSOPHY > EPISTEMOLOGY
PARENTING/FATHERHOOD

Copyright © 2018
Capture Books
5856 S. Lowell Blvd, Suite #32-202
Littleton, Colorado 80123
www.CaptureMeBooks.com
Facebook/Capture Books
Twitter and Facebook/Lynn Byk Author
All rights reserved.
Cover: Kathryn K. Swezy
Interior photos are family possessions.
They are Mr. B's personal mementos of his life and work.
Do not reproduce any part of this book
without permission from the publisher
ISBN 978-0-9971625-6-1 (hard cover).
ISBN-10: 1516845293
ISBN 13: 9780997162509 (large print)
ISBN 978-0-9971625-1-6 (ebook)

DEDICATION

This book showers honor and humor onto all of Mr. B's grandchildren:
Sandy, Jamie, Jessica and James, Jimmy and Guida. It is consigned to the safekeeping of the would-be scientists who refuse to allow passion to dictate evidence,
and to those who learn from history, negotiate politics, and tenaciously shadow their heroes,
following paths of energy and numbers in space.

Disclaimer

The views and conclusions contained herein should not be interpreted as representing the opinions or policies of the US Government, ethnic groups, clubs, religions or corporations within the United States. Mention of trade names or commercial products does not constitute an endorsement by the US Government, Capture Books, or by this author.

"Life is mostly froth and bubble,
Two things stand like stone –
Kindness in another's trouble,
Courage in your own."
— Adam L. Gordon

~

"Through wisdom your days will be many,
and years will be added to your life…
By wisdom a house is built, by understanding it is
established; And by knowledge the rooms are filled
with all
precious and pleasant riches."
— King Solomon

CONTENTS

	Preface	10
1	THE OL' MAN	13
2	AUGUST ~ DISSEMBLE	40
3	SEPTEMBER ~ THIN GRINS	56
4	OCTOBER ~ OCTAVES	115
5	NOVEMBER ~ NESTING	167
6	DECEMBER ~ DECIBELS	197
7	JANUARY ~ JERRY RIGGED	238
8	FEBRUARY ~ FAHRENHEITS	273
9	MARCH ~ MOMENTUM	303
10	APRIL ~ INTERSECTIONS	327
11	MAY ~ BOUQUETS	348
12	JUNE ~ JOY	382
13	JULY ~ REJOINED	417
14	IN RETROSPECT	439
	ACKNOWLEDGMENTS	452
	BOOK CLUB QUESTIONS	456

PREFACE

An adversary could not make me swear in a court of law that what I have written on these pages is absolute fact. I believe fact and truth can sometimes be confused. While a journalist is an ethical creature aiming at facts, and a five-fingered handful will do, a storyteller is a moralist character aiming to impart some truth, though in doing so, the tweaking of facts is occasionally required.

In fact, these stories comprise a period of two years, rather than the detailed year-ish diary I have set forth. There were the first three months in which I observed Mister B's interests, tested him with questions, and jotted down journal entries. These provided me with enough good historical and scientific fact to turn my head and ply my ear. Some people necessarily repeat themselves so as to be heard by others or, perhaps, to steady themselves in a spinning world. Yet when I was growing irritable, then beside myself, with the idea of spending all my days listening to the repetitious stories of a presumably needy old man, I began to notice him adding new details on occasion, and new correlations to current circumstances, so that a life history and scientific career were being declared in such a way that dictation was made possible. Also, Mister B turned out *not* so needy.

Spurred into becoming a discrete note taker, recording the distinct timbre of my father-in-law's articulation, his scientific calculations, wry humor and the colloquialisms from the Greatest Generation, the idea of writing a memoir of our time spent together came into being.

It's true, however, that for me to tell a story in the fashion of historical truth, sporting the kind of humor people like to read, I had to adapt the timing of some events, change names to protect the innocent, and also recolor some voices to better illustrate tension and relief. To that end, my rascally protagonist might well ask, "Whose truth is this, yours or mine?"

I attribute the quality of disclosures and camaraderie enjoyed here to Mr. Byk, who was a pragmatic and hospitable host to my husband and me, and because he had a fine sense of self-editing that took the burden of awkward conversations about his limitations of aging from our shoulders. When he could no longer drive or cook, he didn't argue, complain or critique. His demeanor was mostly gracious and grateful, keeping feelings concerning that acute loss of autonomy to himself. His lack of sentimentality or acting victimized allowed me to fill in the emotional gaps as I was able. I'm not sure I could have been as happy a caregiver to someone who presented a bitter, controlling or critical persona.

Before Mister B's wife, Maudie, passed in 2009, the couple had included us in their process of looking at retirement or an assisted living home, but in each case, they had preferred to stay put at home. When she died, we asked my father-in-law if he would like to live in the main floor guest room of our home. He declined, though he had often mentioned that he liked the view of our garden from the room. Instead, he determined to live on his own, eating boiled hot dogs, shrimp, and eggs, with the occasional Braunschweiger sandwich, or a can of sardines decorated with blue cheese for meals.

He lived alone and drove as needed from age 92 to 97, which is an extraordinary age to have your driver's license and wits about you!

My husband and I watched his father growing more disconnected from friends and family while staying in his home, and Mister B also started getting rather confused in his conversations with us in our once per week visits. We bought him a cell phone, but he could never remember how to use it. He also forgot how to use his house phone.

When he walked, he wobbled so much that we enticed him to let us put his bed on the main floor so that he didn't have to risk coming down the stairs. He joked in return that he would slide down the stairs on his rear-end if it got that bad.

There came a day in the summer of 2013 when we decided to downsize and to look for a temporary home in my father-in-law's neighborhood so that I could simply check in on him on a daily basis. When we broached the subject of our intent and showed him a house we were considering, it took less than a week for him to suggest that we should rather move in "wid the ol' man."

In any serious relationship, the surprise of good humor is the up-sweep to making love soar. To exemplify this bigger-than-life concept, I'll tell you this. I had been journaling, really writing, this book for well over a year, dreading the thought of having to divulge to him the aim of publishing his memoirs, when I finally determined to address it. He and I were coming home from an early eye doctor's appointment followed by a late brunch together, sitting fat and sassy from the rewards; he, beside me in the front seat of my car, was adjusting and readjusting his temporary plastic eye screen. The dark screen scraped repeatedly over a burn wound on his face from a "barnacle" frozen off a few days earlier. I knew it had to be painful.

"I have a proposition for you, Mr. B."

"Oh, I don't want to go anywhere else just now, Sweet Pea. You've already given me a full day, and I don't feel I should go looking for trouble. I'd rather just sit in the dark at home and listen to music."

"Let your pupils return to normal?"

"Yes, Ma'am."

"You don't think trouble can find you in your own living

room?" I rib him.

"Well, of course, when you bring in that gospel stuff, trouble finds me all right."

"Actually, I have a different kind of proposition, which may become another kind of trouble for you."

"Really? I can hardly believe it!" He turns to me all darkly spotted with frozen barnacles and blind.

"Yes, and you can say 'no'." Although now, even under a cloudless autumn sky, I experience a visceral fear that his disagreement would mortally pierce me should he actually reject the idea. "Uh, I am wondering if you would mind... if, I wrote a book based on your life and our conversations, you know, the things you've told me." I focus on the horizon and brace myself for the worst, hoping to God he won't think I've cared for him all this time only to objectify him.

"Well, I'll tell ya, Kiddo, I don't mind one bit because I can't see that anyone would want to read it!" (His voice propels irony but contains no real exclamatory inflection) "I'm no hero. I'm nobody special." He adjusted his sun guard over his wounded face again. "Besides, I have thought about you writing down the things I was telling you, and wondered. I told you that around the time I retired, I thought about writing a math book for stress engineers? And, you know, Maudie's fathea – (in keeping with the accent of his eastern seaboard upbringing, he drops the 'r') – her fathea wrote down his life, and nobody but the family read it. Heh! Maybe some of them didn't bother to read it."

"I think you're a pretty interesting guy, Mr. B, so I'd like to give it a shot." My spirits were rocketed, up, up into the stratosphere with his release.

He pats my leg. "We get along fine, don't we." It's not a question. "Thanks for taking me out for breakfast. It kinda lifts an ol' man's spirits, you might say."

"Sorrow prepares you for joy. It violently sweeps everything out of your house, so that new joy can find space to enter. It shakes the yellow leaves from the bough of your heart, so that fresh, green leaves can grow in their place. It pulls up the rotten roots, so that new roots hidden beneath have room to grow. Whatever sorrow shakes from your heart, far better things will take their place."
— Jalaluddin Rumi

THE OL' MAN

Memorial Day, 2013
It's four o'clock in the afternoon, time for us to visit Joseph John Byk. I climb into the passenger side of my husband Paul's big boy Tonka truck. My hubster received this 1977 F-150 industrial yellow pickup from his parents on his fiftieth birthday. Now, at age 58, he's still a big toddler zooming about with a toy truck in hand. This time, however, he gets to ride inside of his Ford collector series. *Does sex make Paul as happy as his industrial yellow truck?* I wonder. He muscles it around hairpin curves in the mountains. He makes up chores just to drive the junkyard canister around town, and he limps it the three blocks to work and back when his legs are giving him fits. It isn't that I haven't enjoyed playing farm girl in his yellow truck, propelling it for construction or landscaping needs, yet it's *waaaay* down on my list of "best consumer picks," mostly because the roar of the engine always shocks me, and because the passenger's side of the long cab seat slopes into Neverland. Of course normally, I am the passenger trying to hold onto my seat.

"We're taking your dad's car to dinner." This, I pronounce as a flat humorless order as I work open the side vent. Even under the friendly puffy clouds, it feels like the heat of summer already; but that's Colorado for you.

"I know," my husband returns cheerfully. "He won't mind. I just wanna unwind on the way over, okay?"

We've planned to take Mr. B–Mr. B being the nickname his

wife gave him–to dinner at the Garden Club.

He has not been shy about criticizing our any number of other personal choices for outings in the history of our relationship, so we stick to his way now-a-days. The Garden Club is his favorite restaurant, I surmise, because the cashier honors his senior coupons for all three of us or okay, because, he can top off his salad with as many bowls full of tapioca as he likes. He's not used to being told "No". Once, he told me that his marriage consisted of "sixty-seven years of getting my own way". He is not only the headwaters of the family, but he is what I call a brainiac, or more particularly, a retired aerospace engineer.

His dour demeanor in every family photograph depicts a man who has struggled for himself, and who has not particularly enjoyed the journey. Perhaps because he has made himself useful at holiday gatherings, or maybe because he has brought me flowers from his garden, or even because I have always found his way of thinking interesting, we have gotten along well. I can't say as much for his relationships with his son, daughter, or late wife. He is of the age where "providing a living" and surviving politics at work are the marks of success. Life is full of mysteries.

At the top of a curved suburban street, full of houses built in the '70s, my own father-in-law's two-story, reverse-gabled home comes into view. It sports an exterior color of today's unsure Colorado sky. I sigh. Pulling into the concrete drive, my soul quietly curses the appearance of the outmoded facade decorated with a giant X under both of the front bedroom windows. The X's appear like a boxer's puffy face after a match, with two widespread black eyes.

"X marks the spot!" Paul announces. The worn family joke gripes me.

Paul's father is waiting inside, seated in his favorite blue velvet rocker, arms crossed. Tonight he's wearing a pink and teal plaid shirt, blanketed with the light blue fleece we gave him last year, decked on top of his navy blue dress pants. I've seen Mr. B's muscles, sinewy thin. He is altogether on the petite size, but we never let on that he should wear less than a large shirt.

When he sees us walk into his domain, he pulls up his pant leg and sticks out his bird ankle so that we can admire his colorful, striped, cotton knee sock. Thus, he continues to affirm my style choices. Nearing Christmas a year and a half ago, I determined to fulfill Mr. B's meager solicitation for warm knee-high socks. To my dismay, it became apparent that men's knee-highs were out of fashion. Shopping, admittedly, is not my forte, but I had finally located a couple pairs of Pippi Longstocking socks. After buying them, I stumbled upon a tuxedo store selling men's silk knee-highs for a penny prettier that we could really afford. In the end, I stuffed three pairs of them into his Christmas package with the other two pairs of the riskier, striped, long-stockings. As a back door, if he hated them, I'd planned to tell him that they were a joke. To my relief, Mr. B was delighted with all of the socks, but mostly, he got the Christmas jollies from the colorful striped ones. He wears them fashionably under his blue dress pants or his summer Khakis.

"You still wearing those crazy things?" I tease. "Aren't you hot?"

"No, ma'am," Joe shakes his head quickly. "I keep it cool in here."

I look at his thermostat which says "76" in bold letters.

June 20, 2013

First, I must drag myself away from the ongoing minutia to head over to Joe's again. Paperwork swaddles my life like cloth on a mummy. I've been trying to get our silent and deflective insurance company to pay the damages promised in our umbrella policy. Paul's been helping in hiccups, but he's mainly been transplanting bushes to reestablish "curb appeal" at our war-weary hospitality house.

At Joe's, I lay a card on the dining room table while explaining in a loud voice that we can all write something to his great-granddaughter who is spending her summer far away at camp.

"Oh, no. What do I say to a nine-year-old girl?" he asks behind a wrinkled brow. "I don't think that asking her to write a *letter to me* will help her penmanship. I think that she ought to be journaling in a diary all the things she gets to do, like horseback riding and acrobatics, and the dog training that she's learning."

"Go ahead. Why don't you suggest that she begin a diary, Mr. B?"

"I'll get around to it." He sighs and pushes the card away from him over his dining room table.

Joe takes the dinner conversation way back to his old workplace, explaining to us the difference between titanium and steel bolts on a project he once analyzed. Pauly and I look at each other impatiently, wondering once again how to respond to a rocket scientist.

He begins by telling us that at one point in his career, his services were loaned out to McDonnell Aircraft for a rocket capsule project. "First, they asked me to figure out what was going wrong because the capsule kept separating from the rocket shaft in simulated flight. Then, they showed me the blueprints, and later they took me to the actual capsule itself.

"Well, I had to assess the drawing specifications to see if they were correctly engineered. Then, I had to compare the L-brackets they had installed all the way around the shaft to hold the capsule and shaft together." His finger makes a circle platform in the air. He explains this dilemma as if we need to know such details for work in our world. He explains it visually, folding his table napkin into a two thirds angle like an L, thumping the base of it with his forefinger to show us where the bolt went in.

Though he quit smoking cigarettes cold turkey at age fifty, Joe still yams from the side of his mouth as if his lips are clenching that smoke.

"The L-bracket was thick, see, as thick as the diameter of the bolt going through it. So, I examined the bolts themselves. They were made of the new titanium material because titanium was lighter weight and strong, and lightweight is what everyone wants of a flying machine, but see the drawing specifications called for steel. Aha! I had the answer!" he exclaims, slapping the tabletop.

"Titanium may save weight on the rocket, but titanium is only strong when stress-tested vertically. In flight, the projection of speed was forcing the L-bracket to rise and the joint to straighten, making the bolt flex. Steel bolts would have flexed with the L-bracket's force, but titanium bolts were popping their heads off rather than flexing."

"Bolts can flex?" I doubt it.

"Yes, Ma'am. But, substituting titanium for the steel that was called for in the design caused the capsule to break off of the rocket, and that was their problem. McDonnell had to accept a new weight factor by exchanging the titanium bolts for steel bolts if they wanted their rockets to hold together."

"Um, that's nice, Dad," Paul clears his throat and pauses before changing the subject to what happened in his workday at the hospital.

Joe listens with interest, nodding. He seems to drink in anything his son wants to tell him. I'm assuming since Joe has no personal friendships made known to us, that dinner with us is his only meaningful opportunity to use his voice and other social faculties of conversation each week.

In the early '90s, while he still wore large oval glasses, we teased Mr. B that he resembled the grim-faced cartoon character,

Mr. Magoo. He'd shrug with a smile and a leaning of his head, open palm raised as if to imply, "What can ya do?"

When he traveled without eyeglasses in the '90s, people stared at him for a religious reason. Some would approach him to ask if he might be the Pope. When Pope John Paul II visited Colorado, we got Paul's dad a sweatshirt that proclaimed him, indeed, to be the Pope, so that people didn't have to embarrass themselves. Joe particularly liked this joke because he had spent an entire childhood of Sunday mornings confused, as an illiterate second-generation Pole, sitting in an American Polish Catholic church. When it burned to the ground, he had an immediate excuse for swearing off religion. There are very few Polish Catholic churches left in America. The notoriety of looking like someone famous, however? He liked that. Occasionally, Joe would even invite the gawker to make his or her confession.

June 22, 2013

Paul surprises his dad by delivering a new pair of fancy wool socks tonight. The souvenir socks are from our visit to an alpaca ranch, managed by a friend of his. They are brown wool, and slipping into them, Joe exclaims, "I finally made it. I feel *rich*! They are so soft!"

"Have you signed the card we brought last time, Mr. B?" I ask.

"No, no. I don't think a nine-year-old girl wants to hear from an old man like me. I feel silly. Besides, I don't write cursive anymore. I forgot how! My printing is pretty nondescript, too."

"That's all right, Chief," Paul chimes in. "She'd love to know you are thinking about her. Just write about the journal idea. We all need to sign it and get it in the mail tomorrow."

Joe sits down. He studies the card like a student forced to write a book report. Finally, he proceeds to print his suggestion using his architectural box styled hand, to his great-granddaughter. His thoughts require a fifteen minute wait time, and almost the whole inside of the card, both sides, are written over. Then Pauly writes a joke, leaving me with less than an inch at the bottom.

"Hey!" I write. "Your grandpa confiscated the whole card. I'll write more later. Love, Aunt Lynn." Paul wonders if putting in a stick of gum like his aunt used to do in his birthday cards is still appropriate. Writing letters by snail mail is so outmoded, I'm thinking; it now takes a whole family to safely get one card into a stamped envelope and mailed. We are still wondering if we did it right when Joe digs inside his wallet.

"This is what that card needs!" He shoves into the envelope a folded twenty dollar bill. "If I'm bold enough to suggest she write in a diary, at least she won't have to cough up for it!"

This summer, the old man has decided to take on a new project. Sewing isn't exactly new to him because he's made slipcovers and has mended pants. He's sewn together a swimming suit, mended socks, even hemmed his wife's old skirts, but he no longer has a sewing machine. He leads us outside to the back porch and shows us his aluminum glider. "The cushions are beginning to show their stuffing through these worn holes, here and here," he points out with his hard and weathered middle finger. "I've done the upholstering of these cushions once before you know, so I'm assuming I can do it again."

I carefully look at Paul hoping he'll pick up on how harried I feel. I don't have time to babysit him with this project! I'm wrapping up our lawsuit. I'm talking to realtors and construction guys and a stager for our house.

Paul closes his eyelids like blinds against me. Out of the side of his mouth, he sidesteps an argument, "Let's just see how far he gets on his own."

"I called Sandy," Joe begins, "when I started thinking about this project, and she was kind enough to return my old Singer sewing machine to me this week." Joe's granddaughter, Sandy, lives north of Denver in the foothills with her husband and with Joe's nine-year-old great-granddaughter, Christina, and his namesake toddler grandson, Joe-Joe. He leads us into an upstairs bedroom where we see he has set up a card table, a pincushion, and the old gray Singer. Sandy has indeed already managed to find the time to return Mr. B's sewing machine to him. He smiles proudly at the setup.

Then, Mr. B scores a look as bashful as an old mountain goat when he asks us to take him fabric shopping. "Look at me, a man wid an agenda!" He tells us, "Things are too expensive, and I can't remember what kind of material to buy. So, I'm asking for your young folks' opinion." Then muttering, "The last place I went, I walked around and around. Couldn't find one person to talk to me or show me where the sales were."

Joe's balance has been pretty bad these past two years. "They probably didn't want to be liable if you toppled over at their elbow, Mr. B!"

"Well, there's that." His head weaves the air between his shoulders considering this possibility. Then again, he refuses to use a walker or a cane because to do so would be to give in to the dictates of old age. He pins us into the corner of his sewing room. "Do you or don't you have a few minutes to help me find some upholstery on sale?"

We agree, and Mr. B eagerly reminds us that he prides himself on bargain hunting. "My aerospace pension is a case in point. The engineering firm set it up 36 years ago, but I don't mind bragging on myself. I won the bet they made against my longevity. See, they offered to pay me a pension every month instead of disbursing it in one lump sum!" Joe turned 97 in January. He still smiles every time he reminds us, "Those buzzards still have to cough up a paycheck *every month* for me, yeah, huh!"

Based on his older brother Eddy's advice in the early '70s, Mr. B once tried to invest in the stock market. It was just after Joe moved the family to Colorado, but after more research, he quietly removed his money and continued his usual course of saving through measly interest rates earned on bank deposits and government bonds. He, rather, chooses carefully what to spend his money on up front. When we asked him why he continues to forfeit the larger stock market returns for the bank's dwindling interest rates, he shrugged.

"Why would I pay a bunch of industry pricks to manage my hard-earned money? They don't have any loyalty to me. We have never looked each other in the eye. They only care about what's gonna make them a buck. No, I don't trust 'em. I don't trust 'em one bit wid my money."

Mr. B has a softer side to his thriftiness, though. For each summer holiday we've ever hosted at our house, Joe would pick, cut, and bring to me his own bundle of flowers to grace our table. He always tended them in his backyard. He typically busied himself through the friendless hours of summer days with his favorite nursery projects, cutting rose stems to cultivate new roses from them, or transplanting the two varieties of lilacs in his yard, forsythia alike, into the boundaries of his three-quarter acre lawn. After the blooms die, Joe harvests the seeds from his poppies, snapdragons, zinnias, and Johnny jump-ups, propagating and sharing with namely us, his grandkids, and neighbors.

Finding the fabric store by Joe's navigation, we all traipse in together and search out material. He growls. The regular upholstery material we show him is too expensive, so he chooses a black and white checked tablecloth material instead.

Paul and I shrug. At least it'll keep him busy.

Back at home he tears apart the old cushions and begins struggling to sew together the back cover with the enlarged front cover. It is one of those things that is better made by pinning the pattern of the pieces he has ripped apart, to the new material and cutting out the pattern, than by trying to work out the mathematical science of the curve before sewing. I try to help him by pinning the front, carefully gathered, to the back. I tell him that some things cannot be figured out mathematically and must be taken on faith.

"Use the pattern of the old ones, Mr. B."

He attempts to sew "in faith," as he says teasing me, but faith is diametrically opposed to his mathematician's mind, honed by decades spent in the engineering hole at the Department of Defense.

June 24, 2013

I've set up a dinner date for Mr. B with Betty, my 78-year-old book club partner. Betty's house is located near Joe's, so we are taking him to meet her at the garden club for dinner.

"Lynn, you know Dad won't approve."

Mr. B is not what most people would call a gregarious person. We have photographs from many celebrations, including his own fiftieth wedding celebration, where he is looking at the camera with a pug Yoda face held in a parenthesis between fanning ears.

I shrug. "So, we simply don't tell him she'll be there." He's still a good-looking man, I think, with a full head of straight white hair kept cropped at what his hairdresser calls "a one on top and a two on the sides."

Joe has made us promise not to let him fall for another woman, but Betty is not that kind of date. They met each other at our Easter dinner, where they discovered that they had both lived in three of the same cities throughout the years. Betty's late husband was also an engineer. And Betty worked for *Nabisco* when Joe's late wife was teaching home economics to high schoolers. Yet, Betty is *my* friend, not his.

At Easter, Betty, who majored in the Spanish language, listened with good humor to Joe's experience of learning Spanish in his sixties. When he and his wife decided their favorite vacation spot was Mexico, they both learned conversational Spanish, enough to read it and use the proper tenses. Joe seemed pleased with Betty's attention. After she left our Easter gathering, Joe continued to comment, "That gal could sure keep up a conversation! Yeah. I found her to be a very interesting person."

Now, on the way to the garden club for dinner, Joe dismisses our conversation of Betty. I assume he is only pretending he doesn't remember her. Nevertheless, we remind him of all the fun they had using Spanish together at Easter, then we remind him about all the other things they have in common. We don't tell him that Betty has said, "If only he were twenty years younger!"

Tonight, Mr. B's sense of etiquette rises to the occasion when he insists on paying for all of us even though the party now includes Betty's forty-five- year-old engineer son, his wife, and two children. Though our guests are a complete surprise to him, bigger than Hollywood, Joe waves paper in the air. "I have these coupons that need to be used or they will expire." He holds them out to the cashier at the end of the buffet.

My eyebrows lift in merriment at Paul because we know Mr. B used to take the *Denver Post* and clip coupons in his sunny dining room till he said he "got fed up with having to pay for it." Now, he clips coupons from the library's newspaper copy. The man's circumspect ways have, of course, kept him situated in his own home throughout the aging process, which he likes.

Mr. B carries Betty's tray to the table for her, which seems to irritate her son. Betty pats her son's hand and says encouragingly, "Don't worry so much, dear."

June 29, 2013

The next time we visit the old man I ask, "Will you show me the progress on your cushions, Mr. B?"

"Okay. But I'm not too happy." He mutters from the side of his mouth. The toothpick he gnashes drops trails of splinters beside him on the floor. He pushes himself out of his chair and leads me to the dining room table strewn with old and new fabric pieces. "When we gave the Singer to Sandy, I never expected to use it again. Seems I've forgotten how to use it. I did this ten years ago, but…" Joe shakes his head and clears his throat, "things have changed. It was a difficult project then, but now I've sewn the thing together and torn it out by hand three times!" Even when it was going together properly, he could not figure out the mathematics of the gathers and the oversized front turning over the edges of the cushion.

To my dismay, I see the new fabric has multiple small holes in it and realize the project is now beyond his ability.

July 1, 2013

My younger sister Kay, a quilter, agrees to spend part of her day with my father-in-law bolstering his confidence and memory to use his fantastic old Singer sewing machine to make the new cushion he's been "thinking over" for six weeks.

As they are talking, I shuffle through the box of photos he's been keeping on the dining room table. Finding one the image of Maudie sitting in a park in the grass, I wave it under Mister B's nose with a smile.

"Oh, yes! Isn't she a beauty there? I remember that day. She wasn't feeling well. I took a picture of her, and then a policeman passed by. We asked for some directions and explained that she wasn't in top notch condition.

He shouted, "CONGRATULATIONS!" He assumed she was P.G." At this, Mister B falls silent. His nose grows rosy. I see a tear about to fall over his lower eyelash. My chest tightens understanding that she was never going to give birth. But Mister B's sentiments continue in another track. "She looked so good in that coat. It fit her like a glove. I remember taking her to the store to get it. It was the first one she tried on, and my! She looked so nice!" He shakes his head still peering at the photograph. "I said, 'We'll take it!' But then the clerk pulled out that fine mink stole and put it around her shoulders. Well, how could I refuse? She looked like a million bucks!" We all have a laugh and he hands back the photo.

(Maudie, Circa. 1942)

He remembers sewing well, and Joe repeatedly tells my sis how grateful he is for her "patience toward an old guy." To show his gratefulness, he treats us to chilled mango juice and tells some stories about his life with Maudie. Much of the time, Joe recalls his wife, who has been gone well on four years now, in the present tense like, "If I eat these onions, there'll be no kissing for me tonight. Maudie hates onion eaters."

"How did you two meet?" my younger sister asks in her polite voice.

Mr. B's grin seems enormous, and he worries a sewing needle

in his mouth as though it were one of his toothpicks. "She opened the door in her flowing white bathrobe wid red roses covering it. Her sleeves ended in some kind of frill over her hands, and the same frill was on her collar over her neck. She was so classy. Mmm. That was it." He shrugs. "The short story is," his voice flows, "I had met a gal who turned out to be her roommate. I had been going over to ask her to go skating wid me. And like I said, Maudie opened the door. Wow! Did she have a figure on her! She was on a college break from, eh, Columbia Teachers College, and was visiting friends in Oklahoma. So, I *ask*ed her on a picnic for the next day, and she made me many of my favorite foods: pickled beets, sliced tomatoes, center cut ham, boiled eggs. I *ask*ed her to marry me." The Rhode Island's coastal awe remains in Mr. B's pronunciation of 'ask.'

My sis raises an eyebrow "That was quick".

"Well, yes, I guess. Anyway, she phoned her mothea back home to ask her if she could put on a wedding in a week. Her mothea said, 'Give me two.' And so she took a break from college to help her mothea wid the wedding. I wrote her a letter every day we were apart and she called me at night. So we tied the knot."

"He wrote letters in shapes and circles. I've seen some of them," I insert.

Joe stares at the wall and then glares hard at me as if to say, *"This is my story, Deary. Butt. Out."* He looks around. "My proposal letter is sitting right here on the table with us in a stack of photographs." He shuffles through his card box of precious keepsakes. "Look, here it is!" We all look at the plain white envelope. In the return address section, he had typed in black ink,

"This letter contains a proposal. Do not delay a response on any account!"

Where Maudie's name and address in the middle was typed,

he'd typed a description of her address after her name:

The Old Maid Quarters

"Okay. I was a bit crazy for her." He suddenly admits, "She was a Brownlee. Her fathea was the town doctor, oh yeah, very respectable. But way back in Wales, the Brownlees were the upper crust who lived up on the hilltops, and the Greenlees were the ones who lived in the valleys and meadows. Oh, and her mothea was a Carey, from the Carey Salt Mine family. I was moving up!"

He smiles. "The minister was this Kansas bloke named Gardener. After he was done, I asked him, 'What do I owe ya?' He was familiar with the family's notoriety and so he got a bit cheeky, 'Whatever you think your wife is worth to ya.' Well, I told him, 'So far, she isn't worth much.' But I gave him half of the twenty bucks in my wallet cuz I told him I had to keep the other ten to get back home for work, and that was a day's drive away!"

"Ten bucks to get married?!" I can't help but exclaim. In spite of his rude comment in the end, I am happy to learn of his one-time passion for Maudie.

My sister asks if his parents came out for the ceremony.

"Nope. My folks couldn't make it to the wedding, but they shipped me a case of my fathea's dandelion wine. Hey, I remember making that stuff wid him as a kid back in prohibition times, so I knew how good it was. But Maudie's parents were very religious, and after the honeymoon, that wine was nowhere to be found." He chuckles.

"Mr. B?"

"Mmm?"

"Will you take that needle out'a your mouth, please? It isn't a toothpick."

"I know that. You think I'm gonna swallow it?" He pats my leg and winks. "This one's always worrying about me."

July 3, 2013

Let's see. Go to a fireworks festival or paint walls? The multiple walls needing paint prior to taking multi-list pictures seems urgent, also, a distressing itemization of staging projects, before we can list our house, hounds me. This community house on Pearl Street continues to be our 'pearl of great price.' We drop the paintbrushes into a can of water. I've arranged that our friends will meet us in the park a block from Mr. B's place on top of the hill for the fireworks display tonight. The idea is that Paul will manage to get his father to join us for the fireworks in the park.

The yellow truck, loaded with furniture and three canvas lawn chairs, carries us to Mr. B's two-story house in the foothills. His basement is only meant to be transitional storage. Our main purpose in clearing out our own specially designed home, used as a lodge for seminary students in the last few years, is so that it stages well for quick sale.

With the afternoon wind in my face, I wonder why I feel like I've been peddling a bicycle backwards. After six years of trying to make our neighbors and city council be reasonable, we're finally moving on, but I feel like I've peddled into one of those old Frenchy films where the wimpy *fini* climax espouses the meaninglessness of life.

Did I outrun Colorado's municipal zoning tornado? Nope. The heated litigation spun us around like odd tangibles in the whirlwind and spit us out as pieces of trash into an unknown atmosphere. In the aftermath, we must sell low or lose our shirts completely. Anyway, at this point, moving is probably the only way we can manage to love our neighbors. For our part, we just want to dust the sand off our feet and lock the doors on the memories. We've been toying with the idea of building a log cabin near Joe in the foothills with whatever money we can garner from the sale of our house.

The idea of retreating from society entirely sounds like paradise to us, two chastened mice seeking a rat hole, but there's the little matter of Paul's elderly father. There's also that detail of timing. Paul has five years till retirement himself, and he works right here in town.

"We could rent an apartment *near* your dad, Honey, while we build our retirement home. You know, just for a couple of years."

He agrees. It's a good option. The buyer's market prevents us from selling our home at a price that would allow us to transfer the whole ministry into another house. Our hospitality lifestyle has ended.

Paul cajoles his dad into riding with us to the Independence Day celebration by assuring him, "You won't have to walk far. There is a nearby handicap parking area. There will be hot dogs, Dad, and you'll enjoy the fireworks. It's *exciting!*"

Even the idea of hot dogs, his favorite, doesn't tempt the ol' man. "I can see that display from the upstairs' window," he croaks, waving us off.

"But it will be good for you to get outside and take a break from all that sewing." I plead. "Plus our best friends want to meet you, Mr. B. They've heard a lot about you."

"What if I don't want to meet *them*?" he counters. "No, I'm not much for social gatherings. You go and have some fun. You need some blankets? Take these…" He swivels in his chair to grab a blanket from the blue velvet couch and throws it to us. We look at each other and reject Joe's blankets.

"We brought three folding chairs, Dad, one for *you*. Come with us," Paul's voice commands.

"Okay, okay! Since you put it that way." Mr. B growls as he pushes himself up from his swivel rocker. "But seriously, I can see that display from the north bedroom up there." He shakes his head. He pulls his sky-blue fleece over his white T-shirt and stands like the wounded Christ, arms before him offering himself to slaughter. "What are we waiting for?"

We pile into the car and park a few blocks away. Then, we join the parade filing up to the bowl on the hilltop with a gathering crowd. Joe greets our friends who convey how much they've wanted to meet him. Done with the pleasantries, he tucks himself into a canvas chair and starts enjoying a hot dog to the calls of children playing with expensive Independence Day gadgets, chasing each other across the grown-ups' carefully laid blankets.

I relax to see he's enjoying the party when suddenly, clouds begin to plop, plop drops of rain, little gray warnings that freedom celebrations often come with a cost. We pass over a large black garbage bag to Joe. He refuses to touch it until we show him how to make a rain poncho. All of us rip off a corner of our black bags and pull them over our heads.

"I coulda' watched it wid'out the rain at home," Joe mutters. "Is there a potty around here?"

Paul leads his dad over to the temporary toilets, but they immediately return. "I gotta walk my dad home."

"What?"

"He doesn't want to stay in the drizzle. He doesn't want to use those toilets, and he has to *go*."

"But can he walk all the way home? It's at least a mile!" I'm alarmed at the pickle I've put us all in.

"Oh yeah. Probably. He used to walk all over this place. He walked to the Columbine Library all the time. I'll go with him." He waves me goodbye with irritation. "See ya."

It's true. During the '90s with the rise of the "dot com's", Mr. B walked through the park a mile, back and forth, to reach the library and return home when his research was completed. He was interested in learning how a computer works, how the Internet works, how the multimillions were made through "dot-coms".

Joe doesn't own a computer. He just likes to understand what's happening in the world, and the engineer is always curious *how* it happens.

Paul arrives back to the party just in time to see the ten minutes of fireworks we've endured hours of wind and drizzle to enjoy. On our way back to the car, we get lost. Sluicing through the crowds, in vast inlets of multiple parking areas, we become blaming grumps accusing each other.

When we arrive back at Mr. B's house, he opens the door and waves us in to hear our story.

"Like I said, I watched 'em upstairs! You kids shoulda' stayed here." The ol' man's earnest expression finally makes us chuckle.

July 15, 2013

I'm in denial. It's uncomfortable that we won't be transferring our hospitality venture into a new mini-mansion *nearby*, but adding that we may be moving *in* with my father-in-law? I find myself, uncomprehending, taking truckload after truckload of furniture, dishes, pictures, artwork, valuables, linens, pots, and pans into his two-story, faded '70s house. This is transitional. *Storage.*

Notified by the roar of the truck, gears shifting to reverse and the clatter of the transmission yearning to drop onto his driveway, Joe opens the door to wait for a sign of our appearance from Neverland. He quickly motions us inside the house with a secretive smile on his face. We follow him through the Hungarian sounds of the Franz Liszt Chamber Orchestra down the hallway, through the den, and out the back door where his finished work is laid on the glider, and under his freshly laundered loincloths hanging on the clothes-line which stretches across his back porch.

Mr. B is grinning as wide as one of the openings in his Fruit of the Loom displays. "What do you see that's new out here?" he demands.

"Wow, Chief! Good for you!" Paul congratulates his father and rubs his back. The black-and-white checked lounge is plumped and tucked together like a turkey. We sit on the billowing cushions and congratulate him again. Instead of displaying pride, he twiddles the toothpick in his mouth nervously, rolling it between his fingers. Mr. B seems humbled by the task and rather relieved to have finally managed to pull it together.

Surveying Joe's backyard now, from his newly covered glider, my concern is sparked. "Why are your roses dead, Mr. B?" The brown earth covers his dry flowerbeds as well as his three-quarter acre of grass. "Where are your snapdragons and zinnias?" I ask.

"Oh, those flowers are so old. They don't last forever, you know." His aging voice sounds like a swarm of bees.

"But your whole yard is brown, Mr. B!"

"Well, that saves me having to mow." He nudges me with his elbow as if this is a joke.

Joe has lived pretty much isolated for five years since the death of his wife, Maudie. It occurs to me that the wilted beds he once nursed carefully are reflections of his own lack of desire to live.

During our weekly visits these past years, we began to comprehend the impact of loneliness on a person. At 97, nothing is physically wrong with Joe beyond his hearing loss and dimming vision. Yet he seems forgetful, repetitious, or simply stuck finding words to communicate with us. He has previously explained that he is too cheap to water and that it saves him mowing his grass, but in this moment, I realize that it is so far gone, it may not revive next spring. He may be intentionally killing the things he previously nurtured, signaling his own soul drying up. What he cannot admit to us verbally when asked, he is showing us.

Yet as Joe's basement has been filling up with our "junk," as he calls it, I rethink the purpose for moving our things to Joe's house as more than storage while staging our home for a quick sell.

Alarmed, I pick up the hose and begin squirting water on his flowerbeds that were once brilliant. "Just wait 'til we move closer," I tease. "It needs water. That's all. We're gonna have you back in tip-top shape real soon."

"Oh, don't worry about me," he says flapping his hands to close the lid on an imaginary box. Though he can't bring himself to discuss his needs, his tough exterior can no longer hide the fact that his soul is as hard as the cracked, dusty earth of his yard.

Maybe this is why we haven't been able to sell our home or find another one closer to him. Maybe we are to move in with him!

Recently, Joe has repeated, "The loneliness is what is worst." Even two visits a week from us have not staved off his gait becoming wobbly and a loss of memory. He is so thrifty that he has frozen himself, almost to death, by turning down his heat on winter nights. We may not receive that desperate phone call from him in the next instance. We cannot risk him living alone another winter. Also, he cannot see to drive in the dark anymore. He has gotten himself lost going to the emergency room in the middle of the night.

A couple of my friends take care of their parents, but up until now, this queen ant has focused on building a colony elsewhere. Inside, I feel the my soul shift in layers like platelets of an earthquake. I love this man. And yes, the alternative could be dire if I leave him to his loneliness.

"Oh God! Help me be worthy of this task." Our move seems imminent, whether we are able to sell our house or are forced into foreclosure. I am, without explanation, reconciled to help preserve the life of my amazing father-in-law. My lifestyle must be more cohesive, truer than ever. If only my faults don't get in the way to mess things up!

July 20, 2013

For a couple of years now, I've been taking Mr. B to both his eye doctor and his specialist for appointments. He gets shots in one eye for the "mac-stuff" as he calls it. Since it takes a few hours for the dilation to wear off, we hang out together at home on Pearl Street or we go to lunch and chat.

This morning, the receptionist hands over an updated annual form to sign. I summarize it for my father-in-law and ask him if he wants to sign.

He responds slowly. "Oh, I guess so. I don't like indemnifying a doctor. If I were younger, I'd feel like I'm signing my life away, but I'm too old to worry about that now."

"Sometimes I scratch stuff out and initial it when I don't like it."

"You do? Do they refuse service to you then?"

"No, haven't yet."

"Well, good for you, young'un. We see eye-to-eye on it then. That's why I don't go for credit cards. Too many questions!" He reflects leisurely in a flow of consciousness. "There's nothing private anymore. If you tell a doctor or, say a bank or, even a politician something, you don't really know who they are beholden to. You think you've told them alone, but you don't know they have agreements of their own with others, and when push comes to shove, they'd cover their own you know what, rather than protecting you. You are only one customer to them."

He looks at the sheet and wobbles his head over the clipboard, then takes the pen and signs his name with a careful script. "I haven't got much anyway."

He smiles down at the receptionist who takes the clipboard and our source of discussion. Then she waves us into the doctor's office.

His specialist shakes Mr. B's hand then greets me with her typical fast and firm handshake. Nodding her head Mr. B's way, she gives him a thumbs up. "He's quite a guy, eh?"

"What'd she say?"

"She says you're trouble, but my lips are sealed. Your secret's safe."

"This gal's a good partner in crime!" He points at me and ogles with his watery eyes.

Mister B's doctor treats me, not as an encumbrance to her job, but with recognition of our relationship and the value my presence brings to communication and the safety of my father-in-law. She banters with Joe like his other doctors do, and I interpret. When she leaves the room, I tell Mr. B that our lawsuit ended against the City because we refused to be questioned in a marital deposition by the City attorneys. It was an expensive lesson for us to learn as plaintiffs. "The intrusion into our sanctity of marriage aside, my father once told me that the smartest way to keep the government from interfering is to tell them as little as possible to begin with."

"That's a good one!" he agrees. "People think they can trust someone else to keep a secret for 'em, but they're mistaken. The best gate is your own sealed lips. Once it's out, it's out."

July 23, 2013

"Noise has the strength of vibrations to break things apart," Joe declares, agreeing with my sister's complaint. She has come to dinner with us because the fire alarm in her apartment building is driving her and her little dog crazy. "I don't know why they can't seem to get it regulated there! It should turn off as soon as the fire department shows up, but it doesn't, and for hours afterwards, you think it's done, but it keeps cycling through with sharp beeping noises!"

Agreeably Joe maintains, "A human ear has a flimsy membrane

that can only take so much noise. It's like the shell of an aircraft with engine noise. We learned about noise dynamics and propellers and gearboxes at work. You know the bombers?" He pronounces the second b in bombers hard, not silent.

"They were not considered fast planes, and the MiGs could catch up with them in no time because they flew faster, at higher altitudes, and after the bombers dropped their bombs, they would drop lower and kinda be sitting ducks. So, we gave them a couple of high-powered engines, counter rotators, and they would kick in and drive the bomber out of range of the MiGs. But we learned something about the faster engines with the counter rotating propellers when we did that. You see, one propeller would go one way and the other would turn the opposite direction, and the gear box would control them on two shafts." Joe moves his forefingers in two separate circular directions and continues. "But the decibels of noise from them operating next to the flimsy skin of the airplane would eventually break the body and shred it like rags."

Joe chews his toothpick, pulls it out of his mouth and spits out a sliver of wood. "They crashed. See, at 450 miles an hour, the gearbox couldn't keep up with the vibration, compression, and speed. Now, they set these things electronically, but in the beginning, the mechanics had to try to make them work like a Swiss watch under those conditions, and it was nearly impossible."

"What did you do?"

"Me? Well, we decided to turn the front of both the engines to point away from the body at an angle and measure the decibels." He points two fingers on each hand in a 'V' formation, away from an imaginary plane. "We put a shell around them too, to muffle the rumbling. That worked."

My sister quips, "That's what I need! Earmuffs! My head was about to explode."

"You already have a turtle shell," I say. "You are my sister who is most likely to hide in your shell before anyone even sees you!"

"Yup." She nods. "I'm going to have to tell my apartment managers that my nerve endings are too sensitive to live with their fire alarms. I'm out 'a there as soon as possible. Ever see a flying turtle?"

Vultee Attack Bomber, which Joe helped design in 1938-39 Downey, CA

July 25, 2013
Being survivors of a six-year zoning litigation with a city is a feat in humility. Emotions are worn like old, holey work shoes. We've exhausted our resources. In short, we feel like Mr. B's favorite *Braunschweiger*, a sausage stuffed into its natural casings, nearly always smoked.

Mr. B's more vulnerable situation, however, turns our attention in grinding fashion to someone's need other than our own. We were looking at smaller homes to buy closer to Joe's home, enabling us to take care of him on a daily basis as he ages. Of course, we want to maintain our autonomy.

When Maudie broke her hip and was laid up in the rehab center, Joe looked around and got spooked. He made us promise never to put him in a nursing home. "I don't like old people!" he hissed. "I like *young* people."

Since then, we'd assumed that he'd eventually move in with us.

After all, he has planned for years to "kick the bucket" and for that reason, he and Maudie cleaned out their home of valuables and a lot of furniture. I don't know how many times I've heard, "When I kick the bucket" as a tagline to some advice or gift. Thus, in our youth, we built a main floor master in our lodge specially for a surviving parent. That plan is not looking up.

July 29, 2013

The last time I took Joe to his eye doctor, she recommended some pills for his macular degeneration. They turned out to be the size of horse pills, but Mr. B gave his doctor's recommendation a gallant try.

Tonight, we visit him, and he seems shaken. His voice is raspy.

"Are you sick, Mr. B?" I ask, handing him a glass of water. "It sounds like you are dehydrated."

Joe waves the water away then thinks twice and takes a sip. "No, actually. It was those hell-bent horse pills my doctor recommended!" Joe lifts up the remainder of the bottle into his son's view.

"What happened, Dad?" Paul takes back Joe's water glass.

"Well, it was funny. I tried to take one this morning, and it got caught in my throat. I thought about calling 911, but I didn't think they'd get here in time. So, I got into my car and drove myself over to the E.R. I was just about there, and I coughed it out the window. But it must have scratched my throat or something."

Paul and I exchange worried glances.

"Oh, don't bother your heads about it. It was nothing. As you can see, everything turned out all right."

But we do bother our heads about it. The last time we got Joe a cell phone, he received obscene phone calls and texts repeatedly, and he only used it twice. I was always having to remind him how it worked. We have since started talking about getting him a medical alert bracelet, but it's beginning to become clear that the best move of all is to move in with him. I cannot conceive it.

III

Then it is only kindness that makes sense anymore,
only kindness that ties your shoes
and sends you out into the day to mail letters and
purchase bread,
only kindness that raises its head
from the crowd of the world to say
It is I you have been looking for,
and then goes with you everywhere
like a shadow or a friend,:
. Naomi Shihab Nye

AUGUST ~ DISSEMBLE

August 1, 2013

After Joe's television mystery ends, he quickly swivels his chair to address me. "I don't understand these new movies! They're too complicated, and I'm getting too old." He pulls out the toothpick from his lips. "I used to like going to the theater in Woonsocket, though."

"Rhode Island?"

"Yes, Ma'am." He smiles remembering. "Cartoons would play: Happy Hooligan, Felix the Cat, that was the one I liked, and another one, something about Up with Fathea. Then, Fox Tune News would be shown, you know, the news in pictures. We didn't have the news on television yet, only radio. So getting the news in pictures was special. Then, the upcoming films were announced, and finally, we got to see the full-screen feature film. Ten cents for hours of entertainment, not just one show, there was one after another! I could spend the whole afternoon in there." He cups the back of his head in his hands and looks up seeing something quite different than his ceiling.

"That's where I'd be: in the balcony of the U-shaped theater. I'd watch the cigarette-smoking piano player down in the orchestra pit. He'd be watching the shoot-'em-ups too, wid his neck twisted up to the screen for the next cue to play. The actors then were Tom Mix and Hoot Gibson, and there was always a beautiful pony or horse, like a show horse that one of 'em had, and there was a cowboy clown actor in those shows, too. That was also where I first saw 'Phantom of the Opera', and I was so scared, really scared up there in the balcony! It was an all black-and-white film, but it still scared me."

"Ten cent movies is what interests me, Mr. B! Do you know what movies cost nowadays?"

"Nope, but I'm sure we were getting' a deal, what wid double headers and the piano player to boot!"

I smile, waiting, encouraging him to continue.

"It was a tall, three-story theater. I entered the theater at the street level, but past the ticket booth, I found the second floor. The main floor was below the ticket booth level, and the balcony was where us 'ten centers' would have to find our own seats. Seats below were reserved for those who paid higher prices, see? When the movie reel caught on fire, the attendant immediately closed the window so as not to scare the audience, but they could see the smoke coming from behind the ocuscope, or whatever that little window was called. I ran out the exit, and up the stairs, but I had nowhere to go, so I turned and ran down the stairs and somehow I was back inside the theater and everyone was following me single file, and we hurried across the stage behind the screen to find a door. I didn't know *where* to find a door, but everyone was following me anyway!"

"You must'a found a way out cuz here you sit tonight, Mr. B." Again, my grin encourages him.

"Yeah, I must'a ran up and out to Main Street somehow." His blue velvet rocking chair complains and creaks.

"You know? I remember all the names of the stores on the street, one after another!" Joe's remark shows he is incredulous with his own memory. "Starting with the movie theater that I would go to, next door to it was a sewing machine store, then Board and Jones Pharmacy where you could get ice cream. Next to that was the post office and a small plain placard marked high up for Dr. Reid's office after that." Joe seems to look through me making his point. "He used to make house calls to us, which no doctor ever does today. I especially remember him coming to help Mothea deliver my little sista, Wanda."

We continue rocking in our respective chairs as he presses his eyelids closed to remember more.

"All right. Then, there was a men's fancy suit store where the clerks dressed up just like you would like to look if you worked in a bank. The Haberdasher clerks even had their pockets stuffed with white hankies folded three times, and a pin was stuck either in their neck tie at the collar or in their hankies in their pockets. Their pant hemlines hung to 'just so' above their polished shoes." Joe bends down to show me how the hemlines touched the tops of their shoes. "I suppose their socks were silk. I dunno." The ol' man places his hands over his belly contentedly and rocks. "Dressed to the hilt, of course. The clerks showed you how you could look if you had the money and needed their suits. Then there was the meat market, a department store for ladies that I had no reason to enter, *ever*, and a music store, a ladies' millinery shop with very fancy hats, and the bank was on the corner. At the hat shop, they'd let me collect the tissue packing from the hat boxes. I'd hang out there, and once I found a white felt hat that they missed, so I gave it back. All we needed was the tissues, you know, 'cuz we'd use that for toilet paper. We'd cut it into squares and hang a bunch of 'em on a hook in the outhouse. We didn't have toilet paper rolls back then."

Paul tromps up from the basement where he's been organizing storage and into the room. "How you doing? I'm about ready to leave."

"Give me five minutes. Your dad is telling me all the names of the stores on Main Street where he lived in Woonsocket." Paul rolls his eyes and leaves us to it. "I am seriously impressed that you can remember all that, Mr. B!"

"Oh yeah. Well, I was the paper boy." He shrugs and frowns, then leans back in his chair and presses his eyelids closed again. "Across the street, going backwards, there was St. James Hotel. In the basement of the hotel, they had a full string of bowling alleys. During the week, it was pretty quiet, so the owner wouldn't have an assistant down there. But sometimes he was really busy when I came to give him the paper, so he'd ask me to go on down to the pins and set them up. The bowling pins would fall into a bin. So I was scared to death, but I *did* it. I don't remember him giving me anything for it though. That hotel was the new hotel in town. Heh, heh! I always imagined what it would be like to stay there. When Maudie and I got married, I was excited to bring her to my hometown to look at it so I could finally have an excuse to stay there. But Maudie was a bathroom fanatic, and the place just wasn't as new as it used to be." He chuckles. "It wasn't kept up. It smelled like smoke too. We didn't stay there."

"After the hotel was Michelson's Music store where they sold every kind of instrument, then another theater, the fancy one called The Bijou with the Chinese restaurant above it. The Bijou played sexy movies, too. It wasn't for children. Bijou means, 'jewel.' The reason I remember the Chinese restaurant is because when I delivered papers, the owner would have me read the headlines to him, maybe a little more of the story, usually about what was happening in Shanghai. He'd nod and hold up a finger for me to wait. His name was Edwood Chin. His partner was a tall, lanky fellow, William Hoy. I'd see him send Hoy out. That guy would hop over the steps and run to the back of the store. I never saw their wives. Did they have children? I never knew. I never saw who the cooks were in back neither. Hoy would return through the kitchen with a handful of dried lychee nuts, in their paper shells. That, or a flexible rope of something sweet with seeds, like it had been rolled in seeds. I liked either one." He pauses. You know those two Chinese guys were teenagers when they came to Woonsocket? I remember they sat in my second-grade class trying to learn English. Hu." His pursed lips turn downward. "Yeah. And, later on, they would drive back and forth to another business in Boston. That one was probably more profitable. Well, anyway…" He spreads his hands.

"We had a shoe shine shop that was a front for the gambling going on in the back. You know, placing bets on races?" I nod. After that was another meat market that I remember had such clean sawdust all over the floor, real thick, and the butchers always wore two aprons because of the blood. The fresh fruit and vegetable store was in front, and the butcher was behind. An Italian and his daughter ran the fruit and vegetable market. The sidewalk got very wide here, and they had some kind of arrangement with the police for wealthy people, like the Kimbals, to come and park in front of their store, so they could buy their groceries. Later on, during summer breaks from college, I worked at this grocery store on the lower end of Main Street. I sprayed water over the bananas and tomatoes, and sat around a lot, for an hourly wage of twenty-five cents. I was glad to have that job. It paid me about two dollars a day."

"Next to that was *The Woonsocket Call*, our town's newspaper, where my big brother Eddy and his guys hung out. As a kid, I sat on the feet of the painted wooden Indian next door, which was the tobacco store. I sold newspapers to the guys going in to buy tobacco. A lot of 'em were the mill workers. The owners didn't exactly like it, but the sidewalk was free space, and the smokers liked to buy a newspaper with their pipes and cigarettes. Oh! There were two mills in town."

"What kind of mills?"

"Both of 'em were cotton mills, but after the war, the one that my mothea worked at changed into a rayon mill. Our house was located between the two mills." His fingers make the form of an 'H' and Joe points to the middle between the two streets. "There were a few boarding houses, too. One of 'em on the square had these curved steps that went up from the corner of the street." Mr. B moves his forefinger in the air, tracing an arc several times to mime the contour of the steps.

"The old guys would come sit on the steps to warm themselves. I remember one guy, after the Great War, had a gash across his forehead." Joe draws with two fingers across his right temple and hairline. "He told me he was clipped by a bullet that knocked him senseless, and he was aware that he still had some trouble upstairs because of it. I also met another soldier there who had been a pilot."

"Which war?"

"Oh, the first one was the Great War, which wasn't so great, I can assure you. He told me his joystick had gone into his belly when he crashed, and somehow it affected his fingernails. He showed me his fingernails which were all curled."

"Weird. Hmmmm. Did Woonsocket have any other industrial mills?"

"Not really. Just those two. I remember after the war, there was a series of strikes. My fathea was the gardener, and he would go in with my sista, Helen, to work. They were called scabs, I guess. There was a machine gun set up on the top of the roof of each of the mills. So, when the riot makers got too dangerous, the machine guns fired into the billboard across the street to sorta warn them." Mr. B's brows rise recalling his own fright during the exciting, desperate days.

August 5, 2013
Hubster and I duly attend a consultation with a bankruptcy attorney, who explains it's because we have a rental house that we

are terrible candidates for bankruptcy. It carries a mortgage that, in the present market, puts us financially upside down. "You sure you can't sell it for more than the mortgage?"

"We've tried. Not now."

He warns, "And if you short sale it, or lose it in bankruptcy, the mortgage company will come after you for the difference in value when they try to pass it off to someone else." No, he doesn't recommend bankruptcy. Add the loss of one worn yellow truck, which Paul nevertheless adores, or the optional loss of our car in bankruptcy, and the settlement is a bitter cup indeed. Paul pulls his wallet from his pocket anyway, about to make the down payment. He shrugs about his truck. "I figured that," he says. "If the bank comes after us, we'll deal with it later." We don't care about any of the personal cost. We just want *out*.

Yet I hold back Paul's hand. "Wait! Let's pray."

We give God the weekend to save our shirts.

August 7, 2013

"Ah!" I put down the phone. Paul can already tell from the grin on my face. "There's an offer on our house! Oh, God! Thank you! Thank you!"

After a year of trying to sell it, fix it, upgrade it, stage it, paint it, curse it, and cry over it, a realtor shows it to some missionaries moving back to the States. Our realtor sends the buyer's letter with their contract proposal through email.

They explain how they wept when they saw it, and how we built it just for their needs. I put down the computer's top abruptly. "Probably," is all I manage to say, feeling that for six years, the blood of the turnip has been squeezed out of our veins. In resignation and relief, we contract to sell it to them for $100,000 less than the appraisal. Coming with nothing, they've also asked us for a few pieces of our best furniture to sweeten the deal. It's a buyer's market.

August 24, 2013

Joe greets us with his thin-lipped Polish grin each time our sweaty bodies arrive. Although he has repeatedly refused any particular help, he seems delighted to have us finally moving in.

"It's time you threw in the towel with all that messy legal stuff." He says this without any expression of judgment.

Ah, yes. "I got my heart's desire, and there my troubles began." Wasn't that Lev Grossman? Rolling my eyes, my gaze settles on Joe's fridge. He has been eating hotdogs, raisins, shrimp, blue cheese, and crackers. Inside, I find jars of Polish pickles, green olives, two gallons of milk and eggs chilling on the shelves. No snacks, chilled cherries or otherwise, are readily available. He tells me he's been using the toaster we got him awhile back, but I don't see one loaf of bread to prove it. I grab a glass of water.

We decide to go out to lunch to treat those who are helping us move up to Joe's hilltop house. Our specially designed hospitality lodge in the shady glen is cleared out.

"Did you make a bundle on the sale?" Joe asks, then backtracks. "Oh, I'm sorry. That's none of my business."

"That's okay, Dad." My husband's blue eyes sparkle as he explains that we sold it for $100,000 less than the appraisal because of the low market, "but we still made some money, too." He doesn't explain our dashed dream to build a mountain cabin. Paul seems genuinely happy to me. I don't get it.

"Good for you. Good for you."

Feeling isolated, I watch father pat son's arm gently.

Paul and I are well aware the LORD has orchestrated this sale. His signature is all over it. Who would have imagined that missionaries would dare to move in and continue ministry in that hostile neighborhood environment? And, despite having to disclose the litigation to them and the ad-hoc fix-ups of the house during these past couple of years, didn't they weep to find it?

After years of juggling life from a mentality of poverty, stringing out each dollar of a paycheck, borrowing from Peter to pay Paul, we are exuberant to suddenly tithe back to the LORD on the whole sum gained from the sale of our house. Thankfully, we don't belong to a church that investigates how much we make to send out a bill for tithes. I was in disbelief to hear Joe's description of his parent's church. Not being able to give gifts to our own place of worship just felt wrong, and we didn't know how to rectify it 'til now.

August 25, 2013

I grit my teeth. There's nothing like going for the American Dream, rising to the top like the cream, only to be skimmed off and fed to the cat!

With the sun streaming into the yellow faux-finished den, I snap an "exit photo" of my husband resting in our Pearl Street Lodge on our last weekend morning. It seemed peaceful, but when I review the picture, his face appears gaunt and white. His resting head is lobbed to the side of the chair we have agreed to cast off to a neighbor in trade for a woven rug. The good neighbor is probably one of the very few who would miss us. I click 'delete' on this grim photo. Today, we both feel disoriented.

The mail brings us a third traffic ticket. It falls between us like a mallet. It topples the stack of mental bills required simply to move out of the house. With the bank adjustments we must make from day to day, sometimes hour to hour, keeping our accounts viable during this push into oblivion, a traffic ticket feels like a fiery dart pricking and burning us. We argue, confused and overwrought. Will we be able to quietly back out of this city? Erase our footprints behind as we go? The way we should act, full of grace, and meek strength, is not the way we act. Our voices rise heatedly. I am exasperated at everyone and every small broken thing. I remind myself, corralling my pride, that we weren't forced out, exactly. We chose to move, and the Almighty provided the miracle missionary buyers.

I'm just praying the bitterness doesn't kill me.

August 26, 2013

Joe turns from the upstairs bedroom window splattered with the sky's grey afternoon watercolors. He proclaims, "Rain's pouring down!" He's showing me throughout his darkened house without turning on the lights as we go, explaining the purpose for each room as if I'd never before visited.

He is inviting me to use all of the closets for storage. Of course, I will have to donate my wedding gown, which has been taking up most of one bedroom closet all by itself. It hangs in waves, stored in a special garment bag, where Maudie safely kept it for most of these 24 years.

He stands in the center of the barren room. Angled behind him are two chalky walls. The one directly behind him is decked around the mid-section with an aged collection of framed postcards, and below him is the rust-colored, carved carpet.

"I don't know why I'm thinking of this," Joe says, "but I remember a strange sight in my bedroom window when I lived in the attic of Arnold Street. Do you know what a blimp is?"

"I guess I do."

"Well, after the Great War, the Americans tried to compete with the Germans, so they built themselves four of these huge flying machines called dirigibles. Each one could hold up to four biplanes." When I don't react, he adds, "That's a lot, mind you."

I guess four planes inside of a blimp is a lot of weight for an inflatable balloon to carry. "Mr. B, I've actually never considered that blimps were anything but silly advertising gimmicks."

"You think that? Anyway, I remember standing at our bedroom window in the attic watching the October leaves falling down when one of these 700 to 800 feet dirigibles came into view! I watched it spilling out tons of water into the Blackstone River, and I didn't know what I was looking at!" Joe's eyes grow round." I remember it said the city of Los Angeles on the side."

"How old were you?"

"I was little, six or seven years old, but I could read it. Later on, I learned that it balanced itself with ballasts, one in the front and one in the back. When they wanted to gain height, they had to evacuate water to keep their equilibrium. Airships work just like submarines, believe it or not! But, where the Germans filled their Zeppelins with hydrogen," he nods, "which burned," I nod, "the Americans discovered the world's only source of helium in Texas! Believe it or not, there is only one source of helium in the world. As far as I know, Miss, helium, being a non-flammable gas, was what was inside the USS Los Angeles."

Joe's story has caught me like a fish in a net. "I had no idea helium was such a unique commodity, Mr. B."

"Well, I learned most about the helium from the radio coverage. The Germans had built the dirigible for America, believe it or not, based on the Versailles Treaty! It was just flying over our house in Woonsocket on the way to Lakehurst." He shrugs and becomes distracted by the afternoon light suddenly shredded over him. The rain has righted the clouds' equilibrium and the fluffy blimps are passing over Joe's neighborhood with the mountain breeze.

Despite the uneasiness of standing in this room together for so long, I'm not sure whether to excuse myself after Joe leaves off his story, or not. I shift my weight to rest on a hip.

His voice lifts in thought again. "My second job after college was in St. Louis, Missouri, where I was working at the airport, about 1940 or so. I was sleeping at a boarding house in Ferguson, where it was cooler, and another guy, a Navy pilot for one of those dirigibles, came to stay there with me. He was sort of a dandy, you know, with lots of money."

Joe isn't the dramatic type; his hands are stuck in his pockets as he recounts the details, but then he pulls them out to count. "Let's see, I think there was the Macon, the Ohio, the Shenandoah, and the Los Angeles: four dirigibles. He had piloted the USS Macon and survived a crash in it, but his wife had just left him for another officer, and he was down and out. I'll tell ya, he went about selling everything that he ever owned.

"Well, one day he showed me this beautiful Japanese wedding gown. I'm telling you, it was beautiful! It was thick black silk on the skirt with ornate embroidery. The top half was all golden embroidery, and the inside was just as beautiful, full of designs." Joe reaches to the back of his neck and fingers his collar. "At the nape of the neck, there was only one design. I'd never seen anything like that! He asked me if I wanted to buy it from him, and I did. I bought it."

"Wait. Wasn't this before you met Maudie?" I shift my weight from one hip to the other.

"Oh, I hadn't met Maudie! But, it was the most elegant thing I had ever seen. I paid him thirty-five dollars for that gown, and when I married, I gave it to her for a wedding gift. I remember it was a warm thing, but she wore it to her brother's summer wedding. Ooh, she looked fancy…" He smacks his lips and grins.

I begin heading for the door, but Joe isn't budging. "It was too bad for the pilot though. He was so angry and heartbroken about losing his wife that he spent every weekend in St. Louis at one of those rooftop bars where he drank himself silly. He tried to kill himself in his expensive car by taking the one hairy turn back to Ferguson too fast, but all he managed to do was wreck his nice car!

So, he bought himself another extravagant car and tried it again. That road was only a two-lane road, and that curve was a doozy. He succeeded the second time."

Joe peers at the sun-streaked window behind me. He seems to be a forlorn figure standing still in the middle of this large bedroom. But, Mr. B is a silo full of facts that spill out like kernels of grain for no apparent reason, or for every reason in the world, whenever we come to visit. He looks up. "I think he sold some carved Oriental chests to the boarding house matron because when she lost her husband, she sold three of them to me. I kept one. I sent two of them back home to Eddy and Bertha, his wife, and one to Wanda. She kept all of her linen and embroidery in that chest."

"What happened to your elegant wedding gown, Mr. B?"

"Oh, I think Maudie gave it to Victoria, Paul's sista. Victoria has it along with the chest that we gave her. She liked that Oriental stuff." He finally moves his feet to follow me out of the room.

"Heh, heh," He sucks in his cheeks and smacks his lips. "But I still remember how Maudie looked wearing that gown!"

August 31, 2013
Paul has walked to work for years, but today, after carrying another load of belongings to his father's, my hubster bounds out of his cab door. "I can't wait to drive my truck to work now!"

I bet Mr. B's neighbors will be delighted, especially at 5:45 a.m.

I try not to gawk at the giant faded blue X's of Mr. B's exterior barn- styled trim, or wonder what our friends will think of our demise. Paul has assured me that we have enough money from our house to paint his dad's place. But there's a renovation list to get the whole house out of the HUD margin. It makes my head swim. Besides, I'd be ousted if I broached the subject of changing the color, so I bite my lip.

"X marks the spot!" Paul resumes the old joke, raising the hair on my head. My husband's glee, equal to a kid's on Christmas, is particularly annoying. Why so happy? I muse. It's simply that we've escaped financial deconstruction. This is reason enough for him, but I remember his words from time to time during visits with his folks that he could see us living here one day. Not wanting to offend anyone, I politely said nothing and smiled. After all, we still had our ranch-style rental, the first house we renovated. Both Joe and Maudie advised us we would prefer to live in a ranch in our old age so that we didn't have to use stairs. That house is currently under a lease contract to renters, however. Obvious to me today, Paul has won and I have lost. All my renovation work, all my hospitality work, are really valued as a big fat ZERO on our latest family budget. *Nil.*

At least we won't have to pay a mortgage because forty-three years ago when houses were the price of cars, Paul's parents were fortunate enough to buy the house with cash. *How do young people manage such a feat as paying off a house these days?*

On moving day, Paul orders his friends to carry furniture this way and that. He knows the territory. We've decided together that we will give this transition a year. A year is a good time to rest after a tragedy occurs, without making any big decisions, at least that is what the experts say. So, a year with Mr. B is how I've resigned myself to make this move. Compared to what we've been through, I begin to experience the whole move as though we were on a vacation. "It's like a historic hotel," I say under my breath. The surreal feeling is most likely due, however, to finally being lifted out of our "high finance operation."

The fact that our friends are walking backward over the uneven back patio slab carrying furniture, forces my feelings back to earth. I imagine them tripping on the uneven patio and falling onto their backs with cabinets landing on top. "Oh please! Watch your step on the back porch! Some of the patio slabs have sunken."

"Yeah, watch yur step!" Mr. B clears his throat and inquires, looking from his son to me and back, which room would we like to occupy upstairs. When we hesitate, he offers us the master. Is this a test? Of course, we immediately decline. Instead, Paul announces we will need all three empty rooms upstairs.

"How can that be?" Joe asks. "You have that much?"

"Yeah, Dad," Paul shouts into Joe's ear. "We have everything you used to have in this house that you gave us, remember? Plus, everything else we've collected over twenty-four years of marriage is coming here."

Mr. B's mouth hangs open. I don't think he'd really considered this.

"Minus what we've left on Pearl Street for the missionaries," I mumble. It's our pearl of great price, indeed. What is the loss of any memory there? We don't yet know. I left heirloom furniture as part of the price of the settlement, all of our appliances and a bed.

As twenty-six loads of our lives begin to unpile themselves from our truck and our friends' vehicles, Joe continues to complain about his basement filling up with junk. Admittedly, the whole move has been so sudden and traumatizing, that we never had a yard sale.

Me? I can't find a reason to look through any of the boxes going into the basement or to sort things into separate spaces. I watch boxes of legal material pile into a concrete corner. My stomach has failed to relax, it seems, throughout this year. It makes me nauseated, now, to see the small mountain of paper. Has my life amounted to boxes of stored rubbish?

"You'll have time. I'm just worried about the fire hazard. Don't mind me." Joe turns his back on us and shuffles carefully to the garage to find something else to occupy his mind. Joe seems glad to welcome a new project into his garage, probably to distract him from watching the stream of boxes coming over his threshold. The project, specifically, is an antique cherry table we've acquired by trade. He immediately begins to scrape and sand it, sending clouds of sawdust and resin into our noses and boxes. Paul conducts our teams of friendly movers to carry our belongings right past Mr. B into the house and down the stairs on to the hard concrete floors…lining the basement walls.

After lunch with the wrecking crew, I bring Joe a vanilla shake. He doesn't eat or drink anything with chocolate after lunch.

"Thank you, Ma'am. I thank you." He gulps it. His white wrinkled skin is covered by holey khaki shorts and a holey T-shirt full of wood dust from sanding our table. His sagging wrinkled skin covers sinewy arms, and his forehead glistens from the exertion of refinishing our table. "Whatcha gonna do wid it once I'm finished?" he queries.

As I describe my thought of putting it on his back porch for family holidays, Mr. B is pleased by my "oohing and aahing", circling the table, passing the palm of my hand over it. "You know, I gotta show you off, Mr. B. You are our greatest treasure!" And, I believe my own words.

Ш 🖋 ღ

"Given the choice between the experience of pain and nothing, I would choose pain."
— William Faulkner, The Wild Palms

September ~ Thin Grins

September 1, 2013

My 80-year-old father arrives from Oklahoma, eager to help in his kids' transition. He negotiates the cost of a Tuff Shed for us while we await the closing transaction to clear our bank account. When the shed is built in a day, he immediately begins to construct storage shelves inside it.

When he sees the condition of the back patio, he asks, "Whataya gonna do with these sunken slabs back here?"

"I dunno, Dad. Please step carefully."

My sis, Ann, has also mercifully arrived to help me paint and remove old curtains. She winces when she views the framed, plastic covered weather barriers in the windows.

"They are Mr. B's form of window insulation," I explain with a dejected shrug. "He made each wooden frame himself and covered them with plastic to keep out the drafts in winter. But I won't be able to live in this house without being able to see out the windows. And I don't know how I'm gonna approach this situation because apparently, Maudie accepted it." Yesterday, I had praised him for his ingenuity!

She gives me a mama bear hug and sighs. Her presence brings courage in the broiling heat. Her career as a professional decorator instinctively calls her to work on other things. Joe, however, grows silent. He mutters that he doesn't understand why we need to change anything.

I take one of the front window plastics out to show him what he can see of the blue spruce out front and the neighbors' gardens, and for heaven's sake, the blue skies, telling him we can put the liners back into the windows when winter comes.

He concedes to that plan with a joke aimed at himself. "Oh look! Now I'll see what's going on between my neighbors!" He follows closely on our heels, now suspicious.

When we move into the den, he strokes the curtains. He explains how Maudie once picked out designer chintz fabric. And, maybe we should know that all the curtains have leaded liners for additional insulation. I could manage a lodge style form of décor here, so I praise their 43-year-old curtain selection, keeping those depicting western scenes for conciliation purposes.

In the bathroom we will be using, located across the hall from our bedroom, the decorator countertop of 60's Frenchy neon-yellow almost matches the sturdy vinyl sheeted floor with a faded fluorescent yellow and brown speckled pattern. The combination makes the hair on the back of my neck tingle. I'm embarrassed to use the toilet or shower here, and I'm ashamed of myself for this reaction so I shut my mouth.

Having already visited a couple of carpet stores, I am desperate to have the 43-year-old carved, harvest gold carpet replaced before we move in. When the measuring tape comes out, however, Joe reminds us that the nylon nap of this quality-made carpet "will last you forever!" I find he reasons like a low rent landlord. All business, without personal malice. I am tempted to ask him what the difference is between walking on his floors and the floors of a mud hut, but I lock my lips. He has convinced himself, and there have been no guests for twenty years to say otherwise. We forgo the carpet replacement in sad resignation.

Joe also rejects the suggestion of installing an air conditioner. Even in these triple digit temperatures, he doesn't see the need. Joe's body temperature always seems to stay on the cold side, he uses an electric blanket every night. Paul and I swing hot very easily.

Knowing nothing of what our priorities will be living here, I'm again willing to wait. "This is a transition." Then, another whisper under my breath, "This is not my house." I remember I'm practically a guest or an employee with a new job to be done here. I haven't even wet my big toe in this stagnant stream.

September 2, 2013

Joe moves the honey bear and the salt and pepper shakers, like checkers over the grain patterns of the maple breakfast table to illustrate for the company eating his eggs and toast the businesses in the town where he grew up. "The National Biscuit Company was located right next to two spurs and a mainline of the railroad tracks. Next to it was the French church. On the other side of the tracks was the feed and grain store, and right behind that was our house on Collier Street. When my parents first married, they moved into a row house, brick, across the street from the millhouse. But when our family started growing, they had to move to the house on Collier Street. That's the home I remember best. Everybody was poor around there."

"There was a woman on the fourth floor of 48 Collier Street. Her two sons could not get jobs, and they were always getting into trouble. Ooh, I've never seen a woman with so many headaches! I remember she would throw me down some money from her window, and I would run to the pharmacy to get her bromo seltzer for her headaches. Aye-ay-ay!"

"Those four-story houses were the most unusual houses I have ever seen, there in Woonsocket, Mr. B! I cannot imagine carrying groceries up to the fourth floor!"

"Well, that's why we lived on the second floor, heh-heh!" He makes a sucking noise with his lips and points at me and winks.

"We had an outhouse, no inside plumbing, but so did everyone else. Nobody cared if everyone else saw you running to the outhouse. Everyone understood those were the conditions. It's not a crime to be poor. It just doesn't smell so nice." He chuckles. "There were 'honey wagons' to clean out the outhouses ever-so-often."

"What's a honey wagon, Chief?" Paul pops a biscuit with honey between his teeth.

"Heh, not what you think!" Joe snaps his fingers and glances at my dad. "The outhouses had a sloping side, and the wagons came around to open that sloped roof and put a pumping tube into the holes. That's how they cleaned 'em out."

Paul swallows. "Okay. I've seen that in the pine forests, too. They still have those trucks for state parks and campgrounds. 'Honey wagons,' though! Augh. Who are they fooling?"

Mr. B is enjoying being the center of attention. "Yeah. And we bathed in a barrel. Fathea first, then the others. We heated our house with soft coal. There was a coal store in town, next to the fire station. It sold pea-coal, which we didn't use, and bituminous, which was the soft coal we used, and they sold hard coal, too, anthracite, I think it's called. I'm not sure who used that unless it was rich people."

It crosses my mind that all the women in my father-in-law's family died of cancer, except Lucy, who worked outside of the home in the rubber factory making soles for tennis shoes. Before that, she lived in a room of the wealthy Kimbal's home because she worked as their kitchen maid.

My dad offers, "I've heard they use coal to make Coke, too." He's finished his eggs and has mopped them up with his biscuits, downed with a glass of milk.

"Maybe," muses Mr. B, peeling a banana. "The only soda pop I ever tasted there was homemade root beer. My fathea liked to make it." He sits looking at his banana, forgetting to bite into it. "We also had a huge kerosene lamp, not like the small ones they use for decorations these days." He points out the one we gave them for Christmas. "You can get rid of that if you want. It's worthless." We cringe. "The base alone was almost a foot high, so when you carried it from place to place, you had to hold onto it."

"The railroad tracks were directly behind the outhouse, and we strung our laundry between the outhouse and the home by a fixed pulley and a movable pulley."

I consider Mr. B's current string of laundry swinging across the back porch of this house. Maybe it waves to salute his roots. It's a wonder that his wife, a lady of airs, conceded to so many years of looking at swinging undergarments.

"At night time," Mr. B continues, "some of Eddy's friends and I would go swimming in one of the railroad ponds. There were ponds on either side of the railroad, and lots of 'em. I'd swim out to the middle of the pond. There weren't so many mosquitos out in the middle."

"My mothea eventually won the argument for getting into a house with a toilet and a real tub. That was when we moved to Arnold Street. I still remember her stirring the sheets in a twelve-inch high copper pot full of boiled water. Then, she dumped it into the tub and lifted the sheets with a wooden spoon to let the cold water run over them. It was back breaking labor, even with her new tub."

Joe suddenly picks up his breakfast plate and licks off the honey. "When my mothea died, my sista Lucy opened her private wooden chest at the foot of her bed. She had filled it with pressed and folded fine linens, sheets and that kind of thing. Among all those things, Lucy found $4.13. My fathea had always kept the books. He was in charge of the money. I didn't know my mothea was so broke because by then I could have sent her money. But I didn't know. I think she was proud: she had secreted that money away."

September 3, 2013

Mr. B entertains my family, his company, at breakfast this morning by describing the way three astronauts died in their test flight capsule of the space shuttle, Apollo 1. Maybe it's the breakfast burritos we've brought home as opposed to his boiled white egg and dry toast that inspires him.

"You'll hear that astronauts Grissom, White, and Chaffee died in a cabin fire from undetermined causes, but they just don't want to admit it was an engineer's fault. See, the shuttle design called for an aluminum exterior, but some genius signed off on installing T-shaped interior extrusions made of magnesium." Joe's forefinger makes the sign of a 'T' in the air. "The government bought it, even though any high school science teacher could tell you that magnesium flares are used under water because magnesium burns, even in water!"

He slurps the yolk out of his half-shelled egg. "Magnesium was lighter weight than aluminum though, and NASA used it without bothering to isolate it from the electrical wires in the shuttle walls. Well, there was one hundred percent oxygen pumped into the inside of that test capsule, so when the three guys—nice guys by the way—latched themselves into their seats, it only took one spark of energy from all that wiring to create an instantaneous shock, which translated into a flash fire that spread throughout the capsule filled with oxygen into their lungs. It burned up their insides, can you guess why?"

"Because their lungs were also filled with oxygen?" I pipe up.

He winks and points his finger at his good pupil, "And fire follows oxygen. What a tragedy."

My sister, who has been holding a bite of burrito for some time on her fork, clears her throat and asks, "They didn't suffer, did they?"

"Oh no. There was only one of them who got a single word out. Neither of the other two even spoke. It only took a second. Oh, all that stuff is in the records." He waves the story away and bites into his dry toast.

Tragedy must breed appetite. The breakfast dishes hardly require rinsing.

Ducking under the empty clothesline on the back porch later, I tentatively approach my new housemate-cum-father-in-law, who is cleaning a paintbrush in his garage. Our cherry table sits fully expanded in the garage and happily appears to seat at least ten people. Its raw, shining wood appears silky naked after Joe's steady sanding. Seeing the table shining in this small garage feels like an appeasement of our failed hospitality house, thankfully no longer my problem.

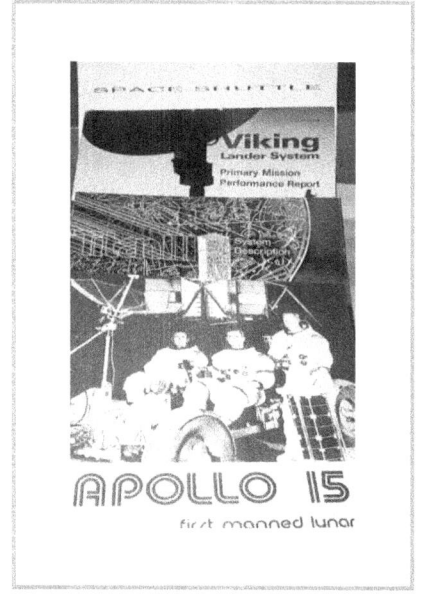

"Oh! You surprised me." His blue eyes suddenly widen when he notices me standing there. Joe's thin white T-shirt has stains and sawdust on it.

Refocusing, my feeling of guilt for the prospect of mortally wounding someone I dearly love, my voice wavers. "May I paint these colors upstairs, Mr. B, in the bedrooms?" I offer Joe a handful of the color cards. Pointing to one, I ask him, "And this pale blue in the den and dining room?" Tears well up and spill over my cheeks from the tension. I'm implying that his own choices are not good enough, but I have tried to mitigate the damage by choosing a steely hue because Joe loves light blues, and this modern color is something I can decorate with.

He pats me on the arm and says with such tenderness, "Only if you stop crying over it. Don't worry about me, Sweet Pea. I'll be fine."

Outside, my father is helping Paul cut studs and screw together benches in his shed. When he realizes that my sister and I intend to make over the den, he tells Joe that he particularly likes Joe's "wood" paneling. "I hate the thought of painting wood white."

I study him in disbelief. He ignores me. Instead, dad supports what he sees as a frail willow of an old man about to be crushed in his daughter's vigor. Mr. B looks at his distressed tennis shoes and then decides that maybe we should wait to paint this room until he's gone, meaning *kicked the bucket*. Satisfied, my father turns to go.

Has my dad been waiting for just the right opportunity to return a decorating favor? A twenty-year-old image of my father's kitchen splattered by the explosion of my experimental caramel sauce from a pressurized can drifts through my mind. He doesn't turn around to see me studying his back as he carries his electrical bag up the stairs. Quickly, my skilled father remedies the ponderous heat inside our upstairs bedroom by installing a ceiling fan. I am numb for hours. "Thank you," I manage without feeling or understanding.

Ann and I carefully tape down painting plastics to the dust boards. I open the first gallon of paint and set it on top of the stepladder. "Let's pray first," I suggest, feeling particularly unsteady. Gulping a breath, I thank the good LORD for my sister's help and ask Him for strength to paint the bedrooms in this heat, and finally, for carefulness so that we can avoid accidents.

Within a wild hair of the "amen," I turn, my foot hits the ladder, and the can of paint topples onto the contoured old carpet well beyond the scope of our carefully laid tarp.

Astounded, my heart skips several beats, then pounding, pumps adrenalin. I grab up the can and start cupping the spilled paint into it in hopeless handfuls. I stifle a scream. I can't cry. I can't think, except to shudder at what Joe might think—that I spilled it on purpose! My sister gasps, shouts, and runs for cloths. We both stand there, searching each other's stunned faces and to the streaks of paint, as if God himself had slapped it over in contravention of our prayer.

Why would the God of redemption and wholeness desire my *brokenness*? This has been my flattened soul's whimper for the past six months!

While I'm freaking over the mystery and dishing the paint back into the container with increasing panic, Ann quickly puts on some music. It begins to lift our spirits, up, up into a surreal "Curley-the-clumsy-Smurf" land. Neither one of us dares to speak. My brain threatens a split.

I've been told the Almighty hates human pride, but *why*? Is He like the Greek god Apollo who dispels human arrogance with arrows? Couldn't be. I'm guessing it must be that knots of pride are like knots found in inferior lumber. Knots look strong, but they cause problems with strength. Seems all my hard knots have fallen out and only the Redeemer's presence, like putty or wood glue, will mend me. Maybe I am whole only because of Him.

Because of my long desperation, I'm beginning to see the importance of integrated relationships. Thank God Ann is here! These family members practically flew to my aid. The movers, were also committed to helping us, their friends.

I cut the paint into the 90-degree corners of the room with a small brush, musing. It must be that when we feel bigger than life, independent, more successful than others, we see ourselves as separated from them, and thankful for the illusion. Friends have proven to be my Savior's hands and feet in our time of need, and good friends gave us good counsel: their love has been our saving grace.

We can, of course, dictate our own lives without messing with another's disapproval. I often reject opinions as interference. In this my silent hour of tragedy, I would prefer to seek my own good in my own manner apart from the good of the community because I'm just that impatient, but God is not me. He loves the world, invites us to rule with Him, slowly, allowing us all kinds of mistakes, and God glories in unity! He doesn't love isolation. The tears come down now, rolling off my upturned face, wetting my shirt like sweat. It goes against the grain of my entire being. I don't understand.

I've been learning, the hard way, that individuality is an oil well needing to be capped off so that the valuable oil can be guided away from a powerful blowout, into usefulness in a community. Arrogance, which separates me from others, only raises a self-sufficient barrier against relationships and ultimately against my Creator. When we are broken, however, we are opened up spiritually to receive help from others and from Him.

Internally wailing, I'm wrestling with these grandiose themes, when my father-in-law comes to inspect our progress with the bedroom painting. As if the accident calls out his name, he turns his eyes downward and then rotates his gaze to survey the extent of the obvious paint spill. The floor opens up–or maybe it doesn't. Everything swirls while we apologize and explain what's happened. He simply offers to clean it up himself. My face burns. I cannot let that happen. I say I will fix it. I have no idea how to fix it. The paint I bought is a specialty paint with *sand in the mix!* My energy ebbs at an all-time low.

I end up calling a carpet cleaning business, but they cannot promise a good result.

Thankfully, mercifully, Paul unrolls the area rug we obtained in a trade last week for our reclining chair. That settles it. As far as we are concerned, the rug covers the paint on the carpet brilliantly. Our bedroom furniture is moved in. What will become of the paint spill at the end of our year with Mr. B? I shove that thought, along with the paint, under the rug.

September 4, 2013
It's certain, absolutely, without question, I won't be able to sleep through my troubles on this uncomfortably narrow bed! Our own bed, the king-sized bed, couldn't fit beyond the bulkhead of the stairs in Joe's house. We thus moved the consolation marriage bed into our newly painted bedroom. I lie on the queen mattress now, staring at the ceiling. I roll around on what used to be our guest bed trying to imagine us sleeping so closely together during the heat of late summer. This sweaty thought makes my muscles tense. Just the thought of it brings on a hot flash.

Life is draining from me like the sand from an hourglass. I feel nothing. More precisely, I feel no purpose. Is this what Joe felt like after Maudie passed? Is this grief? Few in our community were particularly supportive anyway. This grief is only the final door closing on my feelings of belonging.

Outside the bedroom windows, clouds of yellow and gray drift into the form of a dragon and burgeon into a cupid's chubby face. Rain clouds. I've set my hand to a few certain efforts in life, but each has slipped through my fingers. I begin brewing about this fact as I watch the golden cupid's face elongate and darken into a shark's snout. This ceiling over my head; a consolation prize? Geography, moving, unfamiliar maps, neighbors whose windows parallel our windows, whose windows overlook our entire backyard. The doors in this house seem to be shutting and leaving me out. There isn't enough WD-40 oil in the world to reopen them.

My hospitality house and gnarly-fisted litigation nearly caused Paul's financial ruin. There aren't enough boxes of TSP crystals in this world to clean up my mess. There is no reason to it. No rightness.

Paul calls sharply for me to help him with something at the bottom of the stairs. "Where are you?!" I sigh. My pity party, wrapped in laziness, ends. I throw my legs over the side of the bed to go help the Energizer Bunny.

Later, when Paul and I take a lunch break, we bring Mr. B a strawberry mango smoothie. Paul's smile is still boyishly winsome. With his brown shiny hair, though he has his own ailments, he looks strong and fit. His generosity brings humor from the Chief.

"Oh, what's this? Gee-whiz," Joe sings, taking his first sip. "I can't resist this! Why'd you kids do it? Now, I'll just have to go to the bathroom."

September 5, 2013

A vision of a two-story plantation house shining in an oval flashing as if it is a hanging pendant against my chest wakes me this morning. On one side, it is a glad image, in bright sunshine. I peer more closely at the front of the house because that is the only image presenting itself, then the pendant flips and an aged old red exterior is decorated with white front porch pillars.

Instinctively, I believe this is a sacred message, so I pay attention. A friend, Malinda, had once told me that she kept a dream diary and that there were online helps to determine the meanings of dreams for Christians. I check with her by phone and also perform some online research and begin to look up scriptural images. I don't know why I am so compelled to understand this little vision, but I will continue to study the image until I'm satisfied. Its mystery has propelled me into finding a more significant purpose for living here than simply being a place to hang my hat while we reconstruct our lives.

Betty, Joe's new female friend, brings over a salad to serve for lunch. She's in good spirits and has been traveling.

"Hello, Mr. Byk! Do I have some stories to tell you!" She's returned from some charity work with inner-city school children in Detroit. "I thought I went there to serve, but what an experience I had! Those kiddos taught me a thing or two." Joe's eyebrows raise. My dad offers a prayer for the lunch, and Mr. B lets us hold his hands to complete the circle. We chow down.

Betty follows my dad from the dining table to see the new shed. Mr. B, then, takes the opportunity to inform me that he agrees with Albert Einstein's deathbed critique of God. "Albert said something-or-ruther that he wasn't an atheist. The problem of God is just too big for our limited minds. His perspective was that we 'are in the position of a little child entering a huge library filled with books in many languages. The child knows someone must have written those books. It doesn't know how. It doesn't understand the languages in which they are written.' You know a kid grows accustomed to the mysteries of the universal order of things, and also the arrangement of holy books, but he doesn't know what it means." Joe pauses for me to soak up where his dialogue is headed. "So, I agree with Einstein, that even the most intelligent human being should have a certain attitude toward a God that we can see in the universe from earth. We can observe the world obeying certain laws, but people don't really understand these laws. We can only put so much trust in the holy books that men write about them." Joe opens his hands. and his mouth opens in apology and pulls back in a resigned arc for asserting his beliefs.

"Okay," I pause briefly, then argue. "I agree, to a certain extent, that we all see or feel different aspects of God. Different people would be able to touch a leg or trunk of an elephant, from one position only. One feels a leg and describes God like that. One feels a trunk or a neck or ears, and describes God like that. But I don't think we should stick our heads in the sand and act like we can't learn more about God."

"Have you ever heard of the probability curve?" Joe counters. He makes the sign of a bell with his right forefinger. "It's a bell curve. It's one of those statistics that salesmen use, especially insurance people. All the time you'll hear this phrase, 'It's ninety percent certain that...' or some other percentage is used. But they are only quoting you the percentage of the probability curve. You will never hear the second percentage, which is really the *only* one that matters!" Joe's ire towards salesmen is showing. "It's the second percentage of certainty or confirmation that really matters. All students of statistics are taught this, but if it isn't used, you can be sure you are being defrauded, Kid."

Mr. B cocks his head, winks his eye, and points at me. "The percentage of probability should always be backed up by the percentage of certainty, and the percentages should be ninety-five percent with a ninety percent confirmation or certainty to back up the probability. Now that, Kiddo, is a pretty good assurance. Yup!" He nods like the old Star Wars' sage Yoda, closing his eyes. He doesn't come right out and say it, but his analogy means that he hasn't been sold on the probability of any religion being correct enough for him to place his own faith in it.

And yet, God reveals himself to me through his Word, through others, through history, through creation, and the organization of nature's laws. Christ reveals Himself through the record of His life events, and the Holy Spirit's work is revealed through personal answers to my prayers like the assuring dream I had this morning.

September 6, 2013

We all hop into my dad's Dodge van and drive to Centennial Airport to eat lunch at the Perfect Landing restaurant, a place with walls made of windows for the purpose of watching small aircraft use the landing strip. Both my dad and Joe are "wing and lift" oriented souls. My dad flew small Pipers, Mooneys, and Cessna planes the entire time I was growing up, from third grade and after, and Joe helped structurally engineer military aircraft prior to being transferred into space shuttles and rockets.

The parents' voices in low rhythms exchange stories of fighting gusty winds in the flying machines. They discuss the hazards of novice pilots who panic flying too low in the slopes of the Rockies, crashing when they try to pull up or turn. Dad describes a vacation when we flew over the cliffs of the Grand Canyon at sunset, how our stomachs bottomed out as the land suddenly fell away and how deceptive shadows can be. We watch planes take off and land on the strips of black tarmac as the men talk. To see the shiny, white and chrome fuselages turn with flashes of sun's rays and go up into the rolling clouds reminds me of the times I've looked out a plane window to view the world's well-organized, colorful quilt squares with rivers and roads for bindings.

"I remember when you taught me to fly using the pedals on the floor of your plane, Dad. Remember how surprised I was that the wheel was for lift, not turning?" My father winks.

Joe's delight is expressed in a question, "You did that? You learned to fly?"

"I think Christina, Joe's nine-year-old great-granddaughter," I explain for my father's benefit, "is also learning to fly her grandfather's plane."

"Is she?" They both exclaim. "Oh, she's a clever girl!" Joe brags.

September 7, 2013

After some grateful farewells to my dad and sister, I retreat to my room to finish some research waiting there. So far, the messages of the meaning of this week's dream, the images of my father-in-law's house, have been as clear as the proverbial writing on the wall. I've listed all of the possibilities of symbolic meanings. Some of them seemed clearly comforting and hopeful, like the shallow sloping roof meaning the oversight that is light handed and barely visible, the pillars meaning stable leadership and assistance to bear up under the roof's weight, the fact that the pillars were white could mean righteousness or angels, or ready for harvest, glory. A house with two stories means community, camaraderie and multiplication. The ethereal glow means a spiritual purpose or covering. Some of them, though, represent choices ahead of me, like the necklace holding a charm touts a symbolic yoke. Is a yoke guiding a person necessarily negative? Is oversight bad? I have to choose my yoke and live with hierarchy; doesn't everyone? The implications in my dream had the hint of glory.

Then there was the confusing meaning of the red exterior implying neglect or fire. I am not sure if certain images apply to Joe and his personal history. If so, what am I meant to do with this information? Were some meanings applicable to the future and some the past? The image of the cameo ornament or house pendant indicates the outward display of a person's inner delight. That seems promising.

Significant symbols were brought to my attention for a reason. Inherently, I know that the longer I live here, the more I'll comprehend, but this vision has soothed my distress and solidified the fact that we will be living here with God's purposes surrounding us. My entire being feels airy. The symbols of my dream have provided a paradigm shift, transforming discontent to contentment. God sees me. Although He is the same far away Creator of the earth, the universe, the stars, and the sun, this same God cares about tiny me and sees my predicament. This intervention gives me hope in what feels like a wilderness within four walls.

September 8, 2013
Charmayne comes to help me paint today. She walks squarely into the hall entry, sets down her dainty purse on Joe's spindle bench, greets Mr. B, and then sits down in our den to chat before we get to work. She gazes all around her. I realize I'm sitting on pins and needles. Under her feet is the rust colored shag area rug and beneath that is his faux tiled white linoleum. Suddenly, Charm offers that she feels comfortable in this room. With a genuine and happy grin, she pats our couch and coos, "I'm amazed how well your brown living room suite fits in here." She leans back and we chat under the western scenes on the drapes. "I love this place! It's peaceful," she adds. After a while, we put on some music, and she helps me paint the last bedroom in the stifling heat. She used the phrase, *love this place*! Oh, how I love Charmayne!

Mr. B says later, "Your young friend, Char-le-mayne, reminds me of my sista Lucy. They are about the same petite build. Nice figure, your friend."

I've noticed the ol' man hasn't lost his interest in women. He usually likes them tall and lean, like his late wife. He likes them taller than his own five-feet-four inches. "Yup! She's an amazing friend, Mr. B. Not as tall as you normally like, though." I wink.

He pats my arm. "I'm glad you have a sense of humor, Mrs. B. I don't know what I'd do if I had to live with a woman without a sense of humor!"

Within five minutes of trying to find a matching salad fork and spoon in his kitchen, all my good humor evaporates. The violent idea of throwing forks and knives into the linoleum floor, so that they stick, seems injuriously appropriate to me. I'm freaking exasperated! I don't understand Mr. B's kitchen. His mismatched cups and dishes fill cupboards, leaving no room for what is familiar to me, namely our matching cups and dishes, things we've carefully decided upon before acquiring.

Regularly, Mr. B makes my discomfort of cooking for him worse. During any given dinner he describes how much he despises even the smell of Mexican spices, smells that might actually cause him to choke to death at this age should they be foisted upon his senses, and he cannot eat Italian oil or any shiny foods with butter or dressings, mayonnaise or sauces, or he may upchuck right there at the table. When I described these conversations to Mr. B's granddaughter, Sandy, on this visit, she looks at him and says, "You mean *flavor*?" earning instant credits with me.

He shrugs with chagrin. "I guess I'm a little *particular*." Supporting my position, she rolls her eyes and smirks.

What fills his refrigerator is not what we eat, and I've sworn off frying anything or sautéing vegetables. My peanut Thai sauce and sesame oil are put away in deference to his preferences. He apparently believes I'm not getting his tastes right. He tells everyone I make international foods just because I use garlic, basil, and feta cheese. His freezer is stocked up on lima beans, black-eyed peas, and shrimp. His cupboards are stocked with, *surprisingly*, Chicken a la King, - in cans!

How could Maudie have chopped, mixed, and cooked in this dark brown Mediterranean style kitchen all those years? The faded countertops are two feet long on either side of the sink, and half of one side is taken up with a sink drainer. Now, our coffee maker takes up the other half of one counter. My Crock-Pot gets shoved onto the top of the fridge as does the food processor. I'm bereft of my china, blue glassware, and the cherry red cookware given to me by my friends for my fiftieth birthday. These kitchen treasures are lost down the hollow sounding stairs and piled on the concrete basement floor.

Most of our spices are also piled in boxes in the basement, along with everything from our community house kitchen and pictures from guest rooms and sitting rooms. When Joe sees these boxes, which we should have marked, "Tragically Rotting Contents", he complains that we have too much junk. "When will you get rid of it?" What does he think, that I will toss out my household goods?

I can't even make his potato peeler work. As I tromp down the stairs to look for my own peeler, I remember a young missionary couple who only ate beans for a year while living in a village in West Africa. No potato peeler required.

I do my best today to prepare breakfast, lunch, and dinner with only salt and pepper. I cook with a tepid smile for Paul and his father. Love can sure string you along when the silt of your grounding has drained out. Strange feeling, this floating without substance, going through motions without holding the weight of things in my hands.

Tonight, after several days of eating my cooking that doesn't delight anyone's senses, because it's too flavorful for Joe and too bland for us, my father-in-law instructs Paul to take away all of Maudie's pots and pans and her dishes from the kitchen to make room for mine. Pauly explains his dad's orders as I'm playing with his locks of brown hair in the privacy of our bedroom. Mr. B's decision seems out of the blue! Relief floods over me. "Why do you think he's decided this, honey?"

"Mom won't be using the kitchen, and you should be able to cook with your own pots and pans and dishes. That's what he told me."

September 9, 2013

I retrieve a kitchen organizer from a pile in the basement, which allows us to keep half of Mr. B's dish set, and I add some of our dishes to the cabinet, too. Many of Joe's dishes are cracked, so the cracked dishes I put into a box, which Paul then takes out to be picked up by the trash men. Joe asks me where the rest of his dishes are, and I follow his rush to meet the trash truck. From the front door, I hear Joe asking the man hanging off the back of the truck if he can use the cracked dishes. The disheveled trash man laughs at Joe who stands there sheared of his good will. My heart breaks. I can't absorb this. His sacrifice is his salvation, and ours is ours. But who can bear the price?

I buy a twelve-space cubby, which will presumably take up more of the unreasonable small space in the kitchen, but we can possibly fit a lot of staples in it. *Who cares?* I reason. I'm a hermit now. *I'm never inviting my book club here. No parties. Ever. Is there a remainder of friendship in them? Surely, courageous people who have experienced losses themselves will understand.*

Paul and I manage to plug and screw the entire organizer together, following directions and helping one another. This is a most surprising event. We don't argue about it once. In wonder and gladness, I fill up the organizer-cum-pantry with sugar, salt, flour, the waffle maker, a stock pot, cereals, vinegar, and oils.

September 10, 2013

Joe's arm is tucked into mine as we pick our way carefully through the shimmering wet parking lot of a local grocery store. He suddenly laughs out loud. "Do you see those people walking by and staring at us?"

I guess I had noticed some curious glances.

He chuckles again. "We got 'em fooled! They just don't know what to make of an old guy like me with a young babe on his arm!

And I'm enjoying the joke myself!"

Filling up our grocery cart, we make the mistake of choosing a checkout line that runs as painfully slow as an engineer's description of, well, anything. When the cashier finally starts to process our groceries, I notice we have a man as old as gold for our bagger. He's using an oxygen pump. He and Mr. B avoid the elephant in the room, for he is obviously in worse condition than Mr. B. Instinctively, I help push along the groceries from the conveyor belt to the bagger. I have an awkward sense that Mr. B is comparing his comfortable retirement, as he and I as companions have been joking around doing chores together. I assume the man needs the work or he wouldn't be standing up all day bagging groceries in his condition.

I pushed along a large can that he intended to grab. Suddenly, the bagger slaps my hand, hard.

"Oh!" I exclaim, recoiling. "I'm sorry." Then, I wonder why I'm the one apologizing. That old guy makes me feel like Dorothy, in the Wizard of Oz, getting her hand swatted by the grumpy apple tree who catches her stealing apples.

Time goes by, and I snag out a head of lettuce that I should have bagged way back in the produce aisle. Absently, I begin to push along the groceries, and again the old man swats the top of my hand. Sharp!

Joe, having averted his gaze, hasn't a clue that the old bagger has smacked me down twice. Instead, Mr. B grasps the handle of his full grocery cart and joyfully pushes it out to our car. His baby steps have me shuffling beside him in consternation.

"Did you see that old bagger abuse me, Mr. B?" I exclaim. "Why, he could lose his job for slapping me–twice–that is, if I had a mind to complain."

"Who did what? What are you saying, Miss?" He begins unloading the cart, tossing grocery bags like soccer balls to me for loading up the car.

"Oh, nothing." I decide to count my blessings.

September 11, 2013

It's raining. It's been raining for a week. This is not the typical Colorado autumn. We help Joe at the clothesline, unpinning his underwear and Pippi Longstocking socks, bringing them into the house to fold while we watch the news. Crazy storm warnings slip across the TV screen in urgent yellow font accompanied by red signs and orange pictures of mountain sludge and clouds. Joe's grandchildren call to tell us they are surrounded by a moat of water! A trailer court nearby them has washed down the river. Colorado experiences significant and terrible flooding in Estes Park, Longmont, and surrounding communities and again in Colorado Springs. Photographs of cars being carried down the mountain highways in the currents are posted on the news and the Internet. Lives are lost in the mud and debris. Business structures and whole towns are destroyed.

Joe turns to me shaking his head and says, "I dunno if those people will ever be able to rebuild there. A whole community wiped out? No. I don't think so. It's too bad."

Then, he speaks about the trains he saw as a child moving through Woonsocket, filled with orphans, headed west. "Nobody knew what to do with orphans, so they stuck them on trains, and poor, struggling farmers and ranchers from the western states would meet the trains, pick out a couple of kids to adopt as their own, and those kids would work like ranch hands for them. In return, they found belonging, and if the family survived, an inheritance."

The music for his international mystery begins, and we are transported into the world of entertainment. "Everyone experiences loss and tragedy," he says. "Almost everyone. It's part of life."

September 12, 2013

Mr. B suggests we all head off to the mountains for a weekend to spoil ourselves. This is one thing that Joe and Maudie always enjoyed spending their money on. Three weeks out of every year, they lived like royalty in any place that caught their fancy, and free from any annual timeshare baggage and free of cooking chores for Maudie.

Taking the wheel, I roll down the street in our 1995 cherry red Saturn. A grey tree squirrel, a skinny little tucker, runs into the road then hesitates as I slam on my breaks. He avoids the wheels and scuttles back. As we pull into Vail, a black crow struts confidently into the road, then begins sprinting in front of me. Again, I hard brake. But this bird slows down perceptively as if he can calculate the odds according to my speed. "Will you look at that little snot? That crow just slowed down from a trot as if to dare me!" I look into my rearview mirror after passing it by. "Another car is coming behind me and, the crow's hopped around and started back across the road!"

Paul chirps from the back seat, "He's not scared of you. He's got Geiko." That puts Mr. B into the spirit. He begins pointing out all the color in the aspens on the hillside.

Arriving, we take our brunch in the Sonnenalp atrium on Vail Road. Mr. B is pleased with the exquisite garden setting and warm sun rolling between puffy clouds. A yoga group plants itself on the grassy knoll between our table and the river. As the ladies begin to mobilize, each of us snicker at the added entertainment.

"It's free, wid our brunch!" Joe elbows me. He motions with his chin to the grass. I see a row of black stretchy-panted buttocks positioned towards us. "This is the best place of all to eat." He chuckles. "We'll come back here tomorrow."

September 13, 2013

"What kind of higher education did you have to get to become a rocket engineer, Mr. B?" We are lounging with newspapers and a local cuisine journal between us in the lodge of our Americanized Swiss condo. A fire is stirring, just because it's fall in the mountains.

"Oh, I worked for Vultee, then Curtiss-Wright as an engineer and then I taught for a year at the Spartan Company in Oklahoma. After that, I married Maudie," he winks, "and she kinda pushed me to get my Master's in engineering. So we inquired from some colleges and found out that I had to get my past supervisors to write letters to certify the work I'd performed over the five years previous. The plan was that then I had to write a thesis paper, and then Alabama State would give me a Master's designation. Vultee actually wanted me back, and they said as much in their letter." He smiles reporting the complement.

"So, what did you write your thesis on?" I'm wondering, how does one write a thesis in mathematical equations?

"Diagonal Tension Beams. And that's what I took to the Martin Company. Maudie was an excellent typist, and she edited and typed the whole thesis for me, probably several times if I admit it." Involuntarily, Joe's eyebrows rise. "I felt, you know, that it was important to start out recognized for the Masters certificate as well as for my experience."

"Why?"

"Oh, for purposes of a better salary, see, and they did that."

One professor, Dr. Wang, he pronounced it 'Wong,' taught something so different to anything else I was learning. We were used to working on the mathematics of the object, like a rocket or plane, but he taught us about the mathematics of the space around the object."

"*Around* the object?"

"Yes Ma'am. When there is an object sitting in a space of air, people usually focus on the mathematical size and shape and characteristics of the object. Dr. Wang focused on the size and shape and characteristics of the space around the object. I didn't absorb it all in his class, but it fascinated me. My favorite kind of problem eventually came out of a course on conical intersections. They were tricky. Calculating the intersection of cones requires some tricky mathematics because at no point are the dimensions the same."

I decide to rein in these esoteric thoughts before they get too far over my head. "What kind of work did you do on the seaplanes?"

"Oh, the tops of all planes have to have some strapping, and they also have like two hats so that when someone is walking on top of the plane, they can secure their feet against the hats. But someone thought that to make the seaplane lighter, they should eliminate the strapping across the body. And the company bought it. But in the water, see, the space *around* the object, the long tails and under body would take on an amount of water that would cause the upper body to bend out of its structural limits and break apart. So, one of the first jobs I was in charge of the crew that was pumping volumes of water into the aircraft to see what would happen to the top without the strapping.

When I saw it start to deform, I called my boss, and he called his boss, and they all came down to look at it and thanked me for not pouring any more water into the craft because it would have ruined it."

"They had to put the strapping back onto the plane?"

"Yes, both the strapping outside and bulkheads inside the plane to isolate how far the water would travel if it became submerged. I helped design the new strapping and the bulkheads."

September 14, 2013

The greenness of Mr. B's yard strikes all three of us as we pull his 95 Saturn into his driveway after our lovely weekend in Vail. My father-in-law lives half way between the two flooded towns of Estes Park and Colorado Springs, in the foothills of unincorporated Jefferson County, and here the rain innocently begets a second springtime. Joe's grass has greened up to chartreuse and finally turned a deep, cool green.

All three of us decide to go rest from our travels on the back porch. *Rest from rest, imagine that.* Oh, I do happily consider it. Afternoon light romances us with an infusion of gold in all the outdoor tones. The snapdragons, zinnias, and some of Joe's Chicago Peace roses perk up and bloom as if they had been languishing for this long, cool drink.

Paul rambles to his bike and shakes the handlebars to indicate his intentions. We infiltrate our new neighborhood like spies on cycling explorations, reflecting and silent expeditions, through winding paths, under long sunsets in the living colors of autumn and crisp spring. It seems, ironically, we are altogether part of nature's vibrant life rather than morbid death.

Joe waits for us, seated before his international mysteries. When we ask him how the show was tonight he says, "Oh, I wasn't paying much attention. I was thinking about you two. Have you gone down by the river? I used to walk there, miles really, to blow off steam. It's really something!" Joe's scientific dilemmas, ethical versus moral, have haunted him. He has relayed to us often how he sweat his labors.

September 15, 2013

Yum! And it's so simple! Joe says he's never tasted anything so good as his warm soft roll with the crisp light crust, even without a smidge of butter. We went grocery shopping together and picked up some new dinner rolls, so tonight, I warmed them up as instructed and serve them with plain, boiled chicken soup, carrots, and celery. My father-in-law doesn't let butter cross his lips. He simply takes a bite of roll with every bite of dinner and swigs it all down with a gulp of milk.

Joe once gave Paul a tie tack fashioned in the emblem of the first space shuttle, Gemini. "Do you still have that tie tack, Paul?" Mr. B asks over dinner. "It was an award given to the team who worked on the first space shuttle. Each one of us received it, kind of a limited edition if you will."

Paul painfully explains that several years ago, while we were on vacation, the troubled teen who lived with us stole his box of jewelry, together with several other priceless heirlooms. It is something we dearly regret losing but rarely speak about. Joe shrugs as though this news is to be expected.

Paul changes the subject to describe how he has been trying to apply himself at work against some natural resentment. This is because his boss just traded him to another division. "I like my new boss better, and the team keeps telling me how much they need me, but I just feel like the bottom dropped out of everything I know and understood about work at the hospital. My old team wasn't told, so they think I've left them in the lurch of my own accord. It's a mess that I don't know how to explain to anyone. I don't have any motivation."

Paul's dad rises to the occasion by trying to console him. "Very few people actually retire from the aerospace industry without being laid off for lengths of time. That's because whenever a research project is completed, the next project builds on what has already been done, so the specific talent of an engineer might not be needed again. If something in his resume could be plugged into another project, he would be rehired." Joe shrugs again and explains, "I would see people politicking in the aisles between offices, but I wouldn't participate in gossiping or 'brown nosing sessions,' as I called it." He chuckles. "Instead, I tried to be ahead of the game. I kept reading the journals, all the new trends, and new engineering studies. When my project was done, I would apply for a new position on the next team. In that way I was lucky, and eventually, I retired from the same company."

Mr. B squeezes Paul's hand on the table. "You are doing a good job, too, son. I know you work hard, or they wouldn't keep piling you up wid new work. Even if it's hard, or you don't like it, you know that they respect you enough to handle it, and where there's a need, there's job insurance."

September 16, 2013

We are outside in the backyard together. Mr. B examines a broken garden hose. "Hey, kid, let's go down to Ace Hardware." He twiddles his toothpick between his finger and thumb. "They carry all kinds of sizes of things that you can't find at the big box stores." We scramble into the car with him carrying his piece of green hose.

He shuffles into the store and asks a middle-aged male clerk for help, showing him the piece of hose. "I need a clasp or a conduit to mend this here…" The man takes the green piece, looks more closely at it, and reaches up for a fix. He hands the part to Joe saying, "This should do it."

His eyebrows go up automatically, and Mr. B counters, "How do you know which size? Did you measure it? Did I miss that?"

The clerk chuckles and explains that he recognized it was a 5/8ths inch hose, and before he can continue, Joe steps backward, visibly embarrassed. "I apologize," he admits frankly. "Of course you know your own business. I had measured this at home, so I assumed you would have to do the same. I don't mean to offend you."

The clerk smiles kindly. "Oh, I'm not offended at all. I understand your concern." Then he picks up a ruler and measures the hose to prove to Joe that there are two typical sizes of garden hoses, and he is used to recognizing which is which. "No problem at all."

As I watch the entire exchange, I realize it would never have occurred to me that challenging a store clerk's knowledge on a subject important to me was being inappropriate.

The floor in this aisle suddenly feels surreal, like holy ground. Witnessing Mr. B's meekness is something short of witnessing a miracle in an age of entitlement. I feel the same humility witnessing this scene that I normally only feel singing certain songs of worship. How much will I learn by spending time in Joe's presence?

On the way out of the store, Mr. B advises me, "These guys know their stuff. I come here because they give good advice and good help."

September 17, 2013

It's Joe's new breakfast favorite to be served a warm roll with marmalade or strawberry jelly alongside his soft-boiled egg, unpeeled banana and steaming cup of Ovaltine. Breaking an awkward silence, I begin, "Mr. B? What was your mother like?"

Joe stares back with complacent blue eyes. "I never knew my mothea."

I sigh, regretting the question. *This will go nowhere.*

"No. She never learned to speak English, and she kept to herself. Even during the war, I never knew how she felt, who her family was in Poland or anything. She never learned to speak English, at least not that I ever heard, but I think she understood it after a while."

I leave it be. We eat in slow silence. When he notices our dog,

Jester, lying by the table, he begins again.

"She didn't like animals in the house, but she would feed a stray cat outdoors. She cooked on a stove that also served to heat our house. She would use metal tongs to lift up the grate and start the fire in the morning. When it was going, she'd cook us breakfast. Once a year, she would cart kettles of boiling water up the stairs to our room and pour them over the mattresses and the iron springs so that would take care of any bugs in the house. She caught the water underneath with another pan. Ooh, that was hard work! We never had bed bugs that I remember. But once a month she would also scrub the floor on her hands and knees, so maybe that did it."

I begin to worry now that Joe may make comparisons.

"She had a hard life. I wouldn't wish her life on women today. Oh, but my mothea was strong. She was sturdy even though she was smaller than her two sistas." He chuckles. "Oh, I know my mothea liked me. My favorite treat that she made was fresh bread, warm bread, dipped in sugar. I guess it was our version of a donut. That was good. I can still remember how it tasted." Joe smacks his lips.

"Do you know when was she born?"

He surprises me. "In 1888. And she came on a ship to America all by herself in 1907. I never learned why. The Hapsburg Monarchy didn't crumble until 1918. She named the place when she came through Ellis Island as being the Kingdom of Galicia, south of Poland but she didn't name a town. Galicia was invaded by the Russians, then the Germans, then the Ukrainian Nationalists instituted their pogroms that massacred thousands of Poles and Jews. In my mothea's lifetime, I think it was finally taken over by the Russians and perhaps now it belongs to the Ukraine. I believe."

I excuse myself to obtain my laptop from the den. Phonetically sounding out the name of the area of Galicia that he gave me, I type it in to discover his mothea's area of origin was part of the Hungarian Crown for centuries, then in 1867, it was taken by the Austrian-administered part of Austria-Hungary. They called it Cislethania because it was jointly governed by both.

"I didn't know that. What else does that black box say?"

"It says it was near Krakow and Auschwitz and part of a Vienna compromise. Wow." I interject. "I thought they were cities in Germany, not Poland. Do you think your mom sensed how unstable life was there?" He shrugs. "At any rate, I'm glad she got out."

"Hmmm. Yup. The Russians, the Germans, the Hungarians - all wanted to *rule* Poland. In World War II, it was taken by the central powers of Germany, but way before that, when I was a child, I never knew how she felt about politics except that she hated the Germans!"

He stares out the window. "There was a railway that went through the southern part of Poland." Joe clears his throat. "That is why the Germans used those southern towns to establish their death camps. It was convenient." He continues speaking in his methodical manner. "My mothea also had two sistas, an older and a younger one, who also came over by themselves. And they all found husbands here. And as hard as they had it here, they never wanted to go back there. In America, they learned that women could make choices. It had nothing much to do with the war because the war hadn't happened yet. It had to do with the freedom they had as women."

Joe chuckles. "My mothea would cook good meals every day of the week except for Sundays. On Sundays, she'd put out thin sliced beef and lard, and we would have to cook our own meal if we wanted it. I hated that, but she wouldn't budge. Sunday was her day off."

September 18, 2013

A window salesman comes to the house today. Warmer replacement windows are Paul's priority, as well as mine, for our new abode. I take the salesman aside and warn him that Mr. B is a rocket scientist. He will be interrogating him on his product.

Joe brings it. Out comes his critical eye.

When the salesman shines his hot light on both sides of the pane to display the blocked heat, and he brags that this gas barrier between the panes of glass works for both heat and cold, he assures us that his company offers a lifetime warranty. Joe asks him, "Lifetime, you say? Correct me if I misspeak, but that gas won't last as long as the window glass and frames because the seals are not absolute. The gas will eventually leak out." He stares resolutely at the salesman.

Finally, the salesman capitulates. "Okay, I'm not supposed to tell you this, but you already know it. Yes, the gas is only good for the first five years."

"So, the heat and cold barrier will gradually wear off, and our heating bills will grow exponentially." Mr. B corners the man. Two hours later, the guy leaves sweating, grasping our hard-won order for replacing half the aluminum windows in the house.

"I didn't like him. Salesmen are as crooked as a ram's horn. You notice how he told us *afterward* that the gas would evaporate within five years, but the warranty is supposed to be a lifetime warranty? Anyway, you whittled him down on the price like Maudie would've. Good girl! And the windows will be an improvement to the ones we have, I'll admit, and I like that you are investing in the house to make it your own." He pats my back approvingly.

Glad for his approval, and the fact that I will have some warm windows not covered in plastic this winter, I gush, "Thank you, Mr. B, for helping me. I wouldn't have known to ask how long the gas in the windowpanes lasts. You are such a smart cookie!"

Tonight we celebrate life together with a small barbecue, our famously warmed crusty dinner rolls, and thanksgiving. Joe laughs with boyish glee when Paul pulls out the fire grill in the backyard and begins burning papers. Then Paul pulls up some lawn chairs that his father has personally restrung and renovated.

Joe sits in the dark and smiles against the fire glow. "I haven't seen a campfire since I was a boy." That being known, I sift through our new pantry cubby to find marshmallows. What's a campfire without marshmallows to roast? Paul finds three sticks, and all three of us roast a couple. "Uh, I can't eat too much of this sugary stuff. I'll be awake all night!" Joe exclaims.

He leans back and tells Paul the story about the movie theater they had in Woonsocket, his childhood town, where Joe would pay the required dime to get a cheap seat and watch the silent films and later the shoot- 'em-ups.

"We still used the term 'short bits' for a dime. Do you know what a bit is?" Hearing nothing affirmative, Joe explains: "Your little niece knows. I played a game wid her, and she got it. Two bits is a quarter, four bits is fifty cents, and eight bits is a buck. I remember that this theater would take short bits for the show, not exactly twelve and a half cents, you know. It was built on a hillside with an emergency exit off to the side. One day I could smell some smoke, so I ran up the stairs and out the side door before anyone else. There I was, stuck on the ledge of the hill, and the river below it. They managed to put out the fire, and later they built steps like a fire escape from that side door. If the place had burnt, I wouldn't have had time to get back inside and run down to the back of the screen, and out the door. I coulda been fried chicken up there!" In the darkness with sticky marshmallows on our fingertips, we each begin to chuckle.

"But hey, I'm not used to these kinds of fires in my own yard. A campfire in my own backyard. My! If the insurance company knew, maybe they'd raise our rates." He leans back and looks into the starry night sky. "You guys have changed my life! This is living," Joe croons. "Yep."

September 19, 2013

The freezer is now full of take-and-bake packaged dough balls because Joe never seems to tire of my culinary efforts in "home baked rolls," crusty on the outside and soft on the inside. I bake them for breakfast and dinner, and he is one happy diner. He scoops out his marmalade from the jar that he sets directly under his chin so that he can apply it bite by bite onto his roll. So much for sharing, and hasn't he ever learned not to double dip? But when he is happy, he makes sure I know it. He smiles, winks, and kids me and repeats his thanks and approval.

Joe has never let pizza pass his lips. "I don't eat it cuz I wouldn't be kissable if I did," is his excuse. Paul, now at dinner, threatens to starve his dad into tasting pizza, but I'm not sure who would win that battle.

"We're gonna put it on your gravestone, Chief: *The-man-who-never-lived-'cuz-he-refused-to-taste- pizza."*

Mr. B shrugs. "So what!" But with a glass of milk and a roll, I believe Joe may try to swig down Italian night just to please me.

"Did I ever tell ya how expensive these kids were?" Joe indicates toward his son and includes his daughter, Victoria, by implication.

I shake my head, not knowing what will follow.

"Vicky cost us thirty-five dollars to adopt from the Church Mission of Help. Your hubby here cost us a whopping forty-five dollars."

"Forty-five *hundred* dollars, you mean?"

"Nope. Just forty-five dollars." He frowns and nods. Then, he ponders and continues slowly. "The doctors worked for free. I think they donated their time for the babies' sake. And Johnsy, or Mrs. Johns, was quite a woman. When she interviewed Maudie and me, she had this stone-cold way of looking right through us. We didn't know how she really felt about our answers until she called us and told us she had Victoria waiting. Maudie was so nervous, she about wet herself. I was the one who had to go in and pick Vicky up. And when she looked at me, I felt that she had a special knowing, a special intelligence. She was beautiful and so chubby. I remember it vividly like it was yesterday." His eyes grow moist, and he wipes them. "I had to change her diapers at first and wash her because Maude didn't trust herself. Hey, I'm sorry if this bores you. There are some memories that I will never forget."

"You know you don't bore me one bit, Mr. B."

Paul smiles at me and starts picking up finished plates from the table.

"Victoria was from a couple'a politicians back East. She musta had a looker for a mothea. She was assertive and smart, like you, I'd say. But she was a spitter from the get go." He smiles. "Now, Paul, he was a drooler. Oh yeah. When we got your husband from the Church Mission of Hope, Johnsy looked at Maude and said, 'This one has personality. You're gonna love him!' And he did have personality. He would laugh every time Maudie tugged on the shade to roll it up in the morning. Giggle, giggle, and drool! He's *always* had a good personality, too. Nothing seems to ruffle him. And I don't know how Johnsy understood babies at that age, but she knew. She really knew about 'em. Your husband is very sensitive. He feels the smallest slight, very deeply. But he doesn't let it deter him."

This insight moves me deeply because I know it to be true. I'm glad to know Mr. B respects this quality about his son.

September 20, 2013

Joe keeps a collection of small wire brushes and a plastic toothbrush under the sink. These are for cleaning pots and pans and the stovetop. He may not care about the most recent kitchen designs and appliances, but what he has is sparkling clean. He works on the stove while I dust the furniture.

Satisfaction with living in a gracious place is not necessarily the same as living in a rich space. I have gloried in the wealth of architectural feats, bringing nature into a home through a window aptly placed, or the angles of an attic room, the sweetness of a sunny coffee nook. Yet, being "welcomed" into another's sacred place is a humbling turn of events. I'm beginning to recognize that being welcomed into Mr. B's home is a rarity. For three weeks we have observed a sovereign, creative orchestration of peace. It comes as a welcomed envelope with personal freedom and rest tucked inside.

After dusting, I interrupt Mr. B who is attacking my new red skillet with one of his wire brushes. He has made several gouges in it. The black Teflon coating is peeled back, and a knife has been doubling the strength of his removal process. "Oh! Mr. B! This coating isn't meant to come off. It's Teflon coating over the steel pan. It was put there so that things don't stick, so you don't have to work so hard to clean my pots and pans as you did with the old ones."

"Teflon, you say? Okay. I remember the guy who invented that stuff. He put one layer of coating that adhered to the metal, and another layer of non-stick coating to adhere to the first coating. So it works, eh?"

"Yep. It does." *Or it did.*

Joe continues to merge households, scooting over some habits and shelves for us. We have done this so often for others, we know what it means to watch Joe move through this himself to intuitively make us feel comfortable.

"You can get rid of these pictures." He moves around the house, points to a few wall hangings. "But I would appreciate it if you keep this one, and this one, and this one…" He points out several paintings explaining which family member painted them, and the memories acquiring them. He is insistent that we make ourselves at home. "This house is yours now."

If he only knew what I would do with this house if it really was ours! Instead, I touch him on the arm and thank him for telling me about these special decorations and remind him that the house is still his. I assure him I won't be doing much of anything, but of course he must tell me if I step out of line.

"Have I told you the story about this chalk painting of the Indian?" Joe is standing in front of a familiar picture in the upstairs hall. I've heard it, but I let him tell the story again. "I worked with a full-blooded Ojibway Indian from the Detroit area, named George Molby. We were both shipped out as engineering consultants to a plant in Ohio. The guys at the plant never used his name. They always said, "the Indian". They tried to sit me at a table under a shaft with a window at the top, and I got cold there, so I refused to sit there and made them move me to another spot. They put George there instead. But George felt that he couldn't make a stink, or they might get a 'hard on' for him. You know what I'm saying?" He lifts both hands, about to flip his middle fingers, so I quickly nod. Joe shrugs. "So it was that George sat there."

One day in winter, he came to me and I could see how sick he was. He wanted me to accompany him back to the hotel. So I did, but George, he could barely drive himself. When we got there, I called the airlines and told them I was bringing a sick patient on board. They were full up, so I had to drive him through a blizzard to another airport. I bought two tickets for D.C. It was the closest airport to his home. Then, I called our wives to tell them we were coming. His wife was a nurse, and I knew she would know what to do. They met us at the airport, and his wife took him straight to the hospital. We went along wid' 'em and watched 'em put him in a tub of ice. *Ice,* mind you! But that's how they brought down his temperature. After he got better, he gave me this painting to thank me. I'd like to keep it upstairs, here."

I agree. Artwork is precious for a variety of reasons. I start rearranging parts of the main floor instead.

Now, Paul's papa is happy about where I have hung his special paintings. I especially enjoy the spotted bird dog he painted in watercolors, which is hung in our guestroom upstairs, and I have reframed another one: a cowboy breaking a horse, in the entryway. These are works that he painted earlier in life. He also treasures prints that Maudie's Aunt McGregor gave them from the Chicago Art Museum when she was the curator. He has watercolors from various aunts and uncles who dabbled. He removes others that don't mean a thing to him.

Then, he asks me not to remove the paneling or paint the den after all. "Leave it for later?" he suggests. *Later,* meaning *when he is in the grave,* or in the best-case scenario, for when he can comprehend all these changes.

"Of course, Mr. B," I concede.

"You can change a lot of things, but I would also appreciate it if you would leave the formal room as it is." I understand that Joe spends most of his time in this room, and one of Renoir's impressionist paintings of a young girl is like a shrine of beauty to him. He adores her. He tells me that Madam Henriot was Renoir's muse and that the artist painted her on many occasions.

I grew up appreciating a Renoir copy of two girls at a piano in our hallway, but this flushed gal dressed in an evasive bodice of teals with sheer neckline and sleeves is subtly sensuous. I tease him, "Why then, that coquettish Henriot is again another man's muse!" He chuckles and smiles his secretive smile sitting in this blue velvet upholstered chair in the large living room with the white walls.

Beneath the print of frail Henriot busting from her sheer smock is Joe's sideboard, a fine serpentine piece of furniture made without nails. Inside of it, he keeps keys, private papers, a record of house sales from the community which he's kept for ten years, and his tax documents. "You understand it's hard for an old man to change, don't you?"

"Of course," I say, hiding the worry from my voice. Neither Paul nor I have told him that we've kept the low-slung, well-made couch my mother had given us twenty-three years ago. It is only missing from our possessions in the house at this time because it is being recovered at an upholstery shop on Broadway. "Of course." My reply is prompted from the heart. I regret that we may have to store the couch in the basement.

Today, Paul reports from the opened mail that more financial bars are lifted, removed, and reimbursed. We shiver in gladness.

September 21, 2013

On our way to the symphony last weekend, I told Betty about the international mystery theater at our house. Joe and I have a regular date watching mysteries at seven p.m.. Betty agreed this is a wonderful idea and immediately offered to join us. I haven't decided. Joe and I have something going. When we'd visit Joe for dinners before we moved in, I'd beg Paul to wait out an extra hour for the movie so that Joe and I could share our mutual thrill of "movie night." Paul hated reading the captions and would usually fall asleep. We'd tease him when he asked what had happened.

This season, Joe isn't sure what's really going on in the new shows. They are not filled with humor. They are more abstract than last season, and more violent, too. He smiles with his shrug and upturned palms, saying, "It's entertainment." Paul hangs out with us occasionally to watch. It's a nice little family event even if it unnerves me at times. After the show, we try to make sense about the plot and then we say an early goodnight. We all seem to be acting like old folks, going to bed by nine, and getting an abundance of sleep.

September 22, 2013

Munching away together he begins reminiscing. "I think you woulda' liked New England, Lynn. It was a good place to be a kid. I looked up to my eldest sista, Helen, kinda' like I dunno, a substitute mothea sometimes. She would have all kinda' boys come 'round as dates, you know, 'cuz she was so nice and pretty, and talented too. She could play piano and sing. Well, they'd come 'round and we'd all play cards. That's the time I remember playing cards, only then. When I was a youngster. And she'd take me truckin' with her and the boys too."

"Truckin?"

"There were a coupla' guys in town who bought trucks as a way to make money, and they would charge us each a dollar to ride in 'em. They had benches in the open air in back, and they'd drive us to the beach and back. One time I fell asleep, but Helen took care of me.

"Yeah, I liked all my brothers and sistas." He continues. "Eddy was Big Byk, and I was Little Byk. He was really an ox, built like your husband." Mr. B leans forward and squints at me. "Nobody ever had a row with Little Byk 'cuz they had to go through Big Byk first, and that was no fun. He'd take me walking wid him everyplace in town. I remember there was a big pond at the railroad junction. They built the railroad tracks through the pond on banks of land propped up by huge blocks of chiseled stone. The kids would jump off the tresses into this big deep pond, and then climb up the banks on the stone steps to the tracks and jump into the pond again.

"Underneath the water, you could see these huge pipes that held up the railroad tracks. The pipes let the water flow from the river through each of the ponds that were separated by the railroad tracks and out to the river on the other side. One kid, Macky, figured out how to swim through the pipes to the ponds on the other side. He would show off. So, the kids learned how to swim through them. They dared each other, and they'd get to the other side.

"One time in the springtime, there was so much rain falling that the ponds overfilled. The water rose over the tracks and dislodged those massive stones. I couldn't believe the force of so much water! It flowed over the French cemetery next to the river. Coffins were unearthed, and some of them floated down the river that spring!

"There was also a false belief about the sun curing polio back then, too. In the summer, a lot of people crippled up with polio would sit and sun themselves by the pond hoping to get cured, but they never did."

Mr. B smacks his lips. "Eddy didn't take to school, like me. *Hated* it." A frown makes him seem thoughtful, and he shakes his head rousing himself. "I remember he tried to take a correspondence course on electronics, but it didn't interest him. He kept looking for something to do because so many people couldn't get jobs, and he didn't want to be one of 'em! He had a gal to marry! I remember Eddy started out as a newspaper boy at the *Woonsocket Call*. He sold the paper for two cents and earned a half-cent on every paper sold. Then he went to the owner, Buell Hudson, and he told him his plans to marry Bertha. So Buell gave him a job as a janitor at the paper. When the head janitor left, Eddy moved into the head janitor position, and he had that place so spic and span! His bathrooms were the cleanest in town. So, on Friday nights, all the guys in town would line up and take their showers in that bathroom. Buell knew it. But showers were kinda a novelty then, and it was free publicity for the newspaper, so he allowed it."

"Pretty soon, Eddy was working in the hot room where he used his muscle, and he loved it. It was a union job then. The hot room was where these guys would make fifty pound cast iron rollers for the linotype. You see, newspapers were the daily means to all the information those days. Newspapers were printed on linotype. Linotype started with thin, flat plates of lead with the raised letters on them. The words for the story were placed into a tray, with the ads alongside in columns. Then they would roll the tray with some kinda' acid I think, and lay down a piece of metal so that the piece of metal became imprinted with half a page of the day's news. It was fastened to one half of that huge roller that Eddy had cast, and another half of the page was fastened to the other side of the roller. Then, they would roll that page over and over onto paper to make one page of newsprint."

"Quite a production, a daily newspaper!" I say. "I never imagined there were such things as hot rooms for a newspaper."

"Yeah, Eddy loved that job. He stuck with it. That's how he earned my fathea's respect because, you remember, my folks didn't think he was adequate to marry so young? Well, he proved that he had initiative and could stick with a good paying job and get along with people. My own fathea was pretty old when he married my mothea, so by the time I graduated from college, Eddy had to help him out with a lot of things. And he was real good to the folks in their old age. Eddy was generous; he helped where he could."

I chime in, "I remember how kind he was to Paul and me when we were visiting Wanda. He drove us all over New England showing us historic monuments like the Wayside Inn, Minute Men war memorials, Plymouth Rock, Boston Harbor, the ball park, and he treated us to his favorite seafood restaurants along the way."

"Oh yeah, that's one thing about Eddy! He loved to drive! He and Bertha both. She would read to him and he would drive her all over the place.

"But he was funny too. He kept his buggy in my sistas' garage: Wanda and Lucy hid it for him so that no-one knew he even had an automobile. He hid his wealth so that he could live in Section 8 housing in his nineties. Yeah, family sticks together."

Joe chuckles. "Well, ya gotta do whatcha gotta do! He survived, but he had to make sure his girl was taken care of, cuz she was sorta handicapped, so he kept all his money in a trust for her."

"The rain is letting up, Mr. B. What do you want to do?"

"Oh, I'm gonna go fix the Weed Eater, and then, I'm gonna do dog patrol. At my age, I gotta find ways to keep moving!" He pushes himself up from the table. "See ya later, kiddo."

September 23, 2013

Joe has decided to get fit. Every day he hops onto our stationary bike that we left sitting on the back porch. He says it helps his balance. He times himself to ensure he rides it ten minutes a day. I bring him a glass of cool water to keep him hydrated. He refuses the water. "I'm not used to drinking water, Miss." His exercise routine would never be approved by a local gym.

Mr. B's 1977 washing machine is inside spinning our clothes clean. When they are done, I take out the circular brush filter and bring it to the hose outside, like he has shown me, to wash off the lint. We are sitting on the back porch enjoying the wonderful weather, but I wonder how I'll clean the filter when the weather turns freezing.

Sitting in one of his aluminum chairs, under his whitey tighties, his thin T-shirts and other laundry strung from one end of the porch to the other, I imagine stringing the laundry line the other direction as a barrier between his neighbor's back porch and ours. *A little privacy?* That image quickly goes up in smoke. There's a lot more to be fixed on this back porch than the laundry. I lean back to look at the ceiling. The nails protruding through the roof of the low-slung ceiling are another issue that tortures me. I sigh.

Joe spies my glare at his laundry line. "I used to string bits of eel on a line like that, on hooks, and tie it up between two floats. The crabs would appear out of nowhere, jumping from the bottom of the bay, to bite the line. That's how we'd catch 'em!" With nothing to be done, we chat with abandon.

September 24, 2013

I find two popsicles in the freezer and take one outside to Mr. B. He is obviously lost in his own thoughts. "My fathea was nineteen when he took the steamship from his home in Suwalki, Poland to New York. I've never understood that. Why did he leave? He never told me. I knew he had an argument with his brother, and they stopped speaking. So, maybe that was why he came over. But no luggage? Just the shirt on his back?" Joe shakes his head slowly. "It means he traveled 14 days, about 3,700 nautical miles, mind you: nautical miles are about fourteen percent longer than regular American miles. At about nine knots per hour, it took him two weeks on the ship. The boys were in the stern and the girls in the bow."

Mr. B's detailed, mathematical mind is a mystery to me. "I hope he had enough to eat in all that time. Maybe he carried food in a suitcase and ditched the suitcase later?"

"I dunno. It's a mystery. I wish my fathea had talked to me more about it. But, he was always a quiet man. I know that Suwalki [Joe pronounces it Suvalkee] is a border town on the northeastern side of Poland, near Lithuania. I know that my fathea understood and could speak German, too, because one day when he and I were walking together in the forest, we came upon a clearing, and there was a house there. As we drew closer, a man with a rifle jumped up on the porch and pointed it at us. He was drunk and shouting crazy-like in German! It didn't faze my fathea one bit. He calmly spoke back to the man in perfect German, and the man lowered his gun and invited us up to talk for a while. I know my fathea respected the Jews, too, because he always took me to the Jewish shops to do business, and he could converse with them in their way of speaking." Joe leans closer, more intently, towards me. "So, it's a mystery, and I just wish I would have been smart enough to ask him about why he came to America."

"Did he come over with his sister?" He relaxes into his chair.

"I dunno, Miss. She did come over. I know that because she married a Pole and settled in Jersey City. But my fathea never talked about her. Somehow my sista found out about our aunt and introduced us. When I was coming home between semesters in college, I'd stop to see them. They lived above an empty storefront. I think they owned the whole building, but they couldn't seem to rent the store on the first floor. Her married name was Povaja. She had two daughters and two sons. Their youngest son was all eyes and his name was Joe, like me."

"Really? That's odd. Why were you both named Joseph?"

"Well, my fathea's name was Joseph, I guess that explains me but not him. Well anyway, they had an older daughter, who was so nice, real nice. She was pretty. An older man got to marry her and got a mighty nice package. But the younger daughter, Beatrice, yah Beatrice Povaja was her name, she was what you might call sexy. She had a beautiful face, and what a figure! So, I would go there in my ROTC uniform from college and take her out to a movie with her little brother Joe."

"What was the oldest son like?"

"Oh! He was stuck up. He kept to himself. He didn't talk to me. He and his parents were kinda' the same thing, so I would only go visit them for a couple of hours every once in a while. Just to take the younger two out to a movie. My eldest sista Helen told me how to get there, but she also told me not to stay long because Mr. Povaja had been in a railroad car coupling accident where his forearm had been smashed up and he had lost the use of his arm. So, since he couldn't work they never invited me in for dinner, and they didn't have room to keep me overnight, so I never put them out of their way."

"Maybe the kid was only embarrassed and just seemed stuck up."

"Maybe." With a final lick of his chocolate Popsicle, Joe sets the stick on the concrete and continues. "I thought it was funny that my fathea never mentioned he had a sista to me. It was my own sista who introduced us. Hey, did I ever tell you that my fathea wanted to go back to Poland?" He sits up straight to change the subject.

"Yes, I think I remember that story. You said you wouldn't have survived the war if your family had moved back."

"My parents almost split up over it. My fathea got me a passport, you know the one in my wallet, but my mothea refused to go. It was 1922. I was five years old. I remember Mothea was in their bedroom pulling on her stockings saying she would go to live wid her sista' if my fathea left. She agreed that he would take me back to Poland wid him, and she would keep Lucy and the girls. Lucy was her second daughter and was kind of her interpreter. She always went wid my mothea everywhere, like an escort. And I was wid my fathea."

"Your mom never learned to drive or even speak English, did she?"

"Nooooooo."

"So wasn't she afraid of staying in America?"

"Nope. My mothea had grit. She was too proud to speak English and be laughed at. She would take Lucy strolling down to a friend's house every Saturday evening, and they would talk for hours and then come home. I guess one friend is all anyone really needs. But she decided she was *never* going back to Poland." Joe's "r" when pronouncing *never* is left off. If he speaks an "r" at the beginning of a word, he sometimes rolls it, like when he says his mother's maiden name, "Rokosz."

Joe surveys his blossoming rust and yellow colored mums in the garden from his rocker without seeing them. "Eventually, she was able to convince my fathea to be content as a groundskeeper and stay because, well, here I sit. And it was a terrible thing that happened over there in the forties. The Soviet Secret Police arrested so-called 'Polish intelligentsia' along wid the officers and policemen. They were really only landowners, loyalists, factory owners, and probably some lawyers, officials, and priests.

Soviets killed the villagers in the forest of Kaytn, over twenty-five thousand people! Then, the Nazis came and took almost sixty thousand women and children from Volyn and forty thousand from Eastern Galicia, and slaughtered them all. All my parents' relatives and friends disappeared."

"Oh! That's a horrible tragedy!" I find myself sitting up as straight as a sheared piece of lumber.

"You bet. My fathea was certainly glad he stayed wid my mothea. Lucy had organized that we would send her parents and brother packages with winter coats, yarn, canned goods, but then there was nobody left. You know, the oldest brother had to stay at home as a tradition in case there was war. It was too bad."

We pause for some time to consider this. "And when did you graduate college?"

"Let's see, I graduated from the University of Alabama in '38. Just about the time my mothea lost her brother to the war. He was wounded, so they sent him back for repairs. Then, when he got better, they sent him back to the front and he was killed. Yep, yep, it could easily have been me."

"Here you sit with me. And I'm glad, Mr. B."

"Hey. I didn't like you much when I first met you. You had your own ideas and you were kinda pushy. Then, I decided you had the right. You can thank my Slavic mothea who found her American voice to stand up to 'fathea-is-all' for that."

I think about all the Polish jokes that circulated in my childhood schools. We were never taught about these massacres. Remembering Polish jokes, I wonder how cruel jokes get started to circulate about any race, especially when they have already been slaughtered, and all their national boundaries repeatedly changed. Do the strong do it to alleviate their conscience? As if the annihilated ones weren't worthy to survive?

"I told Polish jokes in elementary school, Mr. B." I admit. "I never meant anything by them. Everyone was doing it. I didn't even know any Poles until sixth grade."

"Well, that's the thing about communication. You might not intend any harm when you are speaking, but other people who hear your words may experience terror or pride or laughter depending upon their perspective. Communication is a funny thing. It's got to be thoughtful. If it's not, then an awful lot of alienation takes place. Or forgiveness." He muses aloud. "In 1945, after the war, the Poles reclaimed their own western territory from the Germans, but there was a line, called the Curzon Line, that was a 1931 pact between the Germans and Russians dividing the Eastern half of Poland and making it Bolshevik Russia. Poland had only been a non-Bolshevik republic since 1917, anyway. So, the Poles allowed the Russians to reclaim that northeastern area. It became Lithuania and the Ukraine, I believe."

I collect my computer from the den and rejoin Mr. B. "It says Soviet Russia suddenly became a loving member of the international family of free and democratic nations in 1943, so the British and American powers betrayed Poland and gave the land east of the Curzon Line to Russia. The Curzon Line ran from the Narew River in Northern Poland down to the San River and the Carpathian Mountains.'"

He raises two fingers with enthusiasm, wagging agreement. "Yeah, yeah, the Carpathian Mountains, and the Bug River along Austria to the South," he says. "The Poles had ousted the Ukrainians from Galicia at the end of 1919, but Galicia never formerly joined Poland so they were sitting ducks." Joe is a veritable encyclopedia!

Mr. B chuckles. "You know, ol' Joe?"

"Joseph Stalin?" I take a wild guess that he isn't referring to himself.

"Yep. He was kinda stupid about his friend Hitler. In the middle of World War II, he got wind that Hitler wasn't gonna honor their pact of the demarcation line of Poland and that Hitler was gonna invade the Russian territories east of the Curzon Line. So ol' Joe dismantled all of his fortresses in Russia and moved them up to the Curzon Line to defend the Bolsheviks against the Nazi troops. He rebuilt the Russian fortresses along the river. When the Russians began to lose, they had no fortresses to fall back to, and it was a slaughter."

His blue eyes hold my steady attention in a metal vice. "People are always risked and sacrificed for land."

"Pretty stupid. Land belongs to God."

"Land means power," Joe counters.

September 25, 2013

I realize now, that, there is no way we'll have sufficient energy to remove the furniture again, a process that is required for the installation of new carpet. At least not this year. We are exhausted in every way possible. The floors in Joe's house squawk in rebuttal of every other step, yet the carpet crew contractors I've consulted with have all denied being squeaky floor repair experts. Also, we don't have the money to spend on extensive renovations. The humor of this situation causes me to start calling our 43-year-old carpet the "money carpet." I tell people that the longer we can restrain ourselves from replacing it, the more interest we earn on the money from the sale of our home, stashed in the bank.

At dinner, Joe tells how airplane engineers had to incorporate an additional 1.5 percent factor to the design of the wings on a plane so that the compression of the mass of the plane when landing wouldn't force the wings to yield up and away from the body. He forms a W with his thumbs and forefingers to show us.

"The wings would go up in the heat of landing, and just stay up at that angle. After a short flight time, they would simply break off when landing. You know the Cary Grant pull up? His pull up was the feat of the day, being able to pull up an airplane without the wings breaking off their bolts. So, the problem was solved when we averaged the distance between the stress of gravity and the mass of the load and realized that adding a 1.5 strength factor would just about always ensure the wings would not yield. They still add that factor to airplane designs, you know, today. In fact, they make the skins of airplanes with a mixture of plastic and carbon to help the bodies yield without breaking in the heat of takeoffs and landings."

This, I note in my journal after two weeks' stay in Joe's home: Surprised by how much gladness I feel, and by Mr. B's graciousness. My resentful heart is emptied. I am entertained by Mr. B, filled with peace. Maybe he's the 1.5 factor I needed for stability in this crazy world.

September 26, 2013

For about a year now, ever since Victoria sent him the Ellis Island ledger pages, Mr. B has tried to find the town where his mother came from. Her town was on the border. Was it Lithuanian—or Russian?—now? We couldn't seem to locate it. His daughter, Victoria, researched and found quite a bit of information. Her original Polish maiden name, Rokosz, was changed to Rokos at Ellis Island so that Americans could pronounce it. Victoria gave her father several maps and documents and visas for each of his parents for his birthday present. Joe and I spent hours on the computer last winter looking for the boundaries of Poland in 1888, the year his mother was born, and he searched his library for information without overturning the secret.

"I know mothea lived inland on the border, not on the coast. She and her two sistas came over separately, and one sista settled in Chicago. The younger one settled in Lawrence, Massachusetts, to be closer to my mothea in Woonsocket, Rhode Island. Her name was Carol. We all liked her a lot. My eldest sista, Helen, named one of her children after this aunt Carol."

Mr. B makes another suggestion that I can find more about this Kingdom of Galicia on my computer. I have searched repeatedly, and he enjoys reading the articles, but there is something sad about his search that always ends with more questions.

There's a computer program now that shows how all the boundaries of Europe changed repeatedly through the wars and emperors and kings and through treaties. He enjoys watching it today, and he watches the boundaries of Poland move like the wind on my computer. I look up. "No wonder she didn't want to go home. There was no town to go to! At least not within the Polish boundaries."

"I think I understand what happened now," he says. That settles it.

"We all want to do something to mitigate the pain of loss or to turn grief into something positive, to find a silver lining in the clouds. But I believe there is real value in just standing there, being still, being sad." wrote John Green.

September 27, 2013

Just before our international mystery movie, Paul joins us in the formal living room, where Joe's granddaughter is sitting with us. She has just confided that she grew up feeling like a princess with the velvet rocking chair as her throne. "This was the princess room, and I became a princess whenever I visited. In fact, I still have an odd affinity for opera because it was opera that was always playing when I visited grandma and grandpa."

Paul's dad reflects. "When we moved here to Colorado in

August of 1970, I had a good sum from what we made on our house in Bald'more and a five hundred dollar check from Maudie's fathea, Dr. Brownlee. I can't remember why. Maybe it was for a piece of furniture, or for helping them negotiate a farm contract, or maybe he was just helping us move to a new state. I don't know. He was a congenial man, full of fun. Anyway, we looked at a house on the other side of this subdivision, and I liked it because it had hardwood floors. Real nice."

Oh good, I'm thinking. *Maybe Mr. B's showing his cards! Maybe he would like hardwood floors.*

"But Maudie liked this house because the kitchen was right next to the dining room. So, I gave the realtor our $500 check as a down payment. That was his first day on the job. He was so excited! He told us it was his first day and he'd sold a house already! This house cost us $32.5. That was when the American dream was still alive and attainable, humph."

September 28, 2013

Mr. B cuts into his cinnamon roll and says, "Maudie and I knew a couple. They were our first fast friends in Bald'more." Sitting in our bright morning breakfast room Mr. B tells me, "His name was George Ruple. George and I worked at the same flight plant in Bald'more until it closed. He was the plant's test copilot for all of our airplane projects. Whenever a new design was finished, someone had to take it into the air. That was George."

"Wow. That's not my kind of job," I admit, stunned to think of the risk. "Takes a person of devil-may-care!"

He smiles. "Not my cup of tea neither! Our big project together was taking the bottom off of an old plane and installing a new design with new material. We installed it all right, and we were about to let 'em test it when we got called in because someone had installed some added instrumentation that hadn't been ordered, reported or registered."

"What? Like surveillance equipment?"

He raises both eyebrows and swallows a tasty bite. Then, "It was the mid-'40s. No one knew who was reading that instrumentation or why. I didn't know. Maybe George knew, but he didn't speak up. He didn't offer any information to me or to anyone else as far as I knew. Then, after they removed it, he asked me to test the plane with him. The guy who was giving out the regulation parachutes accidentally pulled the rip line on George's parachute." Mr. B pulls the imaginary handle across his chest.

"They were designed to open up and the wind would do the rest. It just hung there. George got angry. He was mad, and I thought, *who is this guy to be doing a job he knows nothing about?* It shoulda been a sign to me, but I ignored it. The guy went and got another parachute. There were five of us who climbed into the plane."

I'm listening because that's the thing I seem to do exceptionally well these days. So Mr. B continues his tale.

"After we were up over Middle River and heading to the Chesapeake Bay, I noticed the fuselage was twisting. It wasn't supposed to do that, so I got up and went to the tail to test the escape hatches just in case. I realized then, because we were flying so low, that no parachute would have time to deploy anyway. We were only a hundred or so feet in the air! George was flying right above the water. Remember, the top half of the plane was the old half, and the deflection of winds over time had sealed those escape hatches shut. Suddenly I realized, if we crashed, none of us was gonna get out of those bent up hatches alive!"

Joe shakes his head in renewed angst. "I was mad as a hornet, but I sat down and sweated it out 'til we landed. I was newly married, I had my whole career ahead of me, and I had been stupid enough to trust the mechanics and George with my life! Well, you can't talk to the pilot or co-pilot when they are in the air, so I waited 'til we landed. Then I marched back to my office and placed a phone call to George. I told him never to expect me to help him with a test flight again. Other than that, we got along."

"Other than him risking your life," I answer.

"Yeah. And also my reputation. I was a suspect in that added surveillance equipment too, and I never knew what became of that inquiry!" Mr. B sips his steaming broth. Void of angst or malice, he grasps the table knife and knocks the boiled egg in his hand with the heel of the knife to crack the shell.

"There was a lithe, blonde woman who hung around the plant flaunting her figure at George. We all called her 'Blondie,' and she just couldn't wait to get married to George. Mmm, mmm. She was from a large farm in Pennsylvania, and she thought she was the cat's meow, all about her figure and getting her hands on someone of influence. Well, I never liked her, but Maudie liked her, surprisingly. Yeah. The girls would chat, chat, chat." His voice mimics a woman's higher tone. "We used to go on double dates and for weekends with them to Blondie's family farm. She'd show it off all over. Then, after they were married, they asked us to join them going to some cabins they had on the water. We played bridge together, and generally, we had some fun times. Yeah." I hear him sucking his teeth as he nods to the side. Then, Mr. B stops and looks at me oddly.

"George was kind of—well, today you would probably call him gay. I didn't know it at the time, but people began to gossip, you know. But he had married Blondie anyway, and all she could talk about then was getting pregnant. We heard all about it at the cabin. So George finally gave her a son. That was the extent of his commitment." His voice ends with irony. "Yeah. When the plant closed, ol' George musta been seeing some political uppity up on the side because he moved to the Michoud Factory Airfield near

New Orleans and got himself a promotion and a swanky new apartment. He left Blondie to her own devices in Bald'more."

"Where did he go? 'Michad?'" I back up, trying the pronunciation.

"No, Miss. Ya gotta work on that French of yours." He purses his lips comically and repeats, "Michoud. Then, they hired me out too, but only as an engineering consultant, and so when I went down to Michoud, someone there said to me, 'Hey, you gotta make sure to check out Ruple's pad!' And I learned it was something of a rumor about how George was able to afford such an uppity place." Mr. B can't keep the irony out of his voice.

"Well, he was only there for six months because in '53, the Michoud plant closed, and somehow, I don't know quite how, he landed the political appointment of quality controller in Washington, D.C.! Boy, was I surprised. How'd he get that appointment? There was something suspicious about his fancy digs and then how he moved up into government so quickly. Of course, his wife was not at all happy with the man. So, after we had moved to Colorado, Blondie came out and found herself a big house in that nice subdivision by the pond, off of Bowles Avenue, the one I showed you that Maudie and I had looked at. They followed us out here, but George would travel back and forth to Washington, while Blondie started making the rounds looking for a way out! She could swear, that gal! I could never figure out why Maudie liked her." Joe folds his napkin and passes it under his nose to catch a drip.

"Funny thing. It was before they built the dam at Chatfield. So, their place along with most of the neighborhood found themselves deluged in water after one of those big rains in the '70s. They were located on a flood plain. I dunno if they had insurance or not. Blondie immediately divorced George and married some highfalutin' businessman. He was *out*. She had a mouth on her.

Told everybody what a loser he was. I never liked her, but I guess she and Maudie remained friendly, even after the divorce. Maudie had her secrets. Anyway, one day we were driving along the avenue, and I look over and see George driving next to us. What a surprise to see him there!

"I waved him down to pull the cars over and catch up a bit, you know. But Maudie crossed her arms and wouldn't get out of the car. She would hardly look at him. I'd never seen Maudie act like that before! She gave him the cold shoulder like nobody's business! I was actually embarrassed. But he was skinny. Something was wrong. I didn't have to think about it for long because he died real young. Probably about fifty."

"What? That's the end of your story, Mr. B? Didn't you find out what the heck he was up to, or who he was seeing in D.C.?"

"Oh no, Miss. I don't like to inquire into a person's private business." Joe picks up his plate and licks the yolks off, shocking me to pieces.

September 29, 2013

It's rare to find anyone who is using both sides of their brain in an equally intelligent manner. "How did you get so good at crossword puzzles, Mr. B?" I've been watching him for days finishing the *Denver Post* puzzles.

"Well, it keeps my mind working since I don't do designs anymore, Sweet Pea. I'm not all that smart. I'll tell ya, there was a blue magazine, you'll find a stack of 'em, that I collected because they were filled with mathematical problem after problem, mostly done by the Germans, and checked by a group of three editors. So, because I would read those problems, and read the tangents of the people who would write in to find errors with the assumptions of the presenters, then, I would have an idea of how to solve a problem that would come up at work.

"Another thing I did was a no-no, Joe did a no-no, it wasn't

Kosher, but I really didn't care." He thumbs his nose in the air and wiggles his fingers. "I used to get close to some of those German engineers who I respected. There was a Neumann, a physicist, that I would go to when I had a single question, only one at a time mind you, and even though he couldn't speak real good English, he would give me an answer, and I respected him a lot.

"A lot of guys would challenge Neumann, but he was *always* right. I wasn't supposed to follow him around, but that is how I would learn! Neumann was a specialist in following the paths of forces in the air, forces of energy that were held up by structures. Once he and another chief engineer were discussing the fact that cracks were appearing all along the side of an airplane. The chief engineer had beefed up the fuselage where the cracks had appeared, but then other cracks appeared further along past the steel patches, you see, because energy forces each have paths they follow. So, Neumann told the chief engineer to take off all the steel patches except the main intersections, and that worked. That's how I learned about energy force paths and adding the problem of adding too much structure.

"There was another German, a Ph.D, Multhopp, who I followed around, but I would only ask one question at a time. He was kinda bitter about the war, and maybe because he had volunteered as a test pilot, but he crashed on takeoff, so he had a prosthetic leg. I was in the advanced engineering course that the Martin Company in Bald'more offered after work. They placed me in charge of redesigning a seaplane to streamline it. I asked Multhopp, 'How close can you put two engines together? How close before they begin to interfere with one another?' Well, he told me, and I redesigned the wings with four engines set at identical spacing, and each piece was designed in mirror images," Joe draws arcs in the air with the fingers on both hands, "so it was easy to manufacture. Then, I removed all the bulk of the main spine that had been designed in X's and simplified it. Oh, they accepted that work, and it saved them $25,000 per plane. Per plane!" Joe points dramatically at me to emphasize the meaning of what he designed. He lays his hand on his chest and his eyes smirk. "They gave me a bonus of five hundred bucks!

"Oh, when I admired a mathematician or scientist, I would read everything they wrote. I got to know their specialties. One summer day, there was a company picnic. It was one of the very few where I could actually take Maude. So, I went down the line and picked out all my favorite engineers and introduced them to her. I introduced each one by name and title and highlighted their education and their specialty. 'This one, Dr. Multhopp, is a specialist in wind tunnels. This one, Dr. Martin, is a specialist in such 'n such… Oh, she was the cat's meow that day! All the German engineers lived in our subdivision of Bald'more, but they had neveh met my *wife*. Heh, heh. Yeah, it got around who I was, and they liked me. That's how I learned because the Americans were maybe good at drawing or good managers, but they just did not have that German education."

September 30, 2013

My sister had been badgering me about going on a trip with her for her fiftieth birthday celebration. I had agreed to attend only if our house had sold by that time. Now she asks permission from Paul to let me accompany her on a trip overseas. "Where are you going?" he replies.

Kay really wants to travel. Anywhere. The whole world sounds exciting because she hasn't traveled much. I feel conflicted since we have put away a little income from our house, so I pull him aside to ask if we can afford it. Paul says, "Go, go, go! You deserve it." We joke that a vacation is cheaper than trauma therapy or brain retraining that a friend keeps suggesting to me.

Kay and I book a late season river cruise, but I continue to feel awkward imagining what Joe will do being all alone during the hours of the day when Paul is working. I have noticed that if I don't take him to the library or to the grocery store or to a doctor's appointment, he will simply sit in his blue velvet rocker, gazing at Henriot on the wall and nod off to the sounds of Beverly Sills' voice from his record player. He also admires Pavarotti, but he has trouble switching over the records, so I have to be around to shuffle through his selection and switch the records out.

It may be a whole week of Beverly Sills! Imagining Violetta going round and round in Verdi's *La traviata*, takes the wind out of my sails, but Joe scratches the dates onto his calendar. He tells me he's cooked his own breakfasts for many years, and he hasn't forgotten how. "Just don't bring me back any olive oil!" he demands.

III 🖋 ☙

"Come away, O human child!
To the waters and the wild
With a faery, hand in hand,
For the world's more full of weeping than you can understand."
— W.B. Yeats, The Collected Poems of W.B. Yeats

PHOTO: I buy Mr. B a book on the subject of Polish freedom fighters during World War II: "In The Polish Secret War." It describes the cause of the Teutonic Knights in the path they took to develop Poland. From this stepping off point, it evolves into the heroic efforts of those in the Polish resistance during the second world war.

After he devours it, he wants to see maps and geography of Pomerania, Poland by looking inside my black box. He describes the hundreds of villages off the beaten path in Poland before they were eviscerated from the landscape. "Thick forests separated them. Each family had several children, some of 'em up to twelve children! They weren't gonna turn on each other. They trusted each other. Each village was made up of farmers, but between and amongst them, they provided for each other everything they needed, butchers, bakers, milk, the construction of their homes... When they were forced to choose between Stalin and Hitler, they chose Stalin, but that was before they understood that it was the Russians who committed their genocide."

We peer over Internet photographs of beautiful Baltic shores, rolling green fields and a portside village, some castles where the freedom fighters were hidden and fed, and an inexplicable Crooked Forest where it appears a blast knocked all the trees to their knees, but which found their way vertically again.

October ~ Octaves

October 1, 2013

Joe has taken up "dog patrol" as he deemed to label it awhile back. Every morning he carries a grocery bag around the backyard looking for small mounds of poo. Then he scrapes it into the bag with our little rake and shovel. This is distressing because Mr. B is usurping our once a week duties with his every day attention! He shrugs. "Who cares? What else do I have to do? Somebody's gotta do it. It might as well be me. Everyone gets a chore in this household. I need the exercise…" On and on go his excuses. I've stopped arguing with him, but sometimes I hold the bag.

"You know, Kiddo, I remember chasing a fire engine one day when I was just a boy in Woonsocket. I thought I was speedy, oh boy!" He begins. "But, I chased it all the way to the French Quarter, and then I looked around and realized I was lost." He piles his mound of poo into the bag I'm holding.

It's a bright October morning, the sky a clear teal, the aspen quakes its translucent lemon yellow boughs.

"A young man appeared and asked me if I'd lost my way, and I nodded. So, he said, 'Come on,' and I followed him. But, I was suspicious of 'em, so I wouldn't get close to 'em at all. He didn't take me back the way I'd come. He took me through the French cemetery and then over the dam. It was a shortcut, just a block away from a place I recognized, so I turned off there and went home. He was a chief engineer for the American Ringer Corporation. You know what that is?"

I confess my ignorance imagining the Salvation Army bell ringers at Christmastime.

"Well," he puts his shovel and rake against the fence. "It was the kind of thing that you rolled your washing through to wring out the water."

Oh! American Wringer Corporation! My imagination is educated.

"Two rollers, and you cranked on it like this to make them go round." He cranks an imaginary crank.

"I thought you didn't know him." I observe.

"Oh, well, a paperboy can learn an awful lot if he keeps his eyes and ears open. People think they are being private, but they show off their habits, their preferences and their values wid'out realizing it. I found out that he was a well-healed bachelor who lived in the Y.M.C.A. and played tennis!" We dump the doggy bag into the rubbish bin in the garage, and lay aside the rake and scoop.

"Did your mama have a wringer?"

"Oh no, she had her arms. She was a strong woman."

October 2, 2013

Mr. B drives very little nowadays, to the bank perhaps and once a month to Super Cuts which are both in the same strip mall as the grocery store. Today, he wants to go shopping with me "to see how our tastes are gonna collide." He backs his rear-end into my HHR car seat first because his vertebra no longer bend above his hips, gracefully or otherwise. Now, he also bumps the back of his head. "I'm sorry about that bump, Joe. I'm gonna start guiding in your head so that you won't scuff the hair off the top of your noggin."

"I'm used to it."

The older he gets, the more he chats up grocery clerks. Today he compliments one of his favorite clerks, Muliu, on her multi-colored head scarf and then tells me that her boss made her stop wearing "her headdress" a few months ago. "It looks like he let up on that. What's the harm, if she wants to wear it?"

After we unload our groceries at home, I run him over to the library for a couple of hours. He won't get into the car unless I promise him that I have something to do there too. I always tell him I have plenty of research to do there to keep me busy. Sometimes I check out the latest book for our book club.

Today, I'm headed next door to Lucha's Restaurant overlooking the lake. "Our book club is celebrating Betty's 80th birthday, Mr. B."

"She's 80? A spring chicken!" He carefully places one foot in front of the other, headed towards the library doors where I've dropped him. He turns back. "Maybe I should come wid you."

"I would invite you," I delicately apologize, "but it's supposed to be just for us chicks."

"Well, give her my condolences, then, will you?"

Until Mr. B was 85, he strutted across the park, and through huge parking lots, to the library, but in the past few years, he has driven those few blocks so that he can continue to read the latest *Aviation Week*, war books with firsthand accounts, science journals and the *New York Times*. He politely waits for his turn to tackle the "remainder of the crossword puzzles in the daily newspaper after the old guy in the library finishes wid' it," and then Joe attacks it and always completes the puzzle.

Today, when I come to collect him, he growls that he misses "certain older folks when they stop coming to the library." He seems grim. Those friendly nods and passing greetings are the closest thing to friends Joe possesses. And, while they come, they nod to each other and pass off the daily Denver Post because they understand their mutually private society. "The good ones copy the crossword puzzle and don't write on the actual newspaper, but maybe some of them can't afford to copy it. I dunno."

Joe's favorite kind of company, though, is a child. He loves the chatter and mixed-up antics of children, even in the library.

Back home, at dinner, we tell him that we'd like to have his grandkids over soon so they can see how we've trashed his place, a kind of housewarming party. Mr. B sits up straight and immediately asks if we have called them already. "Oh not yet. We wanted to pass it by you first."

"Let 'em come! Let 'em come!" he roars.

October 3, 2013

Biting into our creamy Braunschweiger sandwiches for dinner, I tell Mr. B that he has defied the entire market statistic for heart healthy dieters and food concerns.

Joe frowns. "What-do-you-mean-by-that?" His placid voice rolls out the question like a lazy river, just before he takes a swig of cold milk.

"Well, most of the information I have been taught about healthy choices never include Braunschweiger, or salty pickles, green olives and blue cheese with crackers for dinner! Yet, here you are, the specimen of health."

"Oh, well." Joe bites his sandwich of pork pate wobbling his head from side to side thinking this over. "It's probably because I don't eat butter or mayonnaise." With a push of his finger, he slips slivers of onion back into his sandwich. It's true, this fact probably balances out his other distrust of fats. Mr. B will not eat a tuna sandwich with mayonnaise, or any other kind of sandwich or salad with dressing, including egg salad. When we go to a restaurant, we always order his food to come steamed without anything shiny on it. One time his steak came with a pad of butter on the top and we had to send it back.

"You also have 45 percent iron in your blood which makes you the original Iron Man."

"Heh, heh, that's true! I told you that story? They always like me to give blood. But, it's probably because I eat so much Braunschweiger, and it's full o' iron." Joe cuts through his side of salted tomato, but his thoughts drift.

"What's on your mind, Mr. B?"

"You know that burial plot we have for Maudie at the church?" he begins.

"The columbarium?"

"Yes. That. Do you know that you put the name, 'Joe' on the stone beside Maudie's name?"

"Yes, I know. You've told me already," I admit nervously. "Your name is Joseph. Not Joe."

"Well yeah, you know, if someone were ever to come looking for me, and I can't imagine they would, but they might be confused. That's all."

"Dear Mr. B, I will change it. It's just that Maudie always called you Joe, and that's how I knew you. Now, I know you better."

Mr. B chuckles. "Oh, no matter, Miss. I'm just teasing ya. What do I care whether it says Joe or Joseph? All of my engineering friends are gone, and my family is all gone. What does it matter?"

"Of course it matters how you wish to be remembered. I was just trying to fit in both of your names, you know, the whole thing of Maudie and you on that stone in the garden, and I made a mistake."

"Well, don't worry, kiddo. The main thing is that you can fit me into a jar beside my wife. Just don't make it say I died from eating Braunschweiger after 97 years. I wouldn't want to break a statistic."

"You already have, Mr. B." What would the food and health administration deduce from this healthy ol' man's diet of pickles, whole milk, smoked sausage and white bread? I stuff a pickled slab of Braunschweiger sandwich into my mouth with guilty pleasure.

October 4, 2013
"What's this I found on your driveway, Miss?" Mr. B has sorted out the ads from the paper and thrown them into the trash.

I pass over his strange adjective. "We ordered the Denver Post for ya, Mr. B, just in case we can't get to the library in winter."

"Well, you shouldn't have. *I* wouldn't pay for it. Papers cost too much these days. I used to collect fifteen cents every Saturday from my paper route customers. If you weren't a *regulah*, the daily paper cost ya two cents and the Sunday paper cost ten. Don't waste your money on me. It's too much."

"Not if you can get your daily crossword puzzle, Mr. B, and your news. We think it's a worthy cause. Besides, that's a heck of a turn around for a paper boy!"

Joe smirks and waves me off, but his attention is immediately redirected to the headlines in hand.

Paul and I have ardently taken to peddling our bikes in the cool evenings around the nearby lake. Tonight, he stops his bike beside a bench at the top of the hill overlooking the lake. We watch the calm twilight blue darken. Night stars begin to mirror themselves in the glossy surface of the lake. Paul prefers to sit and watch the stillness through the smoke of a cherry cigar, so I decide to ride around it by myself.

The whirr, whirring of my cruiser tires are the only sounds besides the crickets. I pass a couple of joggers and a few dog walkers and lovers out for their evening stroll. Sound bites of rubbery shoes slap-slapping the concrete and a muffled jingle of the dog's tags breeze by. The intimacy of the moist breezes against my dark form feel mysteriously delightful.

By the time I return to the top of the hill, I am musing glory in my own world.

> Safe and solid, my high mountain,
>   God who trains me fair and well;
> He's my bedrock and high tower
>   His command will surely prevail.
> And, I wonder why you love me,
>   why you bother to rise to my prayer?
> Surely human beings are merely
>   shadows in the smoky air.
>   (Psalm-Hymn 144, by L. L. Larkins)

October 5, 2013

"I only got laid off once, Miss. It was a political move, to save the company money. When I was rehired, they put me into the top secret division where nobody ever bothered me."

"What did you do there?"

"You know, Sweet Pea, the space program had Lockheed working one part of their design, and some other companies working on other parts of their design, and everyone's work was considered top secret to themselves, trade secrets, see? But when it came to modifications, they wanted me to sign off on them. I told them, I couldn't sign off on a design, especially wid all of the new hidden electronics inside of little black boxes, without knowing what kind of gasses they were using, and what the maths were for the blueprints. Oh, they didn't like that. They wanted me to sign off with a gentleman's handshake. It was political. There was only one old timer I trusted. If he told me it was alright, *then* I'd do it."

"So, what kind of modifications did you make yourself?"

"One time I recommended they install a honeycomb aluminum cover on one satellite because the radiation experts were saying that we were losing equipment due to radiation. I asked for half-inch aluminum, and they came up with three-quarters, so I had them split that thickness in one third for the interior and two thirds for the exterior cover, and I designed two covers, one inside of the other, with a blanket of air for insulation between them. Another time, I modified the capsule for the top rocket thruster on a two stage space shuttle. One company did the lower half, and another company designed the rocket, and I did the capsule. They put two tanks of solid burning gook in each level. The first design was fired by a liquid flammable, but then they went to solid."

"Why was that?"

"Oh, because you know, if you pressurize something with a very thin skin, it gives it greater strength, but say someone were to shoot a hole in the skin, then the pressure would release, and the skin would lose its strength!

"Oh, you know those satellites in the atmosphere? They take pictures of everything? Well, they had three of 'em. One rotated one way and was held by a truss system to the middle stationary one, and then the bottom one, which also rotated, utilized the truss system. I removed the truss system. The satellites didn't need all that exterior ribbing. I recommended they place all of the

equipment inside the satellite and support the structure from the center, and also by four husky one-inch bolts that would attach it to the space vehicle."

"Are you talking about the Hubble Space Telescope, Joe?"

"Well, this was before that. What we were taking pictures of was all the things moving on the earth. We could see a submarine surface, and watch the war efforts from above."

"Oh. You were the first Google Earth."

October 6, 2013

Joe and I have been standing at the front window trying to decide what is causing the annoying whining across the street. The young man who lives there is finishing a degree in mechanical engineering. Unable to decipher the rolling, whirring continuous whine, we decide to use the den at the back of the house for a quiet refuge.

"Have you heard of the movie, *Papa Knows Best*? Say what you want, but 'Papa is all' has its value. It was good training to fear our fathea's word, and my fathea made us a family unit, but a lot of people couldn't take that. Especially because of the women. My mothea had to carry boiled water to the bathing barrel for the whole year we lived at number two Arnold Street." He looks up to see me cringing. "I don't hold to it anymore, neither. I believe life was too hard for women back then.

"I guess my fathea was also what you'd call moody. He played cards down in the speakeasy every Friday night for fun, and the men there were his only friends. On the weekends, when my fathea wanted to go into the forest to pick pioppini mushrooms, he always asked me to come wid him. It would rain on a Friday and fathea would nudge me and suggest we go into the forest on Saturday. I guess he needed to get outta the house?" Joe's head wobbles from side to side. "We'd stuff our pockets and buckets with these little mushrooms, no bigger than your finger, on Saturday and bring them home to mothea.

"Mr. Curtis owned the third house we lived in, corner of Boyden and Church Street. There was only one potty in the entire house for all the renters. On the third floor lived a deaf widow. We were supposed to share the bathroom with her, but she was deaf. It created a problem you can imagine: We would walk into the bathroom and see the deaf woman on the potty! If we knocked, she couldn't hear us." He opens his hands and shrugs. "So Mr. Curtis promised to add a john to our apartment, and a tub. He did that for us. He kept his promise and then he died shortly after."

"Well, bless him."

"There was a Russian woman, Ms. Lipski, who would stroll to the end of our block at Church Street and Boyden. She'd stop there and peer around to see what she could gossip about. At least that's what my mothea thought. My mothea didn't like her, but Mrs. Lipski's oldest son had a painted truck and I rode with him to all kinds of mill towns. He just wanted my presence, not as a worker. The Russians were just as jumpy as the rest of us. It was safer for him if he had another guy along. And you know? Maybe I was too young, but that guy wouldn't talk to me!"

I wonder if there's an off chance Joe's parents and this Russian guy didn't talk to him because Joe had his own ongoing soliloquy, even at a young age.

"One place the Russian guy and I went along to was a house belonging to two Jewish brothers. They had a job collecting pulp fiction magazines to return to the publisher for credit or a few dollars. Hey, they even collected *Wiz Bang*, heh. Yeah, it was a lobbying magazine for porn, a small pocket magazine, but it mostly had all kinds of jokes. They'd give me the insides of the magazines for my mothea because they were cheap fuel. She liked to burn them in the stove. Magazines burned easily. But she didn't get the Westerns at first. I got 'em!

"See that cottonwood tree?" It's backyard girth is four times the girth of Joe, and a hundred times his height. I nod, even though the roof of the back porch obstructs all but its ankles from my view.

"I guess I planted it because of the Westerns. There were always cottonwoods in the Westerns I read. Yeah, I loved to read those stories! I'd help the brothers rip off the covers of the magazines, and they'd let me pick out the ones I wanted to take home for fuel. That was my pay. After I read 'em, I'd roll 'em up and tie 'em wid something, and we'd stuff 'em into the stove for fuel, my mothea or me.

"Sometimes inside the magazines, there was a plastic disc for a record player. Yeah. Records were plastic first, not vinyl. Betcha didn't know that! But they didn't last too long.

"One of the Jewish boys was real strict, but the other one became a sailor who traveled the world. In the end, he married a Catholic." Joe continues, shaking his head against that notion. "The people in my family who married Jewish people ended up with tough marriages because interfaith marriages are hard. Parents don't like the awkwardness, or shame, of their kid marrying outside the faith, you know."

"Well, especially after World War II, I presume."

He nods and shrugs. "Just being polite about deeply ingrained things in the family only gets ya so far. When the babies come along, well, it all but ends a marriage."

October 7, 2013

Mr. B and I traverse county roads north of Denver into farming and ranching territory. I am on a mission to pick up freshly packaged meat. He wonders why I would bother to pay for anything but pork. Certainly not a lamb, which tastes despicable to him, except that Maudie used to like it, which compelled him to occasionally take her to the odd restaurant to find roasted leg of lamb. These days, even beef is usually too tough for Mr. B to concern himself with. Nevertheless, for something to do, he has agreed to accompany me into the flatlands of Colorado with a picnic cooler. As we pass by the village towns along the way, he eyes the bungalows on Main Street. Finally, he blurts, "I could never live in one of these places."

"Why not?"

"I dunno! I look at these small houses on such a busy street, and I know I couldn't live here. It would bore me to no end. What would I do here?"

"Oh, you'd probably meet your neighbors and get to know people."

"I would not. I'm too skeptical. You forget my family was from the old country. We learned to be polite, but we never stopped being cynics. My sistas were worse skeptics than me. They never liked people asking them too many questions. 'Why'd they want to know?' they'd say. 'What did they want to know about your history and private life for, and *why* did they want to know it?'" His voice rills recollecting his sistas' voices.

"Oh, Mr. B, most people aren't being nosy or have agendas. They ask questions to get to know someone. They think they are being *polite*. People are very open these days." *Too open!* I agree secretly.

"Well, I don't think asking questions is *polite*. You won't catch me asking questions of you because then you'd start talking religion and pretty soon I'd be trapped."

I throw back my head and laugh. "You're pretty funny!"

He grins. "No. People always have an agenda, and I don't like to help 'em out much. They probably don't even have a library in a small town like this, so there would be nothing that I would consider fun to do. When you get into a good story, it's real fun, that is."

I consider this. Library and fun and what I know of Joe's childhood, collecting magazines for ripping off the covers, turning them in for cash and using the inside pages for heating their house. Hmmm.

"Did you like to go to the library in Woonsocket, Mr. B?"

"I'd deliver papers there. An old man and his sista ran it, and my fathea said they were from a very good family. He said 'good family' like it meant something, so I believed they came from wealth most probably."

"But did you go there *to read*?" I press, trying to get to the bottom of what he thought was fun as a kid. Surely it wasn't the library unless they had story hour.

"Me? Oh, nooooooo, Miss. The only books I ever read were pulp fiction books. Westerns. You know the magazines we collected for the covers to send back to the publishers? I loved the insides of 'em. I'd read those Westerns for hours and then, we'd roll 'em up and pump the stove wid 'em. They burned well!"

Okay. Clearly, there was no library reading in Joe's early years.

I notice the Platte River beside our road, glowing like a deep blue mirror of the Colorado sky in areas and running brown in other sections. "People used to say the Platte was a mile wide and a foot deep." Joe grunts.

"When I was a kid," I divulge, "we played all kinds of games out on the street and in each other's yards with all the neighborhood kids. We ran and played hide-'n-seek, red rover and kickball, and we danced and rode our bikes together. I was also the neighborhood storyteller, and I'd sit on the steps and tell ghost stories in October. We invented fun 'til our parents started calling us inside. We thought it was fun just to be together. And really, that's the way that we got to know one another. It seemed if people went to the same school or to the same church, then the families instantly trusted one another. Otherwise, it was the kids who broke the ice by playing at a friend's house. The parents would ask their kid's friends about their home life, and if they liked what they heard, then the parents would become friends."

Oh, man, Mr. B doesn't seem to have noticed, but the "refuel" light in my dashboard is bright yellow. I limp into the next town and turn into the gas station. After refueling, I confess my predicament to my passenger. "Paul even warned me, but I had completely forgotten!" My face is flushed.

"You were gonna leave me on the side of the road," he accuses with those stern blue eyes.

"Yeah, for those vile farmers to roll you up into a haystack!"

"Now, you've established your reputation wid me, Ma'am. Sorry, I won't let you live it down." He shakes his head sadly and squeezes my arm with his quick vice-like grip.

After picking up the packaged meat, we start the long road home. Joe gazes at the passing carmine cornfields in the low-lying sun with the snow-crusted Rocky peaks in the far distance. "I think you are right about trusting people. It's the kids who break the ice between neighbors. And church. Otherwise, our family was a family of skeptics. That's a hard thing to shake, and I think it's served me well."

October 9, 2013

Trying to please Mr. B's Polish taste buds, I follow instructions from our local grocer to gather and cook a curated collection of wild and cultivated mushrooms—chanterelles, cremini, porcini, morels. As they sauté, I find a new appreciation of the subtle differences in texture and flavor.

This classic French recipe takes a diversity of mushrooms and unites them in an irresistible creamy sauce. Our Chowhound *Wild Mushrooms à la Crème* recipe goes like this.

Total Time: 15 mins
Active Time: 15 mins
Makes: 8 servings

Ingredients (9)

- 4 tablespoons unsalted butter (1/2 stick)
- 1 medium onion, finely chopped
- Salt
- Freshly ground black pepper
- 1 pound wild mushrooms (chanterelles, morels, cèpes a.k.a. porcini, false chanterelles, or the common field mushroom), sliced into 1/4-inch pieces
- Juice of 1/4 lemon
- 1 cup heavy cream
- 1 tablespoon finely chopped Italian parsley
- 1 tablespoon finely chopped chives

This rich, creamy sauce is so versatile: Top baked potatoes or crostini with it. Or turn it into a pasta sauce or a filling in omelets or crêpes.

Instructions.

    1. Set a heavy medium-size saucepan with tightfitting lid over medium-low heat. When the pan is hot, add 2 tablespoons of the butter. When the butter starts to foam, add the onion, season with salt and pepper, cover, and cook over low heat for 5 to 10 minutes, until the onion is translucent and soft but not colored. Remove from heat; keep warm.

    2. Meanwhile, heat a large frying pan over medium-high heat until hot, about 2 minutes. Add 1 tablespoon of the butter and cook until foaming. Add half of the mushrooms and season with salt, pepper, and 1/2 teaspoon lemon juice. Sauté, stirring occasionally, until mushrooms

are browned on both sides, about 2 to 3 minutes. Transfer to a medium bowl. Repeat with remaining butter and mushrooms.

3. Add mushrooms and cream to the cooked onions and bring to a simmer over medium heat until the flavors meld, about 2 to 3 minutes. Add parsley and chives, if using, and stir to combine. Taste and add salt, pepper, or lemon juice as needed. The sauce can be refrigerated for up to 5 days or frozen for up to a month.

Paul and I delight in the delectable bowl. Joe, on the other hand, eats his meal silently and carefully. Finally, he speaks. "This is not something I would normally order, Ma'am."

My heart sinks.

"Well, my mothea used fresh and dried mushrooms to flavor soups and *bigos*, a church potluck dish. She usually sautéed 'em in butter or simmered them in sour cream. I remember one favorite mushroom of the Polish Catholics. Can you pronounce P.R.A.W.D.Z.I.W.E.K?" I explain that I can't even remember the letters in order, so he informs me that this term, "prawdziwek" mushrooms meant that they were noble or real. They were excellent. "My fathea and I would find them in a forest of conifers."

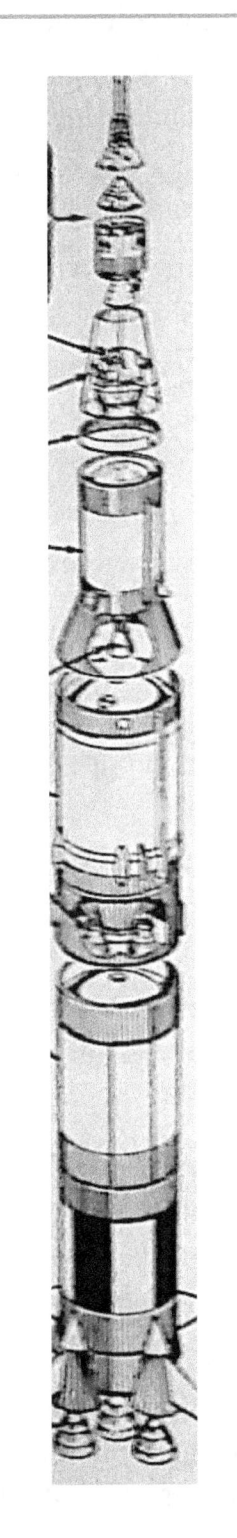

October 10, 2013

"Oooooh, see that missile in the park?" Mr. B points out the window.

"Isn't that an airplane? Everyone always calls this 'Airplane Park,' Joe."

We are passing the pretty and popular park, with the *missile* on display.

"Nope. It's a missile." He takes out his toothpick. "They put a rocket on the end of it, and it went pretty far. I was given the job of reconfiguring the insides of exactly that kind of missile so that it could hold more fuel and go farther."

"What happened?"

"They took me off it cuz cruise missiles took over from the guided missiles. You might call this an intermediate missile because they never figured out how to send it farther."

"What was the *diff* with guided missiles, Joe?"

"Well, Miss, a guided missile was guided by radio waves, like the drones that real aircraft are complaining about now days for being in their airspace. They are just the same as model airplanes, nothing more, maybe a little fancier. But, the cruise missiles could be shot off of submarines or aircraft carriers, destroyers or frigates! They were betta." (Joe holds the "r") He goes back to working on his teeth. After another mile, Joe adds, "Then came sonar. You know in the

'70s, the cold war, the Americans built a ship with the sole purpose of being able to lift metal. They wanted to lift up the Russian sub, K-129 that had sunk, and by use of sonar, the CIA had discovered it. Since the Soviets had abandoned their search, America wanted to study it covertly, so it was all hush, hush. Well, they built a ship called the Hughes Explorer, under the guise of it being a metal collecting ship but, it eventually picked up the K-129 from deep on the ocean floor with a special holster. The problem was, when they were lifting it, all the atomic bombs slipped out of the ship."

"What? Didn't they explode?"

"Oh no, Miss. In the ocean floor, some places are soft earth, down to 100 feet thick, believe it or not. Oh, they were sunk and lost forever, *believe me*."

October 11, 2013

A lone window installer arrives today with two suction cups and a ladder.

I almost refuse him entrance when I see him approach the house solo. Disbelief consumes me that he can replace all these windows without a crew in one day.

He stands at the threshold, patiently listens to my objections, and pragmatically asks me to let him try because he's been in the business for 17 years and always works solo.

Six hours later, he carries the last aluminum window out the door and with them, my fear of having to use Joe's dreaded plastic window coverings for winter. I had to follow the window man around and move furniture to and fro. With the exercise having cleared the cobwebs from my head, I apologize profusely for my earlier abuse. He replaces the blinds, vacuums, washes the replacement windows streak-free, caulks and seals them.

Mr. B inspects the new window above the head of his bed. He whistles and exclaims how pretty it is, testing the window crank.

"You do good work, Mister. But do you recommend that I still wear my knitted cap to bed?"

October 12, 2013
At today's housewarming party, which doubles as a birthday for great grandpa's namesake, little Joe-Joe, Mr. B produces a bouncy ball for the children to play with. Jester, feisty as always, immediately intercepts, swiping the ball, teasing Christina and little Joe with a game of keep away. He wants to play, yet keep the ball himself, so he tosses it around the yard, making the kids chase him for it. Mr. B's jaw forms a lump from clenching his teeth. "Sometimes I like that dog, and sometimes I don't," Joe, works his toothpick. "My mothea would never have had a dog living under her roof."

His granddaughter's laughter rings out. She says, "We have three!"

"They don't seem to hurt your kids, neither," Joe nods as he delves int toe "no mayo" deviled eggs. "Times have changed." Joe puts three at a time on his plate. Sandy and I exchange knowing, secret glances. For years we have kept up a little white lie that there is no mayo in this dish because it is one of Joe's all-time favorites. Just last night I overheard him assuring Paul that mayonnaise would come right up if he was forced to try it after all these years. The kids have brought their grandfather summer garden gifts of fresh tomatoes and canned pickles. We make sandwiches.

"Grandpa, do you remember the time you asked for the plate of tomatoes to be passed, and each of us took one before it got back to you?" His sweet granddaughter has a tender heart for her grandpa, but now Mr. B has a hard time hearing most female voices including hers. So Paul and I shout repetitions of the conversation. "Oh yeah, I remember that one!" he sputters. "You kids were naughty. All the tomatoes were gone when the plate got 'round to me! But, I guess I deserved that. One time when I went to visit Maudie's sista and her husband, I got piggish and when the plate was passed to me, I took all the slices. You should have seen the look on their faces. But, I didn't care one bit." I can only imagine why Maudie never mentioned this tale herself. He smiles blandly, not in the least embarrassed.

Paul helps me clean up after our party. "You know, honey, you are gonna have to leave my dad some notes or a list of things to do while you are gone. Since he refuses to answer the phone, I won't be able to check on him. He's been relying on you for breakfast, and if I'm gone for dinner, what'll he do? I don't trust him to remember how to make his meals or to feed Jester." Our dog, hearing his name, comes to the edge of the kitchen and looks up at us, all eyes.

"I hope the nice days continue throughout October so that Mr. B can walk around the yard. I've been praying our hefty dog won't leave a ball on the stairs, or trip him up or run him over!" Suddenly, I just don't want to go. "I'll leave a list, but you need to be here at dinner," I whisper. "You can't leave him alone all day. And what if Jester runs down the stairs and pushes him over? I'm concerned."

Mr. B shuffles into the kitchen. "Talking vacation days, are ya? Well, I can fix my own breakfasts. I've done it for years. You go and have fun wid your sista!" He leans forward using both my arm and Paul's. "May the cockroaches be small."

October 13, 2013
"How about joining me on a little excursion, Mr. B? It'll break up the boredom of sitting in this room all day." He smiles as I rub his shoulders lightly.

"Nah, not today, Miss. Not unless you find a port-o-potty to put in the back of your vehicle. If I just sit here, seems I don't ever have to go, but as soon as I get in the car, I feel the urgency."

"We can always stop, you know. I have to go sometimes too."

"A port-o-potty and a raincoat, both. That's what I'd need."

I pull back the living room curtains. "It's not gonna rain this morning, Joe. —" Then, it's privacy that dawns on me, not weather, he is referring to.

October 14, 2013

His eyes are trained on the Alabama - LSU football game showing on television. He points at a flock of sparkling pom-pom girls and notifies me that his "athletic grand-daughter could be one of those girls in sequined costumes. Only she's too short. She's not as tall as those gals." I get him to turn his head so that he hears me clearly when I shout, "She's only ten, Joe."

"You think she'll grow? That tall? Well, she's a strong and talented girl, that one. I hope my grand-children are motivated to become athletes. I've heard a rumor that athletes get a decent discount on their college expenses."

It's apparent that Alabama is beating the socks off the other team. Mr. B shines his fingernails on his blue fleece and points at me. "Just remember the Crimson Tide, Miss! They took over the top tonight! Even if you aren't a fan, you gotta hand it to 'em." I am a fan, Mr. B. because you are a fan.

October 15, 2013

My sister and I are having the time of our lives as passengers on a riverboat cruise, in Venice! I recognize bridges and city squares that Joe and I have watched on television together in the foreign mysteries. Gondoliers come to life before my eyes in their striped black and white shirts. Small speedboats and vaporetto barges carry us like taxis wherever our feet cannot navigate on cobblestones. We learn the lion is San Marco's symbol of their patron saint. Every plaza has its own ornately carved stone church, and many have community opera halls. Even though Paul and Joe fill my mind, my senses are captivated by old buildings, classical history, gelato in a cone, artwork on cathedral walls, wine information and pasta-making instructions with dinner after our walking tours. The alleys of Venice are known for high-end fashion stores with full story window scenes that stand out and call a tourist in like any excellent form of media. I recognize some of the leading fashion designers in the world in these exclusive boutiques.

Before we take in an evening of Vivaldi opera, Paul calls me from overseas to tell me that his dad and our dog seem to be getting along fine. His dad has approved of Jester as a good watchdog.

"Keep his toys off of the stairs, honey. And as long as your dad is letting the dog go down the stairs before him in the morning, I think he'll be okay."

"You wrote a list for him?" Paul quizzes.

"Yup. I left it at his place at the table."

"Well, I think he's actually gotten better remembering things since we moved in!" exclaims my husband.

I smile. "Yeah? Let's hope. Oh, and don't forget to clip his toenails."

"What, what? The line is breaking up, dear. I can't hear you anymore."

I laugh at him and roll over the silky bed, staring up at the Murano glass chandelier, feeling my good fortune.

October 20, 2013

Yesterday, I smuggled home some well packaged Italian cheese and pâté in my suitcase for Joe. He is delighted to get pâté for breakfast with his warm roll. I explain that I accomplished this feat because my own family ancestry is rooted in Jesse James, not Queen Victoria.

"Really?"

"Yes. Really."

"Swear to me that you didn't bring back olive oil."

"Would I do that to you, my friend?" What's the point of telling him the latest medical studies prove one lives longer on a Mediterranean diet?

He looks askance. "Maudie couldn't believe they cooked eggs in olive oil! Imagine that, olive oil!" In a jolly mood, he asks questions, and I show him photos on my computer. He wonders how I got the pictures in there. He compares my adventures to a European trip that Maudie took.

"Didn't you go, too?" I ask.

"Oh no… I wanted to dig out the grass around the fence and put the peat in. I got the whole yard done by the time she and Vicky got back." He pauses, shaking his fork over his pâté. "Besides, I don't like Italian food or fancy stuff. Maudie didn't like much of it either. We are a picky bunch."

Joe has taken to wearing his pale blue jacket over his light blue fleece, over his wool shirt over his T-shirt. Winter chill is setting in. Several years ago, I bought him a large sized alpaca wool blue and white snowflake sweater for Christmas. That's how I discovered how much Joe likes blue and white. He wore that thing almost every day of every winter until last winter, when he could no longer mend the holes. I've been searching for another light blue wool sweater like the first one, but in the meantime he looks cuddly in his layers.

"Mr. B? It's freezing up in our bedroom at night. We've opened the vents, and it doesn't seem to help. As soon as you walk half way up the stairs, you can feel the temperature drop ten degrees!" I feel my mouth inadvertently pull to the side, nervous to complain.

"Oh, Vicky used to hate that room because it was so cold. I think us engineers sometimes pull a boner. Mine was to turn down the heating element on the furnace to 90 degrees. It was supposed to be at 150, but I thought I could save money if the fan kept circulating the air at lower temperatures. Now, I've tried, but I can't get my hand back in there with a screwdriver to turn it back."

"Okay, I'm going to ask Paul to get a heating guy to make it stop circulating cold air, then. Is that okay?"

He shrugs, "Sure…" and this time it's his lips that turn downward. "Hey, you know my brother Eddy traveled the world via his vacations every year, and I remember getting a postcard one day. It was from my brother. He was sending me a postcard of the Taj Mahal! Imagine that! I was more concerned wid saving money, but he and Bertha were out there seeing it all. And he risked a lot more wid the stock exchange than I did, too. I thought it was safer to put my money into government bonds, but you know what? The last statement of interest I received on $23,000 said I'd made a dollar and twenty- three cents for two years."

"Well, I'm not sure who came out better, Eddy or you!" I can't resist ribbing him.

"Eh," I see his eyebrows raise. "I have no complaints."

October 21, 2013

At breakfast, Joe's glasses steam up from his hot Ovaltine. He slurps it and delicately slices a piece of mushroom and pork pâté onto his warm roll. "Szynka," he says. "That's what we call pork meat, or pig, in Polish. And Moshlemonkies."

"Moshlemonkies?"

Mr. B drifts to a memory. "I can still smell that particular and pleasing aroma of the mushrooms drying in our room in the attic.

Us kids would go into the forest and pick mushrooms. I could stuff my pockets wid them, 'cuz of my brother Eddy's pants being so large on me. When we'd bring 'em home to my mothea, she would string them together and hang them in the attic where Eddy and I slept. You wouldn't think it, but those darn things smelled so good. I never smelled anything like 'em. When she cooked 'em, they didn't smell. Not that I remember. It was just when they were drying in the attic. They had a sweet earthy aroma."

The image of a mountain slope full of mushrooms on a vacation we took as a family comes to mind. "I remember when all four of us were in the mountains, you wanted to go hiking and bring us back some mushrooms to cook for dinner, but Maudie wouldn't allow it."

"She was afraid that I wouldn't know the difference between the good ones and the poisonous ones. It had been too many years. Maybe I wouldn't. But I think there's a saying about telling the difference. I just can't recall it."

I run to collect my computer and look up edible mushrooms. The sites we read advise us to stick to the same variety to avoid picking a toadstool. Apparently, a silver coin will turn black if it is cooked with a poisonous mushroom, and if animals are seen eating the mushroom, then it is not poisonous. But often dogs eat poisonous mushrooms and die, so it's tricky. I wouldn't want our Jester to keel over. Also, if the top layer of the cap can be peeled, it is not poisonous.

"Hmmmph." Joe listens closely to the information coming from my black box.

"Do you remember the kind you picked? I'm asking because I

used to see fairyrings of them in the neighbor's front lawn, and I wondered if they were poisonous or good to eat."

"Oh, I don't remember anymore. Their tops were white, but the gills underneath were dark. You don't eat mushrooms with white gills. They can kill ya. "White-Fright!" I do remember that. We used to call them moshlemonkies. I don't know why."

The more I read about collecting mushrooms as an amateur, the more I realize how dangerous it could be. There are just too many look-alike poisonous ones.

"Anyway, you can just buy what you want in the grocery store."

"I don't know that any of those would dry like yours did with so sweet an aroma." Mr. B's childhood experience has me jealous. The websites advise that I join a local mycological (fungi) group to avoid danger. This is an education that is localized and seems to be passed on by personal experience alone. I don't want to hunt mushrooms with anyone other than Mr. B. I sigh and close my computer.

"Can you find anything in there, Miss?" he asks.

"I can't find my way back to your childhood to hunt mushrooms with you," I reply sadly.

October 22, 2013

Unfortunately, Mr. B grows what his doctor calls "barnacles" on the side of his face that absorbed the most sun during his years of driving. He gets these sanded or burned off from time to time. I've been noticing that he doesn't seem too concerned about getting rid of them lately, but they must bother him some because he rubs and scratches at them.

Today is our appointment to see his general practitioner. The good doctor listens to Mr. B's lungs and takes his blood pressure. "You are one healthy guy!" she exclaims.

"What did she say?" Joe turns to me.

I repeat her encouraging words.

"Yes, I hate to bother you, Doctor, but could you do something wid these bumps or barnacles as you call them?" He scratches at one behind his ear.

I'm relieved when she freezes them and then cleans out his ears.

"How is he eating?" she asks me.

"Oh, this is my new cook!" Joe interjects, pointing at me. "I have nothing to complain about."

"You are good to go," she declares.

"One more thing? As Joe's doctor, do you think he should drive? Paul doesn't think his dad should renew his driver's license, but I think he needs his license to drive in case of emergency."

The answer? She looks at Joe and shouts in his face, "Mr. Byk, if you can pass the driving test, go ahead." It's official.

October 23, 2013

So, instead of waiting for Mr. B's birthday to take the driving test in January slush and snow, I ask to accompany him to the motor vehicle department this morning just in case.

Two young men cheer him on as he reads the letters in the binoculars at the counter. He labors to hear the clerk's questions, leaning in, and I hear them chuckling at the repetitious exchange, but when the clerk congratulates Mr. B, they clap and keep clapping as his picture is taken. He smiles at them as if they are the entertainment and signs the form.

Maybe it is all the excitement, but suddenly, Joe has a little trouble getting home. "I seem to have lost my compass," he croaks. "The neighborhood has changed. The streets are very busy, and I can't tell where the line in the road is, Miss!"

The clouds hover above us, not creamy or puffy white, but as strange purple and yellow ribbons, blotched arms of an old wounded chief like himself, stretched and sagging with the weight of wet air across the sky. Over the foothills, the cloud-arms appear to be bleeding blue blood. "Looks like winter is here," I observe.

"You know that property you have higher up, that has those deep red rocks on it, Miss?"

"Um, yeah. Watch the road though."

"I am. But the thought came to me about Lang Hancock. Ever heard of him?"

"Don't think so."

"Well, he was a pilot who discovered the world's richest iron ore reserve near Perth, Australia. He was flying over some deep red cliffs, and his compass went crazy. There was nothing wrong with his plane, but he barely made it out of the gorge because of the confusion with his compass."

"Iron messes with a compass?"

"Heck, yeah! It messes with the magnetism. But because he wasn't a good minerals man, he didn't know that iron had that power, so he told everyone that it was a rain storm that had driven him to fly so low into the gorge of red cliffs."

"All he cared about was the wealth from mining that stuff outta there! He did manage to sell it to China for several years, but I think they are in a slump now because Australians decided not to sell it to them anymore."

My father-in-law brakes in odd spots, probably due to multiple limitations, but pulling his Saturn into the driveway, I can see he is rather pleased with himself nonetheless.

At home, I curl into a corner of the dim afternoon light, on our brown couch in the den, and pull out my computer. I search the key words of Joe's story, and find out that his facts are basically correct.

Of his discoveries, Woodward wrote:

This is essentially an iron country, for one cannot travel a mile in the parts where the older rocks appear at the surface, without encountering a lode. It occurs in many forms but the chief are magnetite and hematite which occur in immense lodes and would be of enormous value if cheap labour were abundant. There is enough to supply the whole world. From the large quantity of iron in this Colony it is impossible to work with any degree of accuracy with a magnetic compass.

Lang Hancock was an asbestos miner who, in 1952, says he found the iron ore cliffs while traveling below the clouds in the striking rain of a November storm.

After his story was published, the tale of the storm was discredited because there was no rain at the time. He may have skewed the facts at that time in order to keep the government out of the claim, "as yet undiscovered." Then, by mining and exporting the iron, he made his daughter the wealthiest woman in the world.

In 1890, sixty years earlier though, an English geologist, Harry Page Woodward, wandering around north Pilbara on his donkey, set down his legacy in the *Annual General Report of the Government Geologist*.

Hmm. Time flying reminds me to forage through the refrigerator for dinner, though with a prayer for navigation. I find Joe sitting with his eyes closed in his blue chair. "You were right about that Lang Hancock guy, Mr. B. I looked him up! Smart cookie, that one."

"You betcha." He smiles. "I don't think he ever flew on an empty tank, neither." Then, I notice his wink.

October 24, 2013

Mr. B drifts through memories of his father at breakfast while eating his new favorite Italian pâté. "Have you heard the saying, 'Papa is all?'" Joe's blue eyes are directed at me over the table.

"Yes, um, I have."

"Do you know what it means?"

I guess. "That the father's opinion, his word, is final?"

Joe's head wobbles back and forth across his shoulders. "Well, yes and no. But you got it pretty well. When we lived in the first house, we didn't have a bathtub. My fathea would always get his bath first in the big washtub set in the middle of the kitchen, then the boys, then the girls. My mothea worked hard to pour in the water and carry it out. She was strong." Joe's voice emphasizes *strong*. "She would take this copper washing pot, it was elongated so that it fit over two burners of the stove. She would boil water and put the sheets in it. Then she would take tongs that were spring-loaded and had like a fork of prongs, two on either side, and lift up the boiling pot, and she'd dump it into the bathtub. She rinsed the sheets and even the laundry in the bathtub."

"She didn't have any hired help?"

"No, but my parents rented a cot to a young woman, I remember. She probably helped out, but then she got married and moved to Connecticut. After college, I brought home my first car, which I bought in Saint Louis. My parents asked me to drive them all the way to Connecticut to see this gal and her husband. I think by then they also had a child about to enter college. She was gregarious. The mothea, I mean. My mothea and fathea both liked this gal a lot. But soon after, I heard that they couldn't afford to pay the mortgage on their house, and the bank took it from them. What a mess! They just took it without paying them back any of the investment they had made over the years. Terrible."

The sad memory of what almost happened to us tickles my back with its old creeping fearful fingers. I shiver.

"Yeah, you understand that's why I wanted to buy our house outright! You can't trust the banks, and when you are down and out, how can you fight 'em?" Joe's eyes grow wide in his own horror. I'm thinking the government should invent some anti-corruption laws against this banking practice.

I remove my dishes from the table and come back to sit with Mr. B.

Joe looks at me inquisitively. "What was I saying?"

"You were telling me about your childhood homes in Woonsocket…"

"Oh yeah, oh yeah. The windows rattled in all those houses we lived in, especially the one on Arnold Street. Eddy and I lived in the attic and it was coooooooold in the winter! You wouldn't believe it, but it was really cold up there." He is a baaaahing sheep when he says *cold*.

"I bet I would believe it. Mr. B, don't forget to eat…"

He smiles and thanks me and pops another couple of bites into his mousetrap.

"The windows had ropes with weights on either side of 'em; you know those windows with the eight-inch long steel weights tucked inside the walls?" He says "The windows" not "our windows," like he doesn't own, rent, or manage those windows and may even be a pain to recall them. "When the wind got to going, even those weights would rattle in our walls. Brr!" Joe grabs his arms, shuddering.

"In all three houses we owned in Woonsocket, my fathea would *always* eat first. Slavic families believe 'Papa is all.' My mothea would sit my fathea down, and he and the boys would eat at the table. After they were done, the girls would eat. And my mothea would eat last, I guess. I don't ever remember her eating now that I think of it."

I blurt, "She probably snitched it hot as she was cooking, don't ya think, Mr. B?" I say this because I happen to know several cooks who might do that, of which I may be one.

His eyes open wide. "Well, maybe that's it! But I never agreed to the way it was done. I loved my fathea, but I thought that was going too far. Oh, but my mothea could make the best pies. Oh yeah. And she made me a whole pumpkin pie to myself whenever I brought her a pumpkin."

"You ate the whole thing?"

"Oh yeah! It was good, so good."

"Did your mom go to the market for fresh things every day or did you have a refrigerator?"

"Oh, we didn't own a freezer or a refrigerator!" Joe exclaims. "We had a cellar where my fathea used to bring chickens and sides of pork to butcher for the family."

"I bet that was sanitary." I imagine a headless chicken traipsing through the ruins of bacon and pork chops trimmings.

"Heh, heh, well, I don't know about that, Miss. There was the iceman who came by with a wagon of ice blocks and my mothea would buy ten cents worth of ice. You could buy two bits too, but she only bought ten cents. The iceman would saw through a section and when it broke off, my mothea would take it in her tongs and put it on the top shelf in the cellar. The cellar was the coldest place in the house. The ice would melt slowly and drain over the meat and vegetables into a hole in the floor where it drained into the sewer."

"Did the iceman come every week?"

"Oh no, ma'am, every *day*." He pauses. "Let's see, my mothea didn't like any kind of fish. But she would cook it for my fathea. He would eat anything that came out of the sea, so my mothea would pickle fish for him, but she hated it." Joe downs his soft poached, salted egg in three quick spoonfuls.

"Papa is all." I shrug.

October 25, 2013
My sister, Kay, and I host an Italian dinner for our entire family featuring pumpkin pasta, roast pork, and tiramisu. Since Joe won't eat the pasta, I prepare something I know he'll love. Pork is obviously Mr. B's favorite meat. He loves ham sandwiches, and he'd rather eat a pork loin or a candied ham for a holiday than anything else. Extra crispy bacon with eggs for breakfast and a hot dog dinner for Joe.

On the other hand, I was raised by a Seventh Day Adventist father who believed that eating pork was sinful. The first time I tasted a pork chop was after Paul and I were married, and he pulled his favorite dish out of the broiler.

My mom brings a papaya for appetizers, remembering how much Joe likes it. I think he was introduced to it in Mexico. What a hit! While all of us are raving about stories from the riverboat and the yummy dishes, Joe is hogging the rolls and papaya. Everyone thinks he's adorable. We argue about family scenarios and theology because my mother has decided not to eat pork either, and that is what we've served. We also argue about politics. He acts like he can't hear much, but later he tells me, "Why is there always so much religious talk when your friends and family come around?"

I laugh. "I dunno, Joe! Is there?"

"Yeah," he says, pointing repeatedly at me.

"Well, I'm glad my mom brought that papaya, then, to distract you!"

"Well, yeah. Me too," he says.

"You hogged the whole bowl, you know."

"You had plenty of that I-Taliano food." He nudges me. "I have to hog what I like or people will steal it from me! But people kept stealing it away."

"Oh, we'll get you some more of that stuff."

"Not too much, or I'll get bored of it."

"I doubt that. Not the way you were going at it last night!"

October 26, 2013

"Maybe we could walk a bit. Would you like to walk wid an ol' man around the block?"

"Why not?" So, leaving a downcast Jester at the door, off we trot together. I don't know why I have never noticed how beautiful this town is. There are red maples in the front yards of the neighbors. The hills loom large on the horizon. Cycling around the lake at night with Paul has been thrilling. The trees along the roads are turning every vibrant hue, and it is lasting several weeks in the drawn-out autumn.

Comparing this location to the area in which we used to live, I realize the investment aspect of owning a home. Location is everything related to investment. Our old neighborhood had a run of houses, one after another on block after block, badly needing renovation. Once I discovered the city was intentionally blighting the area so that they could sell it to developers, I became angry at the city powers. It was clear that there was no code enforcement in our neighborhood. Joe is right. Government treats human beings as expendable. My mind wanders along the ungainly curves of our history. That's why we are still trapped upside down with the mortgage on the first home we renovated in that town. We must keep renting it, rather than selling. It wouldn't appraise properly in that neighborhood. So we hold onto it, eeking out the mortgage but not with any joy. Yup. Location is everything related to investment, and here we are.

"What makes you mad, Miss?" Joe interrupts my thoughts.

"Oh, incompetence, I guess. Stupidity. Greed with a lack of compassion for others." Confession time? I hear myself spouting, "And really, I'm just a naturally impatient person."

"Like the flower."

"Impatiens? Ha! Guess so." I look at him holding my arm as we walk slowly down the sidewalk. He doesn't usually ask me questions about myself. "What makes you angry?"

"Me? Oh, I'm too old to be bothered much." He studies the pavement.

"You are not. You have to be honest with me if I upset you, okay?"

"No way!" He exclaims with bubbles in his raised voice. "My life has improved! Why would I upset the apple cart?

"Hey, did I tell you that my fathea was a letter writer for the Poles who settled in Woonsocket, Rhode Island?"

"Nope. Just that he was a gardener." I remeasure my steps to match the shuffled efforts beside me.

"Yeah," Joe pants, redirected. "He maintained work as the groundskeeper for Mr. Kimbal, a self-made man, yeah, have you ever heard that terminology? He told me once that he never had a college degree, but that he was a self-made man! Yeah, I admired him. They had a huge house on the hill. He ran a factory, and he had his hands in the bank somehow. Maybe he was on the board." Joe doesn't remember. He stops to catch his breath and drifts off in his thoughts.

He muses, "Some people just love working wid their hands outdoors. My fathea loved planting things and weeding the Kimbal's garden the best, and those are the best memories I have of my fathea. He was a very quiet man, and he never spoke much with me, but he would take me with him every chance he got. He would take me to collect mushrooms in the forest and also blueberries.

"The only time my fathea came home mad, really mad, was after Mrs. Kimbal wanted her peonies moved from here to there and from there to the other place so many times, that my fathea finally killed them." Mr. B chuckles. "The other time he wasn't very happy was when the Kimbals made a formal visit to my parents to ask if they would be willing to let the Kimbals adopt their eldest girl. My sista, Helen, was extremely pretty and played the piano. They came to visit all dressed up…"

"What in the world?!"

Mr. B begins with his short steps on the sidewalk again.

"Well, we were very poor, and they had the means to give Helen an advantage in life. My parents, of course, declined the offer. The only thing that kept my fathea working for the Kimbals after that was he realized that despite their financial well-being, they were lonely wid'out children. It made him feel sorry for them, so he kept working there."

I notice we only have to cross the street and our front lawn to count this circle of exercise a success.

"Whew! That walk took us a half hour, Mr. B!" He pushes past our dog's eager sniffs of welcome so that he can make it to the bathroom before an accident occurs. I realize sadly that exercise with Mr. B is never going to slim down my waistline.

I go to turn on Mr. B's stereo, and some beautiful guitar music fills the speakers and leaps into my soul. Sometimes when I'm listening to incredible music, the world becomes surreal, like it awakens a different part of my brain and everything seems as highly imaginative as I feel.

"Do you ever get jealous or have envy, Miss?" Joe's question jolts me out of my revelry.

"I don't think of myself as an envious person, but there were times when I had to talk myself out of resenting someone else's musical success, or jealousy when a boy I liked was taken by another girl. You?"

"Oh, it happens. I think I was envious of the Kimbals. Especially when they lived in the big house with the wrap-around porch and the gardens and maids and cooks. I wanted that life. When they died, they left their entire estate to a niece. She came out from Michigan and gave my folks several pieces of quality furniture. One of the pieces is the round Italian table in our front room that I had to refinish."

I nod. "I've always loved that table."

Joe snickers. "My mothea used to iron on it in front of the living room window, so when it was handed down to me, I had to sand and refinish it to get the burns out." I smile because Joe has refinished two of my own tables, and of course, he did his own mother's table, also.

My spirits are soaring with the guitars from Joe's old stereo speakers. Joe must notice my face because he suddenly turns his head toward the living room. "They've been playing some guitar music every day lately. It's new to me, but I like it."

"Me too!"

Joe continues. "My fathea never took to working indoors though. He was happier working outside, except he liked to hide out in the basement of the Kimbal's home in winter, and they let him. There was a wicker rocker down there. The Kimbals were good to him. In the winters, my fathea would take care of the Polish Catholic Church building. I remember walking wid my fathea up the hill in the frigid cold mornings to get the boiler running in the basement. Later on, when the church fell onto hard times, my fathea became the church accountant and treasurer, and he put the priest on a budget. He was tightfisted wid everyone for a few years, and you know? He finally got the church building and the cemetery paid off. Yeah, my fathea was so proud of himself, and I admired him for it. He taught me how to be tightfisted too."

Mr. B smiles to remember the church's celebration after his father had paid off all their debt.

"A year later, a fire started. Maybe the gas lamps. I never knew how, but the whole church burned to the ground."

"Oh! That's terrible! Did the church have insurance?"

"Of course not. Insurance wasn't something most people had back then. Especially cheap Polacks!" Then, he hisses conspiratorially, "When you're a Polack, you can call yourself one but only if you are one." And winks.

"My older brother Eddy decided to transfer his membership from the Polish Catholic Church to the Roman Catholic Church, and I went to college and stopped attending church, Miss, until I met Maudie."

I remember Eddy showing us the brick church with the steep gables a couple of years back. Maybe he felt safer in a brick building.

October 27, 2013

Joe wants to accompany me to the Chevy mechanic in town, so inside the car he entertains his chauffer. "My first job was a drug trafficking salesman, believe it or not. Yup. It started because I used to hang out at the drugstore on Arnold Street. There were two sistas and a man who ran the thing. Some of us kids found that if we would dig up small sassafras roots and bring them to the store, the brother and sista would pay us a nickel. I read somewhere the roots of a sassafras tree can make a tea that 'can be used as an anticoagulant for the blood.' Maudie's fathea, who was a doctor, later on explained to me how that worked."

"We were just kids so we couldn't dig up the bigger roots, but there was a tree by the river that had leaves the druggists wanted, so we would try to lob stones at the branches, or climb it and cut some leaves down for them. They would buy those bundles, too. I don't recall what kind of tree it was, maybe it was sassafras too, but it died giving away the goods anyway."

"Nah, not after you all threw stones at it!" comes my retort.

"Ha! You got it! But the drug store family distilled the dried roots and bark to produce an oil."

"Essential oil? I thought it was only used for soda pop."

"Okay that, but it was also used in tobacco and in soap and perfume. I think they used the leaves of that tree in Southern foods and incense. Anyway, that guy who ran the store also sold peanuts at the ball games, and because I was hanging around there, he would whisper, 'Hey, Joey! Hey Joey! Come wid me!' And so I'd go wid him, and I'd tell the folks that the bag of peanuts were a short bit, and they'd buy 'em from me. They were honest. Only, I can't remember if I got paid for doing it.

"I do remember that my big brother, Eddy, would hang around that store too. He and a bunch of guys. They'd watch the broads go by. And my brother got hot pants for a girl. My mothea was set against it because he was so young. So Eddy started living in the back room of the *Woonsocket Call*. There was a shower, a latrine, and a sink in the back of the typesetting room, so I guessed he was okay. I let my mothea know he was doing fine when she asked. Finally, he decided to get married no matter what. And they did. They were in love, and they stuck it out to the end. They had two daughters whom you've met."

"Why was your mother so set against it?"

"Oh, because she looked French, even though she was really Polish. And Eddy was the oldest. He didn't have an education yet. My mothea didn't think he could provide for a wife anyway wid'out going to college. But he surprised us all. He worked two jobs most of his life. He worked at the newspaper for one, and I can't remember what all else he did. So, they picked me to be the one to go to college."

"When I went to college, it changed all their plans. I was the one my parents determined to rely on. Only…" Joe looks at his hands. "I guess they didn't realize that I would have to move away for four years at college, and then after I got an education, I would have to move to find work! There was nothing for an engineer to do in Woonsocket, so I was *out*.

"Eddy ended up taking on the first son's job as head of the family after all. And I guess he did a good job of it. He rented the second floor of one of those four-story tenement houses and stayed on Pond Street all his life. After my mothea died, my fathea and Lucy took the first floor, and Eddy and Lucy kept both floors clean as a whistle. After my fathea died, Lucy went to live with Wanda in Washington, but the sistas moved back to live near Eddy in their last years. He was so strong. He could have used his size to hurt others, but he didn't. He really took care of the family."

Joe continues as we wait in the car queue for a service repair agent. "I knew my fathea had always been curious, always wanted to visit California, so I invited him out for my last two weeks of work there. He took the bus everywhere all by himself, and he looked at all the plants and flowers, you know, because he was a gardener. He still didn't talk much to me even though I was a workingman like him then, but I'm glad he was able to do that. He wasn't ever much for inside work. I think he would have liked living in California.

"You ever hear of Goethe? No? Oh well. He wrote, —" Suddenly Mr. B shocks the living daylights out of me by quoting poetry. "'You cannot walk among palm trees with impunity, and your sentiments must surely alter in a land where elephants and tigers are at home.' I used to read some poetry because it often has a lot of truth to it. Anyway, my fathea accompanied me in the car as far as St. Louis, where I took him to the train station and we parted ways."

The vehicle repair agent approaches and tags my car, telling us to wait for it in the lobby where hot coffee and donuts await. We sit down with our continental breakfast and Joe continues his story.

"I was only in California for a year, and I determined to leave for a better opportunity. They weren't payin' me much so when I went to tell my boss that I was goin' to take another job in St. Louis, Missouri, he asked me how much more it would take to keep me there. But I didn't like the way he had treated me, so I left.

"A year after that, I married Maudie, and took her to see my family." Joe says, "I was embarrassed to take Maudie to see the house where I grew up on Boyden Street. My mothea was ill, and Maudie didn't getthe reception she deserved. For a gal who kept her Welsh family crest under the glass of her nightstand, it musta been a shock. The paint on our house was peeling badly. I remember it had been peeling throughout high school and college, and suddenly it seemed so unlike her when we drove up to it. I don't know what she thought she was getting herself into. Except that we were married by then." He pauses. "I think my mothea died that year. I remember the last time I saw her, I hugged her over the fence, and she said the pain was 'przenikliwy.' That's Polish for 'biting'." He shakes his head.

"Didn't you ask your father questions about his life on your trip from California?"

"No, I never did. I'm real sorry about that now. We didn't talk much at all. I remember somewhere in New Mexico that he asked me to stop alongside the road. I did, and he got out and just looked around. I never knew what he was looking at. My fathea was going on from St. Louis to visit his brother, whom he had just patched up a row wid."

"So, your dad had a sister and a brother?" The television is blaring the early morning show in the dealership lounge, and I find myself distracted, trying to concentrate on Mr. B's story. Joe doesn't seem to have the same trouble competing with the noise.

"Oh yeah. But I never knew my uncle because he and fathea had parted ways, and they didn't speak the whole time I was growing up. I didn't know if my uncle had stayed in Poland through the war, or if he had come to America. Then one day, my fathea said he was going to visit him after he visited me in California because they'd patched things up." Joe swallows his coffee with a bite of donut and looks up at me incredulously. "That was news to me!"

I try to imagine spending all that time with someone and never asking them what was on their mind. "Did you ever meet your uncle, then?"

"Sometime later. Oh yeah. I stopped by to meet my uncle and his family. I just walked from the train station, stopped on their doorstep, knocked on the door, and introduced myself. And they were real friendly, real nice. But they never did tell me what the disagreement had been."

October 28, 2013
Joe and I are trying to cook chicken soup together. The cleaning and chopping of the carrots, celery, and chicken goes well enough, but then he rejects my boxes of low sodium chicken broth and declares that the boiling chicken will make its own broth. He turns from the gallon and a half stock pot on the stove and announces, "This reminds me of the time I was sent to help out some physicists at a plant determine whether a canister they had made would explode if they dropped it from ten thousand feet in the air."

"How did it turn out?" I'm hoping he cuts to the chase and then moves from the kitchen so that I can finish dinner.

"Well hold on there, Miss. Not so fast. I got there and they showed me the canister and told me what kind of nuclear material was inside."

"Nuclear?"

"Well, yes. I asked them what kind of material they had made the canister from, but nobody could tell me." Joe shakes his wooden spoon over the boiling contents on the stove.

Covertly, I push away from the counter to smell the herbs and spices I'm selecting from a "focus group" for the pot of chicken soup.

"Finally, I forced them to admit they had found the material at a junk yard! Yeah, well, I contacted the junk man, and he said they didn't keep track of things like that. No record existed. It just wasn't done. So then I had to go to the maker of the canister and ask them how the material had reacted in nature. Was it weldable material or not? Some material can be welded, but it won't hold together well. Other material is unweldable completely, and then there is some material that welds very well and holds tight. The manufacturer told me the canisters had been successfully welded. So, with that information, I made my best calculations and sent my report to the physicists. Then, one guy had the nerve to call me and start giving me you-know-what because they weren't paying a stress engineer to simply make a calculated guess whether or not it would explode!"

Joe stops stirring his soup, thumbs his nose at the imaginary caller, and tells me he told the guy off. "Then I flew back to my home plant where my boss asked me how things went, but I couldn't say how it went or even whether I was successful because of the situation with the mystery material. I never did get a call back to help that group of physicists. But why were those educated guys pulling unknown materials from a junkyard in the first place? It beats me. A stress engineer cannot pull calculations from the air. He has to know the kind of materials he's working with!"

I look up to study Mister B's lecturing face. Did he have a clue what he was working on? I can tell my chief cook and bottle washer's ire is up for quite a different reason than my own, so I nod and agree in amazement and wait until much later to add my herbs and spices to his bland soup.

When Joe lifts his bowl and sniffs his dinner, he shakes his forefinger at his wayward assistant. I know I've been caught. "You tried to get one past me today, Miss, but I can smell garlic in here! And what's that green stuff floatin' around?" He pokes at his soup: plop, plop.

Shrugging, out comes my reply, "I don't remember exactly because I cook by putting in a dash of this and that, Mr. B. All I can tell ya is that it didn't come from a junkyard, and it is guaranteed not to explode in your tummy."

"How do you know?" He mutters, wags his head and slurps his soup. "And I thought you might have the makings of an engineer with your curiosity and mechanical inclinations, but this bowl has really set me straight. I was *wrong*!" A giant bite of plain warm roll disappears into his mouth and is chased by a big gulp of milk.

Paul winks at me and mouths an exaggerated, "Thank you!" grinning.

"Oh stop it, you two. Anyone could tell you are in cahoots."

October 29, 2013

"May I speak with Joe, please?" The male voice on the phone is a new kind of evening solicitor. We typically only get recorded political messages or requests for donations to various charities. Our international mystery is about to begin, so Joe is already seated in the living room.

"May I say who's calling?" I respond.

"I'm on his church's search committee. We are raising funds for a new pulpit search. Joe is a deacon here."

I relay this information to Joe and he emphatically waves the phone away. "Nope. Not interested," he says without turning around.

I explain to the caller that Joe hasn't attended his church for several years and that he has declined to take the call.

"Oh! I apologize!" the caller responds and quickly hangs up. It must have been a bit embarrassing, this awkward exchange.

"Why don't you like to go to church anymore, Joe?" I ask after the phone call.

"They only want money. They can't answer my questions. I have no use for church." He lists these reasons on his wrinkled fingers. "Who cares?"

"But you are still listed as a deacon there! Shouldn't you get that taken off?"

"Oh, yes!" he gloats. "Won't everyone be surprised to open my bank deposit box and find my deacon's certificate?" Joe has a secret joke going on. "No." His guttural voice is dismissive. "God and I made a deal. I'm not going back to any church. I had my fill of church when I was a kid anyway. Did I ever tell you about our priest wid the long, long beautiful hands and fingers? Oh, yes, they were perfectly manicured. He was a very handsome man. He spoke only Polish in church. That's what they wanted. Polish liturgy. I couldn't understand a bit of it. But during the week, I would watch my fathea play poker wid him and some friends. And when I got my paper route, I would deliver papers to the priest. One day, I walked up the stairs and turned the corner, and there he was wid his long fingers around a girl's behind. You know her dress was hiked all the way up, and when they heard me comin' they were pulling it down behind her very awkwardly trying to hide what he was doing. But you know, they couldn't hide that. I didn't know what to do, so I just left the paper there. But that priest cornered my fathea and asked him about whether I would keep his secret, and my fathea promised him that I wouldn't say anything. Then, I started getting a dollar from the priest as a special Christmas gift for keeping my mouth shut."

"I'm so sorry, Joe. That's terrible." I finally understand Mr. B's animosity toward religious authority figures.

"Oh, it doesn't matter, kiddo." He shrugs.

October 30, 2013
Clifton Kern's informational lecture together with this "know your mushroom" site on *Chowhound*[1] informs my Polish mushroom collecting education. Mr. B sits and watches the lecture with me. It becomes a game of stories and wit for us. These are several good-tasting, safe, and mostly easy- to-identify mushrooms.

1. Huge Puff Balls are very safe and taste like mild tofu when cooked like French toast. They are the size of a golf ball, softball or basketball. They hide their spoors inside their body by forming a little pore. Until their bodies are hit by raindrops or something else, then they expel their spores by puffing them out of the little pores. They are normally white, but can be tannish.
2. Hydnum or Hedgehog mushrooms look fuzzy white the size of softballs, but they have an icicle toothy covering. They grow on the sides of trees. Very good.
3. Chanterelles are narrow and fluted, funnel-shaped mushrooms that come in golden or black. Excellent edibles and are easily identifiable. They appear like ruffles, with shallow ridges, and do not have actual gills with spoor colors. Black trumpet mushrooms. Garrone describes the texture of black trumpets as "very slight, almost like they're not really there," but the mushrooms' aromatic, cheeselike flavor makes up for that. Chop them finely and add them to eggs, stews, or anything that needs a bold flavor pickup. Black trumpets are harvested in late fall and into winter across the United States. Shelf life: 4 to 10 days, depending on moisture level.
4. A true winter mushroom, the Yellowfoot, is sought for its earthy, woodsy flavor. Its delicate texture breaks down easily in sauces, and it is usually paired with veal or pork,

as well as game dishes such as venison, rabbit, duck, or quail. Don't confuse it with its relative, the golden chanterelle. Shelf life: 4 days.

5. Nothing looks like the morel mushroom with its sponge-like, pitted fish-shaped surface, with the skin looking like the inside of grey-brown nut. Morels grow on oak trees or old apple trees. Its appearance is easily identifiable, and it is about the safest mushroom to eat when cooked. Its shelf life is only 5 days. This springtime mushroom is highly prized for its earthy, smoky flavor and light, veal-like texture. Because it's so strong in flavor, the morel works well with beef and in rich gravies. One popular fresh preparation is to flour and fry morels. But, there are also false morels, with an orangish, convoluted, brain-like surface, which are poisonous.

6. The lobster mushroom gets its distinctive red color from a powdery parasitic fungus that grows on its surface, but don't let that sway you: its walnut-meat texture and mild seafood flavor have made it increasingly popular. Lobster mushrooms are better fresh than dried, and the best time to find them in the U.S. is September. Check them carefully for bugs. Garrone recommends brushing them with olive oil and garlic and grilling, or using them in lobster bisque instead of the real thing. Shelf life: 7 days.

7. Oyster mushrooms grow on trees, in burgeoning white layers with short stalks. Honey mushrooms taste good, but they have a white spoor print, and they have a poisonous look-alike which has a brown or rust spoor print.

a. King trumpet mushroom. In the same family as the oyster mushroom, the king trumpet is larger and denser. Its buttery, sweet flavor makes it a good choice for grilling and as an addition to stews. An "all-around good mushroom," Garrone says. Shelf life: 10 days.

b. Shimeji (pronounced shee-MAY-jhee) refers to about 20 different breeds of oyster mushrooms, the most common of which go by the names brown or white shimeji. Because they often grow on beech trees, they're also known as beech mushrooms. With a firm texture and a delicate shellfish-like flavor, shimeji mushrooms are ideal for pairing with any kind of seafood. Shelf life: 5 days.

c. A member of the shimeji family, pioppini mushrooms

have a flavor similar to porcini but are more peppery. Their firm texture makes them a meaty addition to a stew or stir-fry; you can use the whole mushroom, stem and all. Garrone says the pioppini has become many people's favorite go-to mushroom because it has a lot of flavor. Shelf life: 7 days.

8. Candy cap. Generally only found dried (fresh specimens can sometimes be spotted in December or January in U.S. markets), the candy cap is prized for desserts. It has a distinctive sweet maple scent and flavor that go well in shortbread or cheesecake. Powdered, it can be added to pancake batter as a sweetener for diabetics. It can be expensive, but half an ounce is enough for a gallon of ice cream, says Garrone. Shelf life: 2 to 3 days fresh, 1 year dried.

9. Cauliflower. Picked in the late spring to early fall in Oregon and Washington, cauliflower mushrooms grow in clusters that can weigh as much as 35 pounds. They have the texture of egg noodles and a rainy, lemon-zest flavor, and can be used as a noodle substitute. Garrone recommends chopping and sautéing them as a side dish with herbs and cream. Look for specimens that are as white as possible, in clusters the size of a cauliflower head. Shelf life: 7 days.

10. Black truffle. Brillat-Savarin called the truffle "the diamond of the kitchen." Valued for their aromatic qualities, truffles vary in taste and smell depending on their age and provenance. They're generally harvested in northern Italy, Spain, France, and Oregon. Flavors can range from earthy to green apple to savory garlic, while prices can range from $400 to $1,600 a pound. Look for very firm specimens. Usually shaved over warm food, truffles can also infuse foods; stored with eggs, for example, they will flavor the eggs. Shelf life: 4 days (the aromatics will be lost after that).

11. Fairy-ring. This fall mushroom is imported from Europe and can be found dried year-round. Fairy-ring has a cashew-like flavor makes it ideal for risottos and cream sauces. Garrone also recommends it with fish; he recently made a halibut dish with pecans and fairy ring mushrooms. The dried form of the mushroom has an intense flavor, so just use a little bit. Shelf life: 1 year

dried.
12. Entoloma arbortivum are easily identifiable and fun to find because they are small white mushrooms, with shallow caps, and they grow next to, or among, white malformed blobs which, if you cut into them look like tapioca. Both the odd white blobs and the shallow capped mushrooms are edible and highly prized.
13. Chicken of the woods (poly), growing on top of stumps or at the base of trees, are either orange or yellow with a light or white rim. The stems are tough. People eat the ruffled cap and say they taste like chicken. The thing you have to be careful of is whether it grows on conifers or hardwoods. Hardwoods taste wonderful, but those that grow on conifers get something from the sap that sickens people.
14. Hen of the woods. It looks like a tan hen with its feathers ruffled. It grows at the base of trees. It is very good, but harder to clean because of the ruffled form.

Finding good mushrooms, as opposed to poisonous ones, takes a variety of different keys and differentials, and in case of the black truffle, the occasional trained dog or horney boar. It can be a true test of friendship to determine whether a mushroom you have found and carefully keyed through it's type of skin, spores, cupped vulva at the ground level, veils or ruptured skirts, cap and stalk form, color, color of spoor print, and smell (and occasionally color of blood when cut) is really good and edible to eat. Perhaps it's the identical evil twin! The little brown galerina that can only be differentiated from the winter mushroom by its brown spores and a ring is an example of mushroom trickery.

The tall white genius aminita and North America's translucent and elegantly white destroying angel are both lethal. There are about 20 mushrooms that can make you sick. The Amerita Muscari (the fly mushroom) is blood red, orange, or pink-capped mushroom with a cottage cheese smattering on its cap from the exploding veil. Poisonous Clorophedum Phyllum has green spores and looks lime green as a baby. It grows in a common lawn. As it matures into a white dinner plate size, it develops brown scales. It produces a cholera-like diarrhea and nausea. If you have a child, eliminate these mushrooms from your lawn.

The jack-o-lantern mushroom is orange and has one foot that produces several fruiting mushroom bodies from that base. It will make you terribly nauseous with cholera-like symptoms. Scleroderma mushrooms look similar to the innocent puff-balls, but the fruit will be purple when you section it. Its skin is hard and causes a nasty gastric awareness. A false morel looks like an orange brain pattern. They have an accumulative poisonous effect. People have eaten them and had no effect. When you reach your limit, however, it will suddenly kill you. Mushroom poisoning has a longer latency period than other plants do, say a hemlock. Generally, there are fewer than six lethal mushrooms. You do not know they are lethal until 24 hours later.

Locations for gathering mushrooms matter though. Apple orchards can be sprayed with arsenic insecticides; also mushrooms beside roads can contain lead poisoning from leaded gasoline.

Ш 𝕝 ᏀᎠ

November ~ Nesting

November 1, 2013

The autumn air has gone brisk with a sudden passive-aggressive, musty belch. We are stuck inside today looking at each other over an elegantly laid breakfast table. The advantage of the new picture window installation in the dining room means we can see the entire park-scene of Mr. B's backyard going yellow, with lilac and cottonwood leaves whisked to the ground under cloudy, lavender skies. Joe begins. "This time of year reminds me of mushrooms and beer, mushrooms and eggs, all mushrooms. I don't particularly like mushrooms. But, beer *yes*, I like, even though I don't drink it anymore.

"Have I told you, we rented a place on Arnold Street? Our family was on the third floor, without a bathroom, from the owners who were Irish. Mrs. Brennan became a widow almost immediately after we moved into her place. She had two daughters, oh but she figured out how to make a living as a landlady.

"Underneath our place was hers, and underneath her place, there was a bar room, separated from the house, but it wasn't called a bar. It was a speakeasy club. She kept liquor hidden up in her hallway though. You know, prohibition?" He winks. "Sometimes, inspectors would come to check that no alcohol was being served, so the bartender would go along the first floor and show them how the entire bar was clean, and also the fridge, but they never looked up her staircase or up in her house into the stash she kept there.

"Anyway, even though our landlady worked her speakeasy downstairs, she right away started raising the rent on us. My fathea didn't like that, a 'come-on price' he called it. So, gee whiz, we moved!"

"Did your folks ever buy a house?"

"Aw, no. My fathea rented that home there, our first home, for $1.50 per month. We never owned, we only rented."

November 2, 2013

After washing up the dishes, I carry a cutting board, some peppers, and a knife to the dining room to sit down again at the breakfast table with Mr. B. He asks me the remaining "tricky questions" on his crossword puzzle. Each proves me to be at least his incompetent equal.

"How do stuffed peppers sound for dinner tonight, Mr. B?"

"It depends on what they're stuffed with, I suppose." His head wobbles as his throat pulverizes his words like a coffee grinder.

I begin cutting the fresh green peppers in half, explaining, "I'm boiling rice to mix into the hamburger and tomato sauce which I will fry up later." Immediately, I realize I've let that cursed word "fry" from my lips.

Joe shrugs.

To bear up under the prospect of all the ingredients of dinner being mixed together, then *fried*, his childhood begins to pour out of him, so I get comfortable.

"I would actually get paid a few cents to deliver papers when I was in about seventh or eighth grade, so that's how I got to go to the theater near our house on Arnold Street. The theater was on the hill too, backing up to the river. Our house, at number two Arnold Street, was three stories high, and my brother, Eddy, and I lived in the attic. It was scary for me to sleep way up there where I could look way down on the river below, believe it or not, from the attic window."

I can suddenly see him as a child looking through the single pane glass.

"Mr. B, do you know why it took us so long to get into the war, World War II?"

He rubs his chin and squints back at me. "Well, it's hard to remember that stuff, even if I knew it once. I don't think America wanted to be involved with other people's problems." His voice turns to wine. "We wanted to be the shining star, away from the troubles of the world. 'Let them sort out their own problems, so to speak. We didn't get involved until Pearl Harbor, December 7, 1941. Americans ignored race problems, even in our cities."

"Did Americans really think that all would be well and that people would integrate naturally?" I ignore my cored peppers, listening.

"You know, Miss, I dunno what we thought. People knew we were Polish. We knew they were French, Russian, Chinese, Jewish, or Greek. They had their parties and celebrations, and we had ours. I've always thought that was the best way."

Interesting. I think. Mr. B does still keep others at an arm's distance. I wouldn't call him an elitist exactly, but he does carry about him the grateful atmosphere of having escaped something dire and *unknown*. He is a gentleman who is always pleasant and respectful when the occasion calls for it, but inclusive is a different story.

November 5, 2013

Something goes wrong with Joe's eyesight this morning. During breakfast, he complains that he can't see very well out of his left eye. He says there is a black arc and dot, and otherwise, everything is blurry. I become seriously concerned when he can't make out his crossword puzzle. I immediately pick up the phone to call his eye doctor, and we make an appointment together as Joe describes the facts of what he can see to me so that I can answer the soft spoken medical assistant's questions. His new blindness seems far worse than the macular degeneration that he otherwise endures in his eyes.

We rush to his ophthalmologist, but because of the obstruction of blood, she cannot tell exactly what has occurred. Joe's eye has had a hemorrhage. He leans on me for security as we walk to and from the doctor's office. I can't explain the grief I feel for him. He, on the other hand analyzes the problem, describes it over and over as though repetition will beget understanding, and understanding will clear up his vision.

I don't say that identifying a problem is only half the problem solved.

Mr. B cannot tell that his doctor is holding up two fingers in front of his face. He gets a shot in the eye to arrest the flow of blood. The doctor says the blood may be absorbed over the next few months, but there are no guarantees Joe's vision will improve.

November 6, 2013

This morning, as I am making Joe's boiled egg and heating his roll, he carves a slow path to the kitchen to greet me with a squeeze, "Good morning, Sweet Pea!" It tickles me that he is so genuinely affectionate and happy to see me busy in the kitchen.

I watch as he holds up Maudie's old eye graph with a giant tic-tac-toe grid and studies it. He puts it down and shakes his head. "Growing old isn't for the faint-hearted," he grunts. "Not that you have a choice." Yet, Joe's handicap sticker is a plus for parking his car at the grocery store.

We avoid discussing the prospect of me becoming his permanent chauffer. Today, Joe insists on paying the bill since Paul just helped him clip his nails. "Besides," he adds, "Don't *worry*. I gotta make sure you buy what I can eat!" He smiles when I find a nice ripe papaya to substitute for his morning bananas. Our financial burden, we notice, has become easy. There is no mortgage on this house. Paul compares our situation living here as "a blissful exchange for the old stress!"

There are times I catch my memories globetrotting through various cultures, hosted in many homes around the world, all past adventures. This home Mr. B has offered us is, to me, another graceful lifestyle with its own challenging conversations. It's not so hard. I could be carried along here for a long time.

November 7, 2013

When Paul takes Joe to collect his prescription tonight, they return with a bouquet. Thus, Paul presents me with yellow mums and roses. "What's this for?" I ask, arching my brow.

"Oh just because you have three boys who love and depend on you." Paul smiles. "Yellow's your favorite, right?"

"What? Yes, but *three* boys?"

"Yeah, my dad, me, and Jester. What would we do without you?" Jester looks up at me with his hound dog wonder. Behind Paul, the Star Wars sage smiles to see my blush. This is one anomaly that tells me it was Mr. B who hinted that Pauly should bring flowers to his girl. There are certain perks.

November 8, 2013

Joe is pulling out the magnifying glass for his crossword puzzle, but before he gets involved, I have to ask, "Is there a mathematical equation for deflection, Mr. B?" He has just mentioned the importance of 'deflection,' a term with which I am unfamiliar.

"Oh, yes. That's one of the subjects I wrote about in my Master's thesis. And [he shows his excitement] you can do the problem backwards also to find out the beginning equation! You move backward from the decimals of deflection to the stress of a beam, and then you can find out the measurements of the beam."

"But what was that you said about deflection and decimals?" My curiosity stems from a fleeting philosophical thought the other day that Mr. B had hit on a spiritual concept while vocalizing his mathematical tangents about bridges, arches, and deflections of weight.

"Oh, you can measure anything up, but people usually round up or down the final figure. But it's not really a true figure, and you can theoretically come to a wrong conclusion if you have to round up the answer, which then has several other calculations weighing on it. The only way to get an exact answer is to add into the equation the element of deflection. When you arrive at that answer, you have an accurate answer."

"So, you are saying that it's the amount of stress that a thing can handle that shows the exact strength of the subject's characteristics?"

He shrugs and chuckles. "That's one way of putting it. But of course, no one really calculates the element of shear very well. So when they omit it, that's where these big accidents occur. You know wind shear? It's another kind of stress that's very difficult to predict, so people generally just calculate the stress of deflection. Deflection will take care of most of the issues."

"Hmm. I've heard of windows falling out of skyscrapers and overloaded hotel balconies imploding. Then of course, there was the case of airplanes flying through the steel structures of the Twin Towers. Are shear stressors always a catastrophe?" I'm considering unnatural outside stressors.

"Well, something will suddenly crack, and immediately it tumbles down or splits apart, but shear is an ungodly outside and unusual force. It's shocking."

"Oh, look at that. I've caught you using the term, 'ungodly'."

"Well, but you cornered me," Joe retorts.

November 9, 2013

Trying to divert my gaze from the plastic-wrap styled baseboards installed in the 1970s above Joe's linoleum kitchen floors, a sigh escapes. Wooden baseboards wouldn't match linoleum anyway. My father-in-law's inlaid linoleum is the sturdy, durable kind that wears out exactly when the owners take it out. Rather, it lasts in and out of fashion, kind of like wood flooring, only *not*.

Joe, unbothered, is peeling his banana at "brekkies."

"Will you pass the salt please, Mr. B?" My thoughts must be redirected.

"Sól" He points at the salt to teach me the Polish word for it. "*Sól i pieprz*, salt and pepper." As he passes me the shaker, he starts, "Did I ever tell ya about my experience as a juror?"

"I'm not sure," I admit, willing to be distracted. "Have you only had one experience?"

"Yeah. Maybe they had enough of me. Heh, heh. Well, I got in there, and they called my name, and it was a case of two brothers defrauding a young gal into marrying her for her money. You know. The one brother was the setup and the other did the marrying in Las Vegas. When she finds out about how she's been duped a year or so later, it's because she discovers her empty bank account." Joe's lips grimace.

I'm listening. "Okay, so I have heard about that case somehow." The sun is shining through our dining room window, and our Christmas cactus is wildly blooming in tendrils of translucent ginger red.

"Anyway, this defense attorney stands up and starts talking up the jury about how an engineer thinks and works." Joe sits forward seriously. "I listened to him gab on for a while, and then I stood up and said, 'Don't be an imbecile. That's not at all how it works.' I stood there and told him I was an engineer myself, and he couldn't pull the wool over my eyes."

I begin to chuckle as I stuff my own banana into my mouth. "What happened?"

"Oh, that lawyer went back to his desk and the judge said, 'You are excused from this case. Go wait outside.' And I left."

"I'll bet, Mr. B!" I exclaim laughing with glee. "You were a recalcitrant juror."

"Then, they shuffled me off to another courtroom, and I had to go through the whole thing again. But this time, the judge knew my name real quick like. He called me up to his podium and he gave me a note to give to a clerk on my way out. So I did what he said, and that was the end of my jury service. But I've always wondered how that second judge got to know me so quickly."

Smiling, I tell him that these judges have clerks and earphones and computers with all kinds of access to all kinds of information about us.

He says he followed that case and the dumb-dumb defense attorney all full of himself lost it.

"Of course he did, smarty pants!" I'm impishly proud of Mr. B in the moment.

November 10, 2013

"When I accepted the terms of college, I had to sign on the dotted line that I would join the R.O.T.C., Reserve Officers' Training Corps, before attending my first day of classes. Both Alabama schools were land grant schools, so I wasn't getting out'a that either way. I accepted it. But, after my sophomore year, they took me to Fort Benning in Georgia for six weeks of boot camp wid all my buddies. There were some real military troops gettin' trained, and we were trained to support them, or vise versa.

"We would plant bombs in the ground. When they'd go off, the holes they created provided them with foxholes, and we would build bridges through the rivers for them to blow up. The noise was horrific. The heat was so bad that my clothes were wet all the time. The officers thought they were the cat's meow, but some of them were sadistic sons of bitches.

"They put us through ground chemicals to let us know what they felt like, and we would stream wid sweat and scratch ourselves to death. They put us through tear gas and we came out weeping. One officer lined us all up and told us to set up camp, but my tent was going to be right on top of a bunch of poison ivy! I told him to give me another place, but he refused. I thought if he didn't care, then I didn't care. We had these khaki pants that closed at the boot and laced up, but the next morning I had poison ivy on my lips and all over my legs and of course on my private parts. The next day I reported to sick bay where I was given a bottle of pink lotion to put all over myself. It was terrible. That guy was just plain mean."

"Then, they put me on guard duty, night shift. I couldn't stay awake, and I was terrified because the military guys were getting up through a trap door into our post–x, like our canteen, see, and stealing from us. So, I decided to carry a flashlight and a real bullet. When the dog robber met up wid me, I made sure I told 'em loud enough so that my voice would travel, what I was carrying for anybody who wanted to ambush me or if I would catch them under the post–x. You know, it was built on stilts, see."

"What's a dog robber, Mr. B?"

"Oh, that's what they called the guys where were assigned to one major or one captain, higher up. They were that officer's personal assistant.

"So, then they'd put us into tanks wid light skins, very light. You'd think those tanks were tough, but anyone could put a hole in the skin wid a 50! I wasn't happy wid the Army. I did it all, everything they ordered, but I determined to transfer to the Air Corps as soon as possible, and I did that." Joe's blue eyes are blazing, so that I feel his angst and determination personally. "I hated the Army!"

"They wanted to make it as much like real war as possible, and I believe they achieved their aim, at least wid me! One time, we were allotted rifles and my arms were short, so I couldn't cock it all the way back. I laid there and tried to shoot it twice, and then I held my hand up for the training officer. Well, that guy came around and took my gun but he never looked down the hole! He just put the rifle in line and told me to get back into line, which I did."

Something inside me sees the whole pathetic picture. "Next time my turn came 'round, I grabbed my rifle and hit the ground and the thing exploded, Oh! The noise! It scared me, I'll tell ya, and the guys around me all jumped too. They were not happy wid me, so I kept getting guard duty, night shift." He pauses in his excitement to swallow hard.

"One time, they sent us running across a field with guns firing at our head the whole way. We slid into the foxhole at the other side. But what we didn't know is that they had planted snipers at either end of the line to shoot blanks that ricocheted through the line of men who had just jumped into safety! If they woulda been real bullets, we'd all be dead, most of us. Oh, they knew how to scare the livin' daylights outa ya, yes Ma'am.

"So, when I graduated, I left for California, and it was there, working wid the designing of basic war planes, that the U.S. finally declared war. Just before declarin' it, they sent me a packet of documents to fill out. I knew what was comin', oh yeah. I knew. I told 'em I wanted a *transfer to the Air Corps*. Then, I quit Vultee and moved to Ferguson, Missouri. All my friends from school had been pulled into the Army, and they were afta me too! They were dyin' right 'n left. Oh, sure, they went in as officers and all, but where did that benefit get 'em? Put right at the front of the action."

Joe sputters out and licks his lips. "Hu."

"I was just plain lucky when the army came afta' me in Oklahoma. I had just married Maudie. I had a new car and had saved $3900 in the bank during those four years of work. The military didn't seem to care that I had put in a transfer to the naval Air Corps: I'd gone to that land grant college and they aimed to keep me." He glances up at me from under his brow. "I considered joining the National Guard at that point, but since it came *after* my papers, I thought I'd get in trouble, and they can make a case outa *any*thing. So, there I was trying to figure out who to give that money to, my new wife or my old folks, but the Major, who was working across the street from the airport where I was working for Spartan, had connections. He was the one who got me a permanent deferment so that I could keep training pilots on how to fix their own airplanes." I can almost feel his breathless panic, then relief. "It wasn't too long after that, Alabama sent me my Ph.D in aerospace engineering and we moved to Bald'more, where I stayed for twenty years."

"Which one were you, Mr. B? Tom, Jerry or the Roadrunner?" A chuckle bubbles up as I suck in the breath I've been holding on Joe's behalf.

"What?!" He quits me with a wave of his hand.

November 11, 2013

Joe gets an itch to decorate his formal living room with "found items." He comes up from the basement with a twist in his smile and an idea for the wall above our reupholstered heirloom couch, which was finally delivered.

I am so grateful he keeps complimenting us on our couch because when we moved into his home in September, he'd asked us to keep his formal living room *as is*. We didn't touch it for months, but we also waited until the last minute to tell him about the couch that would arrive this week. He offered to have the mover set it against a wall opposite of his living area. I am grateful that all things worked together for the good, including our heirloom couch. He loves the way the velvet couch resting against the far wall opens up his formal sitting room, and now he's got a decorating idea from the basement! He prods me, "Go see if you can find what I found down there."

I trot downstairs to see if I can locate his secret idea. It's a game. I can't see anything I could believe we would both like to see on the wall. I have already hung one of his favorite paintings, and anything more would be overkill. So I trudge back up the stairs empty-handed. Joe winks and smiles. He carefully trots down the stairs and returns with my carved and painted wooden bowl from Africa and a couple musical instruments. "I think these would fit right here," he says. "We've always had interesting items from museums and travels in the front room because they create conversations." I am astounded. He likes *me*. He thinks these artifacts are so interesting that they need to be shown off. After I hang up the bowl and place the instruments on his side table, he adds, "You also have some decorating talent." Come to discover, Joe likes the eclectic look.

November 16, 2013

Paul and Mr. B's mouths are full of French toast, drooling with syrup and whipped cream. I've tricked Mr. B into gobbling up a butter-fried breakfast food by squirting mounds of whipping cream over the French toast he had previously vehemently objected to. It looks like a dessert. He likes it!

Paul says, "Dad, if whipping cream came in bottles, it would expand if it froze, right? 'Cuz, I remember in Baltimore, when I was a kid, I'd bring in the milk bottles in the winter, and the cream would be piled an inch or so above the top of the bottle, and I'd have to fight off the neighborhood cats licking the cream."

"Oh!" exclaims Joe, patting Paul's hand. "You remember that?"

"Wait. Cats ate the cream from people's milk delivery?" I cringe.

Joe chuckles. "Yep. The dairy used to put a small cylinder of cardboard on the top of the bottles so when the cream floated up to the top of the bottle, and froze a little, it pushed the cardboard lid up." He uses his fingers to show me the frozen expanse of maybe a couple of inches. "Oh yeah. The cats loved it! I loved the ice milk crystals, too, just before the milk froze solid."

"Did I ever tell you about the time I lost your husband in Bald'more?" He smirks, but doesn't look up. "Pauly was only ten years old, and Maudie sent me out to put him on a city bus. Well, I put him on a bus alright. It was just the wrong bus!"

I look over at Paul, and he grins real big.

"He never told you about that? Well, he knew our phone number, and he knew he didn't recognize any of the bus stops, so he just stayed on the bus until the end of the line, and then he asked the bus driver to call us." Joe rears back in his chair and looks me in the eye. "If Maudie was a hating woman, I'd be a goner for losing her precious son in that big city!"

Mr. B's plate lies empty. "I know I said I didn't want your French toast, Miss, but if you'll forgive me, I'll take another piece with some of that cream squirted over it." His head wobbles happily between his shoulders.

November 17, 2013

"When I kick the bucket," — Oh, here we go, and Paul is at work.

"I want you to write 'deceased' on my federal and state tax forms and send a note to social security, Medicare, and Martins maybe within the week. I don't owe nobody anything, that's the way we do it in this family. Cash or nothing, so I shouldn't have any I.O.U. sticking out there." Mr. B has made himself a seat on our brown sofa in the den.

"I want you to take five thousand for funeral expenses and such. Make sure the minister at that Presby church says that official 'dust to dust' bit over me. Since Vicky can't use the house, Pauly will send Vicky my savings account. You and Pauly get this house. I'd give it to you now, but I get a discount on house taxes since I'm an old man, and you would have to pay double it. Why bother wid that rigmarole? We can use the fifteen hundred just as well as they can!"

November 18, 2013
"Mr. B? How did you manage to avoid the draft of World War II?"

He removes his toothpick from his lips to talk to me. "I tried to enlist! Recruiters were traveling around to all the colleges and picking the cream of the crop, one guy from each college to form an Air Corps, part of the army, mind you. The Air Force, as you understand it, wasn't yet enacted as its own military division. All the guys in college were signing up. But, when it came my turn, they turned me down because the recruiting captain said I was color blind, believe it or not. *I* didn't believe 'em, so I *appealed* to the overseer and said, 'I think I can pass it.' So he sent me back in line," Joe gestures with his thumb, "and I went through the physical twice. The second time, okay, I passed. I took tests all day. By nighttime, there was only one other guy left. We took the last test, a depth perception test, and my points of contact were off slightly, so the overseer reversed himself and declared me 'blind as a bat!' I congratulated the other guy and left." He pauses. "Anyway," he shrugs, "I happened to be teaching the engineering students at the Spartan Company, at the Tulsa airport, when the army finally called me up. The telegram ordered me to report to Woonsocket, but instead, I reported to a division in Tulsa, right across the road from where I was working, and they excused me."

"Why?"

"I guess I was better off serving where I was. They needed me there. But I got sick of teaching. Maudie was smart. She had encouraged me to get accredited for my engineering experience in both California and Tulsa. So while I was teaching, I was also writing a thesis so I could get the equivalent of a Ph.D., in work credit, and that's what I eventually did."

"Where is that degree, Joe? Is it framed in your bedroom or something?"

"Oh, you haven't seen it? I guess it's in the basement storage trunks wid all my keepsakes. My certificate reads Aerospace Engineer. I guess you can find it down there if you're that interested. Martin hired me, and we moved to Bald'more. I started work with Martin Company in 1945, based on that certificate and some recommendations. But about that time there was a mass exodus because everyone there knew when the war ended they had to find other work."

"When Maudie and I bought our first home in Bald'more, they wanted to just sell us the house, and lease the land to us. That was the way, but I couldn't see it. So, I told 'em, 'That's not for me. I'll buy the land.' They came back with a price of $1600 more, so we bought that place in '45 for $13,000 cash. When we moved twenty years later, Maudie managed to get $18.5 for it."

"Is that what you used to buy this house?"

"Yes, Miss. Only, this house cost us $36,000 when all was said and done. I'd neveh seen anything like this type a house, so large: the bedrooms, so big!"

I consider that perspective is everything.

He licks his spoon. "It was humble beginnings at Martin's, in Bald'more, at first. I was put onto the design team for plumbing airplanes right away."

"You mean for bathrooms on commercial aircraft?"

He inserts his toothpick again, then takes it out to point with it. "Yes, Ma'am, and believe it or not, some of the plumbing called for such thin sheets of steel that you could squeeze them and crush them with your hand, but they had to be that thin for weight purposes. I used .16 thickness in the tubes."

"Several companies at that time were beginning to see the value of developing commercial airlines for longer flights. That was the vision. There was suddenly a whole group of Germans who came into upper management at Martin.

"They had strong accents. I didn't ask questions. Most of 'em weren't very friendly. Maybe they were wary. I'd see 'em and look away. They were what you might call 'shunned' at first. We didn't know it until much later, but they had cut a deal with the U.S. called Operation Paperclip."

"What do you mean, these were Nazi German engineers?"

"Yeah, the first rocket scientists."

"What? Were they given amnesty?"

"I guess you could call it that. We needed their expertise. They were just engineers and designers, none of 'em were the Gestapo as far as I know, but things were top secret in more ways than one."

He continues, "They were the original Germans who designed the V-2 rocket which had caused such destruction in Britain. Wernher von Braun (Joe pronounces it 'Brown') was the chief developer of the first ballistic missile ever created.

"Braun basically hand-picked his best engineers and offered to surrender this group to the West rather than wait for the Russians. He sent his brother on a bicycle down to the Americans to negotiate the value of the German group, with their designs and some of their rockets made by concentration camp workers in their underground factory. So, the Americans brought 'em over and put them to work on the Titan I rocket. Hey, they weren't all bad. Hitler had given them the choice of working for him or being branded as traitors, so they worked mostly in underground facilities in the mountain and commandeered prisoners of war to do the mechanics of their designs."

My mouth is hanging open.

"I saw Braun but never worked with him. He was hired to work in America's space program in Ft. Bliss, Texas, and then White Sands, New Mexico. NASA began to absorb the US space projects as a private industry since the war was over."

Standing above my chair now, with the aim of turning out the light to make the hike up the stairs to bed, Mr. B stops to explain to me that the group of 'em came from the V-2 rocket center at Peenemunde, on Germany's Baltic coast. "Sorry, Miss, I can never pronounce the name of that place." He sits down on the edge of his blue chair thinking.

I'm trying to digest this anomaly that our space program was developed by SS engineers. "What was your title again?"

"Oh, I wasn't even the head of a stress department at that time. I was nothing compared to them."

"Did you ever experience prejudice from the Germans towards yourself because you were Polish?" I want to know.

"No, no." He leans back in his swivel chair to think it over. "They were very intelligent, their education was much better than any engineering degree in America. I told my opinion to a guy named Multhopp once. There was good reason they thought they were a superior race. I think I remember some very good-looking men in charge of things in Bald'more, and a woman, too. She was the mathematician, and she had her own office. She was smart. I knew there was another group of Germans working down in

Huntsville, Alabama, near the border of Tennessee, where the Marshall plant was. But I never worked down there."

He continues in his flow of consciousness, "Hans Multhopp was the German whose specialty was wind tunnels. I asked him one day what was the optimal spacing between two engine propellers. I thought that the vibrations would matter, but I remember, he didn't think it mattered as long as they weren't close to the fuselage where ice could form on the propellers and get cast off like spinning weights into the frame of the plane."

"Like bullets."

"Yeah. He would write essay papers on fixed-wing aircraft or spacecraft configuration in which the body itself produces lift rather than the wing. We worked on the Gemini Space Shuttle together. But I remember reading the last paper he wrote and I couldn't make heads or tails of it. His aerodynamic experience was well beyond mine, which is why he was hired to help us develop the first shuttles."

"But you were proven right about the vibrations of the engines being too close to the body of the plane, right?"

"Well, for airplanes, yes, but we were starting on spacecraft. Martin Company steered away from the commercial jets and into the space program. I came along into the aerospace division when the airplane work wore thin, so I began helping design the Titan II."

"We were in a race with the Russians by then. They were in such a rush, the management was getting sloppy. Politics were unbearable for some of those guys. In Bald'more, I remember a tall, lanky German who spoke good English, and who had a very funny sense of humor. I don't remember his name, but I liked him, so he was one I would talk to."

Mr. B mentions, "Another guy I worked with was named Neumann," as though he had never before mentioned this scientist to me. "I liked him a lot, and we had some conversations about the Titan II. They wanted to put on a spherical dome, but I determined that it would collapse from the inside. It would pucker in the stress of space flight. So, we recommended using a square root of 2 dome, not a spherical dome. Conical intersections became my favorite projects from there on out.

"Neumann also had me design some unusual shaped connectors. Till then, all the brackets were arcs, but they needed a new bracket that was straight at the bottom where it attached to the dome, and arced at the top at a certain degree, connecting to the steel nose cone."

"Do you know what he did in World War II?" I'm stuck on the problem of morality.

"Well, he wasn't an officer in Europe. He maintained an air fleet, and he had a mind for envisioning engineering solutions, like how a part should match up to another part. For some reason, the others had it out for this guy. What he recommended was always right, but the management would try to find another way to meet the objective. When he got wind of management trying to replace him, Neumann moved to Orlando, Florida, and asked me to come wid him, but I never liked the weather there. It reminded me too much of Alabama and the ROTC!"

Mr. B is producing the odd effect of steering me away from this Nazi quandary in the U.S. space industry. German engineers responsible for the bombings in England literally became the lead engineers in Martin Marietta and NASA personnel. I remind myself that he was born in Rhode Island and never served in the war. He only heard vague stories about what the Germans did to the Poles and the Jews. American movie houses removed any American film footage shown of the horrors until it appeared again in 1961.

"I designed a new connection in the Titan II for him and also a payload fairing."

"What's that?"

He moves his hands in the form of an arc and explains the nose cone that protects the spacecraft against the force of rocket flight. "I had to create a criteria book first, which turned out to be about an inch and a half thick. I asked for Teflon so that when the rocket heated up in the atmosphere, the Teflon would allow some slide. That was my idea."

"But was he one of the German Nazis, this Neumann?"

"No, no, Miss. He was working there long before I came to Bald'more, and before the others, too. He had been reporting German intelligence to Washington; so President Truman finally gave him citizenship."

He was a spy, a congenial spy!

November 19, 2013

I wake up thinking on the fantastical espionage tale between the Nazis kingdom of horror and the Americans' amnesty for the sake of the aerospace race. Do they teach this stuff in schools now that most of the guilty, or forward thinking as the case may be, have died? On the road at the lake where we pause our bikes, I explain Paul's father's most recent conversation to him. He seems as astounded as I am. "Do juries ever grant amnesty for conspirators?" Paul asks huffing up a hill. "I've never heard of that."

"Maybe defense attorneys should consider marketing a criminal defendant's proposed future value to society?"

November 21, 2013

"Have I told you about my brother-in-law, Paul? I was just thinking about him and Helen."

"I'm not sure, Mr. B, but I'd like to listen again."

"Well, he was a German. *Nobody* liked Germans during the

war, especially my mothea. I dunno why, but she was always dead set against 'em."

"Maybe because they killed her brother who stayed home to take care of her parents."

"Yeah, maybe." He clears his throat. "During the war, the German's boats often drew close to the American coastline, so Paul jumped ship, and swam ashore. I dunno if he became official, like going through the rigmarole of becoming a citizen or not, but he was determined to make himself a new life. So, somehow he found my sista, Helen, working at the first fast food restaurant in New York City, called Horn & Hardart, oh, I never liked fast food, but eh, that's where they met, and they started going out. Well, Helen brought him home one evening to meet my folks. She was the eldest, the one who died of cancer later. Boy, was she in love! But my mothea refused to have him in the house. So, I recall that I could see him leaning against the lamp post outside on the street. Waiting to see what would happen. He was out there having a smoke. His knee was up, and his foot was braced against the post. Now, my fathea smoked too, but only at the bar. Nevea at work or at home! That was a no-no."

Joe thinks about all this for a moment then continues. "I decided that I wanted to meet him, so I went out to the lamp post and introduced myself. He told me his name was Paul Eschenroder. I was still young, but my mothea trusted me. So I told him to put out his cigarette, and I'd get her to let him in. I went back to her and told her he was okay. And yeah, she let him in. I don't think she evea really liked him, but she nevea said as much.

"He, on the other hand, loved to talk. He had opinions on everything! Well, they got married. They settled in the Bronx. They had two daughters, and my sista Helen made sure that those girls got a teaching education. It was a benefit of living in New

York. So they went to the State college there because that's where they settled."

"What kind of work did Paul do?"

"Oh, he was kind of a fix-it sort of guy, a natural, like your fathea is. He became a super at an apartment building. You know what a super is?" I nod. "He was the superintendent of the apartments so he collected rent and fixed anything that went awry. He trained this young man to be his apprentice; I guess the guy was like an orphan or something. The kid fell in love with Paul's eldest daughter, Wanda, who Helen named after my youngest sista. The apprentice and their daughter got married pretty youngish."

He adds in an off-hand manner, "She broke up our friendship because she didn't like that I am an outspoken opinionated person, you might say."

"What did you do?"

"I didn't do anything, Miss. But, I gave 'er a piece of my mind. What did she think she was doin' trying to get married when they had no assets built up yet?!" I don't mention that Mister B is putting all the blame on the female.

The name, Wanda, is one of those antique names to my ears. "How could your sisters be that close with so many years between them?"

"Yeah, those sistas were about twelve years apart, and when Wanda grew up she became a lieutenant colonel in the Air Force and traveled all her life. She finally settled in Seattle, so they lost touch, but Helen musta been fond of her. She was a cute baby. And she found a way to make something of herself through the military." Joe spits out the toothpick he's been worrying. I see I'm gonna have to pull out the Dust Buster around his chair again.

"Paul and Helen were like Maudie and my best friends in a way. We enjoyed their company. We really did. They remind me of you two a lot."

"I remember you and Maudie telling us that before." I laugh. "That we agitate well together."

"Yes, Ma'am. You two are like Paul and Helen! They would argue all the time, but then they would make up and they stuck it out. We used to say that they agitated together like a washing machine. I didn't know that Helen had any of her own opinions, really, until she married Paul. Then her opinions came flying out! My! It could be exciting! But I could never figure out how they did it."

"Did what?"

"How they kept loving each other when they argued all the time! I guess people are cut from different cloths. Maudie knew how to treat me. She was real quiet. She'd let me have my say. All the way. In fact, I'd talk myself into a corner, and she'd let me have it. Then, a day or so later, she'd say a little thing, just a little word or suggestion, and I knew I'd been had. You just can't win against a good woman's reason."

"That's funny. I would never be able to keep my mouth shut that long. What ever happened to them, to Paul and Helen?"

"Well, I don't really know. We lost touch wid them. We moved to Colorado, and all the closeness just stopped. I don't know much about them now. Of course, the girls wouldn't have that last name anymore. And I don't think their husbands had college degrees, but they were set because Helen made sure her girls had a good education. She was a smart cookie."

November 24, 2013

Having baked a fat orange pumpkin and pulled out the seeds, I cut the stringy meat and mix into it a little sugar, flour, brown sugar, and egg to make three small custards. I know this isn't the best kind of pumpkin for pies, but maybe it will serve up decently for a side of veggies at dinner. Five minutes before I take it out of the oven, I sprinkle on a topping of pecan pieces and lumps of brown sugar with broken ginger snaps.

Paul dishes into the vegetable bowl several times and mmms and yums. Joe looks over at his son as if he is a monkey on an organ grinder's shoulder. He returns to eating his mound of sweet squash carefully, with small filled teaspoons. "What is this?" he asks, about halfway through.

"It's our pumpkin, Dad. The one we bought from the pumpkin patch." I hold my breath.

"It is? But what's this hodgepodge on top?"

"Way to make a cook feel good, Chief!" Paul looks at me apologetically.

I interrupt. "It's the pecans and brown sugar we just bought, Mr. B. It's safe."

"Oh! I like pumpkin. I just didn't recognize the other lumps and bumps. But surprisingly, it's pretty good! Like dessert even." He looks up and smiles at me. Then, Joe turns and snaps at his son. "How's *that*, Pauly?"

November 28, 2013 Thanksgiving Day

We have typically hosted most holiday meals at our place, but I feel unable to cook the big dinner with everyone's preference of meats in a kitchen with one oven. I'm not the most organized cook. Besides, I've thrown out my gouged red Teflon skillet, and I'm embarrassed, without saying so, that we have a jumble of Mr. B's dishes and ours to serve a crowd of company. Where the china is hidden remains anyone's best guess. When I don't take the initiative, we determine through a unanimous vote that reserving a table for Thanksgiving dinner is the best route to go this year. That way, everyone can eat whatever they wish to order in style.

Before we leave for the restaurant, Joe asks Paul to take him down the street quickly. When they return, Paul thrusts a fistful of beautiful flowers at me. "Why thank you!" I look from one to the other. "Are we making this a habit?"

Joe appears just as bashful, squeezing my arm. "You deserve 'em."

November 29, 2013
There is a bundle of leftover wood in Joe's garage. He and I decide we could probably make a trellis for the Virginia Creeper vine to grow on. It's a warmish day. "No time like the present," he says, though he's a little nervous about putting something on the fence. This is because in 1970, at the beginning of the subdivision, he didn't want all the yards to be fenced in or buckled up, but all his neighbors wanted fences, so they fenced in all three sides of his three-quarter acre backyard for him on their dime. Oh, he enjoys admitting that he didn't dish out a red cent for one fence post, reciting this story to us several times, but he is also careful to cut back his Virginia Creeper to keep it from running up "his neighbor's" fence.

I see nurturing his Virginia Creeper as my opportunity to erect a screen between his neighbor's back porch and ours. Theirs is on a higher plane than ours, making it a bit awkward for the neighbor appearing last on their back porch to remain there because of the issues of privacy. We tend to wave at each other and the last one to arrive retreats into the house. A green enclosure high on a trellis would make the perfect friendly barrier.

I reason with him. "Mr. B, all of your original neighbors have moved. You're the only original left. These new neighbors don't know who built the fence because they *inherited* it. I promise you, they don't care if a vine grows on it. I even bet ya they will be delighted to get some privacy!"

Joe makes me ask them first. The husband is taking out his trash, so I ask him there on the spot. He looks at what we are doing and agrees in an instant. That was easy. We lay out four strips of cedar, and he begins sorting through screws in Paul's cans to find a handful of the right length of wood screw as opposed to the metal screws. I help him sort. When we find a bundle, I begin to drill and screw in the first corner.

"Oh, wait, Miss Tom Boy!" Joe interjects. "Here's a tape measure. Let me measure it up." Joe measures and marks the strips of lattice. I drill. He picks up the drill while I'm screwing in a screw, and he begins drilling, but the blindness in his one eye affects his depth perception and he keeps missing the screw head.

"This reminds me of the fence you and I built at our rental, Mr. B. Remember that?"

"Oh, I do. That was a nice fence, and we had to build it twice because zoning said it was too high." Actually, Joe and I have a history of working through projects together. "You also helped me build the three kitchen door headers in the first house I ever renovated, remember? 'Cuz I needed the opinion of a structural engineer."

"And I was bored at home, so it was fun to come to work in the mornings at your place." He stands to stretch his back. "And I hung drywall in your garage; oh and, I helped your dad build that wooden deck you wanted."

That was my birthday gift, and you painted the back entry, too!" I smile.

"We make a good team." He grunts.

"We do," I agree.

November 30, 2013

Paul and I take our Chevy HHR, after dinner, to hunt down a nativity scene for our church foyer. The first store we find in the dark is an A.R.C. Thrift Store. There, in the window, a plastic baby Jesus is lying between his mother Mary and his father Joseph like an early Christmas present meant just for us, so we scoop up the two feet tall display, and Paul swipes his credit card for them.

Paul makes sure Mary and Joseph are facing out the back window of our HHR so that they appear to be staring down at any unlucky driver following behind us. Enjoying our mischief, we slip into the driveway at Mister B's house, park, and collect Joe from his velvet swivel chair to come view our highbrow nativity. Walking him out to the back of the vehicle, Mister B complains, "It's cold!" We push him along, then turn him to face the back window, showing off our fortunate purchase.

Joe gasps. "What are ya gonna do wid those *idols*?!" he exclaims.

Hardly expecting that kind of reaction, Paul defends us. "Dad, they are Christmas figurines, not idols, for heaven's sake."

"Well, what are ya gonna do wid those idols anyway?" Joe insists.

"It's a nativity scene, Mr. B!" Then I look around to make sure there aren't any joggers passing by to overhear my militaristic response. "We got it at the A.R.C. Thrift Store to make a

Christmas display at church! Only $44.16 to keep Christ in Christmas!" I'm cracking up. Paul ribs his father.

"It's for church, for Christmas, Chief! But, we don't know if it needs new light bulbs or if the wiring still works!" Now we're both shouting.

Mr. B shrugs.

Feeling deflated at the failed joke, we steer him to the front door.

"I thought I raised you bettah than that." He declares, watching his feet and pointing at his son.

"No, Dad. You didn't."

"Where did ya get those idols, did ya say?"

"We got 'em at The A.R.C., down the street, Joe." After three tries, I'm exasperated. Has he forgotten so quickly? Does he not understand? Or, is he being even naughtier than us?

"On Mount Ararat?"

"Oh. My. Goodness. How do you know about Mount Ararat?" We've all found our seats, and Joe has the television remote control in hand.

"I've seen a show or two about how they found that boat, that ark, in Turkey, and then there was an avalanche so that they weren't able to dig it up after they found it. Or, they had made photographs of it, I guess."

"Well yes, and also there's no way one official religion is going to allow another religion to establish the truth it has buried within its boundaries, either."

"If you put it that way, okay."

Paul one-ups both of us: "You've seen the Indiana Jones movie, haven't you, Chief? Raiders of the Lost Ark?"

Mr. B raises an eyebrow. "You slug 'em and I'll kick 'em."

I'm up from my chair and spinning. "That's a completely different ark, funny guy. I'm leaving both of you to go lock our

Christmas idols safely in the car. Choose whatever you want to watch tonight."

As I'm parking the car in the garage, I thank God that clever ol' Mister B can maintain life in his own home since he now has two of us playing his personal chauffeur. Yet, the stunningly archaic term *idol* keeps circling through my thoughts. That's not a term from my father-in-law's Catholic upbringing. Joe knows the difference between idols and a nativity scene. Doesn't he? What the heck is an *idol*, anyway? Into my dusky imaginings comes the visage of our large, fancy house with all its baggage. Maybe somebody's Christmas present will become an idol of happiness only to finally disappoint. I suppose almost anything that we use to identify ourselves with or bow our true identity to, besides the one true God, could be deemed an idol.

Ш 🕯 ෆ

> Oft' times He weaveth sorrow;
> And I in foolish pride
> Forget He sees the upper
> And I the underside.
> He knows, He loves, He cares;
> Nothing this truth can dim.
> He gives the very best to those
> Who leave the choice to Him."
> — Corrie ten Boom

Below is a picture of a turbo jet engine that Joe worked on. It is set in a pod, as if you were standing on the ground looking up at it. The turbine is at the top. The compressor blades (compressors) are at the bottom. They spark the air and send out the exhaust which creates the thrust.

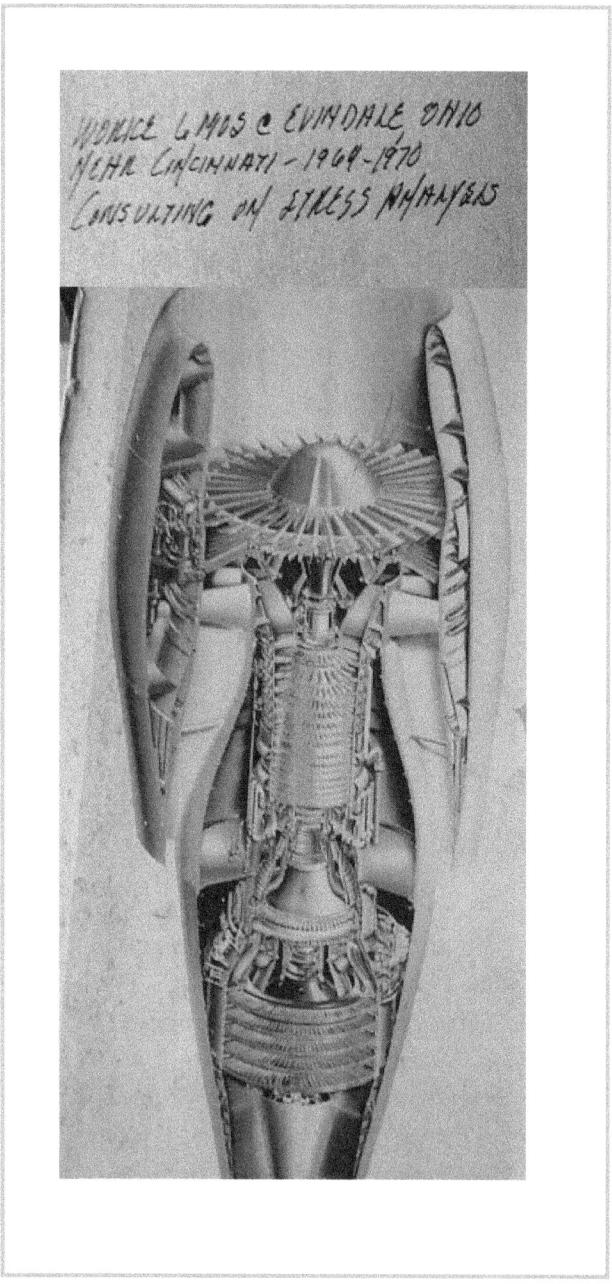

*D*ECEMBER ~
DECIBELS

December 1, 2013
"This is the irrational season
When love blooms bright and wild.
Had Mary been filled with reason
There'd have been no room for the child."
- Madeleine L'Engle

December 2, 2013

Icicles hang from the edges of the eaves like theater curtains around our home. Inside, we are toasty, consuming raw veggies and piping hot chicken noodle soup. Paul and I have a little something extra that Mr. B wouldn't touch.

Slurping up soup, my good friend swallows, shivers, and looks up. "I can feel this warming me all the way down to my gizzard!" Mr. B smiles happily and rubs his tummy."

He looks at our plate of fat, steamed, pork dumplings and comments that they look like his mother's pierógis, all crimped and frilly at the top.

"Do you want to try one, Chief? They are *szinka*!"

"Oh, nooooo. I neveh liked 'em. Back then, I didn't have what you would call a choice. If she put it on the table, I ate it. And the Poles like their pierógis. She made sauerkraut pouches and even prune pierógis."

Paul then discloses winking at me, "My dad couldn't believe that those candles you put in the windows were battery operated, so he opened up the bottom of one to take a look around."

Joe's mouth drops open as he's being ratted out.

I say, "Don't worry, Mr. B. It's the engineer in you, I know."

He shakes his head. "I was just curious, you know. I couldn't help myself. They still work just fine."

"You're just like a little girl who looks under the dress of her new dolly. Curious."

"Well…"

Both Paul and his dad cringe a little.

December 3, 2013
I've been keeping the radio turned off in my car, the HHR, whenever I drive Joe anywhere, mainly because he cannot hear the news, which is what I typically listen to, and also because he would not appreciate my CDs. Today though, thirsting for a taste of my familiar self, my old habits and things I fondly recognize, I stick a Christmas CD into the car's stereo and turn it up so that he can listen. Twinkling guitar riffs seem to glow with the special loop effects used to record them, and I am grinning broadly at this clever festivity, when Joe says, "I hear the noise of guitars, but where's the music?"

Occasionally opinions come forth from his mouth referring to my weight or my cooking or my ornery dog, Jester. In those cases, I have learned to smile and shut my mouth because humor escapes me.

Some people are much more critical than Joe, and their ugly edges don't soften with age. My friends who throw tantrums, or fight back against humorless critics, don't seem to spar better than the silent treatment that comes naturally to me, so I stick with it.

He looks at me steadily for a moment expecting, um, who knows what. Then, he points at the flock of geese in the park beside the road. "They sure like to congregate in winter here." I gaze at the hundreds, perhaps thousands of geese pecking the olive colored grass. Altogether, the geese make a uniform landscaping effect. The soft tweed, a handsome cloth, is made of grey, black, and tan dots flowing through a paisley grid.

I nod, acknowledging that winter holds its own forms of beauty. "Yep. It's good to congregate with those who saddle up to you." We smile at each other as the music plays on. Thankfully, we have arrived at the library.

December 4, 2013

Today I receive a Christmas letter from the missionaries who bought our house. The address of our house, *our house– on Pearl Street–* is affixed as the return address. The combination brandishes such a jolt. *What are they doing in our house, the one I designed and helped build with my own hands*? my emotions demand.

I re-read the letter in partisan disbelief to absorb all the many ways they are appreciating *our house*. Namely: they have people coming and going *like we could not*. They have crowds using it for parties and meetings and extended sleepovers *like we could not*. I can only imagine how the neighbors are writhing, yet it feels like my heart is split into pieces to consider all this goodness that was taken from us by our neighbors' hatred. Stunned, I set aside this Christmas letter to consider. *God! Make it stop!* I had prayed this while being taunted. There were months, during those six years, I longed to lay down and die. An ancient song springs to mind. From the closet upstairs, I pull out my lonely guitar to sing it for my own good:

> Hidden in the hollow of His precious hand,
>   Never foe can follow, never traitor stand;
> We may trust Him fully all for us to do.
>   They who trust Him wholly find Him wholly true.
>   Stayed upon Jehovah, hearts are fully blessed
>   Finding, as He promised, perfect peace and rest.

(Hymn by Frances Havergale)

The presence of God, I realize, is the headspring of joy. Finding purpose for those past events, with gratitude for them, unclogs that river of wellbeing. His presence there, His redemption of the past is a tributary to joy. I think He probably broke the dam that was holding back my river of joy when the missionaries stepped in to buy that house from us. I'm feeling much more than a trickle of joy these days. Once again, I let the flood carry my designer house down the stream away from me. It's the joy I want.

Learning the balance of rest and work in the common day is a second tributary to joy. By journaling my conversations with Joe, I am helped to quietly examine all that is good in my life. Removing the blockages in the river, the situations over which I find myself stumbling, seems like rolling boulders from this present stream of joy.

And for the future, there's hope; hope that the Spirit will care for me since I no longer control my estate, by authority or power, by assets or money or even by physical strength to renovate another house into a home that suits my idea of comfort. The Spirit is my third tributary to future joy. I need these three personal tributaries of joy[1] to be able to care for my father-in-law. I am hidden in the hollow of God's hand.

December 5, 2013

"Did you ever meet her?" Joe shakes his fork over his cut up banana and asks me whether I knew his sister, Wanda. Apparently, he has forgotten that he sent Paul and me to represent the family at Wanda's funeral. Mr. B *Hates* funerals with a capital H. He refused to attend the funeral of his own wife! "I can't take the emotion of a funeral," he confided. "I went to my fathea and mothea's funerals, and that was enough for me."

"Yes, I remember Wanda. She was fascinating." The image of

her is a stout, but well-groomed, grey-headed woman who smiled but kept her cards close to her chest.

"When I first met her, she came through Colorado on her move back to Rhode Island. You took all of us out for dinner: to Mohammed's place." The image of the candlelit harvest table at Thanksgiving, filled with Mr. B's family, is the still life in my mind. I remind him that Paul and I flew out to Providence, Rhode Island, to visit his sisters, twice. "She was a nurse in the Air Force, and I saw a picture of her shaking the President's hand in the hallway of her home; a couple different presidents in fact. Pictures of her with them. She sent us all those beautiful doilies and tablecloths she had knitted or crocheted. Not sure which."

Joe has been listening intently. "She did? She musta liked you."

He starts again. "Did you notice the other men sitting in their car outside of Mohammed's, too, then?"

"Wha… What men?" I'm confused.

Joe's words are measured. "Wanda didn't believe in banks. She was a wealthy person, I gather because she had purchased land in the San Juan Islands and also a ranch in Montana. The reason she was coming through Colorado was that she decided to sell it all and move back to Woonsocket to take care of our sista Lucy and to be near Eddy and Bertha. You know, Wanda's husband Jack had died.

"There was nothing to keep her there. So, she called some uppity up in the military and they granted her a military escort! All the way across country. When she stayed with us that night, the men were outside in their car. I didn't understand it, but she had some kind of power to employ a military escort! You know she was a colonel, not just any ol' nurse."

I think about this for a bit. Then, I disclose a secret. "You know when she appointed Paul as her executor? We went out to stay with her and Lucy. She was very sick with cancer. I couldn't sleep one night, so I went down to the basement and found a book, just a paperback of *Pride and Prejudice*, but it had all kinds of codes in it; underlined and circled. At the time, I didn't understand why, but I learned people did that kind of thing to communicate to others working for the Allies during the war. It was spy material."

"On her walls were paintings and photographs of her husband's airplanes. I also found a book in German, Hitler's *Mein Kampf*. I couldn't read a word of it, but I realized how much of her identity was wrapped up in the war and politics. She came down after me that night and caught me looking through her bookshelf. Instantly, I felt her suspicious nature come to life. I realized I'd accidentally crossed some sort of line of hers. I'd never met someone like that before. 'You think Wanda and Jack were spies, Mr. B?"

"Her husband was a courier pilot during the war. They served together," Joe reflects. He stops eating entirely while he is thinking and talking. "They were very secretive. I didn't know much about their marriage or their war experiences. But she was highly decorated. Something from the war musta haunted Jack terribly. He saw too much. Maybe they *were* spies!" His eyes widen. "I don't know. She never told *me*. Anyway, Jack had his demons. He put a shotgun into his mouth and pulled the trigger. She found him on the sofa. That's the real reason she moved from there."

Now, it's my turn to stop breakfast. "Awful! Oh no."

"Oh yeees," Joe agrees.

I divulge another secret. "Sadly, I think she was in denial about dying. Her closet was full of new clothes sewn by a personal designer, including furs and brand new shoes. When I asked Lucy why they still had tags on them she said that Wanda had just paid for them and hadn't had a chance to wear them yet. I found that to be so odd for a woman planning her funeral. She was someone I would have liked to know better. That's for sure."

"You and me both. You and me both. She was the youngest, but apparently, she was very close with Helen, the oldest girl, because Helen named her daughter after Wanda. The one I never knew personally."

"But Helen was married to an escaped German soldier!" My mind is whirring. "Wouldn't it have been fascinating to have been a fly on the wall in their conversations, Mr. B?"

He smiles like Yoda and nods with closed eyes.

December 6, 2013

Joe likes to get out of the house a couple of times per week. In the local library, he can read in the quiet section with his one good eye and glasses, sometimes pulling out the magnifying lens from his fleece pocket. He'll find a history book or the *New York Times*, or he does the crossword puzzle in the *Denver Post*. It's a Friday visit today.

I look up surprised as Joe meanders over to where I'm sitting. He's come to collect me earlier than normal. "I got an idea, kiddo. You wanna go get some clam chowder wid me? There's a place nearby that uses quahogs in their chowder."

"You're finished reading already?"

"Well, my eyes are tired. The *Aviation Week* only comes every month anymore. Guess news is scarce, I dunno. But, I already read the one on the shelf two times. Let's go on, that is, if you are ready."

How can I refuse? In a few minutes, we find a booth at the Fish Monger and order two delicious bowlfuls.

"Do you think everyone here is Catholic?" he sputters over his soup.

"Why would you think that? I have no idea." Is dementia setting in?

"Well, I had work buddies who only ate fish on Fridays, and this place is rather full. They all look like they're having—

what-cha-call-it—business lunches."

I look around and see one couple deeply absorbed in each other's company. "All except for that young couple holding hands, there."

Joe follows the motion of my head to glimpse the couple in love. "We could hold hands too and have all of the Catholics confused," he hisses in conspiracy. In our amusement, we manage to collide hands with my glass of water. The spill abruptly straightens up the fools.

December 7, 2013
My sister, Liz, confides over lunch that the most awkward moment for her, living with our mother, is when they are both watching a movie and a torrid sex scene ensues.

"Oh really? Huh. I can top that. Imagine the same thing, only sitting with your father-in-law."

December 8, 2013
Paul and I are doing our best to accommodate Mister B's request to do away with some of the "fire hazard" we have stored in his basement, meaning our stored boxes. The boxes Paul chooses first contain bitter documents from our legal appeal. Paul insists that we should rid ourselves of them. I tremble to think what would happen if anyone appealed anything before the statute of limitations runs out. Dragging my feet, I pick up the court transcripts binder. Maybe I should save the certified parts.

In reading over the municipal transcripts one last time, the truth finally sinks in. It isn't what the city's prosecutor says to the jury that I see, but the omissions made to the jury, what he didn't say. Frantically, I sift through each page to find any honest mention of the City's referenced timeframe. There is none. After six years of accusations, appeal, redress, and the city's ducking of discovery, my eyes are opened. Yes, I knew it had been a shady delivery, but I had never quite understood how they had won a guilty verdict from the jury when from my estimation any review of the facts would show we were innocent. Omissions of facts are harder to find.

All of the pain and shame of those moments turn into blood-curdling wrath.

"Look at this, Paul!" I shout at the back door.

"Bring it here," he shouts back from the firepit.

"The City's lawyer never did tell the jury, even in the closing arguments, what year we supposedly violated their new zoning code and building code!" I run at my husband shaking the binder of hubris. "That's how they did it! I finally figured it out! They told them about the codes, they talked about the months, but they never admitted to the jury that we had built our home two years prior to the adoption of the codes! Oh!" My fury!

"Give it over." My husband says calmly. "I'm gonna burn it."

I stand in the grass and stare at him in disbelief. "Really?"

"Really. We are done. We have landed here in a much better place. Let the chips fall where they may. I'm not going to lose my wife over it. You are done, Honey."

He leaves the stick in the firepit and comes to me. He puts his arms around me. He kisses me. He slides the court transcript binder out of my hands. He goes back to his lawn chair, snaps open the rings in the binder and starts pulling out pages of transcripts. He throws the papers, inch by inch, into the flames.

I want to throw up.

December 9, 2013

"In Cali, used to walk a mile and a half from the boarding house where I was living, along the beach highway, passing under a row of eucalyptus trees, and a little ways past a little diner where I liked to stop and eat to get to where I worked my first job at Vultee."

"Were you trying to save gas money?"

"Oh, I didn't have a car yet, Miss, and yes, I *was* trying to save money. But walking wasn't bad except at ten o'clock at night when there were hardly any lights."

"You mean on weekends?"

"Oh no." He raises his eyebrows. "I mean, I worked till ten o'clock at night. Some of the guys worked 'round the clock, and Vultee set up cots for 'em. Yeah… We were on a mission to get the first basic trainer out. We finished the BT-13 in 90 days, believe it or not! That's where I got that Vultee pin that Pauly has tucked away upstairs. Ninety days to design and build a new airplane."

"My goodness. No wonder you burned out on that job."

"Well, they offered us as many sandwiches and as much coffee as we wanted."

"Still, those conditions would never be tolerated today."

Joe smiles a bland oh-well smile. "Downey, California was orange grove country. On Saturdays, I always went to that diner and asked the waiter for a bowl of fruit."

"Oranges?"

"Well, yes Ma'am. The oranges were mixed in with other kinds of fruit. I liked that very much."

Joe draws an imaginary S-curve with his finger. "You know what an integral is? No? Well, I was drafting my design on vellum in pencil and handing it to my supervisor. That guy was a mathematician. He kept handing it back to me with red pencil all over it, and I couldn't get out the red from the vellum, so I went to ask the boss if I needed to write out the integrals and constants of each design like that mathematician wanted. After that, there were no more red marks."

"What's an integral, Mr. B?"

"In calculus, the 'constant' is the limit of any given figure, like the extent of zero or maybe L, whatever it is. But, sometimes you have to make an approximation, so you put that integral sign before the constant, and that ties the limit together with whatever is before it, which creates a derivative function. So, it's a way to tie together two or three variable numbers. We used it a lot because of all the curves on an airplane. It approximated the region of the curves. Once you know what you are doing, Miss, you shouldn't have to report your entire calculus problem on the blueprint, at least I thought so, so I was kinda irritated. Maybe it was my pride, but there were guys who didn't have a college degree working for them then, so I guess they were just checking me out."

My eyebrows go up. I don't bother mentioning in high school I failed the course, *Introduction to Algebra*. My inner designer, however, is moved by the beauty of such concepts. So, I clear my throat. "The way you talk, sometimes, Mr. B, I could aspire to learning calculus, even now."

෴ Ⅲ ≥ 🏛

Directly after this exchange, our prayer group leader at church happens to read the portion in Colossians, chapter one, on the supremacy of the Son of God, like this:

> [15] The Son is the image of the invisible God, the firstborn over all creation. [16] For in Him all things were created: things in heaven and on earth, visible and invisible, whether thrones or powers or rulers or authorities; all things have been created through Him and for Him. [17] He is before all things, and in Him all things hold together. [18] And He is the head of the body, the church; He is the beginning and the firstborn from among the dead, so that in everything He might have the supremacy. [19] For God was pleased to have all His

fullness dwell in Him, [20] and through Him to reconcile to himself all things, whether things on earth or things in heaven, by making peace through His blood, shed on the cross. [21] Once you were alienated from God and were enemies in your minds because of your evil behavior. [22] But now He has reconciled you by Christ's physical body through death to present you holy in his sight, without blemish and free from accusation— (NIV)

The light flashes on, even for this illiterate mathematician. The person of Christ is both the "constant" and the "integral". He is the limit of all scientific possibilities because He is authoritatively God, and he is the integral because He is able to connect the dots and reconcile all things to God by a particular function of being the Son who laid down his own physical life to bridge over our sins while God continued in eternal life. The end of the equation is that we can now be reconciled, free to live to our best equation, without accusation.

December 10, 2013

Joe found some big blue tarps among Paul's boxes in the shed, and he cut and stapled them together to make covers for our bikes during winter. He also makes a cover for Paul's grill. It's one of those uncommonly pleasant winter days in Colorado.

"Here, Mr. B, have some water." I hand over a glass.

He shakes his head. "You just want me to have to run to the bathroom." But he takes a sip. "I couldn't say it when you were so busy moving in. But that city pretty much persecuted you."

"Oh, you got that, Mr. B?" My sarcasm ends with a raised brow. "Yes, we definitely felt targeted and persecuted. We were so surprised that even churches didn't help beyond writing a couple of letters."

"Did you ever wonder why the American Jews didn't help save

the European Jews during the war?" He takes another sip of his water.

"No, I've never thought of it." How does he drum up the ragged edges of any given issue?

"Well, I have. You know, there wasn't really a nation of Israel at the time. Jews lived among all the nations but didn't really have a state. They had sort of a kingdom of tribes or something or ruther." He talks slowly as he considers his story. "No one was the head of 'em. 'Cept the British took control and decided to call their holy lands Palestine. That was around 1920. The Jews in America weren't really immigrants from Palestine. They were Americans who practiced their beliefs amongst themselves and their communities." Joe has forgotten that he is holding a glass of water, so I take it from him and set it on the table next to his chair.

"Do you want to go inside, Mr. B?"

"In a minute, in a minute." He pats the air as if telling me to sit down and leave well enough alone.

"Initially the German government passed civil laws to isolate and impoverish the Jews from German society, like they declared they couldn't take out business loans or housing loans. The Nuremberg Laws were initiated in '35 and declared they weren't really German citizens so that they couldn't vote or hold public offices. But that made the unemployed game to be picked off the streets by the police as anti-social and work-shy. The rumors began about 'the Jewish problem,' as though they were an immoral or diseased people. See, it planted the seed of doubt in people's minds, but it was all libel and slander. Then, the Kristallnacht happened. You know?"

"I know it was the night where the Germans broke all the glass windows of shops owned by Jews."

"Okay. So, their synagogues were burned and 30,000 of them were incarcerated in the camps. That was '38. There was no national government to protect them. The concentration camps had already been established for the prostitutes and drunk and mentally debilitated as a way to clean up the German streets, and no one resisted. The effect of the laws seemed unfortunate and prejudicial, kinda like your experience with the city making up new zoning laws against you. But people assume these kinds of laws won't last beyond the next election." He wags his finger at me and squints his blue eye.

This evokes a bitter laugh from me. I look up into the nails piercing through the blue paneled ceiling of Mr. B's back porch and pull my coat tighter around me. "Okay, well I read a book about the genocide in Rwanda. It was also started by the RTLM radio and television that publicized libel about the Tutsis' intent to take over the government. Once the scare was started, their genocide by the Hutus seemed justifiable. That was just in 1994! I wonder how many people have put together the correlation between gossip and annihilation of others."

"Well, that's the thing. You aren't really sure, and there's no way to prove it one way or the other, and until harm actually comes, you don't even have a legal avenue to trace the path of the dark cloud and assert blame. I think that's why we have so many Jewish lawyers these days. They understand this difficulty and want to stay a step ahead of the game in case it happens again."

"Okay, but you began this conversation by asking me why the Jews in America didn't help."

"Well, I don't know why! I was asking if you did!" He sits up.

"Well, I heard that Jews sent money, but that the Swiss banks held it up. The Palestinian Jews sent money to the Brits for visas to save the children at least, but the Brits sat on it. I also heard that no one knew the extent of the genocide until the Americans and British began liberating the concentration camps."

"Oh, they knew, Miss," Mr. B smirks. "That's why they gave

half of Poland to the Russians. It was the guilt of the world's high commands that created the Palestinian borders and the Israeli State from the so-called holy lands. The powers of the nations are held in the hands of a few, and they make all the decisions. Churchill, Roosevelt, Stalin. Have you seen all the photographs of them sitting together? They knew."

Geez, my old friend sure knows how to put the chill into Winter.

December 11, 2013

On the way to the library, Mr. B tells me that since his family used to send over crates of supplies to their Polish cousins during the war, one time he even sent his winter coat. "They probably never got it," he surmises. "We should have cut the threads in the middle seam to preserve it from the looters of all those packages. We could have mailed it in two different packets. Then, they could have sewn it up when it arrived. It was a beautiful coat, long to the back of the calves." He motions with his hand to show me how long it was on him.

"You know a wool coat will keep you warmer than leather?" Joe asks.

"Really?"

"Yes. There was an officer and a military pilot who got caught in a blizzard together. The officer forced the pilot to trade his leather jacket for the officer's wool coat because the wool was soaking up the snow. But it was the pilot who survived the cold because the wool will keep a body warm no matter how wet it gets."

I'm glad Mr. B has his warm winter jacket on today. He is a survivor, but he is also a generous man. It seems he always has been.

December 12, 2013

We are sorting through old shipping crates in the basement. Joe picks up a yellowed newspaper clipping he's saved. He hands over the photo drawing of an early war plane. "One of the first things I worked on was the BC-3 for the Army Air Corps." He shows me the photograph of a small aircraft. "It was scrapped." He confesses. "Then, I worked on the BT-13 for the Air Force. BT meaning Basic Trainer. Somewhere in the basement, I still have a certificate of award they gave to the whole design team for it."

Joe and the work team got an award for designing it because it was an agile, quality airplane. "In the field, though, it was referred to as 'the Vibrator'. Joe smiles.

I don't understand why an award-winning plane would be given that nickname.

"It didn't have retractable landing gear or a hydraulic system. The flaps were operated by a crank-and-cable system." He explains. "That was noisy! And a two-position propeller had an irritating high-pitched vibration. Also," Mr. B chuckles, "the windows vibrated on takeoff, and if you got close to stall speed in the air, it vibrated violently to warn you. If you were doing fancy maneuvers with it, sometimes the canopy vibrated. It was just so noisy, the pilots nicknamed it 'the Vibrator.'"

"Airplane technology was all *new*. We were doing the best we could! Things got better as they went along." He shrugs.

"Fact is, there would be nothing to improve upon unless there was someone to make the prototype. Whether people recognize you or not, you brought something into existence. You helped to create something really valuable to all of aviation and the wars that followed, and to modern research."

He chuckles. "To engineer is human, as human as any entrepreneurial or artistic pilgrimage."

I'm thinking, yeah, you get the idealistic thrill of an architect's eye and a pilgrim's challenging path. Your tools of navigation can't tell you where the holes in the ice lay, or where the hanging cliffs are, or why bridges collapse.

He interrupts my thoughts. "Being the pioneer makes for some humiliations in life. So, you gotta hand it to the tenacious ones!"

"I understand that concept, Mr. B. Sometimes a cover artist gets the fame for the songwriters' hit because of a single improvement of voice, tempo, or arrangement. Maybe the second artist has a better marketing agent. When you're a developer, people can mistake your excitement for bravado."

December 13, 2013

With a chilled, whipped Jell-O in hand, book club Betty comes to visit her biggest fan at our house, that being Mr. B. "I thought you might need another side for dinner," she explains.

I make a hearty meal of turkey soup with rosemary, pepper, and dumplings and offer a salad on the side. She woofs it down, comparing life and times notes with the old scientist across the table. Betty worked with Nabisco Corporation as a foodie scientist of sorts, and well, she also just possesses that particular engineering eccentricity. I look at my bowl and plate, smiling at how well these two get along.

"Oh my goodness. You lived in Cleveland, Ohio, too?" She elbows me with one arm as she wipes her mouth with the opposite extension. "What serendipity! I've never met another person with so much in common. We've both lived in Fergusson, Woonsocket, Mexico, Bald'more…"

They chat like there's no end to the soup bowl. I pull out an apple pie, warm from the oven, and they gasp with greater delight. This was a good idea to invite Betty tonight.

After dinner, we retire to the blue room for conversation. "Oh dear. Lopsided Henriot is looking askance at us!" I go to straighten her frame.

"Ah, thank you, Sweet Pea. But I like to call her On-ri-o."

"French pronunciation?" Betty asks.

"Yep."

"Ah, noooo. Mr. B just wishes she was ornery."

Betty's laugh flutters across the room. Joe glares like a Tasmanian Devil and shrieks. "She's just mean. Don't you believe her!"

Afterwards, she whispers, "We have so much in *common*! I'm just too young for him."

I embrace my friend, telling her she is always welcome here, as she folds herself into her Camry. I wait to watch her drive away before slipping back into the front doorway like an icicle. No matter how cold it is outside, that is something Mr. B has always done for Paul and me, waiting and waving us off into the distance. It's another one of my father-in-law's endearing habits I'm trying to replicate.

December 14, 2013

Mr. B offers a nod as we get into the car, "I'm proud of you for standing your ground as long as you did, kiddo." He's referring to our city lawsuit, and I'm staring at him because I haven't talked to him much about our lawsuit since we dismissed it and moved in with him. I really don't know how he feels about the right to use one's own residence for religious hospitality. I didn't want to worry him needlessly, so when it continued on over a year, I stopped bringing him the confusing updates.

"You brought over a couple of your pleadings, and I really thought you would win, I really did. Maudie used to be aggressive too. I admired that in her."

"We had a 50/50 chance, I guess. Like everyone else in court does." I try to ignore his choice of description being aggressive rather than assertive.

"Well, not really. It's the tall grasses that get mowed down. Powerful people don't like to be *told*, if you know what I mean. And they got friends in high places. You don't know what goes on behind closed doors. So, I'm glad it's behind ya now." He pats my knee.

"Well, thank you, Mr. B. I appreciate that. It's just that officers, city council people, have immunity according to state law and the city charter. All they have to say is they made a mistake, it wasn't personal, or that it was done in the line of duty, and the judge dismisses them." I sigh the unending sigh.

"What was that word you said? Im*pun*ity?" His blue eyes leer into my face from the passenger's seat.

"Ha, ha! That's pretty good, Mr. B. That's right. Im*pun*ity. You'd think there'd be somebody to stop them, but the feds pretty much take their hands off local matters, so unless the people of a city vote an amendment into their charter to hold city council members liable for the way they vote, there is no way to hold anybody but a couple of peon staff members accountable."

"But it's all done now, right?"

"All but one thing. One party put a lien on our rental house."

"Sons a' bitches!"

His support warms my heart. "Why thank you, Sir! You have a way with words."

December 15, 2013

I listen to Mr. B talking savings strategies with my sis, and her talking with him about the financial training decisions she's made for her son. My nephew compliments Paul as being the one who taught him to save money throughout his work life. He also thanks his mama for teaching him to pay off his credit card and not overextend the debt that he can actually manage. This is a cool reflection, a generational gift I see rippling out. My sister is surprised when I tell her that Mr. B never uses a credit card. If he makes reservations for a hotel stay, he sends a check in with his reservation.

"Yeah," agrees Joe. "Well, credit cards were started in Bald'more. I remember the store that started the idea of giving a card for debts. Then banks took over the idea to consolidate all the stores' credit cards. It was a *ba-a-a-ad* idea because it started the debilitating debt amongst our younger generation we see today. It's no longer a simple short handshake between two people."

December 16, 2013

It's not a welcomed doorbell that breaks into eight o'clock gray of a Sunday morning when one is trying to sleep in. I hold my breath. Paul finally sighs and rolls from under our quilt, puts on a robe, and marches down the stairs. When he returns he says, "Maybe eight o'clock feels like noon at the plumber's family across the street."

"Mmm."

"That was the wife asking us if she could cut some blue spruce branches from our tree. She's making some sort of wreath."

"Mmm."

"I told her to take as much as she wanted."

"Mmm."

He kisses me.

About two o'clock in the afternoon, who rolls around again but the plumber's wife from across the street, carrying a two-foot by two-foot door hanger made of fresh cut blue and green boughs, fat bows, and streams of red and gold ribbons, earthy pine cones, and shiny red bulbs!

Amazed, tears spring to my eyes. Neighbors sure make or break a "neighborhood"!

December 17, 2013

We are celebrating my love's birthday party quietly today. We ask Joe if he would like to join us in the mountains for a special birthday dinner. He waves his hands from his blue chair indicating he declines. "I've had my day. This is your time. You guys go and enjoy it."

Hesitant to leave Paul's father alone at night, we sit in the living room for a while as he rambles about some of his favorite dates with Maudie. "I couldn't have done any of it had I not graduated from college though. I'm very grateful. My fathea told me that I had to save all my earnings from the paper route so that I could go to college. We put it in a bank. But after college, he gave me that account. He said he had never touched it. I could have used it to move to California when I found my first job after the University of Alabama, but I kept saving it and instead, I starved because I was too proud to ask my fathea to send it to me."

Your traveling companion is as important as your destination. Paul and I have had a very good run in marriage. There are times, though, we spin on a dime and wonder why we keep loving each other in the lows of struggles, arguments, and bad humor. These are things our single, idealistic friends don't comprehend about the reality of marriage. They look at us and often say our marriage seems ideal. We don't offer this information to Joe. He already knows. Tonight is a good date to celebrate Paul's thriving life and to talk about our future hopes, which may never come true, but which nevertheless have always been important conversation pieces for us. Paul glances at me as if to say, "Ready?"

Joe misses the clue, leans back in his chair, and continues

talking to the ceiling. "I was so poor after graduation. I went to California to look for work wid a business card from a banker friend of my fathea's in Rhode Island." Mr. B suddenly sits up to emphasize this fact with his gravelly voice, "That's how they gave you a good reference in the old days, you know. So, I met the guy who was also a banker in California, he said he'd do what he could, and he pointed me down the road to a woman who rented rooms in her home."

I glance at Paul, whose knee is beginning to bounce impatiently.

"I didn't have enough money to rent a room from her, and I didn't know how long it would take me to get a job, so she let me stay in her front sunroom on the porch for two weeks, for ten cents a day. I'd walk around and get a feel for the place and put in my resume. But at night I was terribly alone and frightened. I was so hungry." Joe stops rocking and looks at us.

"You kids are lucky. You don't know what it means to be poor." Suddenly, silent tears begin running down his cheeks. He begins to wipe the tears away with the back of his hand. "I tried to save you from it."

Paul and I look wide-eyed at each other. We've never seen him weep except on a rare occasion when he reminisced about Maudie. We've experienced some frightening times ourselves, but we've always seemed to have enough to eat.

I move to where Joe is sitting, rub his back, confiding, "I've experienced that fear, too, Mr. B. You know when I graduated from music school? There was nothing for me to do. I hadn't earned a teacher's degree. It was awful. So, I spent a year in Africa singing in a mixed race African band during Apartheid. When I came home, I didn't have enough money in my pocket to make a phone call. My mom used to tell all her friends how stupidly idealistic her daughter was to think of coming home with a nickel in her pocket! In fact, I had gotten into some trouble. Someone had broken into our band vehicle and stolen my paycheck, my camera. and jewelry. I arrived home pretty broken and poor, though I'd had the adventure of a lifetime. That's why I finally decided to pursue a practical career as a paralegal."

Joe smiles. "Well, what can you do? We all have to learn some things the hard way. I was lucky. As it turned out, that banker was on the board of the Vultee Aircraft Company, and they hired me right away. I had less than a month to spend eating canned beans and a handful of dried dates and sleeping on a porch. Now you two go find yourselves a place to eat."

Paul stands up, relieved.

"I have a theory about life's luck, Mr. B. Wanna hear it?" Since he shrugs I continue. "Luck comes from the same root word as Lucifer. But good fortune comes as a gift from the benevolent God. Sometimes you have the same set of circumstances. One connives to use our circumstances for ill and the other means to use them for glory."

Joe looks at me with watery eyes. "I'm not gonna argue with you, kiddo. I'd lose."

His comment evokes chortles. Paul and I excuse ourselves, and we drive to our favorite hole-in-the-wall overlooking Bear Creek. There, we enjoy T-bone steaks, reveling in our good fortune and Paul's father's legacy to us.

I announce to Paul that my elder sister and her family have decided to come for Christmas, which represents some meal production challenges. I will be cooking special pastas and Mexican foods for each of them as well as preparing a plain, often raw food diet, for Paul's dad. And like normal Americans, my sister's family likes three squares a day. So, explaining to Paul that I've made up a few extra meals, I also advise him that I'll probably need his help in the next couple of weeks. "Sorry, Hon, er…

Happy Birthday!"

"Don't worry, Lynn. I'm taking a couple of days off," he reminds me squeezing my hand. "I'll help wherever I can."

I bellow at Paul on the way home, but of course it's his fault. He's missed both of the turnoffs to our new home. Flying along the way, now, to the east side of the city, I yowl, "Stop! Stop! Stop! What are you *thinking*?" Paul shrugs. "Nothing. I missed the turnoffs, so I was just gonna keep going and drive through our old neighborhood." I sigh in frustration, staring out the window at a silent snowy city. *Still his birthday party,* I think. *Pinch your lips, Deary.*

We've survived many fiery side trips longer than this forty-five minute detour, especially these past seven years. We survived not because we are so sexy or inspiring or gracious. Sometimes survival comes because God maneuvers each of us through the unfitting alleys of our humanity on bald tires. Higher love helps us wander safely through the sour and salty roads.

I squeeze Paul's thigh. "Okay, good idea. Tonight is as good as any to see the old homestead."

December 18, 2013

On our way to register his vehicle title into our names in our new county, freeze-dried snow squeaking beneath our tires, Mr. B takes his toothpick out of his mouth and offers, "My sista Lucy never learned to drive, same as my parents. I dunno. Maybe she was a bit backwards after she got sick and almost died, but my fathea took her out of school, and she was a little different after that, a little different in the head. So she didn't drive. She began working as a housemaid for the Kimbals. She worked inside, and my fathea worked in their huge garden surrounding the lawn. Mr. Kimbal was on the board of the Woonsocket Association of Savings Bank. Oh, they were the 'leaders of the Hoi Pallois' you know, 'had a nice house, a two-foot wall made of stone surrounded it, and it had a screened-in porch. Wow, was it nice! My sista Lucy made a name for herself, and they rented out her services to big shot dinners, because she learned how to arrange big vases of flowers, big flower arrangements, and how to set the silver on the table in decorative ways with all that fancy etiquette stuff, and she learned to bake really well, too. So, she liked to bake for our family after that. But then she found that she could make more money doing piecework at the rubber factory."

"She traded in all her nice manners and sweet surroundings for factory piecework?"

"Some muckety muck from the rubber factory at one of those big dinners offered her a job there. She made so much money doing piecework! She was always working on tennis shoes after that. She could put together more soles in the shortest amount of time than anyone. She always made good money at that."

"Was she sorry that she didn't finish school?"

"I don't think so. I couldn't say for sure," Joe begins slowly. "She never married, but she was a very good cook. And she loved her sweets. She could really bake. And she could knit, like Wanda, too. They kept boxes of it."

"Chocolates?"

"Nah, well maybe. But, boxes of their embroidery and crochet."

"I've discovered you like sweets too, Mr. B! I always thought you didn't like them because after taking us out to dinner, Maudie would order dessert, but you never did. Now I know how much you love your ice cream and a nice piece of pie!"

Joe grins and nods sheepishly. "I just don't like to pay for 'em. That's all." Yet, Joe has always been the perfect host, buying for everyone who ever came out with him and Maudie. "I wasn't raised to order desserts at all, so it was always great to go out with you."

"Mr. B? Does it bother you to give your Saturn to us?" He seems so businesslike, and I'm not sure whether to feel sad or relieved that he edits his activities himself, in all pragmatism, before we have to address a situation.

"Why, no ma'am." His face opens up, surprised. "You two are doing all the driving! Why should I pay the taxes?"

December 19, 2013
Joe has been duly warned that his quiet life is about to radically change. My relatives are coming for Christmas. He asks their names again and again and then writes them in his calendar for memory security. Joe relates a conversation about Tesla coils he had with my fifteen-year-old niece. He asserts, "I liked that young gal. She is particularly smart and also surprisingly humble about it." His head wobbles to and fro thinking over his Christmas propositions. "I admit I am hoping your talented brother-in-law will fix the driveway's overhead lights while he is staying here, but I don't want to ask him directly." I get the message.

December 20, 2013
Early this morning, Pauly-the-birthday-boy, came down the stairs to the smell of something electrical burning on his father's old two-foot Christmas tree. By the time I joined him, he'd carefully removed all of the lights and ornaments. It was obvious that his father's ancient frosted snowmen were the culprit. A couple of their necks were melted through.

"Bring in the coffee, Honey, and come-n-help me. What I want for my birthday, today, is to redecorate the tree!"

The 97-year-old chief draws a grim face to spy the removal of his favorite string of lit snowmen from his tree. Spying this effect, Pauly has an idea. He gives his father a reconstruction job with the tin snips. The chief snips all the faulty wires above each snowman's head. Then, he re-attaches the snipped wires by tying them into loops to hang them as ornaments rather than the strand of lights. Now we have a few Freddy Krueger Christmas ornaments, but hey! It's a bit like some real life holiday memories, right?

"HAPPY BIRHDAY!" My sister's voice carries from the phone at Paul's ear, to where I'm sitting. He explains to her our exciting morning, illuminating the fire hazard of the ancient strand of holiday lights. He starts chuckling, then, as she relates an empathetic story back to him. When he hangs up the phone, he declares, "Your sister said her toilet seat caught on fire while she was sitting on it!"

"What? How could that happen?"

"Because she owns one of those fancy French bidets, and the last time she sat on it, the thing broke. It damaged the electrical wiring. Ha-ha-ha, so it caught on fire with her on the stool! What a funny birthday I'm having already." He grins with all the amusement of a naughty elf.

December 21, 2013

When my Texan relatives arrive this year, they come to join us in quite a different home from our last, but somehow finding enough room doesn't seem to be a spoiler here.

My sister traipsed through the snow-clad town at my side this morning, exclaiming how much better it is than our last town. "Hey, girl? You've traded UP!" She had giggled. People clambered over the decked out streets to chocolate shops, pottery makers, antique outlets. We spent time with my niece decorating pottery today and then bought some steaks on sale at the butcher's storefront for tomorrow's dinner. Here I am again, watching gladness beget gladness.

December 22, 2013

I come downstairs to find Paul, my brother-in-law Kim, and Mr. B watching the end of a WWII movie. "It's the Battle of the Bulge," Paul informs me sideways.

After the ending, Mr. B explains that there were American Germans who decided to fight with the Germans, who the Germans used as double agents. They wore American uniforms and drove American jeeps and they could easily pass into the American check points because they could speak with an American accent. Finally, after many casualties, the Americans wised up. They began asking everyone questions about sports heroes. When the Germans responded incorrectly, they would radio up to the next check point where the Jeeps would be taken over."

When Paul and Kim leave the house, I bring Mr. B a cup of hot tea and sit down with him in the other rocking chair. "Oh thank you, Miss." He warms his lap and hands with the mug. "It's 'dziękuję' in Polish, Miss." He pronounces this, 'Jen-koo-yeh'.

"'Jenkooyeh' is Thanks?" He nods.

"Where was the Battle of the Bulge?"

"Well, the Battle of the Bulge was where we incurred our highest number of casualties. Twenty thousand men out of six hundred thousand died there. Yup. You see, there was this rich multicultural area where coal and iron were mined to provide the Germans with needed resources. The Germans held all of the towns along the English Channel except we took Antwerp. From there, Americans and allies were bulging out into an egg shape, and holding one side of a densely forested area called the Ardennes region of Belgium, and the Germans were pushed back to a holding in Luxembourg on the other side." His brows furrow in concentration. He takes a sip of tea.

"It was the Western Front, late in the war, the fall of forty-four.

Nobody thought they could actually fight in the area, so they were just holding ground until one German officer convinced Hitler that he could command an offensive in one area, and he did that. It was officially called the Ardennes-Alsace campaign, and the Germans' goal was to reclaim the harbor in Antwerp. American successes in weeks earlier had driven the enemy from their Western positions along the Schnee Eifel, creating a salient of poorly- manned, isolated positions over-looking German positions and jutting deep into the German lines. But winter was miserable for our squadrons in the dugouts of the dangerous hills and forests surrounding us, and communications were poorly conveyed because the Germans were jamming our radio waves with phonograph records."

Mr. B leans back his head and rocks a bit in his chair to recollect details.

"The Canadians had helped Montgomery by clearing up the harbor at Antwerp for us to gain shipped-in supplies. But the Germans surprised us! They took advantage of some bad weather for their offensive into our weakest lines of defense, and it split the American and British forces in half."

"The 423rd Infantry instructed Troop B to make their own decision, but when the troopers couldn't find any road for escape, they destroyed their vehicles and broke up into small groups to attempt to reach St. Vith. Without further orders, most of the officers and men surrendered without a fight. By nightfall the next day, nine thousand Americans were rounded up west of the plateau."

"The Germans then circled St. Vith and took captive the 106th Division attempting to retreat from the town of Roth on December 19th, and the 14th Cavalry Group in the Schnee Eifel plateau and Losheim Gap. This was the largest American surrender of the war, the 9,000 troops who surrendered to the Germans. We don't like that publicized because it betrays months of poorly supplied pockets of resistance, lapses in command, and it represents a total of fifteen thousand of our troops captured in the war."

"If we were so badly beaten, then how did we win?" My woefully ignorant knowledge of any war is embarrassing.

"You know there are a lot of things about the Battle of the Bulge that are not portrayed well in the movies or the official accounts. It's not like the American government denies them, but they kinda hide them away."

"Hmmm. What things?" I'm enjoying the epic tragedy telling while I'm gently rocking the joints off of the old blue rocking chair.

"Oh, really, the only reason we won that battle was due to mistakes that turned out well for us, and because of the small tenacious groups of individuals who were being slaughtered, but who held their ground. Like in St. Vith. And because the Germans lost 100,000 troops."

"How were there 'good' mistakes?"

"After the 9,000 men surrendered, America was out of arms, so they put all the newbies at the front wid'out any protection, no guns, no ammo, just a show of force to try to ruse the Germans with a show of bravado. Most of 'em were slaughtered. But there was one or maybe two smart leaders who ordered their men to run around on the battlefield in a Jeep and collect all the weapons they could find to bring 'em back for their units. Ooo, they were *smart*! Another thing was that our allies bombed an incorrect target only to find out it was a petrol and armory supply."

"Yeah, good one!"

"You betcha. The German super heavy tanks couldn't move an inch if they couldn't get gas! Then, there was one battalion that was ordered to take a road leading into Bastogne, B-A-S-T-O-G-N-E," he spells it, "where all the German action planned to converge and take place. Well, the Americans couldn't make it to that road, so they held the road they were on, and it happened to be the southern road the Germans had decided to use for access to Bastogne."

"In another situation, one of our unit's tanks simply followed the Germans into Bastogne and held them there. The Germans kept fighting even without supplies and food, and when supplies were dropped, they used incorrect grid coordinates so the supplies landed on the American troops. And the Americans took another filling station over and offered the gas to all the locals including the French. The Germans were suffocating widout supplies. The French were still using them to sell on the black market after the war. The turning point of the thing was when the 101st Airborne Division reached Bastogne on December 19th. Then, allied forces began bombing German forces and they were able to parachute supplies into Bastogne and send medics in to help by flying them in on gliders. Finally, December 26th, General Patton's 4th Armored Division reached Bastogne to claim it."

Erich Maria Remarque wrote, "We are forlorn like children, and experienced like old men, we are crude and sorrowful and superficial—
I believe we are lost." — All Quiet on the Western Front

At last, I am educated on the greatest American battle of WWII.

December 23, 2013

Joe shuffles carefully through the crowded Christmas parking lot. We've muddled through traffic in slush and ice to the bank, to the gas station, and to the alterations boutique. "All this hullaballoo will be over soon, but I like to be prepared for the holidays. Just when you run outa gas or have an emergency, everything'll be closed." Then, he suddenly runs sideways into me and apologizes, "Oh, excuse me. I seem to be walking sideways more and more these days."

"Maybe you are turning into a crab?"

He's quick on the uptake. "Eh. No. I'm *already* a crab."

(Note to self: Being loveable in misery wins empathy from others.) "I'll make up a couple of those six bags of cranberries we bought for tonight's dinner, Mr. B. That should cheer you up."

"Oh, you are too good to me. Even though they were only a dollar per package last year. I'm not kidding when I say, you know how to make an ol' man happy!"

December 24, 2013

My sister's little dog has managed to drive our own big, strong Jester crazy. We separate them into different bedrooms for the duration of our family Christmas outing, Jester in ours and their pup in theirs.

Upon our return, we find that Jester has shredded the threshold of Joe's forty-three-year-old money carpet at our bedroom door trying to get a mouthful of the little dog across the hall. Now our bedroom carpet not only has dried paint splattered on it but it has also turned into a square yard of shredded wheat. We hiss at each other about whether to show Joe his new house ornament. *No way!*

My sister and her hubby's brief apology is filled with alarm, and they quickly retreat to the guest bedroom.

Paul studies the matter soberly then moves our bedside table, tugs our woven grass rug over, the one that we used to cover the paint spill, drags it another foot, and sets the bedside table back on top of it all. He looks at me with a quirky smirk that says, *Viola!* Again. *No problem.*

And I stare at him with big eyes.

December 25, 2013

Joe explains to all of us at Christmas brunch that he isn't really used to having a lot of people around, but it's fun to hear all the chatter. He says his church used to have fundraising picnics, where "the social organizer, Mr. Furcek, would sell hard liquor to raise money. No beer, that was too cheap. Only the hard stuff."

"Wasn't that during prohibition, Mr. B?" I query.

"Well yes, but that's how they hid it. No one suspected churches! In the winter, they would hold parties in the basement of the church. The men would stand up a collection of straight tree limbs to make a lean-to partition for the bar so that it would separate the men from the women and children. The women would talk and the children would play."

He compliments me on the rice and raisin pudding we are eating. One of his favorite treats is a box of raisins, so I take the risk that he will also like the pudding, and he is pleased. He explains that his father's employer, Mr. Kimbal, "employed two cooks and a maid for their three-story house. Never mind the attic or the basement. So anyway, when I would follow my fathea to work, the cooks would give me a small clear bowl of rice pudding as a treat. I can still feel the raised nubs around the rim of that small glass bowl. And it was good pudding too. I don't see how anybody would complain about yours."

"Mr. Byk? What kind of work did Mr. Kimbal do?" asks my niece.

"Oh, he was the manager of the largest cotton mill east of the Mississippi! I dunno. Maybe he owned it. Also, he was on the board of the Woonsocket Institute of Savings Bank. That was before the banks were insured. It wasn't until 1935 or '36 that Roosevelt enacted the FDIC wid a guarantee for the money people put into their banks."

"Didn't they do away with that guarantee?" interjects my brother-in-law.

"Well, yes and no. They've limited it now. It's not as good as it used to be since the banking collapse." Joe gazes out the window.

"It was a good thing to give the people a government-backed bank, though. I witnessed one bank that went belly up. It was terrible. There was only one door to the bank, a double door, and people were crowding and pushing up against it trying to get in. People got hurt and trampled. Hard-working people who had put their life savings into that bank had no recourse. It was just lost. All lost. What can I say?" He glances back at us and smiles a sad "whatcha gonna do" smile.

"Did your father have money in there?" We all want to know.

"Oh no. I don't think so. But my fathea taught all of us kids to keep our money as close to our chest as possible. I know my sistas, Wanda and Lucy, kept rolls of money in a chest under their beds and between the mattresses."

"Yup. Lucy was still doing that when we went to visit her for Wanda's funeral." I agree. "She got out some of it to make us pay the church tithe while she was stuck at home sick. She was terribly afraid that if she didn't pay them what they asked for, they wouldn't bury her beside her sister. It made me angry that a vulnerable old woman could be so afraid of what the church held over her head to make her pay tithe money."

"Well, that's how a lot of churches operate." Joe is indignant. "It's all business. They can be as immoral as those phone shysters who tell people stories to get into your bank accounts. But I believe she was a rich woman by that time. Nobody knew it. For certain, she always had enough. She and Wanda were very committed to the church regardless. They would make beautiful tablecloths and runners and banners for the holidays. I think they liked it. Lucy would want to be buried with the family. Yup. I'm certain that she was buried beside my parents and Wanda."

Joe opens his package and lifts up the soft sweat pants we purchased for him to keep his legs warm. "Aaaah! I'll wear these!" He exclaims tossing his head. "Two pair? What are they? Long

Johns?"

"Kinda, Chief." Paul explains. "People wear them to exercise in."

"These are super-duper. They'll keep my legs warm! I get so cold these days!" We are happy with his genuine enthusiasm.

His grandchildren hand over their paintings, including a handy night-light hand-painted, and a ball cap colored with "Greatest Grandpa" above the bill. Joe ducks into Pauly's gift of a gray and crimson "A-for-Alabama" sweatshirt pounding a vigorous fist in the air. Betty's choc-chip cookies are shared, one per person, judiciously. A papaya, decked with a bow, together with a tied sack of cinnamon breakfast twists are sniffed and hoarded away.

Joe smiles like a spoiled boy when he opens his new T-shirts, in several colors, new underwear, and new socks. "Guess this means I'm gonna stick around for another year!" He refuses to taste the taffy when he opens it, and instead hands it around to everyone else.

December 26, 2013

My sister's family has gone gallivanting out with other family members. I take Mr. B to get his hair shorn. The receptionist looks at his shaggy head and says, "It hasn't been a month, yet. You're early, but it looks like you need a cut anyway."

He turns to me and frowns. "What was that?"

I alleviate his confusion, "She says my good cooking is making your hair grow too long, too fast!"

He smirks and points his finger at me repeatedly. Then, "I got a shaggy looking hairdo, eh?"

"Like Einstein."

"Maybe I shouldn't waste my money then." He hesitates in all seriousness. "But I'd hate to put you out again, Miss B. I mean since we're already here."

After his haircut and back in the car, Joe remembers aloud, "The British irritated me. I was sent to Britain once to run stress analysis on a British commercial airplane the U.S. Navy intended to retrofit for military use. They repeatedly dismissed my requests for data so that I could perform my analysis! I was being paid to do that work because they were trying to get rid of the fleet by selling it to the U.S. Navy. It was a water boat plane, but see, when America came out with the DC-4, it made their plane look foolish, so they were attempting to reallocate it for another use."

"Reallocate it to America, you mean."

"Well, heck yeah! But I got written up for not being a team player or 'participating well with the group' because I kinda made a scene about it."

Joe was the only stress engineer on the project, and he couldn't get anyone to accommodate his requests for specs and data on the plane. They put him off, and in the end, they apologized, saying the data was lost. "Instead, their meetings went political, you know, on and on about possibilities, prices, and politics. So, I kinda did a nincompoop thing and burst into one of their meetings

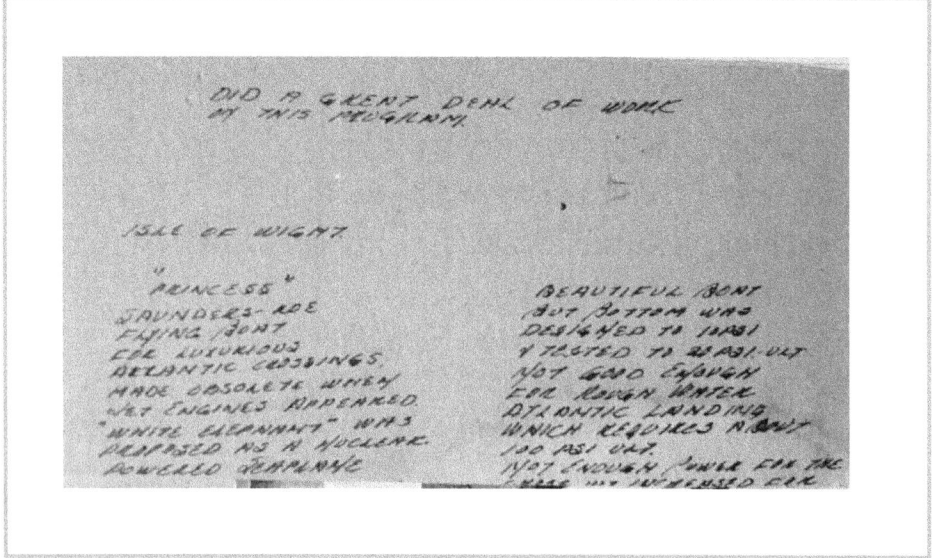

and told 'em all off."

"With what?"

"Well, the British believed in building half scale model planes for testing, but I explained to them that the United States would not accept models for testing. Models could not correctly represent proportional strength of the real materials or the conditions of takeoffs and landings in a factory!" He gets animated and his guttural voice hard, remembering his lecture to the group. He explained to them, "The U.S. military would build actual planes to test and see if they flew correctly. They'd bring them up to speed and keep them there for two minutes. If they passed, more planes were built."

"If they didn't pass, they were scrapped in whole, brand new. MacDonald once scrapped ten brand new airplanes. Skelly scrapped six new planes when they found at the last moment that the plane they built was too small for the engine they built for it!"

"Fru-fru meetings," he says. I see his irritation when he slices the air beside his head repeatedly with an agitated hand.

"What did any of that mean if the rivets failed and the panels fractured? The B-36 was an Army airplane that could handle a whole battalion inside its hull. I told 'em America already had a plane in hand without having to renovate this old commercial water boat, but the Navy wanted their own plane. See? It was a military competition."

Joe told the group he had just read an article on this B-36 plane when he overheard some Englishman saying the British plane he was to analyze was not only a thin-skinned commercial airplane the Navy intended to retrofit for military use, but its bottom hull was built to handle only 10PSI, that's the strength of pounds per square inch, and that it had failed at 20PSI. "Your hull stinks. It's no damn good! We can't use it." When he pronounced his judgment, and the whole deal immediately fell flat. "When it fell flat, they brought me home and put a letter in my file that kept me in my place for several years."

"Eck." I sigh. "Well, that is sometimes the cost of telling people the truth. Sorry, Mr. B. I'm proud of ya though. Does that count?"

December 27, 2013

It's laundry day. The old washer begins to knock obnoxiously as it spins. This has happened a couple of times. Ol' Mr. B believes I'm intentionally and methodically trying to break his washer. "You can't put so much in this one, Miss." He instructs once again. "Here, let me move the clothes around to balance it." I realize there will be no cleaning of the quilts or comforters in this washing machine. Dry cleaning expenses, here we come.

After sharing Joe's guest bath with us for a week, my sister, the designer, with her skilled hubby, take it upon themselves to replace our broken sink and florescent yellow cabinet top and flooring from 1969, with this granite sink kit and stone look-alike flooring. This kindness is a very special gift to me in particular. "Yeah, I was pretty sure you loved that retro French look," she explains with raised brows and a self-satisfied pinch to her mouth.

I'm so happy I'm dancing in circles in my new bathroom renovation. It doesn't even matter that the stone flooring is linoleum. I can't believe the difference a color combination makes.

Mr. B doesn't seem to notice our bathroom. *Just as well*, is my thought. It's safer to not have to explain an insult to him. Later, however, my brother-in-law lets me in on the fact that Joe, indeed, had asked him to compare the stone colored tiles to the quality of the yellow Armstrong rolled linoleum.

"Oh dear!" I mutter. "What did you tell him?"

My brother-in-law had heralded his honest opinion that the Armstrong flooring was his favorite flooring to see in a house, or to work with himself, because the sheets of inlaid linoleum were so sturdy and easy to clean. "I know it will never curl or break on the edges."

I sigh. But I'm still dancing at the transformation of my bathroom into the modern Colorado style.

Ann's husband also fixes some electrical stuff for Paul on his garage workbench and over his desk in the basement. Then he installs a motion detector light in the front of the house for Joe. Now Joe suddenly takes an interest in my quiet, no-nonsense brother-in-law. "He doesn't say much, but hey, that brother-in-law of yours is one talented guy. Very nice of him to help us. Very nice. What's his name? Isn't that a girl's name?"

Mr. B's standoffish manner of sitting grim-faced and solitary in the corner of his formal blue living room livens up considerably. He keeps complimenting Kim on how clever and helpful he is. At dinnertime, I find Joe happily patching the drywall in the garage where Kim fixed the electrical wiring behind the wall.

I may still wonder why I can't get everything I want in life, but it is pretty clear to me that there's a significant reason for living in

Joe's home with him. I'm the wife of a hero! And, Mister B rocks on. I'm good with that.

December 31, 2013
My book club celebrates the holidays with a "white elephant" book swap, a long, demonstrative tradition of female railing and competition. This includes manipulation, theft and downright unladylike sitting on a book so that it cannot be stolen without a struggle and a toppling over, sometimes culminating in tears and ranting wails. We have earned the right to act out our senility this way since our particular book club has been meeting in this obnoxious cycle for 28 years now. The tears, being big girls' tears, are mostly heated laughter. Mostly.

Tonight, when the struggle is over, I've landed upright on two travel and humor books about renovating a castle in Italy's wine country, and renovating an old house in France's Provincial wine country. Oh yes. *Best* "white elephant" party ever!

Ш 𝒟 ᏩᎤ

"Those who do not know how to weep with their whole heart don't know how to laugh either"
— Golda Meir

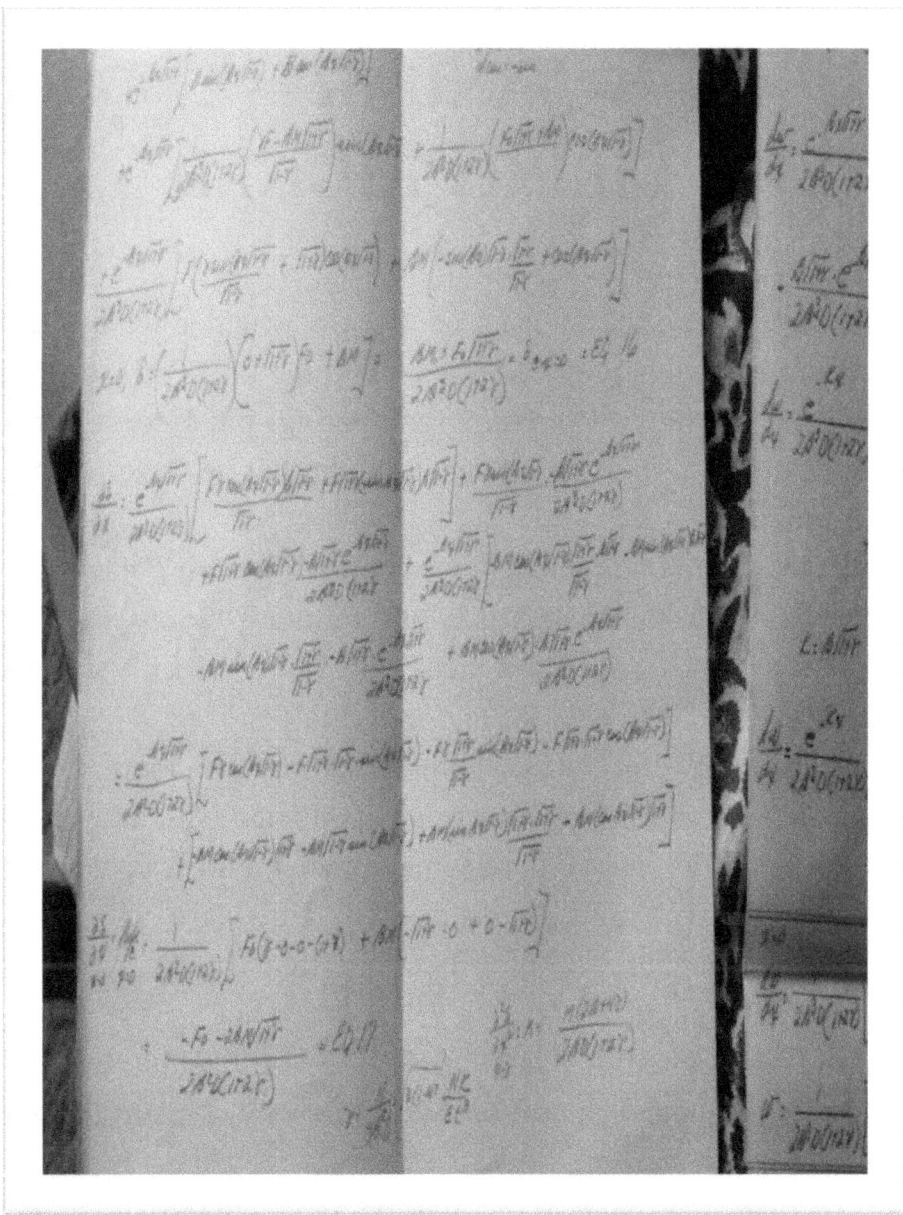

January~ Jerry Rigged

January 1, 2014

The ol' man pointedly asks us tonight whether we are trying to make him an Italian or a Mexican with the kinds of foods we have been serving him. "I'm eating and eating, but I don't know what I'm eating." I tell him it's Greek tonight, but he doesn't have to eat my cooking.

"What? *Me* cook when I get spoiled like this?" he backtracks. "No way!" Normally he winks and mouths, "*Thank you*," ever so quietly to me alone after a meal, so I know he isn't suffering too badly.

Apparently to distract himself from the food tonight, he embellishes on a favorite memory of Mexico. "Maudie and I were eating avocado soup at a very nice place on a bluff. We were at a window overlooking a jungle, and oh, there were colorful macaws or parrots maybe, swooping over the treetops. So multi-colored! Um! What a place that was!"

Instinct ignited, my jaw drops. "Let's go! This plain ol' flank steak, beans, and rice are too boring for any of us to hang around here."

He wags his finger at me over the table. "Pauly, ya gotta watch this one!"

"Oh, don't I know it, Chief, but there are no vacations in the works." I catch his own little sigh. "You remember the time we saw those yellow birds, small birds, flitting through the arches of the Palmetto Restaurant?"

"Oh, yeah. They had beautiful little yellow birds that would eat the crumbs on the ground, and from the leftovers of the plates the waiters had collected from the patrons. That day, the sky was as blue as blue can be."

"Really." I retort. I've always been more about lingering together in an atmosphere of creative reflection than a gourmet meal itself. "We *should* get a set of flying yellow birds or parrots before tomorrow night's dinner is served. I can tell we'll all be happier."

January 2, 2014

I notice Joe has squirted mustard on his peeled egg. He's been doing this lately saying it's a habit from his youth. Closing my eyes against the rising shudder, "Will you please pass the salt, Mr. B?"

Now into January, family visitors have gone and left behind their gifts of the season. I have fallen back into the habit of fixing Mr. B his favorite lean breakfast every morning: a boiled egg, a banana, his special soft roll with a crusty crust, a jar of marmalade under his nose to eat directly from, and a cup as big as a bowl of steaming Ovaltine. "Sól… Sól i pieprz, Miss."

"Okay, sól? *Por favor*?"

"Oh, you!"

This morning, he and I are talking about the width and breadth of the universe, the light years in the solar system, and he is trying to explain to me some mathematics that blow my mind. I say to him, "The psalm writer, King David, wrote this beautiful passage … 'When I consider the heavens, the works of your hands, the moon and the stars, what is man that you are mindful of him or the son of man that you visit him?'" Then, I sing him the psalm.

Psalm 8

When I consider your heavens, the works of your fingers,
the moon and the stars you have placed in their settings to swing there,
what are our minds? What are our souls that you care?--
Why should your kindness dispense here?
     (Psalm-Hymns, verse 2)

"It says all that? Well, I guess you would know. Thank you for the concert, Lynn.. Gee whiz! I neveh know what to expect."

Laughing about this exchange with Paul later, he says to me, "Dad was never funny, never as happy as he is with you, honey."

"Really?"

"Really. My dad has no friends to speak of for a reason, you know. It was my mother who had friends. He likes you. It's like he's getting another chance at happiness. I sometimes think he's getting an all new third life."

"Which is?"

"His childhood, which he seems to have enjoyed because his family spoiled him, His life with mom, which was stressful for a lot of reasons, even though he thought he'd married "up", and now, this happy third season, where it's all come together for him, and he's letting loose his humor and all the stuff he's never been able to tell anyone.else…and I am so proud of you. I really do thank you."

January 3, 2014

It's the doghouse days of frigid January. Ding-dong humor rings in offbeat strokes. Restless people try to reassess their lives and lifestyles, and there's that coming down from all the heights of glitter and lights... down, down to the basement storage.

"Mr. B?" I hand off to him a small slab of barbecued ribs, a favorite dinner of his. He licks his lips and grins. "You look an awful lot like Jester right now." Jester, hearing his name, lifts his head from the carpet, looking from one to the other expectantly.

"He can *wait* for the bones," Joe says with emphasis. "It's my birthday!"

"Tomorrow is your big day, Chief!" This Paul mentions looking over his own larger slab of ruminating pork. "We made your favorites for dinner and we have a surprise for you tomorrow. That's why I brought up your old belt from the University of Alabama to wear."

"Oh yeah? Look at that! It's been awhile!" He turns it over and polishes it with his napkin. "It's gonna snow tomorrow. This is too much already!" He's looking very seriously at his knife and fork stuck into his four-rib dinner. "Too much," he mutters.

"Joe, do you realize how many times you could have lost your life?" I ask. "You were fortunate, especially because you were exempted from the war, but even training in the heat and muck in Alabama's ROTC; swimming in snake-infested ponds..."

"No. Gar-infested ponds!" Joe corrects me. "Those gar were like sharks! They were huge, but they'd get stuck in pools after the Black Warrior River flooded, and then the pools would evaporate."

"Well, you evaded the Alabama sharks then, and the Woonsocket heat!"

"Oh, we thought we had it bad with the temperatures in Woonsocket. I could almost see the humidity hanging in the air there, because you know, Rhode Island is a long state with all those islands of the coast on the east side. But, when I spent my first summer in Tuscaloosa, I thought I would suffocate. I just couldn't breathe in that humidity!" Mr. B seems alarmed even now to remember it.

"Okay, and all the illnesses that don't seem to harm you?"

"In the ROTC, they would sometimes put the guys in jumpsuits with helmets and stick them inside cabins for training exercises, and it was torture, actual *torture* in that heat." The sadness creeps into Joe's tone now.

"You know about land-grant colleges? Under the Morrill Act, Alabama started up one of the first land- grant colleges, which is how poor students like me got offered an education." He shrugs. "My high school counselor suggested it because I needed to make up for my math deficiency. If I wanted to design aircraft that would defy gravity, I had to defy my own gravity! It meant that I could get the education I wanted, but in return, I owed them my time in military service, so that's why I was in the ROTC, sweatin' it out in the thick, wet Alabama woods."

"Your long life is amazing! I thank the Sustainer for lending you to us."

Paul pipes in. "Yeah, Dad. Remember all the times you told us, 'When I kick the bucket, you should know how this tax situation works,' or 'When I kick the bucket, these things in the house will already be divided so there won't be any bickering,' or 'When I kick the bucket, you'll want to know this…'"—we're all chuckling now—"but here you are, turning 98, and healthy as an ox."

"Okay, okay, but ox is our family's namesake. We all live a long time. Eddy was drafted, you know, but when he got his physical, they said he had flat feet. We were all so relieved because they had conscripted him to be a flame thrower and the life expectancy of flame throwers was," he holds up two fingers, "two minutes." Mr. B nods his head once to confirm the ridiculousness of a life in that occupation. "Yeah. He got an F-4 notice; that meant Eddy had flunked out of his military death sentence.

Our friends were mostly cannon fodder. That's what we would say. My brother's friend, also named Eddy, Eddy Schwartz, entered the army in the same unit as his older brother. They specifically asked not to be separated. They wanted to look out for each other, I guess. Anyway, his brother was hiding behind a tank because their tank and the German tank were volleying cannon fire at each other. He looked up to see what was happening to the other side when another bomb exploded and the shrapnel got him. Then, Schwartz was also hit with shrapnel in his chest. They thought he was a goner, so they left him there and took the other wounded. But then someone cleared out a place on another ship and they got him on it. He survived!" Joe pulls off a scaly barnacle from the side of his face, wincing.

"Wow!"

"Yeah, but when he came home with his mended ribs and that horrible scar over his heart, the newspaper did everything they could to keep him from getting his old job back. Imagine that! A wounded vet and they treated him like that. But Schwartz survived the lawsuit, won it, and as far as I know, he had a decent life in Woonsocket."

I am trying to emphasize that God has preserved him, and ask him to consider the purpose of this blessing, but I can't articulate these thoughts well. "Have you ever considered why you've had such a long life, Mr. B?"

Joe rubs the side of his face with a napkin and looks at the dot of blood as he puts it on the table next to his placemat. "Well, when I was in college, I dated a girl who was interested in becoming a fortune teller. She took one look at my hand and said I had a long lifeline."

January 4, 2014

We plan to forge through the snowdrifts in our car tonight for Joe's 98th birthday celebration. Can't wait. Right after we watch *Zorro*, that is. Joe is gleefully laughing at the swashbuckler featuring handsome screen actors Antonio Banderas and Catherine Zeta-Jones and my favorite actor, Anthony Hopkins.

After it finishes, I hand him the present I've been saving. It's a light blue and white wool sweater, size large. Mr. B is so delighted he immediately dresses in it for dinner.

"How does it look, fine Sir? Does it meet your expectations?"

He mimics a lady model with his hip out and turns in slow circles with his hand in the air to show it off. I notice he has the cuffs turned up, and the bottom of the sweater turned up too around his middle, then ask, "Is it too big?"

"Oh no, Miss! It's just right. Wool shrinks, and I like 'em big." He growls again, "Why'r you doing this for me? Birthdays were nothin' when I was a kid."

"Oh, Mr. B! When you get to be 98, you deserve to be celebrated! You sure do look spiffy tonight."

"SPIFFY!" Joe stomps in place and jams the air with his fist. "I thought you might say, 'kissable!'"

I plant a red-lipped smooch on his cheek.

Paul alerts his father to the red imprint and leans over to get a tissue. Joe swats his son's hand. "Leave it."

Joe hasn't been back to a certain French restaurant since Maudie passed. He is delighted to see the place again. Oma, the cook, comes out to greet him with a hug. They catch up for quite some time. Then, the feast begins. She serves us three huge scoops of pâté when Joe orders the appetizer. She heaps up the potatoes and serves us all double portions of meat. The dining room is quiet tonight because of the blizzard outside. Our server says many of the reservations were canceled.

Eventually, the place begins to receive visitors, and Joe expresses his relief that they aren't losing business.

Oma brings us the mousse for dessert herself, and though Joe doesn't usually eat chocolate so late in the evening, he licks it off his spoon down to the bottom.

All the way home, Mr. B thanks us and relives his memories of many happy family outings in that establishment. "You kids spoil me. Thank you very much."

"Happy birthday, Joe! Happy birthday, Dad! Happy Birthday, Mr. B!"

"Oh, you kids did too much," he says shyly with a big grin. "Too much!"

January 5, 2014

"Thanks for saving my life again." Mister B shouts.

"What?"

Joe shakes out the newspaper and sets it beside his breakfast plate. "Yeah, you went out to pick up the newspaper for me. Venturing out on that sheet of ice!

"I'll tell ya, at the beginning of the war the British were *hot* to get some fighter airplanes that could compete with the Germans' swifter machines, so they conscripted Lockheed to make them. A company called North American actually designed the P-51s, a very lightweight fighter, but they went outta business, so it was Lockheed that made the planes.

The engine wouldn't fit in the plane as it was designed, so one day a guy got the idea to try a Merlin engine, and the engine fit the plane so well, and it proved to be faster than the German planes, too! Everyone was happy with that. Lockheed started production for American military then.

We put a tank underneath the pilot and one at his back, and then also a third tank somewhere, so they had longevity. It was war, so pilots didn't expect to make it, but if they got shot in those planes, they were goners. We put six M2 Browning .50 caliber machine guns on the wings, six, believe it or not! The bombers only had ten caliber guns, and they were too heavy to outmaneuver the Germans and Japanese.

"This time last year, there was a big write-up, an obituary for Colonel Fitzroy 'Buck' Newsum." He pauses. "Ever heard of him? No? Well, there was a Negro squadron in Tuskegee, Alabama, trained on the new Mustang P-51s. Bomber pilots began to request the P-51s to escort them into battles because the P-51s were faster than the Japs. The Tuskegee Airmen did so well that they were requested again and again. We lost 63 of these pilots in the war, but we owed them for gaining us the advantage. One of these hot shot pilots made it back to Colorado and he became a Colonel after the fact. Colonel Fitzroy 'Buck' Newsum. Lockheed Martin set him up as the public relations guy in Colorado. He was in all the papers. He died the day after my birthday last year."

January 6, 2014

The washer spins off into the wall, pounding repeatedly because I've stuffed it with our bedroom quilt. "You can't do that, Miss!" exclaims Mr. B, rushing to my side in the laundry room. I swear we are going to have to buy a new washer and dryer set soon. He helps me drag it dripping to the back porch, and we twist the dirty water out of it together. Then he suggests gently, "Maudie knew a good bulk cleaner in town. The washing machine does fine for small loads. So, it would be cheaper to get these big blankets cleaned at a bulk cleaner, Miss." I remember my mother used a bulk cleaner too. But there are very few left.

"Thank you, Mr. B," I apologize. "I should have asked first."

"Oh, that's okay. Let me help you pin it up onto this clothesline here. It'll be dry in a day." I thank him again and sigh.

Colorado winters are so dry that the water drains out of my

quilt pinned up on Joe's clothesline outside and freezes on the concrete patio, but the quilt is indeed dry in a day.

January 7 2014

I am thankful for good humor today when I have to accompany Mr. B into the doctor's office to get not only his barnacles frozen, but also to remove a nuisance of a nose cancer in the ala of his nose.

The assistant greets us, ignores that Mr. B is wearing layers of pants and sweaters, weighs him, then compliments him for gaining five pounds. Looking into his baby blues, she suggests that since he will be getting a nose job done today, he maybe should have consulted a plastic surgeon.

As Dr. Cooper makes Joe comfortable in a reclining position on her clinic table, she gives Joe some numbing medicine with several pricks of a needle. I don't even realize how tense I am until I see Mr. B's hand flinch and clench into a fist. I suddenly feel like throwing up.

He quickly relaxes. He says he's grown comfortable with the realization that he'll be gaining a new nostril when the good doctor is done. She defends herself saying she's trying not to let that happen, that her aim is to dig out the surface skin only for a cancer cell biopsy, then cauterize the base of the cell. I offer him a big diamond earring if she accidently pokes through.

"If that happens, you'll fit right in with the teenagers," Dr. Cooper agrees. She moves efficiently while at the same time chatting about playing piano for her church last weekend. She also thanks Joe for his RX pharmacy chocolate contribution, which he brought as a gift for her today.

After she is finished, Mr. B thanks her for her care and concern. She laughs and replies, "Oh sure, if you call cutting, gouging, freezing, and burning someone care and concern!" Then she pats him on his back and offers to help him down from the medical table.

"By the way:" Mr. B turns, "Should I be ready for a photo session? Since I've joined the lives of the rich and famous, with a nose job, that is."

January 8, 2014
Paul eyes his father's spotted and burnt face with grim concern today.

"Aw, it's nothing. It really doesn't hurt at all, Pauly. It only hurts you to look at it."

Paul shakes his head and informs me that his father wouldn't complain if a shark was hanging off his arm!

January 9, 2014
Tonight after dinner, Mr. B expresses concern about a loved one who has a problem that caused an extended hospital stay for some unusual tests. He and Paul talk it over, and they write out a check to help with the unusual medical bill. It's a gift, not a loan. Both Joe and Maudie were generous to family members over the years. Joe pats Paul's hand with approval and gets teary-eyed remembering his baby's sweet personality. "Pauly, at six months old, used to giggle when we raised the shade in his bedroom. He was our drooler, and he would laugh at anything. He's always had a good personality."

"Yes! Mr. B, through these horrid past few years, your son has always had the happy knack of making people like him! Pauly's congeniality can be infuriating when I'm the one people love to hate. But, my hubster's love also makes me laugh when I've built up a wall or when I get too serious. He makes me love him even when I'm really mad at him, so what can I say? It's a special gift."

I, too, have benefited from the Byk's goodwill since I married their son. Perhaps they were able to help us because they had purchased their own home for cash when they moved to Colorado. Not having a pesky mortgage payment freed them up to help with emergencies and medical needs. They wanted us to enjoy that same freedom. Since then, Mr. and Mrs. Byk would give us large sums for birthdays and Christmas, specifically directed toward paying down our mortgage. Mr. B was proud of how cleverly he gave us just the amount that the IRS allowed without having to pay a penalty. "It's all in the family anyway. Your benefit is our benefit," he'd croon nonchalantly. Within the ten years of living in our first home, we were able to pay it off that way. Actually, we were unprepared for how quickly our mortgage dissolved.

Someone coming from a background with a sliding scale perspective of rewards based on performance would view Mr. B's type of thinking as foreign. A sliding scale is always biased, ruling some types of people out even though they may be family. If you belong to Joseph Byk, though, he rewards you without critical reservation, without skepticism. He may offer an occasional humorous apology for "meddling". To him family is everything. This is just the way it is. He believes what goes around comes around. I consider what his philosophy means to a house rich, but poor in love, family. In the inner city church we are attending, people have lifelong hang-ups and addictions they battle even after turning to Jesus and church members for help gaining a whole new life. There, grace is always extended, even when someone is removed for returning to a disturbed lifestyle, they can return for help almost immediately. The building isn't much to shout about though.

Lately, when my passenger and I have driven by other developments in the area, gated communities or suburbs on a lake, Joe mentions, "We almost bought here, but we had only saved up so much. We didn't want to overspend. Sometimes, I wonder if I made the right decision, but Maudie liked the floor plan at our place. If she liked it, eh, I was happy."

Mr. B looks at me. "The way I see it, we're family and that means we plan to help each other. When one needs it, and I have the means to help, I do. We've been able to because we bought a little further down the block."

January 10, 2014

Mister B carefully crunches his body into the passenger seat beside me. "I hope I'm not too much of a pest. I just needed these tax forms."

"You are the *opposite* of a pest, Mr. B." I pat his arm.
"You say," He huffs, "I'm what? The Officer of the Pests?"

"No, no!" (giggling) "I said, 'you are the OPPOSITE OF A PEST.'"

"Oh." He uses his rolled up 2015 tax booklet in his hand as a baton to swat me. "I thought you'd given me a promotion."

January 11, 2014

Joe hasn't been eating much lunch for a few years now. He has told me that he used to eat crackers with cheese inside them for lunch when he was an engineer. Sometimes he'd go out with a friend to the bar afterwards to unwind. Then he stopped drinking beer and smoking because Maudie threatened him with divorce. He didn't tell me that. That part came from a secret Paul told me years ago. The man's self-control amazes me.

After breakfast the chief does dog patrol in the sloppy, snowy backyard, then comes in to work a crossword puzzle, and if we have nowhere to drive to, he sits in his living room tucked inside of his new sweater over his T-shirt, with his fleece over the top of both, hands stuffed into the pockets. He refuses to eat anything.

"Too much, too much," he growls, putting his nose in the air. "*Za dużo.*"

After all the food we consumed at Christmas time with my relatives, I'm grateful to join into Joe's routine. Dinner continues to be whatever I make of it. Perhaps I can get healthier eating closer to Joe's style. I haven't been going to lunch with friends much because we live so far away now, and there isn't the entire restaurant menu to entice me or the smells of someone else's cooking to defeat my resolve. I find that I am not missing the absence of lunch most days. Since breakfast usually becomes an extended conversation, Joe and I have bonded like good friends.

This morning, he tells me that when he started a newspaper route for the *Woonsocket Call*, he would rise before anyone else in the house so he had to learn to make his own breakfast.

"What did you make for yourself?" I want to know.

Happy to reminisce, he wobbles his head between his shoulders. "I made mostly scrambled eggs. I would start the fire in the stove, and oh, my mothea loved me for doing that. Then, I'd crack about six eggs into a cast iron skillet and mix 'em up. My! They were tasty. I couldn't begin to eat that much today." Joe leaves off mentally comparing the differences in his appetite over the years.

"Paul can eat about twelve of 'em if he's camping. That makes him super hungry."

Joe smiles. "My mothea would have loved to cook for him. He can eat!"

Every morning, I am learning about Joe's childhood, his schooling, siblings, his observations on people who opened the door to him on his paper route.

There was one house he's described a couple of times. "I've never seen such a beautiful house as that teacher and her mothea had. It was clean, very clean, and it didn't have very many things on the wall that I can remember, but the bones of the house were beautiful. It shined, I tell ya. I loved standing in that foyer. I'll never forget it."

"One teacher was a gal who walked to the side of the classroom and taught from there, standing up. But if she turned her face, you could see she was covering something up with powder make-up. One day when I was delivering papers, I saw her walking with a nice looking well-dressed man. They had just married and were buying a house on that street. I was happy for them. She was a very nice person. But I think that thing on her face musta been cancer or something because she didn't live there very long. I think she died within the year."

Mr. B explains to me that only one teacher seemed to take any interest in him throughout school. He was "opposed" to the others. "There were three sistas who taught at our school. They all sat down to teach. I'd argue my point wid one of 'em, and she had it in for me. No. I didn't care to go to school, and I didn't like what the teachers had to say or how they treated most of us. So, I didn't apply myself, and I skipped out of school just to deliver papers, or for whatever reason I could."

"Sometimes, I'd go mow the Kimbals' lawn in the afternoons just so my fathea wouldn't hafta do it. They didn't like mowing on Saturday mornings because people liked to sleep in, so I'd do it after school. I remember the cook there would treat me to rice and raisin pudding. Nothing objectionable about that!"

In his high school, there were three different courses of study, and the teachers would choose for the students depending upon their test performance and apparent aptitudes. Joe was placed into the classical education vein (grammar, logic, rhetoric). Others were placed into practical trade and business education and a third vein was science and mathematics.

When he finished high school, he immediately discovered how deficient he was in mathematics. This was because one of the guys was bantering with his math teacher about college entry exams and discussing equations that were completely above Joe's head. So, he enrolled himself in summer school and also paid for tutoring in mathematics through his first year of college at Alabama Polytechnic Institute, Auburn University. "I studied like mad because by then, I knew I wanted to be an engineer, and I was embarrassed about what I lacked."

I'm learning slowly about Mr. B's politics, his first job, and memories of his parents. But mostly, I'm learning about his character. He's certainly not one to make excuses for himself.

January 12, 2014

Mr. B accompanies me big box store, Costco, for a grocery expedition. He grabs ahold of the cart to ready himself for the long tour, and we dive in. His eyes wander through the aisles of giant packages, wandering much more than his feet and cart, and he tells me he's glad I brought a list. Finally, he pronounces, "Too much! Too much! Za dużo!"

He and I pile up the shopping cart and then argue who's going to pay for it. I whip out my Costco card and slide it through the machine. He concedes when I hand over a wad of cash. "You tricked me, Miss." He wags his head sputtering. On to me now, he thrusts dollar bills into my purse, "to buy gas for your car." He says. "It's all in the family, anyway, Sweet Pea."

Mr. B has never possessed a credit card. That's the shock of it. I've wondered, how did he ever get along in life? Then, when we'd go on family vacations, he would show me by simply paying in cash and giving the registration clerk an extra hundred-dollar bill for incidentals. He plans and then he pays. He saves and then he pays for more. If he doesn't have it, he doesn't buy it. He doesn't need the best or the newest gadgets out there.

For dinner I make grilled chicken with yams and asparagus and an apple pie for dessert. And warm rolls. After Paul prays over the meal, Mr. B looks up and says, "What's all this mmm, mmming about?"

"I'm so happy, Dad!" my husband announces with delight. "I have a life and a wife. And now I have you, too."

"Well, okay then." He winces. "But don't spread it on so thick."

January 13, 2014

Mr. B's Einstein hair mop is being cut, or mowed as the case may be, so he's sitting in the barber chair, which reminds me of a story about my own great-grandpa. Especially because of Mr. B's hearing loss. So, when he pays the bill, I tell him, "You are always asking me for stories of my own. Well, I remembered a good one while you were sitting in the barber chair. Do you wanna hear it?"

"Oh course I do!"

"Okay, well, my mother's grandpa was something of a nincompoop."

"He was? I haven't heard that word for a long, long time."

"Yes, apparently he was. When he was old, he became hard of hearing like you. He was a barber, and his best friend would like to sit and chat with him all day long in the barber's shop. When they both got going, they'd be talking along without really hearing each other. One would be talking about his wife's ailments, and the other would answer about Southern politics. Neither would realize they were carrying on one-sided conversations."

Joe chuckles.

"One day when he was a younger man, my great-grandfather was listening to another guy from out of town getting his beard trimmed. The guy complained that he badly needed some work. My grandfather had an ax to grind against a landowner down the street, and he put one and one together. The landowner's crop wasn't ready for harvest, but my granddad got it into his head how to give this out-of-towner some work. He gave the guy directions to the landowner's field, claiming it was his own. He said he'd been looking for someone to clear it in order to plant another crop. Could the bearded fellow handle that job? Why, sure he could! He was happy to do it. Granddad promised to pay him the next day, after he saw to it."

"Oh! That was mean!" Mr. B's astonishment matches my own.

"Yep. That was the same great-grandpa who was also the town drunk. His wife was a saint though. She was the town's midwife and the mortician who would wash the bodies, and she also kept and raised several of the town's orphans, but she couldn't seem to keep her husband out of trouble."

Mr. B admits, "He was a handful! I can see why."

"One day, because his wife snuck his wages from his pocket and gave them to their eldest daughter for safe keeping, he chased the girl up a hill and then up a tree. He was determined to drink the money away. He ran after her and grabbed back his wages."

"He was a rascal."

"Huh, *yeah*. When the town built a new brick jail, the sheriff put him in it straightaway, first guest. But his friends dynamited the jail wall to get him out. He ran home and hid under the bed. When the sheriff came calling, hat in hand, he had to notify my great-grandmother: "I'm so sorry to inform you that your husband has somehow been blown up in my keep!" She acted all innocent, even wept for the loss of her spouse of fifty years! Meanwhile, the louse was hiding under their bed! I guess she thought he was good for something. I don't know."

January 15, 2014

My companion reminisces about Christmas describing memories of home, eating a large flat square of my family's Poor Man's Bread recipe with raisins and walnuts. "My fathea used to make a huge pan of gingerbread, oh, that was good!" He motions with his arms spread, the size of a large pizza pan, outdoing the size of my Poor Man's Bread pan. "My mothea's pet name for me was Jousou, (Use-yoo)." With that name, she'd call him in after school to have a slice of warm homemade bread dipped on her pile of sugar that she kept in a wooden bucket in her closet. "We should still have that bucket laying around somewhere. It has a handle." Then, he says he's used to stale pastries because when his sister was working, "she would bring home day old pastries from the bakery. The icing was a little hard."

"This isn't stale, Joe, this is fresh. Homemade!" I shout a little, just a little perturbed.

"I don't know if she did it because she had a sweet tooth, which she did, or if it was to save my mothea the trouble. Lucy started bringing home bakery bread so that mothea didn't have to make it anymore."

"I'm kind of in awe of your mother, Mr. B."

"You're what?"

"In awe of her. I admire what you've told me about her."

"Oh, she would'a liked you, too, Sweet Pea."

"You think?"

"Of course! I like you, so she would'a liked you. I was kinda her pet."

I change the subject. "Mr. B, did you remember your medication?"

"Why no! I guess I musta forgot! Good thing you're around,

Miss."

January 16, 2014

"Mr. B, what was the significance of the Gemini Space Shuttle? It didn't land on the moon, did it?"

"Oh no, Ma'am. Not the Gemini. But we had to figure out *how* to land on the moon and how to connect to a space station first. That was the purpose of the Gemini, precisely. Oh, there was high pressure to get it all done before anyone else. And I guess they had to know for a fact that orbiting the moon was possible. It's hard to remember in hindsight."

"So, what was your contribution to the Gemini? Why did they give you a tie tack?"

"Well, Sweet Pea, they never really told us what we were working on at the time. It was only because they gave us the tie tacks that anything was ever confirmed." He pauses. "I remember working on the plumbing, which had to be very lightweight, and I also did some heat calculations for inside the chamber, and I worked the heat calculations for a human being to survive inside there, but I didn't know that my work was being used for a space shuttle at the time. They gave us two chambers that were turned over to our unit just because there was a deadline, not because the team's work prior to ours was actually finished. Because time was up, they just moved it along to us as though they had completed their job. I was mad about that because there were so many discrepancies between the prints and the actual chamber sitting before us, and nobody told us what was missing or where the problems lay, so we had to recalculate everything. One chamber just had too many problems and it was sent to the boneyard in Philly."

"Yes, you've told me about that."

"I did? Hey, it was only about 20 inches of the rocket

midsection's width I was working on when I knew it was a rocket," he spreads his hands apart vertically, about 20 inches, to show me, "Not much."

"Calculations for the conical outer wall of the rocket had to be elongated in the final determinations, not exactly a round sphere. At the top, it was 20 inches, which was a different size to where it attached at the bottom. Then, there were the L-brackets to connect the capsule chamber to the spherical body. They were using the wrong material, so the capsule kept coming off. I suggested they use steel, which flexes in the heat and force of air dynamics. Oh, and you know, I also determined there weren't enough L-brackets. They didn't like that, but I added them anyway and turned the challenge onto *them* to prove me wrong. In the end, they kept them, even though they added to the weight."

January 17, 2014

Augh!!! Note to self: Never read a Provencal book about gardens, truffles, breads, vinegar tasting, olive oil and wine when on a 1,200 calorie diet. Never.

January 18, 2014

Joe is watching me text into my phone by dictating a message to a book lover about the French memoir I've been reading. He shakes his head. "I hope that little blonde-headed girl is getting computer lessons in school." In the moment, he's forgotten his great-granddaughter's name. I pass over this point.

"Why do you say that?"

"Well, because. Without computer training in this modern world, she'll be lost!" Is he reflecting on his own inability to access information via the Internet? "I've heard kids don't wanna go to any of the colleges anymore because they can get all their information from computers! And, anyway, Pauly told me that his friend who is going to the University of Denver hasta pay $62,000 per year! Per year!" His flocculent voice sprays with a certain acid in his words. "It cost me $75 for outa state tuition, and the whole degree cost me $3,500, including *travel*. Maudie graduated from the Teacher's College at Columbia University, and it didn't cost her much more than me. Did Maudie and I ever show you our little ledger books? We did? Both of us kept one. We'd write every nickel we'd spend in them. If I woulda claimed to be a resident, college woulda cost even less. I guess I've always been cheap." He muses. "You realize those black boxes and trick watches they sell nowadays are the Dick Tracy comics of my childhood come to life? Dick Tracy used to have a space-age watch he'd talk into. Now, it's become real stuff!"

January 19, 2014

At breakfast, Joe asks a lot of questions. He is trying to get down to the bottom of our knotty lawsuit from last year. I tell him it taught us that local government can negate an individual's constitutional rights not for reasons of right or wrong, but simply because the wall of police power and deep pockets give them the advantage. "They" incorporated is bigger than us *un*incorporated. This idealist has learned a hard lesson.

"What actually happened, Miss?"

I say I tried this, but that happened, so I tried that, but the other thing happened, and eventually after six years of this disillusionment with the system, I just hung it up, dismissed our claims, and decided to be happy with a huge education of how things *don't* work, and how the Constitution really isn't accessible for private individuals. I hear the bitter edge creeping in. It's been a while since I've had to talk about it to anyone.

Moving my hands as if to block out the memory, I tell him, "Anyhow our heavenly father has underwritten and provided for us, all the way, despite going through all that hell. We're so happy to be living with you now, Mr. B. We feel like we came out of that fire unscathed."

He says, "There are those who do not accept reality, and those are the ones who go mad. They are too rigid, so they can't adjust. But there are those who shrug their shoulders and say, 'What are ya gonna do?' They just keep living life on the terms handed to them. It's healthier. Yup. Ya gotta be a little bit flexible." Joe breaks into song, "Getting to know you, getting to know all about you…" He breaks off. "I can't remember the rest."

Since I've never heard Mr. B sing, we both get a bit ticklish about it. I was so afraid of living as a bitter old woman, but these last few months have been an Oasis, with a capital "O" in my life. Paul and I both feel we are being rejuvenated.

January 20, 2014

Joe breaks into the chocolate-glazed cream puff sitting on his breakfast plate. "I'd scold you, but only nicely for this treat, Mrs. B." He's grinning sloppily with the cream covering his lips.

One of my book club friends allowed me to take the extra cream puff home for Joe last night. So I wrapped it carefully and stuffed it into the fridge to save it for this morning. I have such fond memories of Maudie's warm cream puffs at birthdays, and then Mr. B got into the act, surprising all of us.

"Maudie taught me how to make these, you know." "I know, that's why I knew you'd like a little treat like this." "Is this an éclair?"

"No, it's a cream puff, but they are pretty similar, only the cream puff is more decadent, made with more eggs, I think."

"I'd forgotten." He swallows another bite as my mouth waters. "Wow! Time flies."

"Oh, it wasn't so long ago. If you ever want to try to make them with me, I'm on board." This, I offer in my wildest dreams. But I'm grateful for those delectable memories. Of all Maudie's exotic offerings, like freshly baked prune cake and cherry chocolate muffins, her cream puffs left me speechless. Having a mother-in-law who was a home economics teacher certainly had benefits.

Suddenly Joe sizes up the pastry ball. "These are tricky to make. You wouldn't believe it. It's all in the timing. It has to be right on. And besides the eggs, you wouldn't believe how much butter goes into making these!"

I don't quiz him on this disparity of woofing down a delightful breakfast of pastry, for a guy who won't eat butter. Maybe pastries are like soups, their own food group?

January 21, 2014

Paul and I walk into the empty house and stand in the hallway looking at each other feeling surreal. "We've never been in this house without Dad," Paul says, hugging me tightly to himself.

"You are a star."

"No, you're a trooper. You are the best." We whisper words of comfort into each other's ears.

This morning, I awoke as if an alarm had been triggered. I waited half asleep, but didn't hear anything more. Also Jester didn't whine or move, so I got dressed at my regular pace and headed downstairs. Pretty soon, a sure crash came from Mr. B's room upstairs. I ran back up shouting to him repeatedly, but when he didn't answer I opened his door and found him lying in a pool of blood on the bathroom floor. His head was bathed in *dried* blood. He must have fallen twice! My heart skipped a beat seeing the calamity. Then, I heard him moan, so I quickly sat him up against the shower door and saw the golf ball-sized goose egg on his forehead together with a raw gash the size of his eye. He was too confused to answer my questions, so I immediately called 911.

In the emergency room, Mr. B had come around well enough to bat his one eye at the nurse, exclaiming what a pretty blonde she was. Then, when a darker nurse arrived, he asked her if she was Mexican, because he wanted to ask the difference between *intendo* and *comprendo*. She explained that she was not Mexican. I was smoothing his white head when he peered up at me and said, "You best be careful, you might lose control." When a third nurse arrived, he verbally noticed a birthmark on her left temple and also that she was "P.G." Then he told her that her ponytail was an old fashioned hairstyle. When Paul arrived, he started confessing that he'd patted my knee a few times, hoping Pauly didn't mind because he was so glad to see me when he opened his eyes... Joe trumpeted on about how much it was going to set him back financially for the ride in the ambulance.

"Don't worry about that now, Chief."

"But I keep trying to figure out what happened."

"There was some blood on your sheets, Mr. B. So, I'm thinking you fell twice, and the first time, you went back to bed."

"Maybe. I can't recall. I was trying to put a cold compress on the little pimples of dried blood on my face, and then I was out. I musta fainted. But I've never fainted before."

A paramedic notices Joe's records say he retired from Martin Marietta. She turns to face him to articulate. "What kind of work did you do?"

"I was a poor engineer," Joe doesn't raise his hand to gesture. He lies quietly.

"You were not," I protest. "He was a stress engineer for the Department of Defense."

"Oh! You were? My 16-year-old son wants to go into some kind of computer technology. He just went on a prospective engineer's field trip to Lockheed Martin, and it is one cool facility!" she exclaims.

"Yeah; when you get rid of some of the *cutthroats*." His dry throat sands his words over to her. "Wherever there's money, there's cutthroats to get to it!"

She agrees.

"Anyway, I don't know a thing about computers. I only used two slide rules and my noggin in my work. But if he finds something he likes, let him do it."

One of his nurses, he compliments for having such a smooth complexion, another one for having beautiful straight teeth. Everyone leaves Mr. B's emergency room grinning. The doctor orders x-rays of his head, his neck, his skinned and sore knee, and his hip, which turned out to be fractured. Otherwise, his heart is beating steadily, his blood pressure is within the normal range, and he is answering all questions with clear logic. The nurse who asks him what the year is, is taken aback when he says, "In three years, I'll be 100, so it's 2014."

After the surgeon stitches up his eyebrow and puts three pins into his hip, we get the call. "What does my father-in-law eat? Does he exercise?" Dr. Smith inquires. "His bones are so healthy, the pins attached really well. He should be able to go home and get his therapist in house. What kind of work did he do?"

I love to answer this question. "He was a rocket scientist. We are very proud of our national treasure."

"Yippee!" exclaims the surgeon. "I can't wait for his follow-up visit. I've always wanted to meet a rocket scientist!"

"Well, he'll be happy to tell you a few stories." I'm glad Joe has made Dr. Smith's day.

Later in the afternoon, when the nurses wheel Mr. B in to his hospital room he crunches his belly to look up from the bed and see me standing there.

"You still here? Just wait 'til tomorrow, I'm gonna chase you down the hall."

Paul and I exchange glances wondering about this new uninhibited version of Mr. B. We are in for one crazy recovery. I'm glad he is going into this situation with his core strength. The day after Mr. B's hip surgery, he's determined to be well, sitting up for hours working puzzles.

January 27, 2014

In rehab, Mr. B obediently walks with a walker, whenever it's daylight and nobody catches him going to the bathroom without it.

"My hip doesn't hurt. Really. My forehead hurts worse than my hip, Miss. I'd like to take you out for clam chowder if you could get me outta here." He also said he felt like he's been here for years, but it's only been a week. "Nice place or not, I wanna get outta here!" He squeezes my hand.

"Oh, Mr. B, it's hard to be patient, but your therapist says you are gaining strength and balance every day, so just do the exercises they ask you to do, and you'll be home very soon. We miss you."

"To be honest, I hate, I actually *hate* exercising. I never liked calisthenics or sports at school. P.E. was Pee You! The only thing I like to do is walk to blow off steam and tend my garden." He shakes his head.

I rub his back sympathetically. "Well, I guess you've established it: extraneous exercising does not improve the odds of a long life after all."

A visitor comes to see Mr. B this afternoon, complaining about his work and all the political shenanigans. He sums up the situation, "I'm getting sick of the rigmarole." The visitor happens to be Joe's aide.

Joe studies him. "You gotta enjoy your work. It helps you live longer, not to have all that stress."

"Ignore him." I advise the aide from the side of my mouth. "He's a stress engineer by trade. He always lived with incredible work stress and political pressure his entire career in aerospace. It made him stronger."

Joe leans forward in his chair. "What are you saying, now? You are always conspiring against me."

"Oh, Mr. B, I'm just telling him that at 98, your long years are a gift. There's no rhyme or reason to them. We're just glad you're here."

"There was a chief engineer in Bald'more who moved to the Michoud plant about the time I went down there too, and they put me onto his team. When I would go to talk over a problem wid 'em, Bogema would listen for a while and then reach under the calendar laying on his desk. He'd pull out a sheet of paper wid the answer on it! Yeah. He was so smart! He'd given himself the same problem as he gave to his team to work out. Prior to me asking 'em about it, he'd worked it out because he was curious himself, see. He was always prepared wid his own calculations in case the others failed."

Just then, Joe's granddaughter Jessica arrives, bringing us a book for entertainment, *The One and Only Ivan*. Then, she warms up a basin of water for her grandpa's feet. Mr. B dips his feet into the warm, soapy water and warms up the story he'd begun. "One day, I told Bogema that I'd overheard two guys vying for his Chief of Engineer position. Eh, the climate was always political. It didn't matter if the challenger wasn't as good as Bogema, he'd find a way to discredit him, so Bogema suddenly got a transfer back to Bald'more, and he remained there as Chief Engineer until he retired, I guess."

"Sometimes, it's not worth the effort to fight the destruction of slander, if it's jealousy or greed that motivates it," I agree. "But, it's hard to open up your hand and give up something that you feel belongs to you."

After Joe soaks for a while, Jesse cuts his toenails and for good measure, clips his hair.

By the time she leaves, Mr. B is happy and handsome. "I want to give that girl the Brownlee sconces for helping me. I can put my shoes on now! Remind me to wrap them up for her when I get home. And, I keep thinking what to get you. I owe you. If you hadn't found me when I fell, I would have caught cold there lying on the floor with my hip like this."

"You don't owe me anything but to get better, Mr. B. I'm just glad I happened to be there. Stop worrying about it. Seriously."

"It gives me something to do at night. I *like* to think. Don't take that away from me."

When I start to get down about how narrow my life has become, I count my biggest blessing that cancels out all the other negatives. Mister B is alive and kicking, showing me how to kick in the flood waters of life. Today, he's alive because I was there to hear him fall in his bathroom so that I called emergency. I recently ran across something the apostle Paul wrote to his godson: Children and grandchildren should learn to practice their religion by caring for their families so that they repay their parents and grandparents because this is pleasing to the LORD. (1 Timothy 5:4)

I'm *practicing*.

Quintessential Mr. B:

Mr. B with his nemesis, Jester (2014)

After a Christmas lunch (circa 2011)

below: Joe designed windows for a special ops plane with German glass made from crystals so that a camera could take photos. The electrical box was tucked inside the tail. One, of the three planes made, crashed right after takeoff, with a full tank of fuel, and burned the crew.

ƑEBRUARY~ FAHRENHEITS

February 1, 2014

At dinner, Paul and I wait expectantly for a thumbs up or down from Mr. B on the treat we have brought to him in rehab. "It looks like lemon, but it's not. What is it?" One dear, experimental bite of dessert has been downed by my father-in-law.

Joe has lost over ten pounds since his accident. Now I'm on a mission to entice him to eat. "Mr. B, we are celebrating your recovery, black eye or not. This is a pear tart. You told me how much you liked pears…"

"This is a pear? Well, I'll be. What else is in it?" I watch him picking up the pear half with his fork, peering underneath, then cautiously cutting another bite.

I can tell Joe is suspicious of this new mixed food, even if it does present as mostly pear, mostly *sweet*. "It has an almond crust and an egg custard, and the half pear is sitting on top. It's a natural sweetness, not too sweet, and it has protein in it, Mr. B, so it is very healthy for you." Why am I *selling* this delicious dish?!

Joe carefully swallows another bite of dessert. "Oh well," he is all wide-eyed sarcasm looking at his son. "I should be cured by now."

February 2, 2014

The ol' man has swallowed his pride by following my order to bring his cane. He means to walk through some long hospital corridors for a follow-up visit. Still, he attempts to leave it behind in the car when we arrive until I gently remind him not to forget it.

Then, after navigating the parking lot, he picks it up and carries it inside the hospital.

"Mr. B, how is that gonna help you if you are carrying your cane?" I feel like I'm insulting him by mothering him, yet he obediently sets the heel of the cane onto the floor and does it religiously with every footstep.

"I agree, Miss. It helps me not to wobble, but my therapist said I had a quick recovery response whenever I lost my balance."

"Yes, and I know I'm being bossy, but I'd rather be safe than sorry, even if we are walking in the hospital."

"Okay!"

We are waiting for his follow-up appointment with the hip surgeon when Joe says, caressing his forehead, "My eyebrow *still* hurts, much worse than my hip where the pins are."

The left side of his face is faded green. "I won't hit you there then."

He ribs me with his elbow. "Ya. All other body blows are fine." Our humor is restored. It is further enhanced when his doctor seems to be more interested in Joe's aerospace career than in his bumps and bruises.

To celebrate his clean bill of health, Mr. B suggests going to his favorite pancake house. On the way, he turns to me and says, "I know I'm not quite right, Mrs. B. I have to allow time, as the good doctor says, 'for a full recovery.' My head does feel funny, and I know I overdid it yesterday working in the yard. It's my pride, I guess, but my hip doesn't even hurt! It's my other side that kinda aches at night when I stretch out. This knee." He points with a reprimand.

I wonder why he didn't discuss this with the surgeon. "Do you want to try a chiropractor, Mr. B? We can set you up with ours."

My arm recoils when he grabs it with his hard fingers. "No way! The Brownlees would never approve!"

"But, you told me you went to a chiropractor for your shoulder on your wedding day," I argue, "and he put it back into place for you."

"Oh yeah, but never again. Never again. They wouldn't approve!"

"Mr. B! They are out of the picture now." What could possibly hold him back from seeking help? "The Brownlee doctors are all dead and gone! Even Maudie's surgeon brother is gone. You can do whatever you like. We'll even pay for you to try our chiropractor. Paul loves him."

Joe shakes his head vehemently. "I just couldn't. Doctor Brownlee made me promise."

"Oh Mr. B. You are a Byk, not a Brownlee. You are a thinker. If you wanna go to a different doctor, you can. Nobody will tell on you."

"You…!" He huffs. "I can tell you came from the wrong side-o-the family."

February 3, 2014

With a stretchy knee sleeve supporting Joe's achy knee, we are practicing balance exercises. Mr. B keeps his eyes closed so that when he takes a shower or walks down a dark corridor, he won't pitch forward. Apparently, Joe's limited eyesight has quite a bit to do with his balance, so we practice tacit touch and feeling awareness from the soles of the feet on the floor to whatever any other part of his body happens to be touching. We had to negotiate pretty hard to get the rehab center to let Mr. B out sooner rather than later, and part of the deal was that he continues physical therapy at home. Learning the other aspect of his balance comes from the inner ear, he declares, "It is the inner ear that gave Victoria her balance problem last month, and now I have a balance problem, too."

"You've come a long way in the couple of weeks of rehab." Joe's therapist encourages him.

I add, "And Paul is putting brighter lights in your bathroom and the hallway, Mr. B."

"Okay." He smiles grimly. "But I might want to practice in the dark so's I'll be ready when the other eye goes."

Walking him to his room for a rest, I ask, "Mr. B, what did you work on regarding the Apollo?"

"You know, kiddo, I didn't do much on that. I think the only thing I did was add some brackets that would assimilate the bounce in the landing gear of the Viking Lander to Mars."

"You must have some satisfaction from knowing that you contributed to so many aspects of the space program."

He stops and turns to me. "You know that magazine your sista Liz brought to me, the one with all the Hubble Space Telescope pictures of galaxies? I found that to be so interesting, all the colors out there! I'll be! When I was reading about it, it came to me that our work on the Titan now enables the Hubble to rendezvous. That fact makes me happy."

February 4, 2014

We go to the rehabilitation facility to collect Mr. B and bring him back home today. As he is walking down the hallway for the last time, he thanks everyone he recognizes who nursed him. "Before we go home, Miss, I'd like to stop at that Polish bakery right around the corner. I want some treats to celebrate this day wid you and Paul!"

February 5, 2014

Joe can't wait to reenlist into his old routine, so he waits for me to scrape off the delicate icy snowflakes from the windshield; we're driving to the library. It's been an uncommonly freezing month. Maybe this cold is what spurs Joe to describe how he "directed a project at Martin where they aimed to heat up a canister to 1,000 degrees, but make it man-safe inside."

I turn the heat control to high and hear the scrunching of the snow under my tires as I carefully back down our driveway. "The guy in charge of the project would just sit with his elbow on his knee and smoke. He wasn't getting anywhere, so they put me on the project instead."

"How can someone survive one thousand degree heat?" My breath heaves rolling steam.

"Exactly! It had the director stumped, too. So, I had to find the kind of material that would protect the human being inside of it and also another equipment chamber that maintained a vacuum of 14.7 PSI in the chamber. Nobody in the company could tell me what 'man-rated' meant. So, I thought about it and then looked up pressurized containers in the *Handbook for the Society of American Engineers* to see what they said about it. I learned a few things. I used the standard they provided, and I went and talked to a materials guy I knew who liked me. He gave me some corrugated plastics that could hold up to a flash point of 063. Then, I approved of a half inch steel strap on the upper dome of the first chamber, and a half inch steel plate on the lower dome to hold them together. In the first go around, the instrument capsule sat on the four-legged pedestal. Okay. Copasetic. The plate specs also kept the four feet it all stood on secure. I had to use some queer numbers to make it work, and the steel was rated at 303, wieldable alloy. My boss sat beside me with an elbow on his knee, smoking a cigarette and watching me figure. The bee was on me!

"But there was a second chamber that they wanted to attach to the first chamber. It didn't meet the drawing specs. They had these flanges put on there without a straightening plate. All the welds looked really rough, but they were going forward with it for the buyer. So I told them they needed to keep the flanges straight with steel plates, or else they would curl in the heat. I started redesigning it for a specific heat environment of 1,000 degrees Fahrenheit. 'Hey! Whatcha doin, Byk?' I heard the boss roar. I didn't know he had gone behind my back and had already started building it for testing. His other team got to bitching about it, but they couldn't disprove me, so they finally attached the plates between the flanges and welded them to the walls."

Joe's cane lies between us. I try to focus on the details of what Joe is describing.

"The stupidos had also welded these cylinders alongside the aluminum walls, and I went and advised my boss that the aluminum walls when they were heated, would just turn red hot and all their strength would be lost, and also, that they hadn't accounted for any heat expansion in the tubes they were attaching to the walls. You see that on the coolers on top of industrial roofs. The pipes have to be offset to account for heat expansion on a roof. So, I told my boss to do what he wanted but I wouldn't sign off on that design, and I couldn't help it, the way it had already been welded. The welds were gonna break. He took me off the job, nice guy, and they shipped that whole kebab that weighed tons, by the way, up to the Philadelphia Naval Yard. When they tested it, the first capsule held up, and I think NASA used it and may still use it. But the second capsule flamed up just where I said it would, and they had to re-weld it. They wanted me to sign off on it, and I refused. I told them I was off that job. I wasn't going to be their fall guy. The second capsule went to the scrap heap."

I turn off the car heater and now remove my glasses, showing Joe how they are all steamed up. "You're hot stuff these days!" he exclaims.

"I'm trying to listen to your story, Mr. B. What happened when you wouldn't be their scapegoat?"

"Oh, the buyer wanted a stress analysis report on it, so I provided a stress report. They came back and wanted to know where I got my figures from. It's statistics! I told 'em. I got 'em from the American Society of Mechanical Engineers. What could they say?"

Wow. That was a lot to take in within our five-minute ride to the library. I park and quickly open my door to disembark. You know you're having a hot flash when it's reading -10 degrees, you turn off your car heater and still your sunglasses are fogging up!

February 6, 2014

My sister, Kay, brings over some Omaha Steaks to grill special tonight. Joe, wary because of the work it takes to chew beef, wants to know what's so special about Omaha Steaks.

"Because they come from Omaha, Chief!" Paul shouts.

Joe looks confused, peering from one to another for clarification, then shrugs. "Well, I remember a top secret mission to get some real Omaha steaks once." Doggonit, Mr. B, if you haven't recovered the ball in the field!

"Oh yeah. There were four of us from the Department of

Defense packed into a Volkswagen, believe it or not, who went out to the SEC, to look at a high-tech stealth plane. The Colonel was a real young man, real young, but he sure knew how to order everyone around. There were guard dogs watching the place to make sure none of us got out of line, too. So the Colonel took us around to different ones and commanded them to tell us what it was they needed. As soon as they finished, we were escorted out. So, we four piled into the Volkswagen, a Volkswagen mind you, and drove to a super-duper steak joint. There, we saw a huge old farmer eating the fattest steak you ever saw! Those were Omaha steaks." The ol' man finishes triumphantly.

"Aw, but hush hush, top secret stuff was a real pain, if ya ask me."

"Painful?" comes my sis.

"The black hole?" questions Paul.

"No. Say, if you wanted a file on a particular subject, you had to go get it from a big file room, behind a guard's desk, and not waste time looking. If you didn't know exactly where to find it, you had to ask the guard, and he went in to find it for you. I asked my boss if I could look through his files instead, and he let me."

Joe places both hands on his knees and rocks forward. "Oh, one time, they herded me into a white bright room with nothing but a few old men in it. They asked me a series of questions about weights and masses. Where would I put this kind of mass or that kind of weight on this kind of rocket if the goal was x? I wasn't allowed to ask any clarifying questions, neither. It was a pain, a real pain."

"Just like the movies!" We all agree.

February 7, 2014
I attend a funeral today for my friend, Kathryn, a woman who earned her nursing degree in her fifties, started work at a hospital

immediately and began to take ministry trips to orphans around the world. On her 80th birthday, she said, "I don't believe in birthday wishes, but I'm praying God gives me ten more years to go to the most difficult places in the world to share the good news."

Kathryn's own life was radically changed with that message because after she was abandoned to "A Home For Friendless Children" where she was punished for crying, and where she lived out her teen years, until her maid services were farmed out to serve a certain family. One day this family took her to church where she heard for the first time that Jesus dearly loved her and had a wonderful plan for her life. After that kind of experience, nothing could dissuade her from loving other orphans.

At 88, she single-handedly raised the money to build an orphanage for a group of Cambodian children whose house, which was built on piers above rice paddies, had a rotting floor about to collapse. Two months after the children moved into their new home, the old house was swept away in a hurricane.

Kathryn died halfway through her 90th year. What a life! Today, people from the funeral crowd spontaneously fill the hour and a half with stories: she loved the color purple. Her gentle faith encouraged people to step out of their common limitations in various ways, and sometimes her more insistent faith kept a missions party from turning back in the face of war, political unrest, flooding, leeches in the rivers they crossed, and police threats of arrest, to say nothing of enduring three-hour rides along bumpy, jarring roads. Each time, she touched lives with the truth that the Redeemer can redeem, with purpose, any abuse or abandonment by experiencing the love of His Son, Jesus Christ.

I hadn't visited Kathryn since we had moved in across town with Joe, so I am feeling particularly unworthy and hypocritical to be visiting her only now at her funeral. The main reason for this is, well, she had clung to me unrelenting the last time I visited her, spouting irrational fears that often come with a person's last days. I didn't know how to handle that. What if her fears were rational? I had no power to change anything. I could only pray for her. I add nothing about our relationship to this audience because of my guilt.

As I pass by her casket to put my hand over hers one last time, my eyes fill with tears. She is wearing a white dress with delicate purple flowers with the frilly lavender sweater I had given her for her 89th birthday. Her purple- framed glasses are perched on her nose.

Upon my return from Kathryn's funeral, Joe raises his eyebrow at me. Pointing his crooked finger in rhythm with his words he says, "I was just kidding about changing the name on my gravestone, girl. I don't want one of those obituaries. I don't want a minister. I don't want a soloist. I don't want a church service. You'll have to pay something for those death certificates though. No escaping that. Just put my ashes in where we've planned and say that Psalm, what is it? About the Shepherd." His eyes grow moist and pink around the rims.

"Psalm 23? The LORD is my shepherd?" My own eyes grow misty.

"Yeah, yeah. That's the one. Just say that over the grave, and I'll elbow my Maudie over one more time. 'Hey girl, make room for me."

February 8, 2014
Mr. B cranks up Figaro playing on his stereo to hint that we should join him in the blue room for the Saturday morning opera. *Nothing doing.* Instead, Paul convinces us all to join him in his quest to find tennis shoes at a new shopping mall nearby. He requires sturdy foot support and comfort in his walking shoes for work.

Joe immediately flips the stereo switch to "off" and dons his jacket. Mr. B carries his cane at his side like it's a garden tool.

He's so stubborn about actually using it. Pauly glances at him, annoyed, "Dad! What are ya gonna do with that thing, wallop a dog or something?"

"When I need it, I'll have it." The deliberate answer assures us.

We roll our eyes in exasperation.

In his torn-up grey streaked leathers, Joe stands in the store beside me denying that he also needs shoes or that these multicolored, multi-patterned shoes could ever be worn by an adult his age.

Suddenly he jabs me with his elbow and I see a wild smirk rake over his face. What's Mr. B laughing at?

Spinning toward the target of his gaze, I see he's laughing at the shriveled old lady, white headed, puffs of hair billowing over her plaid coat collar, looking at neon tennis shoes! She is bent over a neon turquoise and pink shoe in particular. Apparently, she thinks these shoes are just her style.

Joe plunks his bottom down, and I call over a salesman. In the end, Paul pays for three pairs of shoes, one for each of us.

Mr. B leans over until his shoulder touches Paul's shoulder in

the front seat of the car. "It would have been less painful for you, Son, if you woulda stayed home and listened to the Saturday morning opera."

Paul leans into his dad's shoulder. "I doubt it."

February 10, 2014

"Acid?" Joe gives me boric acid to pour into my eye. "For my eye, Mr. B? Are you sure?" We both study my red eye in the bathroom mirror.

"Well, yeah. It's not what you think. Maudie got this powder, you see, from the pharmacy, it's over the counter. We used it whenever we had eye irritations. You just dip the tip of your finger into it, and then put it into a little paper cup of warm water, here you go, stir, and then tip it over your eye. Blink a little bit, and it washes your eye out."

"Really?"

"I promise you."

I notice immediately after obeying these instructions that the irritation is gone. Whether it was pink eye or not, the discoloration lessens throughout the next couple of hours until it clears up. Funny, the Byks, who always refused to take vitamins, and who are committed to doctors and drug prescriptions, also used peppermint oil and lavender for ridding their home of summer spiders and ants, and for cleaning off their counters and spraying into the air after a fish dinner. Maybe that is why Mr. B never owned up to having a headache. If he did, I'd anoint him with his kitchen cleaners because lavender oil and peppermint are the best things to clear up headaches.

February 12, 2014

"Crossword puzzles are getting too hard for me!" Joe exclaims with alarm. He puts down the paper. "What do I know about all the new movie stars or the stock market? They don't ask the kind of questions they used to ask." I can tell he is disappointed. After his outburst, he spends most of his day rocking in his blue chair in the darkened room.

Over a steamed lobster and shrimp dinner, splashed with Old Bay's seasoning, and garnished with fresh, warm dinner rolls, Pauly cheers him with tall tales of his daily heroism.

"Pauly, do you remember Middle River?"

My husband, interrupted, responds, "You mean the time we went out to catch crabs in that flat boat with some dead fish we found on the shore, and we caught an eel instead and got pulled over by the harbor patrol because we didn't have life jackets on?"

Mr. B snaps to attention. "Well, since you put it that way, you can just forget it."

Paul relents. "I remember you took mom and Vicky and me there a couplea times. Once you let me beat the heck outa the cat tails on the bank."

"Well, you ran around like a kid *off leash*. What could I do about it?"

February 13, 2014

Mr. B has apparently dried my laundry for me. The shower door has a wire coat rack that is now slung with all of Paul's woolen socks opened up and sticking off the knob ends, eight in all. When Maudie was getting too old to climb the stairs a few years ago, I hired some friends to remodel this entry bath to include the washer

and dryer and add a shower
for her. Today, it appears Dr. Seuss has also moved in.

February 14, 2014
We have a celebration tonight! Many years ago, Mr. B and Maudie found this little restaurant in the oldest working hotel in the state, located in Empire, Colorado. It's called the Peck House, run by Innkeepers Gary and Sally St. Clair. They of course introduced me to the inn when Paul and I married. Since then, our Valentine's Day tradition has been to drive away from the city and all the crowded franchised restaurants. Instead, we make our way up to the Peck House for a romantic fireside dinner. Tonight, we both order a smoked trout appetizer with shrimp to share. Then comes the warm spinach salad. Finally, the main course, which always includes my favorite, the tenderloin with peppercorn sauce. I have a glass of the red wine, and since Paul doesn't drink, he orders their coffee. Now, this coffee happens to be served with a whole side bowl of house-whipped cream and a dish of colorful sugar sprinkles. Delish!

Paul likes to sample the entrée menu and tries different things each time we visit. During our conversation of delight and thankfulness for the Almighty's many graces, Paul finally tells me "For Valentine's Day, I'm taking the blue roofing nails outta your head."

"What?" This strange comment I don't understand.

"I'm telling you that I agree with you about my father's back porch. Half the view from the inside den is his painted blue roof with the roofing nails hanging through, though you gotta admit, they are also painted that lovely shade of blue." He's sly, this one. "I miss not being able to see the trees, too."

"Oh! Honey!" I am exuberant. "I'd be thrilled to open up *your* view!"

"I think we can swing it, if you want to raise the roof or whatever this spring. Check it out. But we also need to re-pour the patio floor because I saw Dad stumble, and almost fall on it, the other day. It seems that anyone who comes over is tripping." My heart soars.

To top off the evening, a simple but fabulous Turtle Sundae is delivered to our table: Two scoops of vanilla ice cream with fudge and pecans, a little whipped cream, and a cherry on top. The owners also drop by the table to explain their plans to retire and close the doors on our favorite date of the year. With this in mind, we buy a little extra smoked trout, shrimp, and pâté to take back to Joe with the sad news. Before we leave, Paul makes a final reservation for my birthday, closing day for the Peck House.

February 15, 2014

I am secretly enjoying a compliment. Joe has been asking us questions about his estate, and when he talks to me alone at breakfast, I just don't feel comfortable answering them. Still, he keeps calling me the "legal eagle" and bats his newest theories around my brain. I tell him Paul and Vicky are the two he needs to consult.

Tonight when Paul tells his dad to keep as much financial autonomy for as long as possible with everything in his own name, Joe pats Paul and me on the back and responds, "I finally found two people I can trust."

"Nobody's perfect, Joe, but we do our best, and you know it works both ways. You are a pretty easy guy to live with!"

"You know, I've thought a lot about what I woulda felt if you weren't here and I couldn't drive myself anywhere. There was a couplea places in town near the grocery store that I looked at, and maybe I woulda been okay there, walking around. But, I woulda felt bad, like maybe nobody cared." He swallows and thinks about that impression. "Leaving my money in different places, not that I have much, but when I think about these organizations that do certain things, I really don't want to give it to them." The sides of his mouth pull back towards each ear as he shrugs. "I trust you. We can really talk, you know, heart to heart. You're good to me, and you gotta leave it somewhere, so I'm happy with my decision."

February 20, 2014
Pauly has bought me flowers, sprouting bulbs in pretty lime green pots. Hoping the warm sunshine will continue, I put them on the porch. Now, Joe is fearlessly swatting at bees on the porch. I ask him, "Please don't make them mad, Mr. B, or I'll have to leave you and go inside."

He stops and tells me once upon a time, a bee he'd swatted didn't die, it was just stunned or wounded. Then another bee came along and scouted around it. Picking the first bee up in its legs, the second bee flew away with the injured bee.

He looks at me with furrowed brow, adding, "I never saw that happen when a bee was killed, so somehow the heroic bee understood that his friend was savable. I am still dumbfounded when I think of it because I realized in that moment how intelligent a bee must really be."

February 21, 2014
At breakfast, Joe contemplates a boring day because it's so

blustery-cold outside. "What do you have planned for the day?"

"Nothing much, Mr. B. Is there something you would like to do?"

"Nah, I'm alright." Long pause…

"Joe, would you like to go to the library today?"

"Oh, if you would like to get out of this house, I sure would agree to that."

He's so cute I can't help but smile.

"I haven't seen you wear those sweat pants since rehab, Mr. B. Would they be warmer to wear today?"

He smirks and bends down to his ankle, pulling up his dress slacks to reveal the blue sweat pants underneath.

"I'm sneaky! I wear 'em every day, Miss. They keep my legs real warm!" I can see he's still wearing his knee sleeve too.

Things pick up a bit when breakfast is served. He says, "Did I ever tell ya about my mothea's dum-dum brother-in-law?"

I'm not sure, so he leans into the table and stops peeling his egg to tell me. "When my wife's sista died in Chicago, the man was bereaved, I'll grant him that. But he had this friend who stepped up as soon as the $10,000 insurance policy arrived to tell him that he would help keep it safe."

Joe pauses for effect. Then he shrugs and goes to peeling his egg. We both start chuckling.

"Poor thing," I say.

"Yeah. But not everyone who saddles up to you is really what they say they are. You gotta' beware." He shrugs blandly. "Once they got your cash, how ya gonna pay a lawyer to get it back for ya?"

I change the subject. "Mr. B, did you remember to take your medication?"

"Why no! I guess I musta forgot!" His voice sounds incredulous, like this forgetting is not a recurring theme.

February 22, 2014

Thick, fluffy snowflakes start floating over the picture windows. It puts me in the mood for hot chocolate this afternoon and Joe says he'd like some if I'm having some. It turns out creamy and rich. He says he did the crossword puzzle in the *Denver Post* at the library and read the *Journal of American Science*, which is based on fact and is not political so that he can trust it.

"What ever happened to the plane you were designing upstairs, Mr. B? You used to show me your progress on that." On winter evenings, Joe used to retire to an upstairs bedroom where he would draft his own airplane designs.

"Well, I determined that my calculations were off on that thing. It woulda crashed because it was unbalanced. I had figured wrong. And there was no way to test it. Who was I gonna get to test it for me? Eh, then I just got bored wid it."

"I guess that's understandable," I admit with some sadness. "But, I bet there's someone out there who could run with your design and adjust it a little, and it would fly."

"You think? Nah…"

Then he tells me about the time he had graduated from college and his professor gave him a signed card of introduction to present to a friend of his in California who was in the aircraft manufacturing business. When the young Joe Byk arrived with his suitcase in Downey, California, fresh off the train, he took his calling card to the bank where the investment banker, Robert Gross, took his card of introduction and made a phone call. Joe was immediately interviewed and hired at the Vultee Aircraft Company.

"Can you look up those names in your fancy gadget there and see what it says?" he asks. "While I was there the chief engineer, Mr. Vultee, and his wife died in a plane accident. That was because, you know, Vultee aircraft V-1s, V-1As and V-11s had sold well overseas. But for some reason, the U.S. Army Air Corps ignored their aircraft, so my boss, Jerry Vultee, and his wife went to Washington D.C. to pitch their planes to the U.S. Army."

I seize my laptop, and we quickly discover the story of Joe's first boss in his career move to Vultee. *The Western Museum of Flight* reports:

> On Saturday, January 29, 1938 Jerry and Sylvia Vultee were flying home from Washington, D.C. in his personal Stinson Reliant SR-9C cabin monoplane, registration number NC17159, after presenting a new aircraft design to the Army. The venerable 1936 Stinson Reliant was popular at the time and featured leather upholstery, walnut instrument panels, and automobile-style roll-down windows. The Stinson Reliant was a rugged aircraft built of fabric-covered welded steel-tubing structures with a single strutbraced double-tapered wing. Powered by a 260hp Lycoming R-680 radial engine, the Reliant carried a pilot plus three or four passengers at speeds close to 165 miles per hour. Pilots appreciated the Reliant's durability, safety, and stability in flight, while passengers enjoyed a comfortable ride in an opulent cabin. The couple was anxious to return to their six-month-old son and home in Glendale California. They departed the TWA Winslow Arizona Airport at 8:35 in the morning and were headed west to Downey California when they were caught in a snowstorm and blizzard. Jerry Vultee was an excellent pilot but had no training in instrument flying and it is believed that he was unable to find his way out of the blinding snow storm. He most likely became disorientated and lost direction. The aircraft disappeared approximately two hours after taking off. Local Oak Creek Canyon ranchers heard the plane flying a crisscross pattern apparently lost in the snow storm trying to find a break in the clouds and then crash... The ranchers' accurate description gave searchers a good direction in which to search, narrowing down the search area. [...] The wreckage was discovered by a Forest Ranger and a couple of C.C.C. workers about noon Sunday, January 30 after an extensive search. Witnesses said that the plane wreck was a terrible sight; little was left

of the plane except a heap of twisted and blackened metal. A small branch of a nearby tree had broken off showing that the plane had come in from the west. The aircraft had slammed into the snow covered ground, about three miles north of Mount Wilson between Sedona and Flagstaff, Arizona. The impact site was only a couple hundred feet from the edge of a deep rocky chasm. The propeller had dug into the ground, breaking off and burying one blade. The plane was found inverted facing west and badly burned. Pieces of the engine and unburned debris were found hurled almost to the brink of the canyon leading to the conclusion that there was no pre-crash fire… It was also believed that the two were fatally injured by the crash and not killed by the flames. Mrs. Vultee was identified by her jewelry and several pieces were recovered and returned to the family. Gerald Vultee's wristwatch had stopped at 9:56 a.m. Two young promising lives were cut short, Gerald Vultee was only 38 at the time and his wife Sylvia Vultee was 27.[1]

The ol' man smiles as he listens to this retelling of history and his memories. He wonders what other parts of his career story can be found in my black box. So, he informs me there was also a very good-looking blond chief engineer who had a plush office upstairs with windows and that he took over the management of making the training planes for the military. He says this man was also the engineer for Howard Hughes. He had a small mustache. And there, we find him, Richard Palmer, though without reference to Hughes.

> Jerry Vultee was succeeded as president and general manager of the Vultee plant by Richard Palmer who became chief engineer in 1940, and the plant was named Vultee Aircraft. A new plane known as the V-12-C was ordered by the Chinese who took 26 in 1939. And the U.S. government ordered training planes in a contract worth $2,986,000 with Vultee in August of the same year.[2]

Joe furrows his brow. "Howard Hughes liked to make a name for himself, so he would fly in a plane one time and then get rid of it," Joe informs me. "There was a plane that he flew that experimented wid new technology. It made all the bolts and seams flush. It was a hit because his flight was successful, but metal fatigue takes time." His hand turns palm up, and he shrugs almost apologetically. "Stress and fatigue were what the airline industry had to fight against."

"One time, early in my career, these upper management guys brought me a piece of corrugated metal and I didn't say much because I didn't think much of it. Planes were falling out of the sky, and no one knew why. Then, the designers tried out different kinds of metals, aluminum, but when the weather turned to snow or rain, the metal would corrode. So we started experimenting wid dimpling the bolts, countersinking, and rivets, a new type of fastener.

"I could see that the metal was developing stress fractures wherever there were holes drilled into the plane, so then we get the orders from above that we had to drill either a hole or a succession of holes beyond the fractures to stop the cracks. You know, you've seen how they repair cracks on glass windshields?" He looks up at me and I nod.

"Theoretically, it works, and it does work. The cracks somehow get stopped and do not proceed beyond the drilled hole, and if they do, then the second hole stops them. But I wouldn't ride in any of those planes. They were stinko. It wasn't a good fix."

He searches the titles of listed online material and I scroll, click on links and turn pages for him as necessary. He reads aloud in his guttural tone: "In Britain, metallurgists at the National Physical Laboratory developed a process of anodizing an alloy of aluminum with a protective coating: Alclad. A man named Charles Ward Hall designed and developed the riveting of aircraft skins, but it was the dimpled tooling for the rivets that evolved over the decade that saved the industry."

Then Joe sees another name he recognizes reading an IInternet page from the online book, *Wings: A History of Aviation from Kites to the Space Age*, by Tom D. Crouch. "Oh, this guy was brilliant!" he exclaims looking at the name of Clarence "Kelly" Johnson. "Yeah, he knew his stuff. I liked him a lot. Look here, it says his plane that he designed, the Electra, was a Lockheed aircraft that maintained the company's sterling reputation." I can tell how excited Joe has become to see some of his memories come to life on my computer screen.

We continue reading this online book. The name of Jack Northrup is recognized for creating the first all-metal airplane. Joe remembers, "He was another smart one." Then, the story turns to the exact problems with metal Joe had described to me. "Duralumin, the tough, light alloy of aluminum used in most aircraft applications since WWI, was subject to intercrystalline corrosion that slowly turned the metal into a white powder." "Glenn Martin, (Martin Company) and other manufacturers saw metal as a uniform material, ideal for… large scale production… However, there were problems." Reports vaguely alluded to repeated deaths from crashes. Martin Company got out of the commercial airline industry completely because of the expense and the risks involved." [P. 321-322] Unlike iron and steel, the process of welding damaged aluminum.

"Oh, aluminum!" Mr. B exclaims. "There was this guy who lost his common sense when he replaced a steel bolt design for the stick controls of a plane with an aluminum bolt, just because it was lighter weight and would be cheaper, mind you. A hot-shot test pilot took it for a spin and brought it back. When they examined the plane, though, that aluminum bolt was worn to a thread, on its test flight! I don't know what got into that designer to decide to switch out something so lightweight as a steel bolt, but so basic to the integrity of the instrument!" Joe's eyes widen and he shrugs helplessly.

"Once I almost lost my job at Martin in Bald'more because I was called into the British engineering board to talk with them about their design for an airplane hull. I told them it was too small, it would never work, and I showed them where it would break. The group was insulted, our company lost the contract, and when the plane was eventually built, it did exactly what I predicted and was discarded! My manager gave me a black mark in my review that followed me for years. It said I wasn't a 'team player'." Joe smirks. "But a week after he filed that report he died of a heart attack from all the political pressure."

He drones on about other ticklish incidents. He's looking over our brown-black and tanned, spiked landscape, gazing through the picture window.

"There was a locked cylinder which was to undergo not only intense friction and flight, but the capsule was also to be exposed to extreme temperatures. They wanted to accept it with flaws, but I explained exactly where the capsule would fail and crack, and why. You know what a parabola curve is? No? Well, it's formed from all the points (x, y) that are equidistant from the directrix and the focus. The line perpendicular to the directrix that splits the parabola up the middle is called the 'axis of symmetry'. The thing was to hold humans, so I used the parabola and redesigned it with new materials." In studies, his work was proved true. This project solidified his reputation.

February 23, 2014

Today, I visit my mother. She has recently begun wearing an oxygen lead and perhaps there are some deep thoughts circulating her mind. She reminds me that she gave me an expensive ring once. "Do you wear it?"

Feeling uneasy, I kinda lie, "Yes of course, sometimes."

I'm using someone else's dishes, silverware, furniture, not my own. I feel like every corner of my life has lost precious pieces. Verizon even deleted all my favorite photos from over the years because I didn't know I was supposed to "upload and save" them before upgrading my cellphone.

Our accountant also asked a similar question recently. "Do you still have those legal documents?" I say, "They're around." But really I don't know where, in the packed boxes, they could be found.

I drive by the house I had designed, labored over, and sacrificed for in order to host lovely amazing people and wonder if it ever mattered. Didn't the LORD enable the sale of it to pass it into the hands of His other kids? Those, who didn't have our baggage and who are mending relational issues in the neighborhood? Aren't they doing practical things we couldn't begin to manage in our legal distress?

In this past year, I've turned a corner. Human rights mean nothing when politicians, the masses, or your neighbors have the power to take you to a cliff and push you over *for the sport of it*. The Constitution, as far as individuals are concerned I learned through difficulty, is relegated to an elegant national history due to the simple fact that average individuals cannot negotiate the courts' new rules without an attorney; or, I should say, without the necessary funds to hire an attorney. *Same thing.*

It tickles me to see people debate so many political theories in this particular highly incorporated, global world.

Instead, I've discovered a power to live peacefully, even thrive in poverty and persecution. I learned this strange fact as a Christian who has faced her worst fears. Due to God's steady Word of comfort and truth, and His amazing presence walking me through the valley of the shadow of death, I now fear no evil. His rod and staff have comforted me, do comfort me... and not like in the manner of some kind of consolation prize, but in the manner of having found real riches in secret places.

A basement full of things in boxes containing knotted legal facts doesn't whet a desire to lift a finger to unravel it.

I look into the mirror and realize my life is now considered "over the hill". As Mr. B likes to tell me, I'd do best to save more than spend. There's a sad surrealness, however, for this idealist to have intentionally allowed myself to become lost. Where are my newspaper clippings? My records? My dreams, journals, desires? Paul's love notes? I'm suddenly considering the great fortune of people who are never forced out of a home. They easily find their lives in the same old drawers. Mr. B is such a one, leaving only to play on vacation for a couple of weeks and then to return *home*. He has chosen a simple life, but he is not a simpleton.

If you have a purpose to live and someone who loves you, you can leave your past behind and be remade. I look around. Things that were once the height of quality are dated, holey, and frayed. But, this home is the vessel that has kept my soul afloat, and my activities loved and humored. Thank you, dear God, for giving us this humble, rich home.

It's mostly surreal because I am content being reduced! Is it because I have found belonging here in a new home? How was it for the displaced Jews? Ethiopians? Serbs? Native Americans? Rwandans? Do survivors ever find contentment, without landmarks of their history?

February 24, 2014
"I had my appendix out when I was 33, or maybe 35, just after we moved to Bald'more."

"How about age 34?"

"Smarty pants! Yeah."

"I remember the best engineer I ever knew was called Mr. Bergama. He was Czech. He was the chief engineer for Martin Company in Bald'more. One day a guy I liked came down and opened a scroll with only a few inches of the top drawing showing. He asked me to sign off on it like it was nothin'. I examined some of the specs on the blueprint and refused to sign off on it. I told the guy 'nothin' doing'." Joe hisses over the table at me. "What was he *hiding*? His superiors wanted a fall guy. So, I refused explaining *any*thing to the other engineer except that I had not done the work myself and therefore could not guarantee it.

Pretty soon Mr. Bergama came down to see what was going on. His boss was a hot-headed Jew, not that Jews didn't have plenty to be hot-headed over at the time. So Bergama explained he'd been asking another engineer to sign off on these drawings, but that guy had gone to the hospital with a brain tumor.

So, Bergama asked me to come along with him upstairs to see the boss. That's when I found out that the drawings were related to flying-by-wire, and a new instrumentation they wanted to install on the wing to check the weight of the wire mechanicals. Okay, fine." Joe shrugs.

"But this boss laid into Bergama because of the guy in the hospital, and he kept saying, 'Joe's right, Joe's right!' I didn't know what was going on. Well, Bergama was getting the pressure both ways so we let him have his say, and we went back to work. The company we were selling to rejected that design bid. There were so many rush situations and politics in the field, we all just had to learn to be quiet when things exploded."

February 25, 2014

Slivers of snow and sleet are dusting off on the shoulders of the sky above through mid-day, so I bake a chocolate pecan cake. Joe says, "In all my life, I don't think I've ever eaten cake at 2:30 in the afternoon."

I say, "Didn't you ever go to a birthday party?" It's nice and hot and the icing is more liquid than not.

"Oh, no... not that I remember."

He takes a sip of his Mandarin orange tea, swigging down a serious chocolate bite. "Our address alone would'a stopped any of those kind of invitations."

"Why?" I'm wondering if it was being Polish in a half French "Canuck" town, as Mr. B has described the situation.

"Ah, no. It was the typical rich versus poor. They could tell how poor we were because I always had to wear my big brother's hand-me-down pants, wid a rope to hold 'em up, and let me tell ya, they were LARGE. I had a best friend who went to kindergarten wid me, and followed me to college in Alabama. Joe Paczkowski. We were both poor. Everybody could see how poor we were from grade school up. The teacher played into it too.

"No time like the present, then, to eat chocolate cake in the afternoon."

"Heh, yeah. Don't tell Paul. He'll be jealous."

"Want another piece?"

"Oh, I'd better not," Joe hands me his plate. "But this makes up for everything I was holding against ya."

Later that afternoon, Joe gets curious about what he can see of his hometown of Woonsockett on my computer. I look up what he remembers to be his address, and "Yup, that's it!" He shakes his finger at the screen. "Except, let's see, the porch was different. I think they enclosed the porch. Can you turn it around and let me see the back side?"

That is the beginning of an hour of looking along all the surrounding streets and the railroad tracks where he used to walk. Much of it seems to have disappeared. We cannot seem to find many of the places he remembers, and he is disappointed. Finally, I look up a map, and we see the highlighted section saying, "Urban

Redevelopment Area."

"Oh," he says matter-of-factly. "That makes sense. It was pretty old, and we lived in a poor area."

I am always strung out by his emotional meekness. He never expects anything, or if he does, he adjusts accordingly. Mr. B is a study in living gracefully.

Our pastor preached on something similar earlier this week: we made a searching and fearless moral inventory of ourselves. It seemed to be a message on humility or meekness: "Why should any living mortal, or any man, offer complaint in view of his sins? Let us examine and probe our ways, and let us return to the LORD. We lift up our heart and hands toward God in heaven." (Lamentations 3:39-40)

How can I explain to Joe how righteous his attitudes seem to be?

February 27, 2014

Joe tells me about his mother's death today. He says that since she didn't drive, she asked him and his older sister, Lucy, to accompany her on the bus to the sanitarium. It took all morning to get to the stop and then walk to the place. After her visit, the doctor came out and showed him the x-ray of her chest. "It wasn't an x-ray exactly. It was like when you put your hand inside a lamp, and you can see through your hand." Joe describes a fluoroscope procedure that consisted of putting his mother behind a fluorescent screen.

"All I can remember is that her lungs looked like a tree. They were all full of cancer. It looked like branches. He said she wouldn't live long. I don't remember her complaining, but what a way to go. The doctor gave her medications so that she wouldn't suffer. She died."

"How old were you?"

"I was in college and had almost four years into the ROTC,

between '34 and '38. I was an officer in the Air Corp, right field top secret commission. So, I had to leave and finish college. My sistas helped her till she died."

February 28, 2014
We celebrate Maudie's birthday today. My sister comes over to

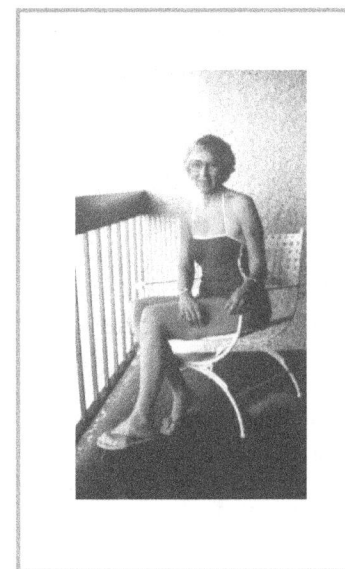

compare her recent vacation to Hawaii with Joe's memories of Hawaiian holidays with his wife. She shows him some pictures.

Then, he pulls out his stacks of photographs from the living room bureau drawer. Several good ones of himself in his ROTC uniform and with Maudie all dressed up are set out for examination among the three of us. He gets to one of her in a swimming suit and explains, "I made this swimming suit for my wife in 1973. It was wool to keep her warm. It was lined also so that it didn't irritate her skin. Wait, not this picture. This was 1984, in Mexico. She loved Mexico. That was the place we went for vacation because Hawaii was too far, and they both packed about the same punch. Oh, here is the picture wid her in the swimming suit I made her!" He handles the photograph with love and pride.

I tell my sister that Maudie and Joe both learned to speak Spanish late in life so that they could communicate with Mexicans better.

"I thought you said Joe doesn't like Mexican food." Kay's eyebrows furrow. "How did you handle Mexican restaurants, Mr. B?"

"Well, we ate a lot of fish and broiled meats, fresh salads, and papaya."

Joe's eyes glint in the morning sunlight to remember. "Yes, especially me. Maudie was more courageous. I'd let her eat those sauces. We both liked tortilla soup though. Umm, that was good stuff!"

My eyebrow arches. I realize when Mr. B admits he likes tortilla soup, that soup to him is its own food group. I have mixed up all manner of things into a soup and he's fine with it. Even creamed peas and onions are not gravy, but soup! Otherwise, each of the foods I serve him must occupy each their own place on his plate for him to happily down it all. He even picks out his lettuce from the salad to separate it from the carrots. "Is this finger food?" he once asked me as he ate his salad with his fingers. His antics don't bother me so much, but Joe's fancy sorority wife must have had a rich strain of forbearance in her blue blood genes!

Joe shrugs. "Lobster was cheap there and yeah, I liked papaya as soon as I tasted it. The hot afternoons, I liked their ice cream. Aw, I'm not that picky."

"The source of all humor is
not laughter, but sorrow."
— Mark Twain

March ~ Momentum

March 1, 2014

I can't wait to plant some of my seeds. It's been so warm that false spring is heralding tricky deceit on every gardener in Colorado. I plant some peas, lettuce, sweet peas flower seeds, and sunflower seeds, poking them into the damp spongy soil with my finger.

Joe used to bring me a vase of snipped sweet peas whenever Paul and I hosted family barbecues. He told me once that sweet peas are one of those special flowers that require some freezes to grow and blossom. And what a surprise it was for me to first experience the sweet fragrance they exude! When, in grade school, I learned that sweet peas are my birth month flower, I was completely bewildered and embarrassed to have a pea rather than a rose. Then, Mr. B's gardening set me straight. So I particularly take his advice to heart. My few hard freezes in life have been timely for my personal assurance of fragrant bloom.

March 2, 2014

Before we head out to my mother and sister's home for dinner, Paul wants to stop at the pharmacy to pick up a prescription. He grabs the first parking space he can find with the blue and white handicap symbol. He flips down the sun visor, then in frustration exclaims, "Oh man, we forgot the handicap sticker in the other car. Well, I'll just run in and run out. You think you two will be okay?" Mr. B looks over at me and sputters, "We won't get a ticket if they take one look at me!"

It's been a few months since Joe has wanted to go out to dinner anywhere with us. We've been eating through the cupboards and the freezer, and I was happy to see him agree to a dinner date with my mother and sis.

Welcomed into their home with cheerful pats on the back and arms, my mother explains that she has decided to fry up a personal favorite, though it's limited guest pleaser. "Lamb liver and onions!" She hugs me with a sly giggle. My sister rolls her eyes as Paul mutters, "Oh no."

Liz shows us the lamb chops she has prepared for cosmopolitan tastebuds. "Don't tell Joe what he's eating, either way."

I feel very nervous about this outing, and thankful that I've brought cucumber and tomatoes to pile onto my father-in-law's plate.

"We have a papaya too, for Mr. B. We know he loves that."

"Shew! Thank you!"

He sits down across the table from me and eats quietly, keeping to himself. This is a bad sign. Then Paul says, "What do you think of the liver and onions, Dad?" I kick Paul under the table. "What?!" He barks at me.

"This is *liver*? I wondered what I was eating." I wait for it. He swallows another bite. "This tastes good." He nods and looks up at all of us. "You know, Maudie used to make liver in bacon grease, and we'd eat that. But this is real good also."

Wanting to encourage this discourse, I add. "I like the lamb liver better than calf liver because it is more mild and not gristly. I like the caramelized onions too, Mom." She smiles appreciatively.

He looks up from his busy eating and agrees. "Yeah. I like this."

Afterwards, we joke around and clean up the plates. Then, we head into the T.V. room. They have a fun chef's movie for us to watch, but the language is incorrigible. Tense, I keep looking at Mr. B to see if he's had enough. He's leaning back on a pillow watching the large screen with his eyes wide open. I'm glad they have closed captions on. I offer to serve the tiramisu we brought. Still, Mr. B smiles up at the screen, then down at his dessert, then up at the screen. The movie ends well. Everyone's happy.

When we finally leave, Mr. B chatters excitedly about how clear the picture was, how the movie gave him quite an education because he was under the impression that foul language had gone out of fashion, how good my mother looked, and Liz was downright skinny. Then he commented how surprisingly good the lamb was, chops and liver both, and how much he appreciated the invitation. I place a phone call of gratification to Mom and Liz. They chuckle like two pleased hens. Then I hear a gasp.

"What is it?"

"Well, we completely forgot to serve Joe the papaya!"

"I guess you didn't need that trick after all." Sigh.

March 5, 2015

We are sitting in the living room talking about why people put ashes on their foreheads for Lent when Joe asks, "Why don't you go to church closer to home?"

Thinking on my feet, I say, "Because we like our church, because of the people, so it would be kind of hard to change now. And our church is doing what churches should be doing. Why? Would you come with us if we went to a church closer to home?"

"Oh, no." Joe growls then lays back his head on his favorite blue chair. "For a long time now, I've thought about starting my own church."

"You have?" No one could be more surprised. "What kind of church?"

"It wouldn't be this denomination or that. It would be a practical church. The people would agree together and have a common interest. The preacher would work for the people, not be the main face of the church. I'm not a believer in these guys who are too busy to talk to me if I am a member. And they always ask for money! That's all they are really interested in, so I give it." He shrugs. "Who cares? It's just money. What does it matter if I give it to them or someone else? Money comes and goes, but it doesn't buy trust between people." Silence. "And the most important thing that churches should teach is how to live this life."

After he describes his practical church, I think for a while, then say, "Joe, it sounds like a great club. We could call it the Joe-Co Club. But I'm not sure about it being a church because you didn't mention worship." As I hear myself speaking, I remember that the term "church" was an ancient word used before Christ, to mean any assembly of people.

Shrugging nonchalantly in his blue velvet rocker, Joe trumps me. "I don't know about that. I think anything we do that goes along wid what God wants would meet his approval."

"You have a point there. You have a pretty good definition of both church and worship at that, Mr. B!"

"But I have to think about it some more."

Indeed, if Joe hasn't come to some conclusions about how to start a church at age 98, I do believe it is an impossible human task.

March 6, 2014

Joe often can't see me when he walks into the den because I sit in front of the picture window. He comes in today from walking around the lawn doing "poo poo duty" and stops to examine whether I am sitting in my spot.

"Yup. There you are, young lady!" He yells as if he's spotted the Blue Angels themselves flying in formation overhead.

"Yup. Here I am, Mr. B. Just working on my computer."

"Well, why don't you ask that computer when spring is really coming to stay this year!"

I chuckle. "It doesn't foretell the future, Mr. B!"

"It doesn't? I thought you could just pump it for any kind of information you wanted and it would pump out an answer!"

I can tell he's teasing me, but I also think he is a little jealous that I spend so much time "pumping" my laptop. He also experiments in the library occasionally to see what he can find on a computer. And he has read up on every computer, how it works, the history of its technology, and the trading of stocks on various brands. Maybe I'll get him one.

March 8, 2014

My companion is talking war times tonight. And since he can't tell that his voice is doing double time with the television, I hit the mute control for the mystery, which is a rerun anyway.

He tells me that just before WWII, the Russians decided they wanted to secure the northern shores of the Baltic Sea to keep their enemies from accessing St. Petersburg (Leningrad) through Finland. The vulnerable access to the Imperial capital was only 20 minutes by land through Finland. But the Finns, of course, weren't happy with that decision, so Russia invaded Finland with manpower only, no tanks. It was called the Winter War. It began with the Soviet invasion of Finland on November 30, 1939 (three months after the outbreak of World War II), and ended with the Moscow Peace Treaty on March 13, 1940. Joe says the Russians were "stupidos" not to send tanks.

"So Finland put up bunches of barbed wire, with occasional openings, which forced the Russian troops through them. Then, the Finns slaughtered them and took hundreds of prisoners."

"I've never heard that the Finns played an integral part in the war!" Sometimes I feel slighted by my prior educators since moving in with my father-in-law.

"Well, eventually, because the troops kept coming, the Russians prevailed, but with very few Finn casualties. When the Russian army released their men from Finland's prisoner of war camps, they put their defamed soldiers on trains, and no one ever heard from them again!" He says emphatically, "There is no record about what happened: to become a Russian soldier meant to give one's life for Russia. If you got captured, it was considered shameful, so the Russians killed their own. The whole thing was a waste of lives, yeah. The League of Nations quickly deemed the attack illegal and expelled the Soviet Union from Finland just before Christmas, 1939."

March 10, 2014
This is the sixth anniversary of Maudie's death. He is so sure it was four days earlier, that he hobbled across the house to his sideboard and pulled out her death certificate. "Here. Read this. What does it say?" And when we looked at the death certificate, he was confused. I know his confusion is due to the fact that four days prior to her death he had to take her to hospice. March sixth is the day when he really lost her.

"Do you want to buy some flowers to put on her grave today?" I worry that I've needlessly upset him by reminding him about his wife's death.

"No. I pay that church to put flowers on her grave and I assume they are doing it. But I don't like to go there. That is not where my memories are."

March 12, 2014
Paul and I have a terrific insatiable taste for pizza. I order standard pepperoni and sausage, and then make a ham sandwich for Joe with a side of cottage cheese and tomato. He has finished his dinner by the time our decadent pie arrives. Paul tenderly places it onto the middle of the table and opens the box lid.

We peer inside and then shovel out two large triangles. Joe peers inside too. He begins with, "What's the circles? What's that smell? Why do people like that stuff? How healthy can it be?"

Finally, Paul says, "Chief, this is so good! You just don't know until you've tried a piece. Here, just try a bite, Dad." He shoves his triangle over to his father's nose.

Joe swings at it with venom. "No way!" Then he points a bony finger at his son. "How dare you bring this abomination into my house! What will the neighbors' think? You are ruining my reputation, and anyone could smell it being brought to the door."

"Ah, you're jealous, Mr. B! I can see you're intrigued by it. Come on, just try a bite. Then, you'll know what you're missing."

He thinks for all of three seconds about this. Then, "Listen. If you bring me a bowl of ice cream, I won't report ya."

March 13, 2014

Paul and I hired construction guys to demo and raise the roof of the outside back porch so that we can see the trees and sky through the back window of the house rather than the underside of the old porch roof.

Joe, being the shortest of us three, didn't 'get' it. "Why do you kids need to waste money?"

The job, which was done in a week, even has ol' Joe smiling. After running from all his questions, and ducking from his repeated engineering suggestions and accidentally losing his structural drawings meant to aid our work, Joe comes out *smiling*. Especially since he didn't have to put a penny into it.

When Joe's porch roof ended up four feet higher than last week, we could see his park-like backyard from the den. He oohed and aaahed. "You are one courageous young lady," he said. "I would never have done that in a million years!"

"Why not?" I ask, "It's not because you wouldn't have thought of it."

"Maybe," he says, "But I'm too cheap. That's why I used to hang my clothes on the line from the roof. It saves the cost of the electric dryer."

Whoops. I guess we are going to have to restring his solar powered, non-politically correct clothesline somewhere in the back yard, but it won't be under the porch roof in front of the picture window or impeding the vision of his backyard park anymore. *Sigh.*

March 14, 2014

Mr. B and I, with upturned faces, admire the new porch roof. "They did a difficult thing here, Miss." He points. "See, the side wings of the porch? They are sculpted like the wings of an airplane. See where the porch meets the house? Up there, the side wings are about a foot in height narrower than at the end of the porch, and yet the roof still slopes down at an angle correctly."

"You sayin' you like it?"

"Nice job." He nods. I breathe a sigh of pleasure.

"I'll let the guys know, Joe. Just wait till we paint it pale blue for ya, though. You'll like it even more. It'll feel like the sky above you."

Smiling, he takes a seat in his black and white gingham glider and then looks evenly at me; so I also take a seat. "You know, I mainly worked in the mid-sections of the fuselage, the bulkheads, the landing gear, from planes to space shuttles and even the reconnaissance satellites that could spy on the paths of submarines on the bottom of the ocean. But, there was one project they assigned to me that had to do with the wings of an American Airlines plane."

"Hum, what was that about? Just a minute. Lemme go in and get us some coats."

When I return, Joe places his coat over his knees and begins to explain that commercial airlines were getting design and engineering bids from just about anywhere, and the Martin Company landed some of them. "We were entering the cold war phase. We finished with the Titans, and American Airlines had a commercial plane, a 202 and a 303 flying, and right when we were finishing the 404 for 'em, one of their planes crashed. It was tragic. One day, my boss had me look over parts of the wreckage. I noted that there was corrosion all over the wings. That kind of corrosion meant that the plane couldn't take the stress of turbulence. It was determined that the new metal they had used on the wings should have been coated with a protective layer, and since it wasn't, the corrosions on the wings during turbulence had caused the flight to fail. Well, I had just finished designing the bulkhead in the 404, transferring the tension and tolerance loads from the cockpit, the paths of determining where tensions from the landing gear would be unloaded, and creating a tolerance for them around the plane and through the bulkhead; of course, taking into account how wind shear on the wing intersected with the fuselage."

"Okay." I'm shivering in a bit of my own wind shear, but interested.

"So they brought me the spar of the wing from the crashed plane and told me to redesign it. It's one of those tricky problems because I had to design a scarf splice with a 14-inch U-shaped gusset,-" he holds up both hands facing me with his thumbs touching to indicate that the U was shallow at the bottom, - "to taper the width," he wiggles his pinkies at the sides, "to unload the forces gradually into the splice."

"I'm not sure I understand, Mr. B."

"One time some engineers came to the principal German engineer, George Neumann, to ask him a question. They had bulked up the frame of a plane after they noticed that the skin was cracking, but after their redesign flew for a while, new fissures occurred. George told 'em that they had to unload the forces gradually, not reinforce the load, so that's what I did on the commercial airliner, too." He clears his throat and appears to be thinking.

"You have to guide the forces from the wind on top of the wing to the bottom of the wing to release them."

"Okay."

"I remember I added eight bolts, recessed from the edge. Some were half-inch and some were three-quarter inch bolts, to distribute the tensions of wind shear. Do you know what a bushing is? No? It's like a pile of washers, only it's one piece, a reinforcement, that is pressed into the previous hole that has been reamed out. Everything has to be smooth and clean! New steel bolts are pressed into the bushings, countersunk, so that they don't stick up above the surface of the wing. The detail is what mattered, Miss. There were two layers to match drill. And, since the wing comes into the fuselage at one angle, and the spar comes into the wing at another angle, and a third factor, wind shear, forces the wing to turn downward in flight, bending at a third angle, the bolts had to be specially tooled and machined with threads at a certain angle, and a specified number of threads. See, the radius of something can present a hell of a lot of problems. The bolts had to be a close fit, cleaned; bushings cleaned and oiled, but on the radius, there had to be a bit of space left for movement. The goal was to make sure there was no movement of the bolts in turbulence, see."

"Oh, once you know what you're doing, it goes pretty fast. So, I designed this eighth of an inch U-shaped aluminum gusset, plied it with eight steel bolts and bushings, and American Airlines had their new plane." He looks up and points at the wings of our new back porch. "That's why I appreciate this kinda work, Kiddo."

March 15, 2014
Paul's dad is sporting a huge sparkly-green bow tie with a green

bowling cap. I have green sparkly ears on and Paul wears a fine top hat with ribbons. "Looks like we've all been to the Haberdasher's!" Joe jokes in high spirits. We are meeting our Greek friends for breakfast at a fun Creole bistro named Lucile's. "It may be a bit early to celebrate St. Paddy's Day," I admit to our server.

"No, ma'am. People have been whooping it up for a few days already."

I'm just feeling a heady silliness these days. Our friends love Mr. B, and Mr. B finally approves of our friends, especially that Paul's best buddy also happens to be adopted. He can tell they have a special bond. On the way home from our silly breakfast with them, Joe says, "You know the Patron Saint of Engineers is Saint Patrick, and our school used to do this shin-dig called Show and Tell. It was our engineering class' form of Saint Patty's Day parade. Well, I'm not Irish, you see, and I couldn't, for the life of me, figure out what to present for the class. So, I finally just brought over our Franklin glider and hooked it up to the back of the building. That way, if anybody was interested, they could come and sit in it for a while."

"Come on, Joe. Did you blow them all away by bringing a real glider you had made to school?"

He shakes his head adamantly and touches my arm. "Oh no. Several of us contributed to building it. There were primary and secondary gliders, and it was only a primary glider, you know, the bare bones kind. I crashed it once and so did another guy in our club. I almost got thrown out!"

"How did you get it into the air? Did you cart it to the airport?"

"Well, yes and no," says Joe. "Those were the days when you could rent a car, and tow it behind you on the road to get a lift into the air, and then you hit the release and the rope would release."

What a rush! My hand goes out the car window to feel like I'm sailing through chilly wind. "Gliders seem so dangerous, Mr. B."

"Oh, but trusting the fuel in airplanes isn't foolproof neither! If chemicals are altered or the fuel is too thick, bad fuel can take down a flight."

"Man, I've flown so many times, and I'm glad I never knew about all the risks involved. Some people I know refuse to fly."

"Well, I'll tell ya, many technicalities were involved in developing the space program. From the type of fuel they used to the materials on the skins of the vessels and the weight, the design of the body, tail, and wings — the engines, the timing of lift and launch, everything *matters* in flight or the fall from space is disastrous!" He leans into me. "It's all math."

Turning into our block he comes to life again. "Engineers and mathematicians today are taught to use those computers. All of our work, the work of geniuses before us, is installed into today's computer systems. But we didn't know everything! There are still problems to be solved, and no-one left to solve them because they rely on assumptions and medians and generalities in the computers."

By the time we park in the driveway, I can tell he's more than a bit irritated. "There are principals and theorems that the best scientists need to know and rely on in order to make their own experiments and space vessels work. The problem today is that students don't have to know and practice these things. They take too much for granted, and there are just too many variables. Too many pluses and minuses. Those fractions, one way or the other, add up. You have to know what you are doing or BOOM." He doesn't say this with any volume. He says it deliberately which gives it an eerie air.

"There was a rocket launch that went bad one time in the NASA program because the missile was released from the rocket before it had built up sufficient thrust. The pad umbilical sent a shutdown signal to the engines, the wings collapsed back into the body as they were designed to, but it was a premature computer cue. The Titan fell back onto the pad and exploded."

March 17, 2014

Joe sips his morning Ovaltine with a spoon, like usual, and opens up, "I don't know if that medication the rehab place gave me is doing *anah* good." Then, to emphasize his point, "I don't like it, Sweet Pea. I really don't. I don't like the way it makes me feel at night."

After questioning him about some details, we place a call to his doctor and request he be allowed to discontinue the use. After his doctor agrees to take him off of this pill, he complains, "What are we gonna do about all this extra medication, though? I have two more bottles! Should I throw it down the toilet, or what?"

I relay this information to his doctor and she tells me that we can donate it to a doctor's mission trip. Mr. B is satisfied with that.

While I'm thinking how important it is for Joe to be able to discuss his medications, and jointly determine their effectiveness at his age, he changes the subject to discuss how his father died. "He knew he was dying. My fathea had five close friends from the bar who played cards wid him."

With the foresight to realize nobody would want to trudge through the February ice and mud to attend his funeral, he gave Joe's big brother some taxi money and told him to invite these buddies to his funeral when the time came, by sending taxis and paying their cab or bus fares. Joe winks and hammers his finger into the breakfast table. "To make sure they had no excuse, see? Sure enough, the day of the funeral came in the middle of the deep freeze of a Rhode Island winter." He breaks his morning bacon, extra crispy, with a fork and scoops it into his mouth with the utensil.

"There was another problem *howevah*. The ground was frozen 'bout two feet deep! Now, me and my fathea had been to the cemetery many times over the years, and we had smelled the bodies being saved in the building for spring thaw burials. So, my fathea, by all means instructed me to make sure they buried him right away." Shaking his head, Mr. B announces, "The grave diggers had a hell of a time digging that hole." He clears his throat.

"On the way to the cemetery after the funeral, the wagon wheel got stuck in the mud, and the casket almost fell out of the back end. They all worked together to get the wagon back onto the road and the casket stabilized. I remember looking around and the church was empty except for my brothea and sistas and those four card playin' guys who acted as pallbearers. They all buried my fathea together in that miserable cold weather. In the ground."

Finishing my own breakfast with many thoughts rumbling around, I decide to ask. "Mr. B, why is it that you eat bacon with your fork and you eat salad with your fingers?"

He shrugs. "I hate to touch the fat."

Ah, he *does* know that he's eating fat.

March 18, 2014

Joe has been complaining about needing new pickles. He loves Polish pickles. Ogórkies, he calls them (Ogórek). The ones we have in the fridge have too many spices in them. "Poles don't like garlic," he informs me. Every time we go shopping at the new grocery store, there are no Polish pickles to be found.

One day, he announces, "I know the old store has 'em. Let's go get 'em." And off to the old store we go. The clerk helps us look the pickle section over, but it is Joe who finally spots the barrel jar all on his own. It's in front of the row of Kosher Dills, so we seek out whether there is a whole row of pickles of the Polish variety. There's only one jar located way in the back of an empty space.

"That's because they are so popular," claims Joe.

"Or, maybe it's because they don't intend to order anymore," I say. Together we agree, "Then let's take both!"

Tonight, I open one of the famous jars of Polish pickles and make Joe a ham sandwich on Jewish rye... his favorite, ignoring the obvious conundrum. You'd think I had cooked him a five-course meal. He is so delighted that he rattles off all kinds of stories between bites. After a while, though, he scoots the jar closer with his fork to have a smell.

"I smell GARLIC," he roars.

"But Poles don't like GARLIC," I say, confused. "Besides, how could you smell it with the ham, Swiss, and rye?"

"Oh, believe me. I can smell it. Here. Read the ingredients for me, if ya can." Dim-eyed Joe pushes the barrel jar across the table in my direction. Aloud I read, "Cucumber, Water, Vinegar, GARLIC!, dill, sodium, GARLIC OIL, etc... Mr. B! You and the Poles must love garlic after all."

Joe stops munching. "What's garlic got to do wid Polish pickles?"

"I dunno, but when I cook something with garlic in it, you can't complain ever again. Poles like garlic as much as the Italians." I'm smirking.

Joe reaches way back in his memory. His eyes close. "Nope. The farmer never brought garlic. He always brought my mothea cucumbers and dill."

"Oh well, have another. They taste particularly good with the bread."

"You know? You are right." He spears another wedge and gobbles it up.

March 20, 2014

Fracking is such a big issue in Colorado these days. All three of us are enjoying the sunset together from the back porch, willing our new plants to spread their toes and wings and flourish along the edges of our little resort we're creating here, barking at Jester to run around the grass rather than tip-toe through the tulips.

Joe compares last night's news debate on fracking to an experience he had once. "You know Maudie's family owned the Carey Salt Mines? Well, they also had acres of farmland. There was an oil company that presented the family a 'Standard Lease Agreement' to allow the oil company to drill for oil on the land. They asked me to look it over. Well, I went to the attorney and I told 'em. 'You don't have a lot of facts in this lease. I want it written into the contract:

1) A beginning and an ending date to the lease. Why? Because you know if there is no end, you can just up and leave us wid'out warning or you can stay beyond your welcome.

2) The family needs a map of where the rigs will be and how close to the neighbor's property they will be.

3) We want an agreement on how you're gonna store the chemicals.

4) Where you're gonna put the access roads onto the property and off of the property.

5) An escrow account at such and such a bank so that at the end of the lease, when you walk off the property, we can correct the mess you made.

6) Who is gonna clean up the mess you make?

7) And we want 18% of the water rights and mineral rights, nothing less.'" Joe says, "They quickly declined our counter offer." He shrugs… "Shysters."

March 22, 2014

My father-in-law peels his egg and begins, "When I was making my own TV…"

"Hold on there, Joe. You made your own TV?"

"Heh-heh, actually, I put together a kit, and I didn't do it very well at that because I didn't have the tools to align the picture properly." He briefly looks up from his breakfast and smiles. "I finally had to take the thing back to the store to get it adjusted properly." He shakes his head.

"You know Maudie and I would go to Haussner's restaurant in Bald'more, and we would meet other young people, a lot of them were just on dates, but we invited them over to watch our new TV set. It was such a novelty in 1950, you know. So, we stuck it in the hall closet and we put chairs in the long hallway, and all these couples started coming over for Friday night fight nights. All the guys loved to watch the fighting on TV and the gals, you know…"

"The gals liked to watch the guys." I interject.

"Well yeah, you get the picture, heh-heh," he says spooning out a bite of soft boiled egg from the shell. "Sometimes we had to kinda ignore the philandering going on in our apartment, but those were the days. Everybody had so much fun. You know that three of those couples got hitched from all the fun we had, and we were good friends wid them until Maudie died. Now, say if Jack calls me, we can't hear each other on the phone anymore, but I still like him and another couple who have survived, like me."

Since the guys are still laying the back patio for us, Joe asks if I am up to walking around the block in the sunshine, and since I am, he wonders if I would allow him to walk with me. We walk it in fifteen minutes. He seems to be much more steady, not as wobbly. He won't hold my arm today.

"I don't want to be an invalid," he declares. "Also, what would the neighbors say if I attached myself to a young babe?"

March 23, 2014
Our Christmas cactus is wildly blooming, the second time in six

months. Long pink exotic funnel blossoms! Joe thinks the thing is possessed because it has never bloomed in March before. Maybe I remember putting Miracle Grow on it in early December trying to get it to bloom at Christmas? But I'm not sure.

"I had a dream I was gonna live to be a hundred and two, last night!" Joe confides excitedly as he stares at the cactus. "I'm coming outa that hip thing, that fall I had, don't you think, Miss?" Of course, I agree, but I've noticed he has a significant swing in good days and not so good. "Oh, I know I'm losing my memory, Kid, but I've still got something inside me."

"Yup, you are definitely amazing." I return, coming to admire the cactus flowers with him.

Our stint of transitional living with Joe is beginning to sound more like a whole new life. I believe I'd best come to terms with that. And, when I buy some black jeans for Paul today, the kind he likes to wear for work, an immediate advantage comes to light. Paul tries the jeans on after work but they are a bit too small. I explain this to Joe at dinner and suggest that he could have them, saving me the effort of returning them.

Paul objects. "No-way…Dad would look like a rock star!"

Joe looks up from his bowl of cottage cheese. He polishes the back of his fingernails on his 98-year old chest. "When ya got it, ya got it, Kid."

March 28, 2014

Paul and I have been given a long weekend at a friend's "recabinated" trailer situated on a vista overlooking fishing lakes and snaking streams, near Buena Vista. Excitement in the air, we relax and take delight for getting time away together in this winter splendor. We unpack, light the cabin stove, and unwind. Paul, then, pulls out a pan and starts cooking the first meal on his weekend agenda to spoil me. I curl into the couch to begin re-reading some great parts of the *Jesus Manifesto,* a book that contains things that I should have recognized from Sunday School, but the magnanimity of which has somehow escaped me for fifty years.

When Jesus left the earth, He left us with relationship. This is pivotal in understanding my faith. Christ is the Tree of *Life*, not the tree of theology, not the tree of knowledge, not a tree of good and evil. In order to break off bad habits, we need relationship!

As Paul serves me his yummy chili and garlic bread, I tell him my new discovery. "You know how I've always said that church should be more like close friends of a twelve-step group? You know how each one gets a few minutes to help another person who names the topic? Well, it's true! Christianity is supposed to be a living body of members who help each other. This body life surpasses the knowledge of good and evil." Paul perks up. "The authors suggest that true meaning of righteous living means living in community in many aspects. Following Jesus is not solely an individual experience. It's not a magic prayer inviting this God into your heart! It's more the model of repentance and sponsoring used in a twelve-step program!"

"I know," says Paul matter-of-factly, which unnerves me. How could he know something that's taken me fifty years to understand?

Living in community with Paul's father has brought home the necessity of family unity, family serving family. In sickness and in health. There seems to be a false interpretation of the Bible spawned from the secular Enlightenment and the Age of Rationalism that God is pragmatic and predicable and basically doting on American individuals so long as we achieve a moral standard. But what about the question of suffering? The feel-good stuff can't hold up the needs of aging and sick people, or the stumblers and doubters. They need hands-on help. I'm startled, and impressed now, that we should approach the Bible's teachings through communal and even global relationships. Like a triangle with vines intertwined, with God as head, I expect we would understand many of the mysteries contained in scripture if we filtered them through a sense of belonging to one another.

"We think it begins with us, but not really. We enter into the flowing river of the historical church, and many cultures, when we meet Christ, Honey." Paul pours boiling water into the washtub and dishcloth.

As we clean up the cabin kitchen together, I feel the chilly breeze coming through this newly-opened door. "We can't interpret Christianity through our own narrow nationalism, race, history, or personal whims. Ah! Maybe that's what baptism implies." These thoughts inspire me to continue to learn from our priceless Mr. B's experiences and to actively show him the respect he is due. Revelation is always veiled in mystery because we cannot completely understand the history or culture in which the Word was written. Nevertheless, it is alive today. Jesus is the full expression of the Godhead made flesh. He said, "The Scriptures point to Me!" The Lodestar of heaven is Christ Jesus, and he left us with the Holy Spirit. He left us with mentors, siblings, and parents, as well. These all guide us and they put checks on us.

"Read something to me, Lynn." My husband plops onto the couch and turns his body to lay his head on my lap.

"Okay." I pick up the book and flip to a dog-eared page. "So the fullness of Christ can never be accessed through the frontal lobe alone. That's why Jesus did not leave His disciples with CliffsNotes for a systematic theology. He left them with breath and body. He didn't leave them with a coherent and clear belief system by which to love God and others. He gave them wounds to touch and hands to heal. He didn't leave them with intellectual belief or a 'Christian worldview.' He left them with a relational faith and an indwelling presence." (*Jesus Manifesto* by Leonard Sweet and

Frank Viola.)

"Your chili-onion breath! You're so fortunate that I love you!" Paul grimaces. Yeah, I am.

In all this world, I feel like I've landed my ship on a desert island. Only, I've discovered a sense of purpose and belonging with Paul and his father. I know that Mr. B is thriving, too, because he says he feels the same way. He has his routine and his ownership and the people he loves surrounding him. He is able to contribute, and he gets loved back in ordinary, incidental ways, ways that let us know our relationship is bigger than a scheduled visit.

Tonight, Paul and I stand outside with our chins in the air, gawking. Then, I find a pencil in the guest book to note something about our visit:

> The Stars! The Stars! The black lion angels
>> With twinkling planets for eyes
>> and fiery galaxies for freckles,
>> as though we had never noticed Jupiter, Venus and Mars,
>> the Norwegian Horse, the Dipper, the Hunter, the Kite,--
>> The studded King's cloak and swaths of moonless jewels
>> refracted of the sun's light.
>
> We gaze and nudge each other with elbows and open mouths
> And then we bow uncomprehending the sight.
> Our hearts pump as though the lion angel had stopped his prowling
>> to pant over us.

March 30, 2014
We come home this afternoon refreshed and eager to see how Joe

managed with his nemesis, Jester the dog. We find him sitting in his rocker in the back porch sun with the dog lying at his feet. "Oh, we get along alright." Joe nudges the dog with his toe. "We just have to come to an understanding, that's all."

"Which is?"

"Which is that your dog's the boss. I'm not!"

March 31, 2014

Yesterday our ol' man also finished digging out a redundant sprinkler line. I, therefore, felt compelled to help him carry, dump, and spread wheelbarrows of recycled dirt while the professionals pieced together our new patio.

I'm exhausted, but Joe wants to keep raking, so we rake. He says when he was in college the guys he really felt sorry for were the ones who worked President Hoover's programs in exchange for schooling. They bunked in an old barn behind Joe's dorm. They had a single light bulb, and they had one bathroom. He said the guys would be so tired after digging public hiking trails in the red earth of Arkansas, that they didn't bother to take off their boots so there was a steady trail of red earth in and out of the shower room. "Now, that was hard work," he says.

Our porch roof has been lifted. Our flagstone patio is almost finished being laid by professionals who don't mind their backs breaking for the right fee.

Warm spring days are in and out, in and out.

Mr. B and I have redesigned a new place in the backyard for the leftover flagstone that the professional workers took out of the old patch.

Joe methodically works beside me picking up chunks of flagstone, eyeing the right fitting, and laying each piece like a puzzle onto the grass. At the end of the day, we think we have a good casual second patio fitted together. Paul, however, isn't sure.

When he looks it over after work he vetoes it being in the grass, but for the time being, we argue, we are exhausted and we have no other place to put it. It stays.

I keep looking at the flower and vegetable seeds I bought last fall, yearning to plant them. Finally, I stick my fingers into the soil and poke the lettuce, spinach, and peas in. I have already poked down the sweet pea flowers, and now Joe puts a few more along the soil line of the chicken wire. Does this satiate my spring fever? Oh no. Warm evenings after work, Paul and I have worked to lay a path of flagstone leading from the back corner of the yard to the back porch. We've laid it on top of cardboard to smother unwanted grass between the roses and shrubs. Today, I'm raking, spreading the mulch between the flagstones.

I hear a voice calling to me from its shaded position under the porch roof. "Whatcha doing there?"

"After this path is finished," I huff, "I just want to plant shrubs along the curves to outline it. Different blooms and colors at different times will give

us something new to look at in different seasons. I'm just puttin' in a row of these daylilies today." I point at the pile of grassy clumps. I don't admit that there is a master plan sketching itself in the back of my mind. I'd like to build a walking path leading all the way around Mr. B's yard, surrounded by trees, bushes, grasses and flowers for the purpose of lingering at different focal points and meditating on sayings, like "a seed must die before it can grow old," or at a fountain, "clean hands and clean heart." It's sort of my idea of a labyrinth, only reversing the inner design space to the exterior of the yard. Maybe I should come "clean" with my design to Mr. B… Hmm.

"You guys are making my park look smaller with all these gadgets you are putting in." Joe complains wagging his head

I shout back. "Mr. B, we are making less grass for you to cut! Besides, you don't have to help me if you don't want to."

Mr. B saddles up to me, removing the toothpick from his lips. "Oh, no. I'm not gonna let you take all the credit. I see what you're aiming at. Besides I gotta help you stay young and fit, Miss."

> "Someone I loved once gave me
> a box full of darkness.
> It took me years to understand
> that this, too, was a gift."
> — Mary Oliver, Thirst

𝒜PRIL ~
INTERSECTIONS

April 1, 2014

Mr. B gets introduced to the nail salon today. Paul said, "Just take him. Don't tell 'em where you're going." This, because his father always fights our suggestion he try a real pedicure with me. Pauly hates giving his papa a nail clipping, and yet a nail clipping is a necessity, smelly business or not. "We can't ask Jessica to do his nails either, granddaughter or not."

"Where are ya taking me?" says the chief bending, but not really bending, his behind into my HHR. The top of the door clips his head and his cap falls off this time. "Gimmee some o' that olive oil of yours, and I'll slip right in next time." I pull his knitted winter cap back over his head.

"Well, it's not to the hairdressers, 'cuz we were just there!" He's so curious, looking around the road as we go, trying to guess.

"It's a surprise." He's frowning and I'm grinning even as I pull into the parking space before a large pink sign that reads, "NAILS". I take him by the arm and lead him inside the place.

"Aye-yi-yi, Miss!... This place is for girls!" He gargles out the words, bewildered. Still, he obediently removes his shoes, lets me pull off his socks, hike up his pants together with his sweat pants till they rest above his knees. A young Vietnamese girl lifts up the armrest and helps him scoot into the salon chair with the kneading massage machine inside. When it starts its job, his body begins to bubble like a foaming machine. "How do ya calm this thing down?" He shouts. The calm manicurist tries a few different settings before he agrees to try one.

When she gets going on his nails he turns to me. "Pauly should use his glasses when he does this. He always takes a little extra besides the nail."

"I told ya you'd like the professionals, Mr. B."

"Oh, they're good. They're real good." Then, he proceeds to ask his manicurist questions about North and South Vietnam. She's confused and asks my manicurist what he is saying. My manicurist begins to interpret, but when she answers, Joe can't hear her soft dialogue, so he keeps talking about North Vietnam helping the Americans, which eventually earned them the right to come to America with passports. "They were mountain people," he informs all of us. The two manicurists speak cautiously between themselves.

When the foot massage begins, Joe relaxes a bit into his massage chair. "Boy! This is the works!" Then he explains how his sister, Lucy, used to get a hot pail of water to treat their father to a pedicure. "Oh, he loved it! You know, Papa is all… but, my mothea neveh got one as far as I knew." As we are leaving, Mr. B declares he is a new man and ready for the party!

"What party's that, Mr. B?" Have I forgotten an event?

"The April Fool's Day party! No, Miss. That was truly a surprise. Especially because I never had a pedicure before. *Wow-wee!* But, I hope you are headed straight home. Otherwise, I'll have to run into the woods somewhere." Heaven forbid Mr. B uses a public restroom. The woods might be just the place to hide.

April 2, 2014

Today, my sister asks me to go shopping for Yew trees. I research them and supposing I am immune from the temptation, agree to go. After a couple of hours shopping, we end up shoving my entire car full of pots, large and small, bags of seeds, and soil, giggling with pleasure. Happy fools.

Joe confronts me, "I read the tags on all those pots you bought. I see those red twiggy things are gonna expand. You see the volunteers off to the side? I don't want you to plant so much that we have no back yard left."

I reply, not mentioning that he is the one who wants me to plant six-foot round and twelve-feet tall pampas grass. "Joe, red twig dogwoods do grow a bit wider, maybe double their width, but I've never seen one expand so much that it takes over a yard."

Joe sighs like a martyr. "Oh well, if they do I'm a courageous sorta guy."

April 3, 2014
On the way back from the doctor's, Joe takes me to lunch. He begins talking about his days working as a stress engineer in Baltimore. Both his boss and the company's chief draftsman were staunch Catholics. "They presumed I was also Catholic due to my Polish heritage." He explains, "We would all eat lunch together and the two of 'em would begin to assert religious ideas and argue," Joe leans in and hisses, "especially contraceptives, numbers of children a family should have, and how to raise them. They would go on and on about other hot issues in the church. Sometimes they would ask me outright, whether I wanted to be asked or not," he complains. "They wanted to know my own perspective on the issue at hand. Boy! Was that a conundrum!" He leans forward with an exasperated wide-eyed appeal. "Ya don't know what to say because in those circumstances, you only have to say the wrong thing once and you've made an enemy out of somebody who liked you prior to opening your mouth. You had to be a *diplomat*." He draws out the term in his voice of cunning. "I would just put an end to it by saying something like, 'I can see both of your perspectives, but it's time for me to get back to work now.' Or in jest, 'I think you each made a good point, but ya talked

about it so much, lunch time is about over.'"

"Mr. B, I've read that the Poles are still a very prejudiced people against the Jews."

"You did? I wonder why? The Jews have made a comeback around the world you know."

"I'm not sure why the British gave them a home country after the war."

"Well, probably because after the war, most of them tried to come back to their homes, but found other people living there. The survivors had no proof that the home was theirs, so they had to immigrate and start all over. The Jews in Poland had big, beautiful houses. Much better than the Poles at that time. It was pure greed that made the Poles point out Jewish families to the Germans and Ukrainian Nationalists. They knew if they could force an evacuation, that big home would be available to move into." He pauses.

"They say the war was a matter of religion, Catholics against Jews, but it was just pure spite. I wouldn't doubt that it still exists." He gazes at nothing and says the strangest thing. "In my life, I've learned that people are expendable."

"What?"

"Yeah. My boss had me analyzing what went wrong on military airplanes when they crashed and especially the seaplane P5M that they were using to guard the straight between Taiwan and the mainland. China was always trying to get that island and it was America that kept them out. The military would ask for volunteers to try out the new designs, and many times they failed and the man was lost. One time the factory women making the plane used the wrong size hole drill, bigger than the screw, on the metal parts. The military was so desperate for planes, that they put the thing together and sent it out anyway. Of course, the vibrations shook the thing apart...who knows how long it lasted.

"Take the B19 bomber. They had a problem wid the turret that hung below the plane. It was such a small place that they would conscript small guys, only 5'3", to man the two 50's, that's what they called the guns hanging below the plane there. The guy would sit in that small spot, but if he got wounded or the mechanics failed, the flyers couldn't bring the thing back up into the plane so that the guy could get out!" Joe hisses over his breakfast plate at me again. "The pilot would just have to land and the small gunner would be sacrificed. He was squashed down there so tightly that his knees were almost in his face, and the guns were between his legs. So, you can imagine what happened to the poor guy if there was a mechanical failure, and it happened more than once, I'll tell ya."

"Augh!" I lose my appetite.

He was stuck designing mechanical parts that he knew would kill guys in wartime! No wonder Joe has issues about the goodness of God. That wasn't the first time in his career that he'd encountered the choice between a safe income and the death of others, or the loss of career coupled with personal suffering. I remember how he refused to vilify the Nazi engineers who came to work with him in the aerospace industry.

"I tried to suggest changes to the design, but there was no money. It killed me. It really did.

"Another thing we worked to redesign was a plane's tail that would break off. If the pilot had to land in the stormy ocean, the tail could break off. Our work was on the front and bottom of the plane because they only had one full bulkhead at the front, a large open space in the middle and then a half bulkhead at the back. You know the Titanic? It taught us that half bulkheads are worthless because the water can fill up and spill into the next space. In the case of this plane, the weight of the full bulkhead would cause it to sheer off of the plane, so we had to figure out a way to balance it. I told them to put in a full bulkhead at the back and seal off the middle section so that the guys would at least have a chance to put on their safety gear before the thing sank into the ocean like a tin can. Also, the middle was so open, that the guys were trying to shield themselves from the force of the crash wid their parachutes, but even if they survived the knocking around, they would sink too quickly to get outta there. The board again vetoed my design suggestion because it would cost too much money."

"They were fortunate to have you, Joe." I replied seriously. "I'm sorry about the way those things turned out."

"Well, not for me. For them!"

He shudders at the thought. "Another problem they had wid some of the planes was that the bombs were preset to explode within minutes of separating from the plane. But when there was a crash into the ocean, the bombs would be wrenched apart from the plane and then they would explode under water, maybe on the floor of the sea, see? A ship captain called in one time because explosions were going on in the ocean beside his ship. That's what happened."

Joe is silent for a few moments remembering those early days. Then he says, "When the chief draftsman was promoted to someplace in Florida, he wanted to take me wid him as his chief structural engineer. I told him, 'I don't take to the weather in Florida. It's too stormy and mucky down there.' I also didn't take to California neither. It wasn't my style.

"So, we moved to Colorado, and we liked it. That's when I quit smoking. Maudie and I both liked the weather, so we'd hike. We used to hike all over the place. Whenever we learned of a new trail, we'd go find it. She always had bad feet, but she never complained. That's where we got these blue spruce, Scottish pine, and lodge pole pine trees. And we also picked up some driftwood, too. You can't find pieces like that much anymore."

"We appreciate your driftwood, Mr. B. We moved the ones you gave us from house to house, and now we've brought it back to you."

Joe looks happy and nods. "Paul loved the outdoors, too. He wouldn't hike wid his parents, mind you. We were too old fashioned, but he hiked a lot wid his buddies. And little Victoria found a stable nearby and they used to let her ride a horse. I still remember before the rest of these houses were built and the neighbors put up their fences that she could ride right up to our back door. Colorado was a nice place to raise the kids."

April 4, 2014

"Paul, has your father ever told you about his feelings in designing parts of planes that ended up killing gunners in World War II?"

"No. My dad never talked to me growing up. Think about it. He would paint in the winter, garden in the summer, or watch sports on television. He never hugged me as a teenager. He never told me he loved me 'til I married you. He would get drunk on the sofa until mom threatened to leave him, and then he quit drinking cold turkey. If my sister or I were crying or distressed in any way, he would say, 'Go see your mother.' That was it. I've learned more about my dad through your conversations than I ever knew."

"Oh, well it isn't me *in particular*. People do change over forty years' time, both parents and children do, if they try a little. I'm glad you are both spending quality time together now."

He agrees. Living in community is a good thing whether with a stranger or with my father-in-law. There are times when someone is able to give and that one is the strong blessing to others. Then, the tables turn, and the next one is the strong one who is a blessing to the rest. If I am not giving or serving from my heart, I am simply missing out on how rich life could be. Why then, does it so often feel like a sacrifice, only to be taught this lesson once again?

I am a forgetter and a slow learner.

April 7, 2014

Mr. B asks me to fax his insurance card to his provider. So we climbed in the car and did that. Then he needs a prescription filled and a can of nuts. We walk into the grocery store together and come out with our basket full. Mocking the tone of a rich man's chauffeur, I attempt a Brit's accent. "Do you require an hour, at the library, Mr. B?"

He turns suddenly to applaud our execution of a morning, "Wow! You solved all my problems in an hour and we still have time for books!"

I look at the wide empty soccer park of stark, winter grass and note, "Where are the geese, Mr. B?"

"The heat?"

"No, the GEESE."

"Where's the *beef*? Oh, you're trying to be funny."

"No, the GEESE! In the park!" I flutter my arms and point.

"A *treat*? You don't have to overreact like that."

In the library, he forgets that he's already picked up the federal tax forms, so he makes his way over to pick up a couple more.

On the way home, then, he taps his tax documents and spouts, "Hey, I think we should get a deduction for my blindness. Can you look into that?"

"You aren't exactly blind, Mr. B. You've been reading for the last hour."

"Well, I know," he admits, "but there has to be some sort of standard you can find out about, and you know I am blind in the one eye and I have this *muscular deterioration* too."

I about lose it with the "muscular deterioration" and am pursing my lips, trying to hide my amusement, when he said, "You know, if I could get another $1,200 off my taxes, you and me could go out to Ted's Montana Grill!" He wraps his hand in the crook of my elbow and snuggles up.

"Now you're thinking, Mr. B., but really, you've already made my day."

April 11, 2014

We are recycling stuff, sort of. Our pastor spoke about hoarding and so Paul and I decided to unload our discontent. It's time to start cleaning out our basement and give to the poor. That was yesterday.

Joe has been sanding smooth the rough patches all over our old lawn furniture, and he sets about painting it today. I declare he is going to live longer than me. After a day of hard labor, heaving boxes up the stairs, from basement to the garage, my back agrees with my sentimental heart and rebels against giving our mementoes to the poor. I decide, instead, to seek out spine therapy and then test my therapist's worth by going shopping for some new cushions for Mr. B's rejuvenated chair efforts instead.

April 14, 2014

"HAPPY HOLY WEEK!" I announce to Joe who squints at me from the bottom stair. "I'm not awake yet, Miss."

"OH, HOW I LOVE A GOOD MYSTERY!" I'm thinking about that medical sign with the serpent on the pole today, that weird sign of healing and help. Jesus said his death was like Moses' serpent lifted up. Yesterday, our pastor mentioned the serpent on the standard lifted up by Moses in the wilderness. God told Moses to lift it up amongst the tents of the Israelites so that all those who were dying of plague could trust His direction, look at the serpent as instructed, and be renewed to health. Such a weird prescription.

"What?" he baits me.

We take our seats for breakfast, and I ask him if he knows where the medical insignia came from. He frowns and acknowledges that it is a strange sign of healing but has never asked about it.

I pray silently and then tell him the biblical history. Joe holds up his hands to stop me. "I love a good mystery too," he says.

My heart plummets, but I find another way. "Don't you think it is a tell-tale sign that churches do not use the insignia that hospitals dare to use? Maybe we'd all run from a church that used that sign rather than an empty cross! But Jesus himself used it. The striking conundrum is that in fact, Jesus said he became the Creator's curse for us so that all of humanity, and all of nature, could be freed from the curse."

Joe's mind is engaged. I can see it. He bleats, "Why'd ya wake up thinking about THAT?"

"I've been thinking about it since yesterday, Joe! Christ's plan was to be made a despicable spectacle, lower than our lowest soul, so that we could inherit new life. All we have to do is look at him and trust God's prescription."

Joe shrugs and thanks me for breakfast. "You made all my favorites today. I thank ya." The sliced papaya, boiled egg, and hot Ovaltine were accompanied today by a yummy bear claw each. "Where'd you get the bear claws?" he asks.

"Oh, that son of yours thought we were worth a treat, I guess. He bought them last night." I pause. Then I shout at Joe, "Do you remember the biblical story of Lucifer, the angel?"

"Who? Oh, oh, Lucifer, yes. I mean, not really."

"Well, Lucifer was the most talented, privileged, and beautiful angel in heaven, but when he began to take all the credit for himself and say he was like God, he was sentenced for his pride and cast down by God Himself. God cursed Lucifer to earth to crawl on his belly like a serpent and be despised forever."

"Humph." Joe is listening.

"When Jesus hallowed that dishonorable image for himself, we have to acknowledge the full truth of his humility in accepting his Father's curse, becoming sin for us, being slimed by evil, sliding into its skin so that we might trust his plan, obey his instructions, and be free from it. He was the only one who could conquer the powers of sin, but it is still a mystery!"

I pick up the plates and wash up the dishes. Mr. B sits there thinking rather than cleaning the stovetop as is his normal routine. When I sit in the den with the dog as my bear rug, Mr. B meanders in and looks at me. "What gets me is why that particular thing, a reptile? The lowest of the low. Why not something else?"

April 15, 2014

We have been looking forward to spending my birthday with Mr. B and the double event of his favorite restaurant closing down, the Peck House in Empire, Colorado. Joe dislikes sad events like funerals or changes that certify endings. He refused to attend his own wife's funeral, and waited for us at home to console him after it occurred. But it's my birthday, and we won't take no for an answer. Besides, he would be embarrassed to offend me, so he joins in the festivities.

Joe insists I take the front passenger's seat in his 1995 red Saturn with only 39,000 miles riding on it. It's rather spectacular to have two men complimenting me on how special I look tonight and how much they celebrate me. Three car doors shut us in like a vault, and our seatbelts whirl into their locked positions.

Passing over Genesee Park, we spy a herd of big horn sheep. Their horns are huge round shells, like giant crustaceans. Their wooly white coats are molting.

The sunset glows off of the far mountain in rosy snowcaps. It has been a long time since Mr. B has allowed himself this pleasure.

We order his favorite openers, shrimp cocktail, smoked trout, and Chef Gary's duck breast pâté. No liver here. Joe's cheeks begin to shine. Then, he orders chicken masala. Paul and I take our time through the warm spinach salads and onto the tenderloin entrées. It's hard to believe this dining room will shortly become the owner's bedroom and office. Mrs. St. Clair brings me a bag of springtime luncheon napkins from her gift shop. "For your birthday. I saw you admiring these, and I won't be needing them." Now, my cheeks are shining. We top off our fabulous memories with the Peck House Turtle Sundae. Joe is chuckling with delight. "I had forgotten how good this place is. It's a shame that all good things must come to an end, isn't it?" He licks his spoon. "I won't be able to sleep tonight, but I'll have lots of good things to think about." He closes his eyes appreciatively, like Yoda.

"Here you go, Miss B." Mr. B hands me a card and a little box. Inside is his wife's silver sailing boat pin. "I sure have enjoyed having you around this year. I hope I haven't been too much of a bother."

"Oh, Mr. B, I wouldn't have any of these memories if it weren't for you. My life is full and rich with you in it." I get a little weepy realizing how true my sentiment is.

Mr. B tells us that he never spent the night there because it was a little old fashioned for him.

"It's a *historic* hotel, Joe!" I say.

"What's that?"

"It's a historic hotel, Joe!" I shout in my deeper *inside* voice.

"Did I ever tell ya about the fancy hotel in Woonsocket that I yearned to look inside of for years? My best friend, Joe Paczkowski, worked there in high school. He'd tell me all about it, and I was jealous. So, when Maudie and I were getting hitched, or just before, I picked her up at Columbia University and took her to meet my parents. While we were in town, we went to inquire about the rooms in that hotel. They had a 'special' going on. So, we asked to see the room. It was clean, but really old. Old fashioned. Then, we walked down the stairs and a couple of guys were smoking in the bay window. All the desire to stay there wid my new bride for our honeymoon dissolved. That's the thing about dreams. Sometimes they work out, and sometimes they don't."

"Lynn's old fashioned, Dad. We've stayed here a couple of times over the years."

"Sometimes old fashioned is a good thing," Joe concedes with a wink.

"Oh, you are just flattering her now," Paul challenges his papa.

"Well, she cooks most of my meals. I gotta be careful. I don't want any rat poisoning in the stew." He's really on a roll with his belly full of memorable food.

"No way, Dad. She'd never do that. She loves you. Besides, she's much more direct than that." Paul nudges me, and I kick him under the table.

"Heh, heh, you're tellin' me. She gets right in there with the religion thing." He turns to me. "You know, you remind me of the nicest guy I knew in college. His name was Tom Arnson. He was hot and heavy with his gal whom he married that year. He'd come in late and hav'ta beg my homework off of me. We did everything together. Except church. He was religious too. I wouldn't listen to him, so he got his pastor to come out 'ta visit me, but after awhile, the pastor left and I never saw him again.

"When the war started and Tommy got conscripted, they asked him to be the quality control guy. It was a good job. Then, after the war, someone handed him a job in government writing letters to people who had written to their congressman. We stayed in touch for several years. I've always wondered what happened to him. He's probably dead for sure since he was older than me."

I wish Tom would have maintained his personal integrity with

Joe, without cheating on his homework. I've decided since living with Joe that memories of people stand out either as an ornament in life or as a demon. They are each there for a reason, but sometimes we have to get real old, maybe older than Joe, to understand what that reason was. I want to be an ornament, not a copycat cheater.

April 18, 2014

I'm explaining to Joe that my Greek girlfriend has invited us all to Easter dinner with her family. Joe tells me that there was one Greek man, a short Greek man, who lived down the block from him in Woonsocket. "I delivered papers to him."

"One Greek in a town of Poles and French Canadians? How did he do?"

"Just one. He ran a gambling establishment. The only one that the police didn't raid. He ran it for years. People would cross state boundaries to gamble there. They'd stay half the night. No one ever bothered 'em. I think he musta been into the police somehow. Anyway, in the morning, I would take my papers down there, and no matter how full that establishment had been during the night, it was silent as a sleeping cat by morning. I remember standing on the porch and looking at the sun's rays filtering through. It was spic and span on that porch except for the dust or pollen floating in the sun."

"Interesting!" I think Joe is a poet in his own right.

"Think so?" He raises his eyebrows at me. "What's more interesting is that the short Greek guy could stand in front of a bar, and suddenly, he could bend his knees and jump from that position onto the top of the bar. Standing straight up! You wouldn't believe it, but I saw it with my own eyes. No running or anything, just standing there, and suddenly jump up on the bar."

"Maybe that's what kept the police away."

"Yeah, maybe." Joe chuckles, reviewing the scene in his mind.

April 23, 2014

We tell Joe that we've decided to put our rental house on the market. He nods in acknowledgement. We explain, "Housing sales are finally up, and even if we can break even, we won't have to be dealing with renters coming and going, and the upkeep of the thing. After all of these years, we haven't made any money on it."

He nods again. "I think you pretty much have to have a rental property paid down to the nubs before you go off and make cash from it. It's like any asset. It's not really your asset until it's paid for."

I start making phone calls for exterior painters. Then we call to notify the renters and finally I post a friendly notice on the door with the dates. We're on a roll.

April 24, 2014

A visceral repugnance rises in me towards the duplicitous priest who mortally wounded Mr. B's conscience as a child. As an adult then, Joe brought his questions to a Protestant minister, then Maudie's denominational preference. That minister could not look him in the eye to discuss the issues. Instead, he shuffled papers and waffled. So, when Joe declares, "That's why I have no confidence in religion or let's say religious *people*," I find I can't hold back from relaying the story of young Samuel who lived with the Hebrew high priest, Eli, and Eli's two sons, Hophni and Phinehas, boys which Eli refused to discipline.

Maybe to Eli, his fatherly love for his sons felt more tangible than his love for God? Maybe he feared the wickedness growing inside of his rebel adult sons more than he feared God? The bare facts of the biblical story seem to display God's loving kindness as overly forbearing for what impatient victims might consider too long, yet not only does criminal activity come to an end, but there is a final reckoning.[1]

Eli's sons, also priests, were stealing the people's designated offerings and meat meant for sacrifices to God for their own personal use. The people were giving to God their best lambs, their best doves, their best fatty cuts, but the offerings didn't arrive at a holy destination. Additionally, Eli's sons were fornicating and abusing young women who came into the temple to worship.

One night in the temple's sleeping quarters, the Lord of All spoke to the young servant boy, Samuel. On the third visit:

> The Lord came and called again, "Samuel! Samuel!"
>
> Samuel replied, "Speak, your servant is listening."
>
> Then the Lord said to Samuel, "I am about to do a shocking thing in Israel. (Both ears of everyone who hears it will tingle.) I am going to carry out all my threats against Eli and his family, from beginning to end. I have warned him that judgment is coming upon his family forever because his sons are blaspheming God and he hasn't disciplined them. So I have vowed that the sins of Eli and his sons will never be forgiven by sacrifices or offerings."

Soon, there was a battle against Israel, and in one day, Eli's three sons were slaughtered and the ark of the Lord was captured by the enemy. When Eli heard the news, he fell over in his chair and died.[2]

My words are blurting swords as I explain to Joe that though we may not see it, we can be sure of the High Judge's decree against leaders who are licentious in their representation of him. God takes a leader's perverse representation of his character very seriously. Jesus said, "It is better that a millstone be hung around the neck, and the person be tossed into the sea, than that person offend a child."

Joe's eyes widen. He is listening closely.

Maybe the "unforgivable sin" does exist. In our popular culture, I am tempted to emphasize the overarching grace and love of God for any behavior, but I realize I must not emphasize it at the expense of failing to represent this God who is righteous in his integrity toward others. I may like the talk that Christianity is all about mercy, but sometimes knowing justice will be served is a source of mercy to victims. I must remember He is holy and can embody both mercy and judgment perfectly.

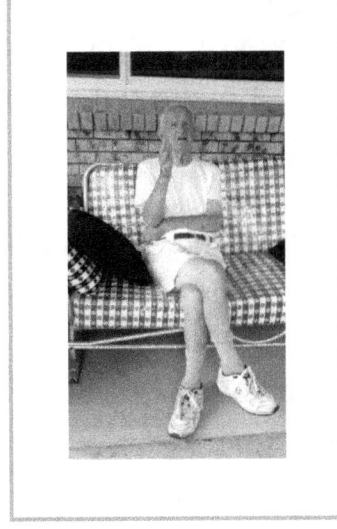

April 28, 2014

I start filling a wheelbarrow with pinkish gravel. Then I dump it onto the weed barrier cloth which we've already laid over the mud pit that was left when we reappointed Joe's flagstone to the back corner of our 'resort'.

Now, we're making an all new patio. Not exactly "we". Joe suns himself. He watches me work. He's said before that he's not one for landscape gravel because "the leaves of the trees tend to muck it up eventually, and then the rock is hard to clean." It's clear, after the fifth load in the wheelbarrow, that he's determined to make me spread the pink gravel by myself. When I explain that I intend to lay down the red concrete squares like a checkerboard onto the gravel, however, he perks up. "I once laid black and white linoleum in the basement of the first house that Maudie and I bought. It was Maudie's idea to lay it on the diagonal, and I liked the math puzzle so I did it. It became the playroom for your hubby and his sista. I put in speakers for the music to play, and I finished the walls in knotty pine. Wow! It was pretty!"

"Oh yeah? I've heard that story before. I would have liked to have seen it. That was the house with the mulberry trees in front?"

Joe chuckles. "Yeah! I built a platform in the one by the front porch. I can still remember little Victoria sitting pretty in her tree house, playing wid her dolls. Oh, she was jealous over that tree house. She never wanted Paul to sit in it."

His face darkens. "You know the story about what occurred after we sold that place? A Russian couple bought it. But they hadn't lived there even *a year* when the neighbors realized that they hadn't seen 'em coming or going. So, they called in the police. The back door had been broken up with an ax, and they found that couple in the basement all cut to pieces. What a terrible thing!" He shakes his head, as though the thought of all that blood and terror on his children's playroom floor has haunted his dreams.

"Oh. My! I'm glad you got outta there."

"Well, I've thought about that a lot, and I don't think it woulda happened if we continued to live there. I think that couple was something different than they put forth to us."

By the end of the day, Paul is cheering us on and helping with the finishing details. We've filled up our serpentine walkway with a pink checkerboard pattern that reminds me of something Alice in Wonderland might have encountered.

"Ooo. I approve of that." Joe points with the toothpick from his lips and then returns it to whittle it away.

Paul releases the dog from the back door, like a horse from the gate. He skids to a stop and slowly tests the checkerboard squares, gingerly placing one paw and then another onto them.

"Yes! It works! Jester's beeline from the back door to the back fence has just been interrupted!" Paul laughs. "Perhaps, Chief, we'll save some lawn by slowing him down."

April 29, 2014
How delightful to walk in the front doorway and be able to look straight through the house, out the picture window and see a picture! To see the trees and sky in the back yard rather than blue rafters. Teamwork can reap rich rewards! Since it is another hot spring day, we go out to shoot the breeze under the new porch fan. Heat for the ol' man; fan for me.

After work, Paul brings us cherry limeades to cool us in the late afternoon rays. Joe takes a few sips, and lies back on his tablecloth lounger, propping the back of his head up with his hands, listening to us exchange the events of the day. After a while listening to Paul and I banter, Mr. B swivels on his bones to sit up, breaking into our conversation. "It's a heck of a lot o' fun to watch you two enjoying this backyard! I hope you like this house when I'm gone. It'll be good to you." Then he slurps up some of his icy green cool drink. Mr. B's goodwill and protective generosity is still something I feel unaccustomed to. "Thank you," and "we are happy here with you," seem to be the only appropriate responses.

In Joe's presence, I notice my own bad behaviors more acutely. Usually, if Paul had hurt me, I'd make sure he knew about it. The ol' man, however, is different. He has a way of teasing us when we disagree with him. When I over-water the plants and they drain onto his carpet, he would rather get a dishcloth to come help, than rail on me. When Paul and I argue, Mr. B leans into us like a little boy watching a wrestling match. "Fight! Fight! Fight!" he shouts in glee. That kind of thing tends to shut our mouths quickly. He takes care of the problem in a way that also shows some humor.

April 30, 2014
Joe and I have been theorizing all day about whether his sprinkler heads can water his entire backyard. I'm impressed that he put this system together forty years ago and has been able to keep it

running. But I also remember the condition of the yard when we moved in last summer, and that was after a few weeks of making sure to water it. I don't believe the rotating heads are up to date. Joe thinks the modern plastic heads are faulty and unnecessary. He would rather take the blame for not watering than switch out the sprinkler heads.

Mostly he insists that sprinkler system installers these days are money hogs. He insists we should save our money rather than consult with an installer. So we take a gander to ACE hardware before we do our grocery shopping, and Joe picks out some new washers and a couple fittings. I ask the sales guys about our sprinkler head problem missing whole sections of the lawn. They point out the 600 series of heads suitable for our water pressure of 60psi and size of yard. I carry them in my arms like a baby to the counter, following Joe like an obedient squaw. Then I set them down. He makes no comment. He pays the bill and we carry on with our day.

Mr. B pulls out a pencil, and his glasses from their case, both tucked into his shirt pocket. I remember that my dad always kept his drafting pencils in his shirt pocket. Joe searches the living room chest of drawers to find his original drawing of the back yard, complete with speculations, done decades ago. Placing another piece of transparent paper over the top, he begins to mark on it with red pencil showing where he's buried the pipes and sprinkler heads. We argue the pros and cons of moving the heads away from the fence and into the yard, and then decide that we should keep the old heads on until we try it out. I agree if we don't need the new sprinkler pop ups, that we'll return them.

I get up and make us sandwiches and leftover soup. He doesn't complain about the leftover soup, even though he generally will not eat leftovers. He tells Paul. "Oh yeah, your wife and I get along all right, even though we didn't like each other all day. And she knows how to talk you out of anything!"

Paul laughs and agrees wholeheartedly.

"What's this?" I demand. "We discussed it, your dad drew pictures, and we came to a *mutual* decision." I roll my eyes at both of them.

"Never mind," coos Joe. "I forgive her everything because she made me a decent dinner." He picks up his bowl and slurps broth.

"In the midst of happiness or despair
in sorrow or in joy
in pleasure or in pain:
Do what is right and you will be at peace."
— Jess Rothenberg,
The Catastrophic History of You and Me

May ~
Bouquets

May Day, May 1, 2014

Joe's appearance surprises me this morning. He is wearing his khaki shorts with working pockets down the thighs and a gold and green checked summer dress shirt. His white knees and shins look a bit rubbery above his gray anklets and worn tennis shoes. He doesn't even have his wool sweater on. "If I wear it ALL the time, it'll wear out," he contends. "By the way, isn't this May Day?"

I acknowledge it is and ask him if he would like some pole ribbons and flower baskets. He laughs, then notices that I've placed his breakfast in solitary on the table. "Aren't you eating this morning?"

"I'm going out, remember? To meet some friends."

"Oh yeah, oh yeah. Well, have fun." He shrugs, trying on buoyancy.

Then, while I am having brunch with girlfriends, Joe actually hooks up the sprinkler system, then plants a pot full of florescent pink geraniums, vivid blue salvia, and an ornamental grass in his favorite wooden trough planter.

In the afternoon, he rests in the sun and watches me dig new holes to transplant shade-loving plants out of holes where I had mistakenly placed them. "Why are you digging up my yard again?" he grouses.

"Well, it's hard to gauge the sun's course from season to season!" He just nods and smiles at me. I know I'm pushing him a little bit by planting new bushes in his yard. That's why he's watching me like Garfield, not budging to help. I put my new nursery plants into the old holes. The research tells me we are going to have a beautiful yard now, in all four seasons!

We both work hard today, but I'm the only one who seems to be sweating in the sun. Barely managing to put a salad together for dinner, I ask Paul to grill the salmon. I must have gotten heat exhaustion. I'm gulping glasses of cold water and orange juice. My heart beats erratically, and I sit back in the chair and close my eyes. Paul tries to nuzzle kiss me and joke, but I push him away with a claustrophobic urgency.

Joe immediately leads me to our newly upholstered couch and suggests I lie down. Then, he picks up his lap blanket and gently places it around me. Not satisfied, he goes and unfolds another afghan and lays that over me, tucking in my toes on one end, and my shoulders on the other. His sweet concern feels like a mother's care. I feel better enough, within an hour, to rise up, watch a mystery with Joe while drinking another two glasses of water. "Aw, thank you, Mr. B, for taking such good care of me!"

He swivels in his blue plush rocker swivel chair and smiles at me. "The expression on your face showed me something was wrong. It was nothing," he says. "We all feel down sometimes."

May 2, 2014

Mr. B waits at the door for me after breakfast with his comfy blue fleece thrown over his wooly blue shoulder. He's making sure we leave for his doctor's appointment early so that we can stop by the Chocolate RX store in historic downtown Littleton. In addition to his doctor checking his ears, he plans to ask her to "put that solution on my barnacles here and here." He points to a few rough patches on his face and ears. "They come from the sun, by the way. But, she can take care of the new ones," he confides.

I know he always buys his doctor a box of chocolates at Christmas, but today he wants to treat her special. "She always takes good care of me and Maudie. Always. A little friendship usually helps every situation." Joe often talks about his late wife in the present tense.

He surprises me by wanting to park around the corner, a ways to walk. When we arrive, he picks out the milk chocolate toffee. "Do you approve?"

"Oh, I think I heard her say last time when you brought her a mixed box at Christmas, that she prefers the dark chocolate."

"You did? Why thank you! You just saved my life and reputation. What kind do you like best?"

I shrug. "Oh, probably the dark."

Joe picks up another box.

"No, no, Joe. I couldn't eat that. Just one piece if anything."

"No way!" he exclaims. "I owe you for saving my life. You don't buy a girl the wrong chocolates!"

May 5, 2014

We have two spring robins who are chased by our dog every morning in the yard. Joe says he's had a pair of robins here for years. He suddenly discloses, "There is a strange relationship between the robins and the sparrows. I've witnessed it on several occasions, that the robin tilts his head toward the ground listening for movement of worms or bugs. Then the robin dips his beak into the ground and pulls out its prey. Every time a worm comes out of the ground the robin jerks his head back with a tug, and then pauses a moment with the worm on the ground before he takes it away or eats it. In the moment after the tug, and with the worm lying on the ground, a sparrow, who has been watching a short distance away, will often zoom in and take the fresh worm from the robin. Here's the question. Does the sparrow steal the worm, or does the robin give the worm?"

Mr. B's story reminds me of Jesus' comments: "Look at the birds. They don't plant or harvest or store food in barns, for your heavenly Father feeds them. And aren't you far more valuable to him than they are? So don't be afraid; you are more valuable to God than a whole flock of sparrows." (Matthew 6:26 NLT)

May 6, 2014

Joe has added a navy-blue hoodie to his normal combination of T-shirt, long-sleeved cotton shirt, and wool sweater this morning. The hoodie substitutes for his pale blue fleece. Below this, he has donned knee-high khaki stockings to match his khaki shorts in celebration for all the sunshine we've been having.

"You look nice today, Mr. B," I say as I place his French toast and blueberries in front of him.

"What's that you say?"

"I say you are looking fit as a camp counselor this morning."

"Let's get to it!" he declares with unusual vigor as he hands me the sprinkler drawing he's been working on. I'm not sure if he means to get to work on sprinklers, or on breakfast, but I join him at the table with our steaming cups of Ovaltine.

He motions to indicate my tank top. "Aren't you freezing? It's 67 degrees in here, according to the thermostat. *Subterranean temperatures!*"

Thankfully, I can blame the coolness on Paul's fine scheme to open all the doors and windows before he leaves for work to cool down the house. We close them up before the air warms up. That way, the air in the house stays cooler long into the day when the sun has been beating on it for a while.

"If you say so," comes my retort.

"You aren't freezing, Miss?" He clasps his hot mug of creamy chocolate and inhales the steam, shivering just a little in delight.

"Nope. I think I'll do some weeding outside before it gets too hot to work."

He studies me in such a way that I realize he hasn't understood my statement. "What's that?" he finally says.

"Mr. B, it would help us communicate if you could hear me."

"What'd you say, Miss?"

His answer unnerves me because I'm not sure if he's joking or if he really doesn't understand.

"Maybe we need to visit your doctor to get the wax cleaned from your ears!"

"Oh, I don't need to hear you." His resolute denial angers me.

"I need you to hear me, cuz one-sided conversations just don't cut it!"

"Maybe. I don't mean to make you angry, Miss, but I just don't want all the fuss of a hearing aid."

"Well, I don't want to yell at you for the rest of my life! Paul is getting hard of hearing too, and I feel like I'm yelling at both of you all of the time!" I give him the silent treatment throughout breakfast to emphasize what the lack of conversation might mean in the future. Being social is not a one-sided affair! Getting old may not be for the faint-hearted, as Joe is fond of saying, but it's almost as hard on the caregivers!

Joe has been complaining all month that I am force-feeding him. "Too much! I can't get through it." I ignore him. Paul usually cleans up what Joe can't eat, so the food usually disappears, but that is not what concerns me. Yesterday at brekkies, Joe almost couldn't finish his banana. Today, he doesn't bother to peel it. It stays on his plate with half his pile of soggy French toast. "I dunno why," he says, "but I'm just not hungry this morning."

My resolution for silence dissolves. Joe's complete lack of appetite is alarming me, but I shrug. "Don't worry about it, Joe. We had a big dinner last night. Let me wash up and you can work on the sprinkler system." No, getting old isn't for the feint-hearted, as Mr. B is fond of saying, but it's almost as hard on the caregivers.

May 7, 2014

Joe recites what he ate for breakfast at Paul's bidding. Then, he announces that he cut the grass today and that he is more tired than hungry. Without skipping a beat, he proceeds to describe how he learned to make eggs for his breakfast, before attending to his boyhood paper route. "Sometimes six eggs at a time!" Thinking about this pendulum swing, the ol' man confesses, "I dunno why I wasn't hungry this morning."

Paul looks at me for a reading and I glance towards him with concern.

"Maybe it needs some salt, Mr. B," I suggest, unwilling to remove his plate just yet.

"What day is it? Is there boxing tonight?" He frowns at the clock in the formal living room.

Paul reminds his father that it's only on Saturday night.

"When did you become a fan of boxing, Mr. B?

"Oh! Long time ago. Remember the Clinton Oval I've told you about in Woonsocket? Well, there was a barn next to it, owned by the company my mothea worked for. Us boys would climb on top of the roof to watch the boxing matches at night. The baseball games were mostly in the afternoon, but all the boxing matches were at night. Never get it outta my blood now." He looks up and shakes his head, then reaches for the salt. "All those guys are probably dead."

"I didn't know your mother worked outside the home."

"She worked a cotton loom in the night. Evening shift, I think. I remember that my brother Eddy and I would walk around to her work just about as she was taking a break at night. We'd walk past the cotton factory, and she'd be out on one of the upper porches. She'd wave to us and we'd keep walking around the French quarter, in the dark, and then back home."

"Oh my goodness. No wonder you didn't know much about your mother. It wasn't only that she never learned English; she worked so much!"

"Yes, she did. I'd go walking to the Kimbals to pick up my fathea after work. We'd walk home together, and my mothea would have dinner waiting for us. Then, she'd run off to the cotton factory to do her looming, and on break we'd walk down and check to see she was all right." Joe manages to eat about half of his supper. "I can still hear the clickety-clack of those looms from the street as we approached."

"Your family seemed to take good care of each other, Mr. B."

"Well, yes. I don't remember any of us kids fighting or not getting along really. We all watched out for each other. Members of our family always walked in two's."

I remember as a high school camp counselor a feeling of jealousy watching two young sisters helping and confiding in each other as best friends do. How could they enjoy and love each other so well? It was a mystery.

Suddenly, I'm glad we've come to live with Joe.

May 8, 2014

Mr. B insists he should come with me to the doctor today. We haven't walked but 20 yards when he murmurs, "For some reason, I feel very tired. I need to stop here." We turn and sit, I on the bench beside him. On the way home the urgency of mortality hangs about my neck. Should I ask Joe what kind of "deal" he made with God? Should I ask him what he believes about the person of Jesus? I pray quickly and decide it's best to go to the heart of the matter. Suddenly sweating, I hear myself blurting out, "What do you believe about Jesus, Mr. B?"

"What?" Joe says, craning his neck toward me. I repeat the awkward question two more times before he gets it.

"Oh, I don't think… I just am not interested in that religious stuff. I dunno. I never have been. My family never had a Bible in the house. I never read it."

"But I know you went to church for years with Maudie."

"Yes, and a girl I went out wid before her once gave me a Bible." He emphatically pauses. "I didn't read it. I don't bother wid that stuff."

"But Joe, what if the Bible has the words of *life*? You seem *very* interested in life, from my perspective."

"Oh. Not. *That way*." His gravelly voice explains deliberately, in an eerie fatherly tone. "I had plenty to be curious about. It was interesting to discover that say an aluminum floor had to be .064 in thickness. I was interested that at 800 degrees the insulation of a space capsule smoldered, you know, flash points. I studied thin skins on airplanes and how to keep them from buckling. Then, you know, I was in the unit that studied nuts and bolts and why they would wiggle loose from their fittings from the vibrations. Believe it or not, if you x-rayed weldable stainless steel, you could see specs of dirt in the manufactured nuts and bolts. It was an interesting cause of a piece's decline. I was interested in the definition of weldable stainless steel being 302w or lw, low carbon. I was interested to handle a bolt the size of my hand." He holds up his palm.

"Of course, my science is way out now. They rely on computers. They use plastics to make the skins of airplanes these days. I'd say it's moot, wouldn't you? Oh, I used to love to work mathematical stress problems, and at one time, I thought I'd like to write a book about solving mathematical stressors. I'm glad now I didn't bother because who was gonna read it? Computers give engineers all the answers they want!"

I feel there is nothing more to say ever again. My heart has sprung an aneurism.

But, Joe isn't finished. "And in the fifties, I had to study nuclear sciences because that was everything in those days… I always believed the politics would slow down, but they continued to be in a rush to solve the next puzzle right till I retired. Hurry this, rush that… There was a guy who was mad at me for taking time to figure out some specs one time. My bracket additions were messing up his scheduling in the other room, always pressure, always pressure. Finally, a real nice guy came out to find me. He told me what all the fuss was about. He said they had tested the first design on something against my specs determination and it had done exactly as I predicted, so now they were waiting on a new design from me. But, I had to design it out of nothing! Nothing, I tell ya! Oh, the bee was on *me*!" Joe is incredulous, talking about everything he studied to further his career. Most of it seems to have filled an important niche in time, but has very little to do with eternity.

My heart plummets with no recourse for argument because that is exactly how Mr. B has designed this exchange. He is intentionally averting the person of Jesus for our entire thirty-minute drive, and that's nothing after filibustering the Divine for over ninety years. He appears to avoid testing God's spiritual engineering, or designs, by consuming his lifetime with sciences that seem important to society in the moment. Yet, the end of the self-made man is a temple built on redundant recitals, accepted now as a humbled man's reflections. I have no words. Not that he wanted me to continue conversing on this subject.

His course repels me. I have hoped to enjoy him forever in eternity, and I have accidentally fallen in love with him, but I now despair that he refuses to entertain any thought of a good God who will judge the living and the dead according to His own standards. By the time I arrive home I know my path is to continue to serve him in every practical way I have been serving him, but for me, the core of the apple has rotted out.

I find my anger to be a curious response to his avoidance. He most certainly must realize how limited his time is. Does Joe think he will simply cease to exist when he dies? Maybe this belief is how Mr. B manages to keep a stiff upper lip towards his Creator. Or, maybe I'm entertaining an angel unawares. An angel has no need of a personal savior. He could avoid the topic until the mysteries of Pluto are unraveled and just be fine with it!

Paul ends his day praying for his dad. I am mute. Stuck in stalemate.

May 9, 2014

Mr. B's favorite is clam chowder and crab cakes, so long as they aren't made with mayonnaise. Joe downs the homemade soup, but won't touch the kale "super food" salad that is our side dish tonight. Paul takes a bite to show him it is safe. "There's a lot of good things in here, Dad."

Joe pushes it around his plate, "Yeah, I can tell it's a real hodge-podge."

"What's hodge-podge?" Paul asks.

"Looks like the devil swept up the floor!" Joe rejoins.

So much for deli "super foods" at our place. "Well, then eat your crab cakes. You love crab cakes."

"My belly button is protruding, I've eaten so much already. Don't push an ol' man."

May 10, 2014

Joe walks around the garden in the chilly gusts of wind, happy with garden hydrangeas and decorative grasses and flagstone. "I can't argue too much about what you've done here," he says. "Especially, this one I like." He points to a five petal, tropical-looking hardy hydrangea. I sense there is something reminiscent of his elegant Maudie when he looks over it, his smile sweet. "Mmm. When I see how everything fits, I like it." His voice growls. "It's nice."

His comments compel a hug from me. Mr. B likes hugs and small pats on the back or on his hands, like all of us do. He acts as bashful as a Disney character, smiling whenever I touch him.

I've set an appointment to meet with an exterior house painter in the afternoon, and when he arrives, Joe throws up his hands and isolates in the blue velvet living room while I show the painter the exterior. When the painter goes back to his truck to work up the bid, Joe announces himself in the den and gives me the rigmarole about the prices these days, the lack of work ethic, brushing versus spraying, watered down paints, protecting windows, and that it is too moist these days to paint a house anyway. At last, Joe grumbles, "This painter will probably take you to the cleaners. I don't want any part of that."

"Let's just wait and see what he says, Mr. B. And," I concede, "I'll be sure to make him put it into the contract that he will tape off the windows with plastic. You are right about all of these things, of course."

The painter knocks on the door, enters, and the three of us sit on the edge of our business seats in the den. He informs us he and his partner do the painting themselves. He always tapes plastic over the windows. He has a Better Business Bureau rating of A+ and stresses there is a warranty on the Sherman Williams paint, including the sheen, for nine years. He tells us he will power wash the house one day in late July, let it dry, and then he will come back to knock off anything that didn't come off with the wash. The first week in August, they will caulk the house and then paint. He tells us he lives in the area and that he's been working here for quite a few years.

I ask him if the price will stay the same if I get a handyman to remove the Xs from beneath the front windows. "What?" Joe interrupts. "You're gonna take away my X-rating? How will I bring in the extra income if I can't get customers?"

Our Sherman Williams salesman seems more flustered at this outburst than me. I tell him it's an inside joke and threaten Mr. B to order pizza tonight if he can't behave himself.

There is a pregnant pause, then the salesman describes approximately how long the various phases of the painting process will take and then he presents the price. Happy with the price, and with a go-ahead from Paul, Joe announces that he will be paying two thirds of the price since he knew the house needed paint before we moved in. With great relief we sign the paperwork and the painter leaves happy. Finally, Joe sets the date for the end of July to make sure the summer rains are past and the house has a chance to dry out real good.

Joe turns to me and smiles. "It's good that he lives in the area. I liked him. He didn't perform like a salesman. He told it like it is, and I agreed wid him." Then Joe gives me the eagle eye. "The only thing I don't approve of is why nine years guarantee and not ten? Ten's a nice round figure. I think there may be something shady about nine."

"Thank you, Joe, for offering to contribute to this project. I really appreciate it."

"Well, even though it's your house, I don't want you two using up all your savings for things around here. It was my responsibility, and I let it slide. I can't see you using your retirement savings. You've spent too much already. You gotta cinch up your belts and save it for your old age. Believe me, I know about the costs of old age." Joe is always lecturing us about not saving enough. We feel like we are doing the best we can.

I grin. "Okay and yessir, Mr. B!"

May 11, 2014 Mother's Day

A big freeze, predicted by the weather announcers for this week, has arrived. After weeks of landscaping weather, our spirits dive with the thermostat to feel Colorado's whimsical temperatures dip below freezing and delve under new storm clouds. Initially, Paul is bundled up on the back porch having coffee, and I join him in my wool robe and stocking feet.

When the sleet starts, Joe eventually joins us bundled up, complaining loudly about the shenanigans of Colorado weather. I offer him a cup of the steaming brew and bring it. Then I slip on my shoes and begin to carry out every empty flower bucket we have to turn over onto our new plants. Mr. B and I dearly hope they won't freeze given a little cover.

Paul pulls out boxes of blue camping tarps and clear plastics he has salvaged from hospital deliveries at work. "You'll be glad I brought these home, now," he informs us with pride. Joe begins to unfold the plastics and we all lay covers over our flowering roses, iris, and wisteria. Then, we race inside to begin preparing the Mother's Day meal for my mom and sister and her son. Joe brings over a brown towel and begins rubbing my damp and dripping hair. I smile and thank him.

"Oh, I'm very selfish, you know. It's my investment I'm protecting." He winks.

"Yeah, yeah, yeah." But it's Joe whose nose and cheeks are rosy. "You may have overdone it, yourself, Mr. B. You gotta stop working so hard!"

"Maybe." He sniffs.

A plateful of papaya, and playing Revolution together, he talks up my cooking up to my mom and says his itchy skin is better because of it.

They look at me.

"That's the first I've heard of my healing powers, Mr. B."

He glances over. "Well, I don't want ya to get a big head."

May 12, 2014

I think Joe has caught a cold. He is sniffling at breakfast and says he won't argue with my diagnosis. He says he'll be better in a day because he's taken two aspirin.

With my healing powers, I prep chicken and rice soup for dinner, chop, chop, chop, and then go up to my room to lie down and do some reading. When I return downstairs, Joe is sullen and bored. He is mad at me for sleeping and staying to myself today. "Grumpy guy," I tease. But he denies it. "I'm making chicken soup for you because you have a cold, Mr. B."

"Whatever you say," He retorts.

When he starts smelling dinner bubbling, however, he chippers up. Then he turns on the stereo to add a concerto as a background for dinner. Yet, at dinner, he doesn't respond to any of our discussion or direct questions. Finally, pointing to his ears he declares, "I can't hear you."

Then I notice he's quietly admitted to my diagnosis by putting cotton in his ears.

May 13, 2014

All better today. Joe's 24-hour cold is gone with the sleet which is also long gone. We shop right after breakfast together and buy him some bear claws for brekkies. Then, I take Joe to the library. All is well.

May 14, 2014

Mr. B bites into his plain *Braunschweiger* sandwich on Jewish rye with gusto. Me too. He's won me over. "You know, Missy, after Maudie died, I started shopping on my own, and I went to the meat counter and asked for *Braunschweiger.* Guess what they gave me. Liverwurst! Yuk! I hate liverwurst. Well, I told the deli guy *no way*, I wanted *Braunschweiger!* He didn't know what the heck I wanted, and he insisted that liverwurst was *Braunschweiger,* but I could taste the difference, you know, I really could. That guy didn't last long. You know something else? I like the plain ol' store brand *Braunschweiger in the lunchmeat section."*

"That's because it tastes like goose pâté, Mr. B."

"Yeah. Yeah, it does." He smiles and eats the whole sandwich, pushing the sides of onions and tomatoes into his mouth.

After dinner, there are so few dishes, I get them rinsed and into the dishwasher in a couple of minutes, and wipe off the countertops. Joe walks into the kitchen and stands beside the dishwasher with his mouth open in mock shock. Then he says, "You're too quick for me!"

"It's fine, Mr. B. There were hardly any dishes to do tonight."

"Oh, that doesn't matter one whit! It's against the union rules. Now, we're gonna have to fine you."

May 15, 2014

We are headed out to find an 0-ring for a sprinkler valve. As we open the garage door and proceed to climb into the car, all the potted plants that had to be moved into the garage during the Mother's Day freeze, now call out to Joe.

"Hey, I want to put the planters back on the porch in the sunshine," Mr. B asserts as he backs into the passenger's seat of my car.

"Okay, but wait to move that big wooden boat one. Pauly can

help you when he gets off work."

The regular home improvement stores do not stock washers to repair our 40-year-old sprinkler valves. Joe is disappointed. We head home and he finishes digging out one old washer, which appears to have melted into the grooves of the valve. He inserts an O-ring and appears to be contentedly working, so I go to read a passage in my book for book club. Later, I go check on Mr. B.

In the afternoon sunshine, Joe has managed to pull out the large planter from the garage where we have been hiding it from the freezing cold. One minute it is off the patio. The next minute, I see it sitting in its spot filled with happy flowers. "That thing must weigh a hundred pounds, Mr. B! *How in the world*?"

"It didn't hurt me one bit. I have a secret to moving it."

"What's your secret, then?"

"Can't tell ya." Joe looks at his shoes and shakes his head solemnly. "If I did, all the *old* people would start doing it, and then those nursing homes would empty out."

"What a calamity," I agree dryly. "I'm gonna have to start spying on ya."

Joe shrugs. "As you like."

May 17, 2014

When my mom and sister arrive to play games with us today, they sit first outside on the porch and gaze at all the new work we have finished. I explain that we like to sit out here for hours smelling the iris and lilacs. While they chit-chat, I cut some stems and replace the old ones in the lavender vase sitting on the dining room table, soon to become our game table. Then, I seat myself down beside Mr. B out back.

"Did you use the sprinkler guy we recommended?" Liz asks.

"No, actually. Mr. B was able to put it together."

"You probably saved yourself about nine hundred dollars

then!" she exclaims. "That's what we paid," rolling her eyes.

Joe rocks in his rocker. His hands remain folded and there rests a contented smile on his face. "You smell that?" he asks. "The breeze brings the lilac's scent up here on the porch. It's a nice way to spend the day."

Joe decides to be polite and join the festivities. He comes inside to learn how to play a new game with us. The fragrance in the dining room is thick and sweet. Liz keeps coaching Mr. B with the

board and his options for moving his pieces. Yet, he continues to be confused about the cards in his hand and the playing board. Finally, after an hour, he begins to describe his particular confusion, and I realize his eyes are playing tricks on him. He is color blind just enough that with his other eye issues, the Settler's game is really no fun for him. Besides that, he makes me repeat most of what Liz explains to him because he can't hear her voice as well as mine.

"Why can you only understand Lynn and not me, Mr. B?"

"What?"

"Why can't you understand me, but you can understand *her*?" she asks again.

"What did she say, Miss?"

I repeat the question for him wondering if he is being more

ornery than usual.

"Why, I don't know. I can't tell ya." He shrugs.

"It's a special grace," I say. Whether Mr. B is exaggerating right now, I believe it to be a necessity.

Afterwards, Joe refuses to take any credit for winning because my sister has coached him the entire way. When we ask him to play again, he stands up and puts out the palms of his hands to the table. "No way!"

Journal scenario: Played Settlers of Catan for hours today with my mom and sister. They are all into real estate and stock strategies. Joe won.

Moral of the Story: Always bet on Joe.

May 18, 2014

Sitting outside on the patio, Joe begins telling me again about an arm of the family which settled far away from the others. The grandparents had given their eldest daughter and her new groom a large piece of farm property with a house on it for their wedding present. The groom disappointed them, however, especially when he drove his truck across the furrows of his field towards the hospital road instead of through the furrows with his wife in late pregnancy. To let it be known in the will, the grandparents cut their son-in-law out of any ownership in their trust. His wife died before him, so he turned his children against the grandparents, and they have continued to play the victim. "They called us ever-so-often begging for loans."

Mr. B defends his case. "Really, the only time this family ever contacted me and Maudie was to complain about their health or to describe a teen pregnancy and to ask for money. That's why I told Maudie that it was my policy and that she would do well to adopt it: never lend a relative money. If you have it and want to give some to the cause, that's one thing. But otherwise, stay out of it. If you lend a relative money, they always take their time paying you back. The last time Maudie's cousin called me, I told her to call a bank. Banks lend money, not relatives. After all, we had teenagers of our own!" He explains this to the gentle breezes wafting over his park-sized lawn as much as to me.

"No. Seriously. Stay away from these people or I'll never hear the end of it." For a case in point, he adds, "Yeah, it was this young man who sued to break up the grandparents' family trust, wouldn't ya know, because he or his branch of the family needed their share of the money at the time, and they got it. No one fought them. It seems that no matter how much money they have, it always sifts through their fingers. I dunno. Maybe their health is such that they needed it."

Joe gets chilly easily in the morning shade of the patio. He pushes himself up now and opens the back door to enter the house. Frowning and squinting to see the den stalls him. It's a slow process. I follow him in.

He heads to the living room to sit down in his blue velvet lounger which still swivels, but when he rocks in it, the mechanics click with sounds as regular as a clock's inner workings. He looks up at me. "I dunno about you, but my agenda is plum full today. Don't ask me to do much wid ya."

"Okay then, Mr. B! But don't you want to go to the paint store with me in about an hour?'

"Well, I could probably manage that." Click, click, click….

May 19, 2014

Betty drops by the house to bring a gift of tickets for Paul and me to see *Porgy and Bess*. She tells Joe that she has a friend from out of town visiting and the woman is in too poor of health to make it to the show. He shows her outside to the back porch, and she admires all the new flagstone patio and blooming flowerbeds.

"What's this?" She points to a brown vine no longer clinging to its support.

"Oh, that? It's a clematis that has apparently seen it's day."

"Well, yeah," Betty agrees. "You should take that out. It doesn't fit with everything else you have going here."

May 20, 2014

Paul left for work, today, hacking. He was back home the next hour. He accuses the guy who was sitting next to him at *Porgy and Bess*: "He kept turning his head my way to cough, and protecting his wife on the other side of him!"

"Do colds travel that fast?" My hubby is ill so rarely that both Joe and I are taken aback. I put him to bed and give him cold medicine, tucking him in, and closing the blinds. Then, I go downstairs to poach gooey eggs for Joe.

In spite of the bouquet of fresh yellow iris and lilacs sitting on the table, Mr. B's head is all taken up with scary thoughts of illness. He tells me again that he takes two aspirin for a cold in the morning, and again two aspirin at night before bed. Within a day or two, the cold is gone. What's wrong with
Pauly? Orange juice should help him. Why isn't he eating? I explain that all he wanted to do was sleep for now. We'll feed him later.

Mr. B tells me that his eldest sister almost lost her life to some illness when she was ten. After that, she had headaches. But the other kids in the family were always healthy, never sick.

Joe says, "I remember I had the mumps when I was young. My face was swollen. Then there were two times when I was sick wid the flu as a full-grown man. Those were the only times I was ever sick. The first time, I volunteered to be a guinea pig for a new Chinese flu vaccine, and I was standing in line and there were guys fainting and falling down flat from the shot." Joe chuckles.

"Immediately, I began to run a temperature of 104, and it laid me out flat. Doctor Bailey had to come to the house to treat me. Then, I became sick wid the flu again in Tulsa, and again, I was laid out flat. I couldn't risk that anymore, so I began to take the regular flu vaccine and I have never been sick since."

"With anything?"

"Wid anything. Maudie used to say I never get sick, and I don't. I don't know why. You don't appreciate your good health until you learn what it is to be sick. Do you get sick?"

"Not so much anymore since I've been taking those shots. They seem to help my immune system. But I used to get deathly sick with about anything blowing in the wind."

"Well, some people got it, and some people don't," he says as guilty as a two-faced penny.

May 21, 2014

In the morning, my father-in-law and I thrust shovels into the ground by the fence to wheedle out the crabgrass and other weeds starting to show their legs. Then we take turns digging another hole. My companion begins to philosophize. "Some people don't know the difference between good grass and weeds. They let bind weed—you know that one with the white flower?—take over their yard. They just cut the dandelions and clover and all the weeds at the same time and in the same way as they cut their grass! It's not the same thing, and if you don't take care of it right when the weed is small, then it takes no time for 'em to overrun a yard. Then, it overruns the neighbor's yard too." He lectures. "No, you can't mask that sort of thing. I think people are too busy these days to take care of their own weeds, and look how they spread out!"

"I think it takes more than one person in the family to look after all the weeds, don't you, Mr. B?"

"Oh yeah, it takes teamwork," he agrees.

We returned the dead clematis that failed to overwinter in Mr. B's yard. He wants to drive over to the nursery with me, so we exchange the dead vine for a five-foot tall, profusely *living* vine with plate-sized white blossoms. "Wow!" he exclaims. "It's a beauty!"

Since the lilacs fencing our yard only bloom for about two weeks each year, I decide I want to get the clematis to grow up into the mature lilac shrubs to get them to appear like they are re-blooming.

"Can we do that?" he worries. "Will it kill the lilac?"

"I'll look it up." Okay, the Internet nursery describes their own experiment with this very thing – mixing clematis with mature lilac bushes - and I show the happy results in pictures to Joe.

He thanks me for looking into my black box to get the answer that this idea should work. Joe mentions, "Your yard is getting to be a habit for you. A good habit, mind you." I'm immensely glad for his help because the lilac branches are poking my neck and pulling my hair, and the sweat is running down my red face. Joe doesn't sweat much.

Paul climbs out of his sick bed to grill some ribs for our four o'clock dinner. We all sit in the shade of the porch smelling the savory flavors out of the steaming meat. "Hey, Honey, you know Dad said that he *likes* the yard? He told me that he likes what we've done." Paul tosses his head indicating towards the flowerbeds.

"Yes! He told me too." We speak as though Joe isn't sitting right here. Joe smiles as he leans back in his aluminum frame rocking chair and listens. Twenty feet beyond him, in the drip line of the lilac, the glorious white blooms have picked up their heads against the grey cedar fence, and they shout!

May 22, 2014

Lately, I've been waking up because of the bird chatter outdoors. Then, the thought comes to me, "Why don't you go out on the porch to spend time with the LORD?" So, this week I've been taking up the invitational nudge. Today, I flip open to the book of Esther, about two-thirds of the way through. The passage is familiar. I notice I've underlined Esther's prayer to her husband the king, Ahasuerus (Xerxes), to revoke his own edict. It was made in response to evil Haman's request to kill all of the Jews in 127 provinces. Since Esther opened the king's eyes to Haman's evil schemes, Haman has been put to death, but his scheme has outlived him, already having been made law. *It's alive and well.* The story continues that Esther prostrates herself before her husband and begs him to do something. "Please revoke the edict you have already sent out! How can I survive if my family and my nation are exterminated?"

The king responds immediately by sending out another edict, which he also endorses as "irrevocable." All the Jews who may be attacked because of Haman's deception, from India to Ethiopia, are to be armed and ready to defend themselves. They are charged to kill anyone who tries to kill them, including women and children. On the dreaded day appointed for war, all the Hebrews in the towns in which the edict arrived are saved. The record states many people convert to the Jewish faith themselves in reverence for the power they must wield over the king to make him change his mind.

I put down my Bible and gaze out at the twittering birds and the dewy grass. The scent of the lilacs and yellow iris drapes this pleasurable experience. I bow and open my hands to God, imagining the daily way He feeds the sparrows. He has promised that He will take care of his children better than the way He cares for the sparrows. I recall Joe's story about watching the sparrow steal the worm from the robin. My hands remain open.

Then, I hear God's impression over my own: "The government

is not the King. I am the King. Those people you pleaded with in court for your house, your ministry, your lifestyle, they are not the King. I am the King. You are in My Kingdom, and you only need to ask Me. Ask again what you think you need."

With open hands, I ask God for a fresh start, for replenishing the savings on the investment that was stolen from us.

Suddenly, I garner a new perspective:

> "You pouted because you didn't get the appraised price from your house when the missionaries bought it. You were only grateful that I saved you from bankruptcy. Yet, wouldn't you agree? You worked these past few years doing what you wanted to do in your home, and I provided you with a nest egg from the sale of the house. Would you have saved that much money had you worked for another business all those years? Maybe you don't get *all* that you put on your wish list, but I am providing for all your needs, including a savings account. Trust Me to provide in the sale of your rental, too."

Tears wash my cheeks. I am humbled by this revelation. God covers His own with a superior protection to human justice. He uses common injustices to drive us into deeper faith and relationship with Him and with those in His kingdom. He really sees us, and He never leaves us or forsakes us even when we are faced with desperate situations and choices.

May 23, 2014

Joe asks me during afternoon tea time to ask my black box how to propagate clematis. He clarifies, "I used to dig down and get a root, but sometimes they wouldn't survive. I wanna know what I was doing wrong."

I find and read to him the Internet nursery directions. "Cut off three to four inches of the green vine, leave only one green leaf. Stick the major part of the vine into the ground with the leaf above the ground. Put a little homemade greenhouse over the top."

"What's that last part?" He's chewing on a toothpick.

"You know, the thing you used to do with old soda bottles?"

"What?"

I shout. "You cut the tops of the bottles off, you know, the spout, and then you turned them over onto the little sprig, and it would act as a greenhouse!"

"Oh, oh, oh. That." He is so low key. "I know," Mr. B is thinking. "Yes, we could use an orange juice container from the fridge."

"You wanna clone the white clematis we bought the other day already?" I can't help smiling because it's his unique way of saying he approves of the purchase, but also that he could double the investment.

He shrugs. "Why not? How long does it take?"

I look down at the computer. "It says it takes two months to get rooted, so we would probably see it starting to grow in late summer."

"I know another way to do it too. Yeah. I used to take old glass milk bottles. I soaked a string in gasoline. Then, I tied it around the glass bottle at the place where I wanted it to break. Then, I lit it on fire, and when it was all burning, I'd dip that end into a tub of cold water. The shock of the fire and the cold water would make the glass break at just the right spot. I had my greenhouse." He smiles at me knowing full well that he's just taught me something new.

"I dare ya!"

May 24, 2014

Paul's been coughing like a croupy baby. Then, of course, I catch it. Joe still doesn't seem to be affected. I can count the number of nights I've been sleeping in our guest room by the three pairs of shoes I've kicked off beside the bed.

This morning begins our anniversary; Paul decides to cook us breakfast, even if I don't want to eat it in bed. Joe is a little skeptical about eating breakfast cooked by a guy hacking up a lung even if the guy is his own son.

I must be getting better because it all tastes so yummy. I tell Paul his breakfast is better than any Hallmark anniversary card.

We sit outside on the porch with black coffee afterwards. "I made breakfast with something new, something old and something blue," announces my husband. "To celebrate wedding day!"

I know he thinks he's clever, but I instantly regret eating breakfast.

"Guess what the new, old, and blue are!" he demands cheerfully.

"Well, the eggs, orange juice and English muffins were new."

"Yes."

"And I have no idea about the old or blue."

"Guess."

"Okay, the grape jelly? Or, the lilacs in the bouquet?" I know purple and lavender are stretching the concept of blue, but perhaps my husband is a bit color blind. "I know I didn't taste any blue cheese in the scrambled eggs."

"Nope!" He trumpets. "I win. You lose!" He encircles my shoulders and draws me close to his beautiful face. "It's my true blue eyes watching breakfast until it was served, and my old heart's love for you."

May 25, 2014

It's Sunday morning. Paul and I coughed through the night again. At breakfast, I hear Joe coughing a little. "Mr. B, do you think you've caught our cold?" I sneak a concerned look at Paul.

"Oh, no. It may be allergies. I get 'em in the spring." Then he points at the cottonwood in our yard. "Son, do you remember planting that tree wid me?"

Paul remembers. "I remember it, about forty years ago. Didn't we plant another one first?"

"Yup. But I made the mistake of staking it to the ground like you've done wid your, whatchacallit? Gala apple tree there. Guess what happened?"

I don't know. We don't know.

"It needed to grow its own root strength to support it through the spring storms in Colorado. I had staked it, so it didn't grow into its natural strength. When I took the stake off the next year, the first storm blew it over, and it split. I didn't like it, so we planted the cottonwood. Maudie and I always like the snow in springtime, and it shades the whole lawn at different times of the day." He turns to address me, "Miss, I wouldn't mind if you looked up in your black box how long that tree might live."

When I find the answer, I bring my black box to the dining room table. "A cottonwood tree lives for approximately 70 years. However, there are some that have lived over 100 years. Cottonwoods are part of the willow family." Joe takes a couple of minutes trying to read my screen. His eyesight has improved, but it is hard to focus on this unfamiliar thing.

"A hundred years! Why that tree will outlast all of us!" he exclaims.

"Maybe us, but not you, Mr. B."

May 26, 2014

It's not only Memorial Day, but this Saturday was our anniversary, and here we sit on a ruined weekend in the Emergent Care. A doctor orders scripts for the earache that is threatening to split my eardrum asunder. Paul complains that even taking every medicine offered over-the-counter for colds, our mutual bronchitis still seems to feed off of one another rather than dry up.

Apparently now, the medics have determined that there is no drug to cure bronchitis. Instead, after waiting for hours, the on-call doctor writes us each a script for more over- the-counter meds and a day of rest from work. I look at mine and laugh ruefully. "Shall I show my prescription for a day off work to Mr. B?"

Paul isn't amused at any of this, but he drives through McDonald's and buys three large packets of hot, salty fries before heading home. We find Mr. B sitting on the porch enjoying the warmth, and although he refuses the fries verbally, he immediately scoots up to the packet on the table and thrusts the hot potatoes, to the last crumb, into his mouth while they are still hot. "You bought too much," he says shoving the last nibble into his mouth.

"Looks like just enough," I report.

He changes the subject. "You know, there was a guy in the neighborhood who used to gather all the children together on mornings like this. They would parade through the streets banging on boxes and pots and pans. And there is a B-15 at the county airport that sells rides to tourists."

Paul nods.

"But why haven't I seen any airplanes or heard about any parades this year? Was there a picnic at the park or anything?"

"I dunno, Dad." My bleary-eyed honey is ready for a nap. "We didn't see anything going on, but we were only looking for meds. What a waste of a holiday." Paul tromps inside to find a bed. I'm right behind him. "I'm sorry, Mr. B. I guess we kinda messed up on all the tradition this year. You still aren't coughing?"

"Oh no. I'm fine, kiddo. Go get your nap." He folds his hands over his lap and leans back against his nylon-strung patio chair.

I'm relieved to be hitting the pillow, but the mystery of Mr. B's iron health fills my head.

May 27, 2014

Picking up his boiled egg, Joe asks me how it's going with our renter's move out of our rental house and into her mother's home.

"It's not," I announce. "She was moving there, but she's already moving out. Her mom can't abide all her stuff."

Joe thinks about it as he peels his egg. "When you come to the end of your life, the things that bring you comfort aren't things. You and Pauly bring me comfort." He briefly looks at me, then continues. "My mothea's eldest sista, the one in Chicago, was a pushy type. She offered to keep my mothea's younger sista's son, while he was going to medical college. His name was Zagorski. He became Dr. Zagorski, and he eventually married a pretty redheaded Polish girl. They settled in Iron Town, Massachusetts. But this aunt in Chicago didn't have kids of her own, and she didn't really love him, you know. So she offered him something, yes, but she complained when she didn't get something in return. I think she musta needed help around her place. My cousin was a poor college kid, and this aunt was kinda' selfish. I remember hearing her comment on the boy's habits that weren't good enough for her. She told my mothea that he wouldn't pay rent.

"Now, I don't know how much of her complaint was true because that's the thing about those kind of rifts in the family. The comments just lie there unconfirmed and anyone can believe whatever they want. My mothea loved her younger sista, so we didn't want to believe anything bad about her son." Joe salts his egg and gulps it, cold.

"One time I came home from college and found that elder sista from Chicago in my mothea's kitchen talking about insurance and money. Yeah. She caused a real problem between my mothea and fathea wid all her talking about fearful things and him needing to get insurance for my mothea." I realize we have wandered far from our original conversation, but Joe continues his flow of consciousness.

"To settle it, my fathea took me wid him to a lawyer, and he drew up a will and gave everything he had to my mothea, and paid the lawyer ten bucks. Ten bucks for a will, mind you! My mothea was happy after that. But you know, my fathea told me that when one spouse dies, the other one automatically gets everything anyway. So, maybe it was a waste of money. Money causes all kinds of family feuds."

"Fear causes fighting too," I chime.

"It was a waste of money anyway because my mothea died before my fathea!" Joe rouses emphatically. "Well, I guess there was a fifty-fifty chance of that." He pauses. "That sista in Chicago, I can't remember her name, but she was the one who died and left $10,000 of insurance to her husband, and he let someone 'hold' it for him while he was grieving and never saw it again. Yeah." He chuckles. "You can't control very much in your old age, especially if you are grieving!"

Joe peels his banana now and continues. "Now, her younger sista had a car, and she could drive up from Lawrence to see my mothea. They would read letters from the family together. But I never understood what they said. I remember my sista, Lucy, got us involved wid sending regular packages over to Poland during the war. The relatives had written to ask for help. It must have been very hard on them or they wouldn't have asked. But that's all I ever knew. My mothea was tight-lipped about it."

"Or maybe she spoke Polish, and you spoke English."

"Could be. Let's see," continues Mr. B peering into the maple grain of our table. "I remember the favorite sista was a larger built woman than my mothea. She was like a strong farm woman, and we loved her. She was delightful. My fathea also got along wid her husband except that they would surprise us wid their visits, and he would kinda' rib my fathea about being grouchy. My mothea didn't care. Maybe my mothea had kinda planned it behind Fathea's back? I dunno. They'd usually come up on Sunday afternoons and the two of 'em would talk and talk and talk."

"In Polish?"

"Oh yes." Joe's watery eyes get large. "Of course. And I never understood a word of it. But one time, my mothea was so delighted that she made the Zagorski family my fathea's Sunday favorite: hot dogs! And my fathea lectured her about that."

"Hot dogs? He was upset about hot dogs?"

Joe nods without judgment.

I try to imagine why. "Was it because Sunday was her day off from cooking for the family?"

"Oh, I don't know why. My fathea loved to make us Indian style hot dogs, for the fun of it. It was as close to camping out as we got. Maybe he had plans for 'em. He didn't like surprises."

"What's Indian style hot dogs?"

"Oh, well, we heated our house with hard coal, sometimes Lucy and I brought home soft coal that the railroad engineers would throw off to us when they saw us collecting the bits of hard coal along the line."

"What's the difference?"

"Soft coal smoked up the house. It was meant to be going to commercial destinations, not for residential use. It was called bitmus. My mothea hated it. But anyway, my fathea would take the tongs and pull off the iron lids from the top of the stove so that the fire would burn, and then we put the hot dogs on a stick. The smoke would billow into the room. We'd cook 'em there together, and they'd get charcoal black and then we'd eat 'em."

"Oh. My. Gosh. Mr. B! That poisonous smoke probably stuck to the walls and ceilings of your house!"

He shrugs. "Probably, but what can ya do? We didn't know anything about it then."

"You still like blackened hot dogs, Mr. B." I grin.

Joe's thoughts drift away. "I'd like to try to make a table for your vegetable garden," he says suddenly. "Yes, about table height. How would that be, Kiddo? Then we can work on either side and neither of us has to bend over. I saw some lumber your husband stored up in the rafters of the garage."

"Maybe you should draw it up first." I'm hesitant because I've been waiting to build a raised garden to plant seeds, but I'm not at all sure a raised platform is necessary, but then again it could be this summer's project for Mr. B. "Could you just build a raised garden bed with scrap wood, instead? I don't think it needs to be as high as a table." I'm gently trying to steer him away from the bunk bed garden idea.

Shortly, I hear the roaring of our circular saw and run outside to find Mr. B. sawing furring strips. "Oh! I'm just reinforcing the sides of this cedar box so that when we put the whole thing on stilts, the dirt won't fall out."

Okay. I can tell he's bored with the traditional raised bed and wants to experiment. But I've still got a cold-clogged head. "I'll just watch. When you are done with that, you should have some orange juice."

"Okay!" He says smiling. "Thank you, Ma'am."

Whether it works out is not so important, I decide, as giving him something to do. I retreat to my room, grab a good book, and return to Joe's glider to read while the use of his circular saw torments my whole being.

May 28, 2014

Today while I am languishing in bed, Joe finishes reinforcing the cedar slats on the raised planter for our vegetables. He lifts up the square, fastened on a cedar crossbar to stabilize it, and then stands on a chair for some leverage to drill the sidebar supports on. The heat rises, broiling me like a stuffed tomato upstairs and so I roll myself out of bed and down the stairs to take a look. He's admiring his work and appreciates me admiring it with him. Within a few minutes, I am lying flat out on the couch. This bronchial thing has knocked me over. Outside, I hear Joe starting the lawn mower. He's finished by the time Paul comes home from work with some more meds. He cleans the grass out of Joe's clogged mower, and we make hamburgers for dinner with sides of applesauce and rabbit food. When we all bow our heads to pray, Paul and I thank God for Joe's strength and health.

Mr. B purses his lips.

"It was hard work pushing that mower around you know." Joe's blue eyes are directed at me. It takes me a few minutes to realize he is arguing about who should get the credit for his strength.

May 30, 2014

We are finally going away for the weekend and Joe has had the dates penned on his calendar for a month, but the closer it gets the more he'd like us to stay put, this morning being a case in point. At breakfast I receive a phone call from an old friend on Pearl Street. Joe suddenly can't recall that we lived on Pearl Street. Then he can't remember what to feed Jester while we're gone. He can barely hear my voice and asks me to repeat myself repeatedly.

"If you're leaving me because I can't hear you, I'll tell ya right now that I've got your fathea's extra hearing aid upstairs on my dresser, the one he sent up here for me to experiment with, and I intend to start using it."

"That's great, Joe. Really? Well, I'll believe it when I see it."

Complaints about the woodpile needing to be moved right away come next. "It's a snake pit. It's a fire hazard!" He then wants to know what kind of range my phone has, can I hear my phone ring all the way to the back of the yard?

"Oh it's by satellite, Mr. B. We can get phone calls way up in the mountains!"

"Oh well. Why don't ya just stay here and get your calls then?"

"Mr. B, I would, but it's our anniversary."

He gets a smirk on his face, but he says nothing about that. Instead, "Is it a motel or a hotel?"

"It's a hotel."

"How many rooms?"

"I can't remember."

"Have you been there before? Have you checked it out?"

"No, but there were pictures and a full description on the Internet and we aren't afraid of a little adventure now and then."

"Well, I wanna give you a little cash so that you can eat a nice meal at the Stanley Hotel, since you can't afford to stay there."

"No. No. That's all right! We just didn't want to stay there, Mr. B. We want to stay in the Swiss Chalet."

"*Swiss*, you say? Swiss *should* be clean enough, but I still want to give you something to eat on. Maudie and I had a wonderful dinner at the Stanley once, and you kids should check it out. Lemme know if it's still any good."

"Thank you, Mr. B. That's very sweet of you." I give him a little hug goodbye and then look out the dining room window in surprise. "Is it snowing outside?"

Joe yams out the side of his mouth. "Look at that! It must be time for Lady Cottonwood to spread her magic around the neighborhood!"

June ~ Joy

June 1, 2014

Paul and I dug up and collected the stringy root of a winter creeper from alongside the road on our return home from Estes Park. They turn a deep Christmassy red on the hillsides in winter. The root is pretty dry by the time we roll up to Joe's house. So, I immediately put the stopper in the kitchen sink and fill it up with the root in the water as Paul goes to make a weekend report to his father.

After we all chat for a while on the porch out back, I refill the sink with water and go upstairs to unpack.

Paul comes up snickering a few minutes later. He lies on the bed with his arms outstretched while a big sigh and a couple of tears roll out of him. "Guess what just happened, Honey?"

"What?"

"My dad went inside for something. Then he came and confronted me with a plunger in his hand. He was worried that the kitchen sink was all plugged up, He said he needed help getting a monster root out."

June 2, 2014

Paul and I sneak out to the store and return with a window air conditioner. Gloating, after installing it, we sit in front of the cool breeze in the living room and grin at each other. It quickly brings down the thermostat from 74 to 67. That'll do! Joe complains that it's Alaska indoors, and he goes to spend most of his day out on the back porch.

June 3, 2014

I have just backed up Paul's yellow truck to the gate beside the house. Mr. B is determined to help me dish out the yard of topsoil and pieces of flagstone to complete another section of the path around the backyard park. He opens the blue shed doors and comes forth with two shovels. I pull up the wheelbarrow but, to open the tailgate of Paul's truck, we take turns pulling, yanking, examining, and pounding on the latches to no avail. I finally succumb to scooping out shovels of dirt over the side of the truck bed, using a completely different set of higher body muscles, in order to fill up one wheelbarrow, dump it, and fill a second. At that point, I call a mechanical friend for help. Meanwhile, Mr. B is steadily examining the problem, twisting and probing and pushing the tailgate with a screwdriver. As soon as I set down my cell phone, he shouts: "GOT IT!" I hear the tailgate grating and squawking as it lunges into a horizontal landing: truck bed wide open for business.

"My goodness, Mr. B! You just performed a miracle!" My admiration gushes.

Shy, he quips, "Eh, no ma'am, it was just a matter of perseverance."

"But perseverance these days is a miracle, and you just made my day."

He accepts my quick hug and pat on his back with a grin, wiping off the sweat of his brow.

By the time my hubster walks through the door, Joe is leaning on his shovel, overlooking a raised vegetable bed, and I am laying the final piece of flagstone. I hear Joe raise his dry voice to his son. "You're late, Pauly. You are just plain late for the party!"

Paul is carrying two glasses of cool, clear water. He walks around studying our newest backyard creation. "Well, well. Look at what you two landscapers managed to do today." He hands one glass to his father. "This is one party I'm glad I missed, Chief. But, hey, you two should go into business together!" My man hands me the other glass, rolls up his sleeves, and kisses me hello. "Can I help you clean up the tools?"

"Yeah." His father gulps. "And, then you can take us to dinner, big boy."

June 4, 2014
The ol' man gives Paul half of his tuna steak tonight. He says he isn't hungry, but he eats all of his lettuce and cottage cheese, and he also downs a second helping of homemade tapioca. I guess he's all right.

"May I ask why, Mr. B, do you hate salad dressing and heap up the cottage cheese over your greens instead?"

"You may ask."

I allow Joe's droll reply to take its toll and he finally patronizes us. "Oh, I suppose cottage cheese and blue cheese are somewhat Polish cheeses. They are the only cheeses we ever got in our home. I dunno how to answer your question, Miss, other than that."

Paul is happy to down the other half of the Chief's fish. He makes it clear in ten different ways how yummy tuna fish is. Later, Paul informs me that his father doesn't like tuna unless it is baked with green olives. Imagine! Olives.

I've been watching Joe during our movie lately. I think he's been nodding off. Tonight, he definitely snored through half of it. He is embarrassed, especially when he admits he hadn't seen it before. "Must be old age catchin' up wid me." He shakes his head briskly.

June 6, 2014
I see our first swallowtail butterfly flitting around the tops of the snapdragons and roses this morning. Watching it for a moment

grants me the same carefree feeling.

After a hard day's labor getting our rental cleaned, painted, and new lights installed throughout the house, I arrive home to find Joe completely bored. "Don't leave wid'out me tomorrow," he says. "There's nothing for an old guy to do around here."

"Why didn't you eat your papaya, Mr. B?" I'm a little alarmed to see the bowl of papaya I had sliced for him still sitting in the fridge.

"Oh, I just haven't been hungry lately. That's a sign of old age, you know. Not being hungry."

Paul is going to see some friends tonight, so Mr. B and I run out for a dinner date at the garden club. Shoving lettuce into his mouth with his fingers, Joe points and snickers at a huge teenager, good-looking sportsman, in plaid boxer-like shorts hanging down his buttocks, calf high socks, and oversized jersey. He starts chuckling.

"The way that guy swaggers reminds me of one of my roommates in college. The guy was the son of a German lawyer, and he was a football star back in his hometown, but he'd gotten this gal pregnant, and so he left the state and went to college to avoid the gossips… and the responsibilities. Nah, he wasn't serious about college. He eventually dropped out. After I graduated and went to California, he wrote to my parents and got my new address. Then he wrote to me that he'd done it again and gotten another girl pregnant. He wanted to know if he could come stay with me. Well, he'd done it twice, so I wasn't impressed. I wrote back that I was looking for work and that he could only join me if he brought his own money wid him while he was looking for a job. Guess what?" Joe leans towards me with his eyebrows in the sky. "I never did hear from that guy again! Heh, heh, heh. Heck! He's probably dead now. He'd be old like me. I believe all those guys I went to college wid would be dead by now." He studies his food.

"Hmm."

"We don't expect you to expire so long as you keep eating, Mr. B, so don't forget that your pudding and muffins are waiting for you."

"Oh yeah." He gurgles joyfully and rambles down the carpeted aisle to scoop up dessert. We sit in silence for a while, Joe resembling Yoda, munching contentedly on the iron-building raisins in his tapioca. He suddenly looks at me and asks if Pauly ever wonders about his birth parents.

"No. No. I don't think so. He never mentions anything like that. He's always been glad that you and Maudie were his folks."

"Well you know, he could go looking for 'em, but they might not be alive anyway. They'd be in their eighties."

"Guess you're right!" I hadn't considered their age since I also hadn't thought about Paul's birth parents for years. "How did you pick his name?"

"Oh, we named him after my middle name and Maudie's favorite brother who was the doctor, and my sista's husband the German, who leapt off the spy boat. We covered all the bases because his other middle name was my father's first name, and all together, it equaled John Paul, like the Pope!"

"Oh, but you are the one who's the Pope!"

"Oh *that*, you kids are funny. You know life isn't worth living if you can't have some fun. You know, Victoria? We named her from the English side of the Carey family. Queen Victoria is in Maude's heritage somewhere, so there is always a girl named Victoria in the daughters."

After a minute he adds, "I'm glad Pauly's happy wid us. It would'a broke Maudie's heart if he wanted to look for them while she was alive. You know those set-ups they put on the television from time to time? Sometimes you read about 'em in the newspaper? Some adopted kid locates his birth parents? But you never do hear about all those parents they find that don't have a happy ending, do you? They only publish the success stories. But there are lots of 'em who wished they'd never found out."

"I believe you are right, Mr. B. Smarty Pants. Anyway, he never talks about it."

"I believe I'll go get me a little more tapioca." Smiling, he pushes himself out of the booth and weaves down the aisle.

June 9, 2014

My sister and mother join us for soup and salad tonight. We are celebrating together that Mother is walking on her own now, without a cane, and is no longer using oxygen. Mr. B greets them in his hoodie explaining that they'll be having dinner with him in the "refrigerator" tonight.

We point to our new air conditioner in the window. "He can always put on a hoodie, but I can't take anything more off," I explain.

Quickly assessing the situation, my sister pipes, "Mr. B? I hear that refrigerators keep things from getting old."

"A-ha!" Joe laughs and pats the clever one on the back.

"Is that a cottonwood there?" She notices the white fairytale floaters wafting in the breeze.

"Shush!" My shoe presses on her toe under the table as I clock forward the conversation. "Mom, it's your play."

"I thought female cottonwoods were outlawed." Undeterred, she continues to gaze through the picture window. "So, Lynn, are you growing that apple tree and pine tree on either side to take its place when you cut it down?"

Mr. B looks at me. Mom makes her play.

Would anyone report me if I strangled my sis? "Uh, Mr. B grew up reading Westerns," I explain, "and there were always cottonwoods by the river in those settings, so when he moved here and saw a sapling growing in the field out back, he and Paul transplanted it here. It's a legacy."

"Oh."

"It's your turn. Besides, personally, I think the white fuzzy seeds are romantic, and anyway it shades the entire backyard throughout the day."

Joe smiles, keeping his head in his cards.

"People are allergic to them." She bends over her cards to study her next play.

After my family leaves, Mr. B turns to me. "Gee whiz, your sista is pushy."

June 10, 2014

Yesterday, Mr. B helped us again at our rental house to get it ready to sell. He replaced two holey bathroom screens, and he washed windows all around the house. He did pretty good for a 98-year-old blind guy. I went behind him and swiped at the streaks when he wasn't looking. Still, he definitely saved me time.

This morning, when I am complimenting him on his stamina, he says, "No. I don't have anywhere near the strength you have. I'm practically as old as Methuselah." Distracted, he points excitedly. "Just look at that swallowtail in among those big pink roses! What a sight!"

I rib him as I get up to follow the bobbing yellow wings and fluttering tail through the window. "No bringing up religion, Mr. B."

That gets him going. He tells me that this Sunday when my nephew was visiting, he enjoyed him a lot. He enjoyed his work conversation about getting stem cells out of middle-aged men's belly fat and growing limbs or gluing bones together with those cells. He said he doesn't like it when he talks about religion all the time. I confess that we talk about religion because my nephew and

I like puzzles. It's like a game to us. There are a lot of mysteries in the scriptures. I admit that I know he doesn't like it though, and I'm glad he enjoyed this Sunday's conversation better. I tell him that religion is woven through life, but the core of our faith is really simple. The whole of the Bible points to the main gospel story. It's just that God's Son came in the flesh, identified with humanity, and died to pay the penalty for our sins. He proved he has the power over life and death by rising from the dead. That's the only thing that really matters in all of our banter.

He suddenly explains about the Scottish red-haired woman who owned the house in Auburn, Alabama, when he was taking preparatory college math courses. "She reamed me for taking the Lord's name in vain."

Now, this also happens to be a red-haired subject for me. So, I tell him, "It wouldn't break our relationship up, but I also feel that way, Mr. B. It's not a moral issue. But I can take people's swearing a lot better than I can take people using God's name in vain. It's because we have a personal relationship with the Lord that we feel that way."

He shakes his head. "Okay, but I think people should keep those opinions to themselves."

"So you think good men should keep quiet so that evil can abound."

He looks up astonished. "Now I can tell I'm not gonna win this point!" His wry humor pulls out another grin from me.

I've noticed that the framed watercolor behind Joe's head is tilting to the side on the wall. I'll have to fix it.

"Well, it's like if I were to mock or say something mean about Maudie or maybe I disparage your mother. You love them and you wouldn't look too kindly on that, would you? It shows that I'm not giving them the respect that you know they deserve."

He's studying his egg. He doesn't verbally respond. Then he

picks up the salt and continues. "And then there was this pastor in Tulsa. Man, his 'flock' or whatever you want to call it, treated him as though he was 'The Man.' But he was a sourpuss. And when I talked to him about my problems, he didn't have the answers. He talked like it was a business. He was just sour."

"I'm so sorry, Mr. B. I used to be like that. There are a lot of people who think that to be holy, they have to be hard and lack humor. It's not the Lord you are seeing in them. It's their own narrow selves. They aren't allowing God's love or good humor to expand them at *all*. They are just trying so hard to be *moral*, but that's very different than being *good*. Goodness includes compassion and fun and play, just like you do here teasing us. And when we watch Jester playing with the fallen cottonwood branches, running around the yard. He makes us all laugh and life is good! Actually, I know some grim people like that pastor too. They suck out the good blood from everyone's life. It's sad."

"You know that religious Italian family that I told you about? The Lumbards? They would have me over for dinner wid their son who was my college friend. I liked them a lot. They were good people. And they always prayed before meals. But boys will be boys, and the boys would sometimes leave the family prayers behind when they left the table. I didn't fault 'em for it. I just thought that religion is for certain times and places, but not for real life."

"Oh dear." The leaning watercolor on the wall seems to mimic my odd feeling about those people who made religious "good ol' boy" deals in Mr. B's past. "For a long time, I wondered how God could love people who spend half their time sliding under the wire with the minimum required, and half the time defrauding others. Why is He forbearing? Or, disinterested, maybe? I used to get so mad at people like that. I'd write them off my list of friends. But I have to admit, now, that I also forget His power whenever it is convenient for me to get away with something. So, why does God keep loving and wooing people?

"Then, there are those who say they are Christians, but do terrible things; they cuss and moan, slander and gossip, steal from and extort others. The only way I can accept that God loves sinners is that I view Him as a parent and the church people as His little children. We are all in different stages of our journey with him, and sometimes I think that God acts like you might if you saw your son Pauly messing up. God may shake his head at the way we act. He has to do something about *it* because wrong is wrong. But on the other hand, he smiles and says, 'That's my kid and I'm always gonna defend *him*.'"

I can't stand that crooked watercolor anymore, and I jump up to straighten it behind Mr. B's head. It startles the poor guy. He looks at me with watery Polish eyes.

"Thanks, Sweet Pea. You may be religious, but you don't suck out the good from my life." Mr. B smiles and catches and grasps my hand. Ditching his hand, I give him a warm hug. "What's that for, Miss?"

I don't explain how unfounded my fears were that I would lose out on "being me" when I moved into his house to be his companion and cook. "I love our life with you, Mr. B." Yes, a sense of belonging can prove to be better than a sense of individuality.

June 13, 2014
It's the day before Father's Day when our rental finally goes into the Multi-List, for sale. Our realtor raises the price another $10,000 after he sees what kind of work we have finished. Then the first lady who visits puts in a full price offer, and we also get a backup offer. At home, Joe pats my arm remarking, "I disagreed wid you when you were putting in those hardwood floors."

"You did?"

"Of course. I thought it was frivolous spending. But I have to admit that every day I walked into that house, and I knew you'd get the best price for it. People like quality. You can't get hardwood floors in new houses, and you did a good job wid all the matching woodwork. I admit. I like that place. Congratulations, girl! I can admit when I'm wrong, yeah. I'm big enough." He pats my shoulder.

Paul and I are so happy and grateful for the high price we were able to contract. It is as though the appraisal money we lost on Pearl has been restored to us through the rental. We just keep welling up with exclamations, laughter, and thanking God that in everything, He keeps His promises. Although I have often felt like a failure for all the work I did in that town to no avail, in the end, the housing investments are paying off. We might not have sold Pearl for its appraisal value, but we still made a lot of money on it for the seven years we held it; made enough to do some needed renovations on our home with Joe.

"Do you like the hardwood enough to replace the carpet with it, Mr. B?"

"Only if you put the used carpet downstairs. I don't wanna *waste* it."

June 14, 2014 Father's Day

As I'm serving up Mr. B's favorite thick-sliced, extra crispy bacon for his special Father's Day breakfast, an image of a father, wearing an orthodox cap, appearing in my memory over the years reoccurs. He came into the café where I often ate solo in my young adult years. He came to have lunch with a young boy, whom I took to be his son. The man was instructing the boy on important issues in life. I could overhear their interaction in which he relayed stories both from scripture and his own life. He so tenderly explained the difference between the boy's choices, then his opportunities, including moral terms and implications to others. This gave me an odd out-of-body sensation: gladness, craving, and loss. It raised the standard for what family could mean to me.

Although he is really my husband's father, Joe shows fatherly tenderness towards me through his teasing and stories. I learn from him. Our Father often places displaced individuals, without community or children of their own, into a new *family*.

After I give Mr. B his own special card, he asks me if I'd called my own father.

I explain that my father called me because he'd received my Father's Day card.

"You did? What for?" He pretends jealousy and then winks.

"Yep. I thanked him for being a hero at so many times in my life. I thanked him for teaching me to write my letters in first grade. I thanked him for making a bean bag toss and puppet theater for Christmas gifts when he and my mom were too poor to buy gifts. I thanked him for encouraging the love of music in me because he used to let me hang out with him in "men's quartet" performances. I also thanked him for Sunday afternoon mountain drives. And he gave me my first guitar, my first bike, and my first car!"

"Wow, that was a nice Fathea's Day card."

"Yup. I felt like writing him a letter. You know, he helped me with several cars, actually, including getting one back from New York when it was stolen from me through fraud! He was brave, Mr. B! He went right into the guy's workplace and told this guy's boss he wanted to talk with someone who had subleased his daughter's car and then failed to make payments. When the guy appeared, my dad made him hand over the keys. Then he bought new tires for it and drove it back to me from New York!"

"I also lived with him in his bachelor's pad when I returned from mission work. And here's a story for ya, Mr. B."

Rusty embarrassment colors my voice. "Overseas, in Africa, I had learned to put a can of sweetened condensed milk into a pot of boiling water to turn it into caramel cream. Like a pressure cooker. Only, I forgot the can of milk was still on the stove when I left his house that day. Oh, boy! The thing exploded, and tiny caramel dots were plastered all over his kitchen. No matter how hard I searched and scraped, we always found a few more brown caramel drops. Every Father's Day, I have to thank him again for not holding that bomb against me."

Joe's wide eyes are rimmed with merriment.

"You know, when my dad sold that house, he had to clean the kitchen from top to bottom, and when he moved the refrigerator, there were still hard drops of caramel candy on the walls!"

"Oh, that's a good story," Joe admits. He absently shuffles his food with his fork.

"Mr. B. You are the only person I have ever known to cut his bacon and chicken with a knife and yet pick up and eat your salad with your fingers!"

He shrugs and grins. "Really? I may have an idiosyncrasy."

"I also thanked him for teaching me how to use a computer because I made the most money I could because of this skill. Computers in the workplace were a brand new technology, and he taught me how to use the WordStar software for typing documents. You know he was the one who wrote the system for fixing power outages at Public Service Company on the Front Range?"

"Your fathea's a smart cookie. I know that. Quiet, but smart."

"Remember my first house with Paul?"

He mmm-hmms.

"Well, my dad re-built our first master bedroom closet in that old house. So, I thanked him for that. It was a long letter, Mr. B."

"Well, I painted your back hallway for ya, and drywalled your garage, Miss, and I didn't see that on my Fathea's Day card..." Joe whines, and then touches my hand. "Just kidding ya."

"Yes you did, Mr. B. You worked hard!" Suddenly, reflecting on what all my renovations meant to others who offered their muscle, my enthusiasm deflates with the air in my seat cushion. "But, oh man, there were a couple of very tender moments during our ordeal with the zoning lawsuit too. My dad gave us our first thousand dollars to file our appeal, even when the attorneys flaked out and didn't do their job. It gave me such hope to have his respect and financial backing. When they were convicting us of violating their new zoning regulation, my dad also wrote the judge the most amazing letter about how much he respects me. It really made me cry. I didn't know how he felt till then. I guess it takes some drama to get those kinds of things out of someone so reserved, eh?"

"Well, I saw it last summer, when he came to visit and helped you with that shed."

"Yeah, he did that for us before the closing on our house when we had no money."

"I watched your dad build the shelves inside the shed and install ceiling fans in your bedrooms. And Miss, you were in *very poor humor* those days."

Nodding, I laugh and admit it. Then I tell Joe that my dad also loves Paul and encourages us as a married couple. "I'm so glad God gave my dad to me! And I'm so glad God gave me you. You are my adopted dad, Mr. B."

"Heh, heh. My kids and I always had a joke like that. I used to thank them for choosing me, and they would thank me for choosing them."

"Oh, that's sweet!" Our eyes mist.

"Well, I always felt adoption was just like birthing the baby. There is no difference. When you love someone, you commit to them for twenty-five years, and you either enjoy them or you don't. So, what's the difference?"

"You've certainly committed to your kids for more than twenty-five years, though. Mr. B, you are the gift that keeps on giving!"

"Ah, no, Sweetie. Thank you for saying so, but you guys have helped me in my old age. What more could I want? You know that package that Victoria sent, cans of salmon from the Seattle Pier, a card that shows she grew up aways back and knows the difference now between a good dad and a bad one? That card of hers was fun to read! And she spoiled me with chocolates. So, you know, it all comes back in one way or another."

I'm glad it's come back around for Joe.

June 15, 2014

We're driving on our way to our rental to bring back some brooms and cleaning supplies. Joe says matter-of-factly, "Maybe you can stop by the garden shop on the way home. I've been wanting to buy you another clematis vine."

"For me? What? Why?" I turn towards him with an awkward grin. "Wait. Is it because I won't let you prune the white one again?" A laugh escapes, followed by a round of coughing.

"Heh, heh. I suppose we'll always disagree about that severe pruning indication, but no. That cutting that I've started off of your white clematis is not gonna grow fast enough for me. And I want to plant one around that stump at the base of the tree that Paul and I cut down earlier. I want to have one that I can prune and take care of all on my own. I want the credit."

"You want a competition to see who is right about pruning?"

"Well, yes!" He pats my knee. "Oh, excuse me. I forgot myself."

On the way home, Joe and I stop to search the garden shop for just the right clematis, one that grows on a trellis and blooms for a long time. The one we picked was purple and advertised as having a nice fragrance. He also buys a couple of other petunias for the planters we haven't yet filled up.

The two clerks at the nursery counter ask if Joe qualifies for their Veteran's special on the plants this week.

"What did she say?" he wants to know.

"You look like you may be a veteran," she clarifies, but not loudly.

"Oh, he's not a veteran." I hiss. Then I lift my voice. "Mr. B's a rocket scientist!" to clarify his own honorable contribution to the United States for her. Joe does hear this and looks towards his feet, shaking his head. The gals load him up with his plants, and much flattery of marriage proposals due to his fine etiquette and intelligence, but they don't give him a discount.

"What was that all *about*?" He seems embarrassed as we push his cart through the threshold and water mister. Instantly, he is delighted. "Oh! Let's do that again!" he says.

Back home, in the heat of a violent sun, the kind of sun that naked people bathe in until their skin boils into brown spots, Joe and I tackle a hole in the ground. He chops at roots near the stump, then I take a turn, back and forth. Too quickly, I have to rest in the shade. Soon, even Mr. B saddles up to the shaded patio and plops into his glider. I rouse my remaining energy to get us a hydrating drink. After a bit, Joe trudges out to finish digging. Finally, I bring out the water hose, sprinkling it liberally in the hole and in our mouths, on my sweaty head. We congratulate each other as the cool stream flows around our new plant. Out comes my white flag: "The breeder of this clematis is Polish, and it blooms profusely, up to 2,000 blooms a summer! So, you will definitely win this contest." I hug him and thank him for being so sweet.

"Well, I want you to think of me each time you look at this. Will you?"

"Of course Mr. B, how could I forget? I'm only avoiding giving you a hug right now because of my cold. But I hope you'll stick around to watch it grow!"

"I do, too. I do, too," he spouts with robust hope. We collect the hose and spade and empty pot and take them to the patio, where we collapse in the shade of afternoon heat, exhausted.

Jester is gnawing at a ball in the grass. As soon as he sees me sit down he gets up and runs over, mounting my lap for pets, kisses, and hugs. When I push him off, he turns about and looks expectantly again at me. Joe glares at him. "Look at that, he wants more, so he's offering his other side! That dog is spoiled. A-hem. Just like you spoil me, I guess. Which of us do you like more?"

"Well! I just don't know!" My sandpaper voice teases. "Of course Jester doesn't bring me flowers. You have the edge there."

"Good to know." Joe nods sharply. "But you just haven't trained him right. My mothea would never approve of his manners." He pushes himself up and goes inside the house. In a minute he returns with Victoria's chocolates. He opens it under my nose and waves the box around. "He doesn't bring you chocolates neither!"

June 16, 2014

My cold has gone to my chest. I'm hacking like an angry dog. So for dinner, Paul brings home three hoagies with a side of McDonald's French fries. After I sit at my seat, Paul pounds on my back like a masseuse.

"What cha doin' to our gal?" Joe demands, going into the kitchen and coming out with a knife.

"Just giving her a respiratory treatment, Dad! Put down that knife!"

Joe sits and cuts his six-inch hoagie sandwich in half and offers one half to Paul.

"No way." I hear myself barking. "Eat that, Joe! That's not too much." I insist.

Paul takes his dad's sandwich and bites into it.

"Oh!" I slam down my drink. He's on my list now. The list that describes the sandwich after it's fully processed. Each of them catch my eyes of fire, but I'm too exhausted to argue with them.

Paul sets down the bitten hoagie and slides it back onto his dad's paper wrapper. He sits to unwrap his own hoagie. "Just try it, Dad."

Joe takes a couple more bites and puts it back onto Paul's wrapper. Paul looks at me evenly and says, "You'll make a friend if you give it to the dog, Chief."

"Oh! A friend, you say?" Joe gets up and walks over to Jester's bowl. He bends all the way down and places his extra bites of sandwich into the bowl. Jester immediately rises and trots over to dig into his treat. He raises his head to see Mr. B staring down at him. The visual exchange is a cartoon played in slow motion. "Us boys gotta stick together," he says patting the dog's behind.

Beaten, I start to giggle and the giggling spurs me into a fit of coughing.

"Come with me, Honey." Paul pulls my arm up and I follow him upstairs. He leads me into the bathroom, shuts the door, and leans over to start the shower running hot. Pretty soon the steam is rolling in streaks down the walls and the mirrors are like clouds. "Breathe that in and cough as hard as you can, Honey. Get your lungs moving." The care for the frail in this house is decidedly circular. Oh, how I love my honey.

June 17, 2014

After the many times I've demurred, book club is finally coming here to Joe's house, where I live. Tonight they're coming. I'm feeling a little better thankfully, and anyway, I just couldn't cancel.

So, I begin dusting, methodically, dusting to calm my nerves.

Joe seems more excited to have them visit than I am: Betty, Chris, Charmayne, Merry Rose, Nancy, Liz, Suzie and Susan, Meegan, Meridith, Sarah Jane, and Linda, touting her great-grandbaby named Rainbow enter, each greeting Mr. B as if he were a rock star. "Are you coming out to eat with us?"

"Oh, no, girls. This is your night. You enjoy it."

"But, I have a whole bowl of chilled shrimp, Mr. B." I press. "Your favorite."

"Well, maybe I'll take one or two." He waffles. I hand him a luncheon plate.

Outside, the girls are exclaiming about our beautiful cherry wood table. "What's the story on this, Lynn? 'Cuz we know you have one."

"Only one. It's the table we acquired through a yard sale trade as we were moving in last year, and Joe refinished it for us all by himself." Still more exclamations of wonder. Mr. B becomes our featured entertainment.

The evening musk and spice of our oriental lilies is meandering through the noses of this celebrated group of friends.

The girls walk the breadth of green lawn, bending over the beds of classically scented Mr. Lincoln roses, snapdragons, wisteria, and sweet peas. "Who is the gardener?" Merry Rose is the famous gardener in our group and the one asking.

I admit that Joe mows it all. "Front and back. We both work on the gardens together." Finally, I show off the flagstone patio Joe and I laid together.

"Oh, my word! How old is he?" come the questions.

"Ninety-eight."

"Ninety-eight and still mowing this huge back yard and laying flagstone?" Glowing eyes are roundly incredulous.

"Oh, it gives me something to do." Joe intervenes, as he

accepts a plate of shrimp.

Lady Cottonwood seems to have stopped shedding cotton for our special event, and I thank her.

As the twilight deepens and the solar lamps begin to burn soft light, Linda begins to talk about her breast cancer, which has metastasized into her bones. "I couldn't figure out why my ribs hurt. I just couldn't remember doing anything to my ribs or my back. So well, this explained it." With great drama, she describes how traumatized she felt with the initial diagnosis, thinking she would only have three months to live. "That's why I scheduled my Life's-a-Beach party, gals. I'm having as much fun as possible this summer," she ruffles tufts of Rainbow's hair, "and my accountant said to cash in my retirement and buy furniture that will make me comfortable." She is glad that her doctor is aggressively treating her and gives her a couple of years in prognosis to enjoy her new great-grandbabies.

As I get ready for bed an image of a stark water glass comes to mind. My life is like a glass. Since I've been meditating in the psalms this year, I've been re-thinking whether there really are wicked people who have been taken over by their evil ways, and corrupt choices, as opposed to righteous people, who are gracious, kind, and loving. People who are redeemed show their actions aligning themselves to their soul's condition. But there are so many gray areas of life. Though this is not a politically correct conviction, I agree with the psalms that describes two kinds of souls; yet how does it happen?

The meaning of the water glass occurs to me, that our lives begin as empty, transparent glasses. We make choices all the time to fill them up with good or bad. Nobody else can pour directly into our glass because we have a lid on it that only we control. At the moment when we take our last breath, when our lives are full of memories that we have made, our reactions to others and life events, our initiations of actions toward God and others on this earth, are those memories filled with God's living water or are they filled with shriveled, self-centered depravity, and left-over smudges of others whom we let in and out? Are the evil memories washed and covered over by the blood of Christ and His forgiveness? If so, every memory is redeemed. Our glass, full or evaporated, is our life.

June 18, 2014

Joe starts breakfast with strawberries and cottage cheese today. He had mentioned the other day that breakfast needed a change every once in a while. So, Paul also bought him bear claws, his favorite pastry. With a full mouth he starts to ask me about Suzie. "She sure is a nice gal. She's very quick and pleasant. What does she do for a living?"

"Oh, she's an artist."

"Really? What does she paint?"

"Not portraits, not people, but not exactly landscapes either. I've been to a couple of her art shows. She's a modern multi-media artist but in a nice way. I think you'd like her work."

"Another one of those? You sure have a lot of artist friends!"

"Yup. You don't seem to mind inviting my bunch of hooligans into your home, either."

"Well, you know, I've gotten used to you. You know Maudie had an artist friend. She was Spanish. It was her husband really. We went to a park once for an art opening, and nobody was there but these huge nudes! Nude pictures, that is. Finally, people came, just one at a time. It was the strangest party I'd ever been too. They weren't dressed up like Maudie and me, neither."

"Well, you probably didn't want to be in a crowd all looking at nudes anyway."

"There was this one nude who was reaching up for something,

kind of a side view, and of course that exposed everything."

"Of course! I'm surprised you didn't buy one!"

"Where would I put it, where that mirror is hanging in the living room?" Joe teases. "No, I actually didn't think much of the artwork, but it was sort of a statement because it was nudity out in the open, and I think there had just been a lawsuit that determined it was all right."

"Did you remember Linda?"

"Oh yes, that young woman who fixed Thanksgiving dinner for us in that huge house across from the governor's mansion. One of your best friends. I know. She has cancer. I didn't say anything to her about it. I didn't know how she would take it."

"That's okay, Mr. B."

"What does Suzie's husband do?"

"She's never been married."

"What? Someone's missing out, then. Someone is missing out."

He shakes his head. "Well, what do you have on the agenda for today, girl?"

"Oh, Mr. B, I am just worn out from all that work yesterday, and from getting the house ready, and my allergies! How can you still be acting like the Little Train that Could?" I am floored.

"Come on. I can't sit around listening to music today. Give me something to do."

"Okay, let's take the leaf out of the table and put the chairs back into the shed." He follows me out to the porch.

"I think you should put some plastic or something between the chairs to keep them from scratching each other."

I find some sheets of cardboard inside the shed and begin cutting squares to set between the chairs we are stacking.

"You are a real smart girl, real down to earth. I enjoy your company. And you know what? Lots of your friends commented to me on the flowers out here. That was real nice. When you first moved in, Lynn, I would have thought you liked sweets for a treat. Boy, I was wrong. I can sure see that it's flowers you like."

"You have a beautiful yard, Mr. B. I'm glad we can share it. Living with you has been like the Hokey Pokey Clinic. It's been a place to turn myself around." I give him a hug. "My friend Rosie said because of the orientation of her deck, it gets the hot sun in summer and no sun in winter. Location. Location. Location." I sing. "That's what my realtor mom's slogan was. I think Rosie was a mite bit jealous of the positioning of our porch to the sun."

"It faces straight southeast, you know."

"Does it? Even when I came to visit years ago I always noticed how sheltered the back porch was with perfect sun exposure." I don't admit I felt it was the main redeeming factor of the house.

How things have changed in a year! Now, I understand the stories in these walls. I'm experiencing many of the reasons my husband and his parents found peace and contentment here. The house snob in me has been routed. In fact, the tiny house fad makes a lot of sense to me now. It's about financial freedom. Being free of debt feels like a daily miracle and puts the happiness back inside our conversations and past times.

We congratulate each other on many days of yard design and planting, sitting in the shade watching the sprinklers water, talking.

"Paul and I both love our bike rides around the lake. And autumn near the foothills is delicious."

"You have a lot of perks living here. I hope you don't sell this place after I'm gone. I'd like you to enjoy it. That is until you can't take care of it anymore. But when you are old, it will be hard to let it go. You know, I have t' tell ya. I was wrong about your ideas: the flagstone patio and raising the roof. I really like them both. You have good ideas, and I'm man enough to admit it."

"Except you still disagree with me about how much to prune roses and clematis." I nudge him.

He shrugs, and his blue eyes twinkle. "Even the best partners disagree on some things."

June 19, 2014

"The local swimming pool looks to be full of children!" Joe watches out the side window on our ride back from fixing a couple of details at our rental for the new buyer.

"It's hot!" I respond. "I wish I dared go into that pool right now. But my nose is running so badly, it makes me remember what kids do in the water!"

"Darn tooten." His elbow shoots at me. "I remember we used to have a monster of a natural swimming pool in Woonsocket. It wasn't a big pond, but on Fridays, all the French kids would go there for their weekly baths. None of them had bathtubs at home. So, they'd just wear cut offs and hop in. It had a big fountain in the middle, but it was filthy dirty. I hated it. Besides, you had to bring someone along to watch that your clothes didn't get stolen! The bathhouse didn't have lockers like they do these days."

"I thought you said you didn't have a bathtub either."

"I didn't. My folks finally got one the year I went off to college."

"So, how do you know that the French kids took their baths in the pool? You musta' been there too!" My elbow juts out to gently rib him.

"Ahhhh, Smarty. You caught me! Yes, I had to swim there too. For the same reason. But Eddy and I waited 'til it was nighttime and we swam in the nude. We didn't go at the same time as the French." We look at each other with amusement. "I was sure glad when they got a bathtub. It wasn't much, but it was refreshing. My mama loved that tub, too. She used it back home, almost every day, for washing laundry."

"But by then, I was in Alabama for most of the year, doing

summer school to catch up with math and science in the summer. Auburn used to be Polytechnic Institute. I took my deficiency course there over the first summer. I remember it was called, "The Strength of Materials." *Ah, so that was the beginning of Mr. Byk's interest in structural engineering, I think...* "And the only way to cool off was by swimming in a homemade pond. Tommy and I would go.

"You know Maudie's mothea's family, the Careys? Well, they owned Carey Salt. So they had a big pool that the whole family shared. It was so clean the water sparkled. Maudie would call her cousin, and they'd go swimming. It had a nice big bathhouse also. You never had to worry about kids taking your clothes from it, cuz it was practically empty all the time!"

He hears me still coughing roughly from the lingering bronchitis mixed with sudden allergies. "You sound like you're on your deathbed, Sweet Pea. Betta get you home," patting my arm. "I dunno why some people have all the good genes. Seems like they don't have to do nothin' and they survive. Like me. I survived Maudie. And she had all the advantages. I don't understand it."

"Well, I consider you a miracle, just so ya know. All my survival genes reside upstairs with the Lord."

"It must be your cold, but I haven't been able to hear you very well for a month." Joe mutters.

Come to think of it, all your genes are from the Creator too, I think. But with my cold, I am too fatigued to shout.

June 20, 2014

"Smells good! Um! Wish I could stay for dinner, but I gotta go now." Paul runs out the door. I'm serving salmon straight from the can for Joe, and with the leftovers from book club; I've fixed my mother's famous salmon cakes for myself.

Since Father's Day, there have been several cans of Alaskan

salmon sitting in our cubby shelf, and plain ol' Joe declares he wants to eat it from the can like a cat. With his appetite of late, Joe would never have opened up a can for an afternoon snack, so it was up to me to set it under his nose for dinner. I'm glad to watch him gobble the contents, reminding myself to let Victoria know it was a hit.

"Guess I'm gonna have to eat all these yummy salmon cakes for breakfast, Mr. B, if you won't help me with 'em tonight."

"Oh nooooo. This is plenty." Joe exclaims as he stuffs bites of canned salmon into his mouth. "My fathea would eat anything that came outta the sea. It's a wonder too. He came from an inland town."

"Where did he pick up his taste for it then?" I wonder.

"Heh, heh. Exactly." The retort is emphatic. "That's what I always wondered. He would eat the strangest things. I've never seen 'em since. Anything that crawled out of the mud or the sea."

"Are you sure you don't wanna try the salmon patties, Mr. B? They're better than your crab cakes, I'll bet ya."

"I've gone to restaurants where if you press the top of the crab cake, the mayo oozes out. I can't stand that. This is an expensive gift just like it is! Canned salmon cost me six bucks at the local grocery store!" He shakes his fork. "I used to eat outta the can like this all the time before you came and changed my life." He shakes his fork over the can the way my husband shakes his fork over something he savors. "I wonder what it cost her at the coast. Victoria said in her letter that they can the salmon right on the wharf as it comes in. Mmm. It must be pretty fresh." He continues, "I don't think I'll eat that blue cheese neither, Miss. This salmon is plenty salty. Juicy. It tastes better with its own juice. Not dry like the cans at the grocery store. And thank you for the olives and tomatoes, too."

I look up to see the framed watercolor tilted so badly on the wall again that I wonder why it hasn't fallen off its hanger. While I'm thinking about it, I move to straighten it. There!

"I think I bump into that when I'm watering plants," admits Joe. "There's another one, the cowboy I painted in the hallway, that's been getting in my way too." So, it's probably crooked too, is the implication.

"Okay. I'll fix it."

"Do you remember that saying your fathea has? 'If you can't get what you want, do with what you've got.'"

I smile.

"Well, I tell ya. These little cans come in handy. Do you know what I used 'em for?"

"For nuts and bolts? My dad would'a done that."

"NOPE. Far from it."

"For flower seeds?" But, I know he uses pill bottles for that.

"NOPE. You'll never guess. I dug the postholes of the fence with one of these. I laid down and dug until the hole reached to my shoulder. Six of 'em. Then I quit."

"Oh my goodness, Mr. B! Why didn't you use a spade?"

"I didn't have one. The one we have now is from *your* house."

"Well, why didn't you call for help or get us to bring it over?"

"Because like your fathea says, 'If you can't get what you want, do with what you've got.' I didn't want to go out and buy a spade just for that small portion of the fence."

"Oh, I can assure you, my dad has plenty of tools. He buys what he needs for the job if he doesn't already have it. Anyway, I thought you said the neighbors built all three fences around your house because you didn't want to participate in building fences."

He looks up and winks. "Okay, yes, you caught me, but then I had to do that bit in the front on both sides of the house or it would'a looked funny."

June 21, 2014

This year, I have been reflecting on cultural snapshots of another way of life, a rich family code of loyalty. A deeply private code of integrity. During my first year at Joe's, I was transformed from a harried person, desperate and selfishly grief-stricken to becoming a more patient person who embodied what I say I believe about family and community. Full of languid conversations over hour-long breakfasts, I have enjoyed the fragrance of rain in the grass and hours in the library with a view of the lake, ducks and geese covering the landscaping. We've avoided fowl scat in the nearby park by enjoying the summer gardening in our own backyard, waking to bird songs and ending our days under profoundly blustery clouds streaked with gold and silver sunsets.

Joe's park-like backyard has provided plenty of work for us, with quick rewards. We needed some quick turnover rewards. Under the new porch roof, thunderstorms and shady afternoon talks have become priceless. Life is so good that my traffic tickets will be falling off my record soon: no new ones are replacing them. The fragrance of sweet peas rises on the backyard trellis today. First day of summer. Longest day of the year.

June 22, 2014

Mr. B's outfit this morning puts a grin on my face. He sports his duck-billed cap over his ears, and he's wearing his grandson's Navy Carl Vincent sweatshirt in navy blue without any other shirt underneath. The effect is that of being a summer camp counselor. Seeing my expression, he shoots a fist into the air. "I'm ready to cut the lawn!" It occurs to me, he'd be great at teaching seed and plant reproduction in a camp program, even at his age!

Betty calls today to say she had talked with a couple of the gals who felt the book club evening was an especially satisfying one. They loved the rose scents, the musky, spicy fragrance of our

Stargazer lilies, and asked about hiring out Paul's grilling services. They had introduced themselves to Mr. B with warm hugs, compliments, and smiles. Some even sat down to visit with him. Meegan invited me to help her throw Linda's beach party based on this book club party. Okay, I did invite my book club to Joe's house after all. Just maybe they are the most loyal friends a gal could have.

"Mr. B?"

"Yep?"

"Would you mind terribly if I asked that good handyman who's been helping us at the rental to come over here and replace those X's on the front of your house with cedar shakes?"

"But how will people know which house to come to if we take the X's off the front?"

"Oh, probably the address will tell them."

Mr. B pauses, stares at me with his blue-eyed, shocking glare, then breaks out laughing. He shakes his head. "It's your house anyway. You might as well do as you wish."

I hear my pent-up breath escaping like air from a balloon.

June 23, 2014

Joe plans to work again on the raised flowerbed after breakfast. I suggest it may be too late in the season to use it this year, plus we need a way to keep the bunnies and squirrels out of it. None of us are handy enough to build the greenhouse at the back of the yard that I've been wanting. When the sale of the rental closes, maybe we'll hire someone to build it. I have the perfect spot for it at the back fence between our house and the neighbor's windows.

He hears a noise and goes to peer through the window. He points to the sky. "See that?"

"The low-flying plane? Yes."

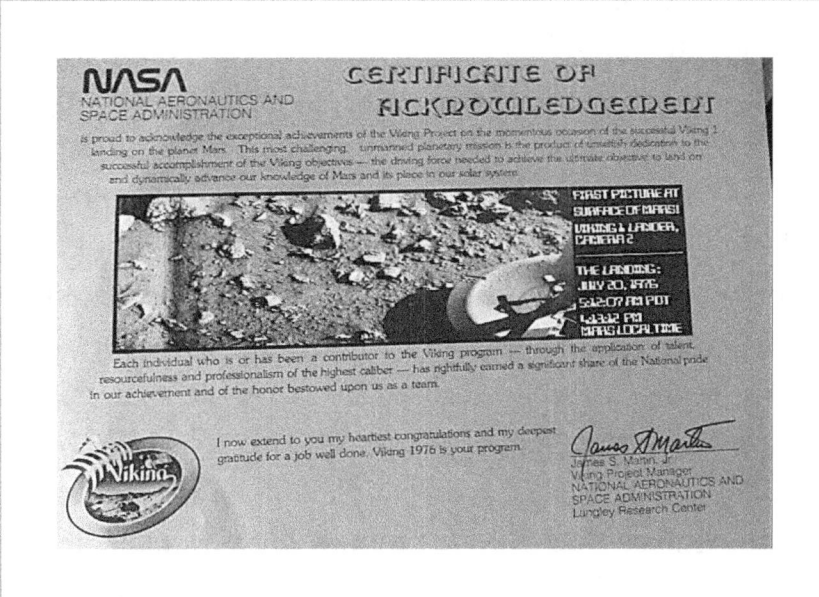

"Okay, that's the B15 I was telling you about that gives rides to customers. I think it flies out of Jefferson County Airport."

"Did you do any of the design on that plane, Mr. B?"

"Not that one, no." He returns to the breakfast table and stares at his eggs.

He tells me that he did design a bulkhead in a plane once that failed. He shrugs. "Nobody said anything to me. My wages didn't get docked; I didn't get a reprimand or anything. But I knew it, and it kinda' stung. Everybody heard about it, too. I was embarrassed. Soon after it failed, another engineer who was an MIT graduate also had his bulkhead design fail. It really affected the man. He started sitting at the back of planes when we had to travel together. He sat alone at lunch, and pretty soon he found a different job."

"Hummm. Wonder why. Mr. B, don't forget to eat."

He picks up his fork. "I dunno. I thought maybe because he was an MIT graduate, he put more pressure on himself, or maybe his boss did. But they didn't pressure me or call me out. So, I just kept studying the problem and working on new problems so that I would be better prepared."

"Wow. Good thinking!"

"Well, I discovered it was hard to keep a job. I needed to keep up with new inventions, and so I kept designing new stress points for things I was reading about. It was all theoretical, mind you, blue print designs. The idea of building models didn't hold water, see. One guy, who competed with me, got laughed outa the room after he took one of his own designs and built a model wid it. Everybody knew the nature of the strength of the materials we used didn't translate into model scale because strength changes with proportions and stressors. You can't maintain the same ratios of integral strength or thickness in a model. So, I kept up with things in the industry that others experimented with in my own method, on paper. That way, every time a new project came up, in went my resume with the new information I had been studying. That's how I became one of the few to ever retire from Martin.

"One time, they moved me into the mechanical engineering section for armament. They were designing a rotating gun, fired by electricity, for a plane." It's not enough to point with his fork; Joe's full body moves one way and then the next, to mimic the circular movement of the gun. "It rotated up and down and pointed every which way, like an eye. Well, they were using a casting I didn't approve of and cylindrical bearings for rotating the gun, so I went to the library and researched the applications.

"When I read an article that stated the use was not a proper application for these roller bearings, I immediately went and told the project engineer that they were not recommended for this kind of application. Well, he blew me off because he said it was cheaper to manufacture it that way. The wrong way was cheaper, mind you." He cocks his finger at me and clicks his tongue. "When they put the gun on the nose of the plane and toted it down to Aberdeen Proving Ground, the gun exploded with its first shot. I never heard another thing about cylindrical bearings."

Joe dismisses the subject with a downward wave of the hand. "They only laid me off once, but they rehired me right away. That's why I get two pensions. But, hey, at least I could handle the pressure. I had three bosses that sat around not knowing anything about what they were hired to produce. It would come to evaluation day, and they would evaluate me, but when they asked what I was doing, all I could think was that they should know what I was doing! They should know, not ask! All three of those bosses died of heart attacks. One guy who was really lazy was driving a Volkswagen in the country and got hit by a truck. Bam!"

I notice Joe isn't eating his breakfast. All he wants to do is talk. "One time, they put me on a project where I was supposed to design a ski for landing gear for an airplane. I wasn't aware there was a boss to report to, nobody ever introduced themselves to me. But one day a man came and asked to speak wid me about the project. The man tried to quiz me on other structural issues of the plane, but I smelled a skunk. I told him I didn't know or care about any other aspect of the design because my particular contract *only* concerned the landing gear ski. Yeah, I thought, *This guy is the boss, and he's asking me?* The man couldn't take the political pressure that ensued. He died a week later." Joe pauses. "Some dumb knuckle thought it would be cheaper to use one ski instead of two. I designed it with a six-foot leg base between the hull of the seaplane and the ski so that it could potentially plow through six-foot waves. It was a flop. Soon as they took it out to test, it crashed."

"Why did it crash?"

"Because no one considered the instability of the waves. Two skis stabilize a plane." He looks around the floor where his chair is sitting. "Where is that dog? I've worked myself up with all these stories, and I just can't eat!"

June 24, 2014
"Mr. B? Are you shivering out here, or are you just tired?" Joe is wrapped up outside, in a blanket, lying on his black-and-white-checked glider.

"What's that, Ma'am?" He murmurs.

I repeat myself, and he sits up with considerable effort to watch my lips.

"When our rental sells, I'm gonna get you some new ears." I hand over a glass of peach juice.

"Oh no. I won't wear 'em, Miss."

"But you can't hear us, and I can't be shouting my life away! Don't you want to be able to communicate with us? Your hearing is getting worse."

"As long as you put a plate on the table for me, that's all the communication I need." He's emphatic. Darn it.

"But, you mowed the back lawn today, and you mowed the front lawn two days ago, so you've got to be exhausted."

At dinner though, he refuses to eat any meat, and he barely eats the avocado salad and plate of tomatoes.

"I'm not gonna allow you to do any more work, Mr. B, if you don't eat some protein."

He wobbles his head nonchalantly over his shoulders. "Tomorrow's my day off, anyway."

Always a smart guy.

June 25, 2014
Joe assesses the situation. He is eager to help my sister fix her table and chairs which are missing dowels and screws. "They don't make quality furniture like they used to."

"I had to get in on this wealth of helpfulness you have going on over there!" she admits, giggling.

Mr. B is happy to have something new to do, so he sits to enjoys a cup of coffee with her, drawing it out, and sends me to the store to buy a 7/64" drill bit that drills through steel.

In the aisle, the guy tries to sell me a titanium drill bit.

"Oh no!" I respond recalling Mr. B's analysis of titanium last year. "I have to get steel because titanium will break if there is any torque or flex going in."

"Is that so?"

"A rocket scientist taught me that."

At my sister's I hand him the steel bits and explain how I deflected the titanium one. He laughs. "See? You do need to know these things!"

On the way home, Joe gets disoriented. Finally he exclaims, "You sure know your way around this town!"

"Well, I've lived around here for most of my life."

"Like a homing pigeon." He makes a bet on whether we'll arrive before the incoming black storm comes down this side of the foothills. We're just inside the door as rain begins to pelt the streets. "Family is everything, you know, Miss. I'm glad we could help your sis out today."

June 29, 2014

Yesterday, my friend saddled with terminal cancer put on the best summer outdoor party ever, her Life's-a-Beach party. Paul and I helped set up tables around the shores of Meegan's shady turtle pond. Paul played grill chef for some of the hundreds of attendees while I manned the dessert tables. And - since we were on a roll - we figured we'd help tear it all down. Today, his joints are suffering for it, and I too feel as flat as a beaten coin.

"Let's take a drive somewhere and go to breakfast," I suggest.

"Okay!" Pauly agrees. It's one of our favorite things to do, exploring.

We give the back yard a drink, and then take a lazy drive, through the foothills. Paul follows the raging canyon river to where ever it is flowing. Paul's daddy starts poking him. "Why ya going around in circles? Where are we headed? I've seen this before!" We eventually try a new restaurant on a river at the Golden Hotel. Joe comes alive. He's delighted. His gaze lingers over the gals loitering in sleeveless shirts, and racing in cycling shorts, or walking along the path below. The sparkling river backdrop also provides us fresh air. He almost topples over twisting to see one distraction and then another, but he exclaims again, "what a nice place we landed in: good food and oh my! Great views." Then, "Did ya hear the news about the Italian priest this week? He was defrosted and declawed. They caught one!" He's on a roll and keeps us and our waitress chipper for an hour. She suggests that we might like to come again on a Thursday evening when they have live jazz bands or blue grass music. "Oh no," grouches Joe. "I couldn't take that kind of music, either one. It's noise to me."

"We could leave you at home, or you could come and suffer."

"Okay. When you put it that way. What'd you feed that girl, anyway? She's getting mighty sassy."

Paul leans in and whispers. "She's eating the same thing you are, Chief."

III

"Yes" Said Gandalf; "for it will be better to ride back three together than one alone. Well, here at last, dear friends, on the shores of the Sea comes the end of our fellowship in Middle-earth. Go in peace! I will not say: do not weep; for not all tears are an evil."
— J.R.R. Tolkien, The Return of the King

July ~
REJOINED

July 1, 2014

Erik, our blessed handyman arrives precisely at 8:30 a.m. while I'm putting Joe's breakfast onto the table. I get him settled quickly and run out to discuss the business at hand. This is an exciting day for me! Erik climbs up the ladder, pries off the four-foot blue X's under each of the bedroom windows, and my heart skips a beat both at the ugliness revealed but also at my daring ownership of Mr. B's house! Then Eric begins to nail a row of cedar shakes into the three-foot by four-foot squares. By the beginning of the third row, I feel a weight lift like wings plucked it from my shoulders, and a great happiness floods over me. Erik laughs to hear me clapping my hands, triumphant.

Then, he proceeds to re-appropriate a pile of leftover 1" x 8" pine boards from our rental as window trims all around the second story windows. I can see that a little house trim makes a world of difference in curb appeal.

"Mr. B! Come outside and look at the difference!"

"Na-naaaa, Miss. I'll wait 'til tomorrow." He rocks in his velvet blue rocker in the dark formal living room, holding his arms tight against his body.

"Are you cold in here, Mr. B?"

"Well, I can get that blanket if I am." He grimaces.

"I'll bring your fleece. Are you sure you don't want to see the outside? Walking will warm you up. It's almost a hundred degrees outside."

I give him his fleece jacket and he gets up to slip it over his arms. "That's all right. Thank ya, Miss. I'm fine here for now." I realize he's grieving the loss of the home he has recognized for 44 years and is working up the courage to face the future.

"Okay. But three of your neighbors have come by to compliment us on the new trim."

"Traitors!" he says, reaching to flip on his stereo to the classical station.

July 3, 2014

On the back end of the chili mishaps yesterday, I decide to try something new with chicken for dinner to please Mr. B. I flip on his classical music station for inspiration. Debussy's airy melodies and open rhythms entertain me.

Two cups of limeade, one can of ginger ale, three chicken breasts sprinkled heavily with mint and basil all go into the Crock Pot on low. Then, I make herbed wild rice with a pad of butter. I put the dinner rolls into the oven to warm. In a quart saucepan after the chicken breasts are cooked, I pour all the broth. Two carrots are sliced on an angle, as Maudie taught me, a handful of baby portabella mushrooms and several celery stalks are dumped into the broth and simmered. Finally, I add a tablespoon of sour cream and a tablespoon of flour, mixing it all to thicken slightly. It looks like a soup Oma would make at Joe's favorite restaurant. When I set the different serving dishes onto the table, I add a bowl of chow mein noodles, telling the boys that they can either eat the dishes separately, or, pile them all up together.

To my surprise, Mr. B eagerly begins to pile it up together in his bowl. He tastes it and begins to *mmm*, asking me what the light flavors are. I explain that he is basically tasting only mint, lime, and ginger for flavoring. We can tell he loves it. He doesn't pick up the salt and pepper shaker the entire meal but continues to discuss how delicious and tasty the dish is.

Finally, he looks at me and says with all sincerity. "You can throw out all your other spices!"

July 4, 2014
Remembering our fireworks in the park ordeal from last year, we make solid plans to let Joe watch them from his bedroom window.

As for ourselves, we meet our best friends at Hudson Gardens this year, where we roam paths between the flower beds for ideas. Eating a bucket of grilled chicken and a plate of brownies, we wait out the late afternoon rainstorm under umbrellas, and then revel through an evening of retro stage bands afterwards. The night sky is filled with patriotic tunes and a half hour of squealing, spinning, exploding colors of fireworks set to the rhythms, and beats of each song, flying and popping overhead. Independence Day!

July 6, 2014
Paul and I walk with arms around each other's waists through the parking lot with great expectations. Closing day is here!

We sit staring at strangers for three hours as bits and pieces of the HUD-approved documents and title documents wind through the fax machine and then over the table to the signatories.

"What was it about the house that sold you?" I want to know.

The husband answers. "As soon as we walked in, we knew. All the attention to detail, the woodwork and nooks, and I liked the clean mechanicals. She, of course, had her eyes on the walls." He nods at his wife. "We felt instantly, after six months of looking, that this was our home."

Something inside of me resonates with his joy, and I am deeply satisfied that my style of work paid off.

When all the paperwork is finally signed, Paul and I practically dance outta there. We squeeze each other tightly before curling our bodies into the car. Over a celebration dinner in an old world upscale Italian restaurant, he continually extends his hands to hold and caress mine, and he spontaneously breaks out in thankful prayers. "Do you realize, WE'RE FREE?"

We grin such big, fat, cheesy grins that the waitress immediately asks what we're celebrating.

"Oh! We just had our closing on our second house in a year, and we are debt free!" Paul announces without reserve.

"Wow! That's an accomplishment! Are you 'fix and flippers'?" she asks.

"Ha! Maybe that was the initial goal, but we over-built," I admit, "and then we lived in the house, suffered with renters and mortgages for a few years, and this year with the turn of the market we decided to try to sell it. It finally paid us off!" It was a simplistic answer to all that we've been through.

"And, we have a mortgage-free home, Sweetie. Oh, the Chief told me he was gonna sleep well tonight when we left for our closing."

"He did?"

"Of course, he did. He's always wanted us to be debt free. That's why they helped us pay off our first house, but we jumped back into debt. I hope we've learned a few lessons this go 'round."

"I certainly have." Reflecting out the window at the late lit summer scene, my flow of conscientiousness continues. "I've learned that we plan and do our best, but that we are human and also make mistakes. Despite these ups and downs, God treats us like his kids. He rewards our efforts and saves us from destruction. Not only are we out of debt, but we have a happy home and savings, Honey! The years that felt like someone had planted a horde of termites against us have not only been swept away, but we have been restored in our persons in fundamental ways."

We sip from our glasses. We feed each other tastes of pasta and salads, and grin like teenagers at prom. Our souls are filled up with joy and okay, fatness, eating this feast to the old crooner's romance tunes.

Watching tables of happy families do the same around us, we make a game of guessing what the conversations are. Paul pretends he knows what the kids are saying and why their papa and mama respond the way they do, explaining everything to me in tidy comic fashion. I find it weird to watch the activity of the subjects match up perfectly to his narrative. We feel drunk with happiness. Mr. B would never consent to this dining establishment. Oh well, some things, even now, are our special moments alone.

July 7, 2014

Dad arrives like a flying hero to the rescue. He totes his electrician's bag, and diagnoses a problem with wiring we are having at Joe's house. After my father hooks up some electrical lights and outlets in the basement bathroom, we decide to book reservations at the White Fence Farm, a family-oriented petting zoo and restaurant. We eat and then roam into the barn to stay for the hootenanny held there afterwards. Joe's expressions are hilarious throughout. He's apparently never been to a concert with those knee-slapping, heart-break-wailing types of gray-haired singers holding guitars.

"Which kind of guitar do you play?" he asks. I point one out that looks similar. He compliments the lead guitarist playing Johnny Cash's "Busted", and the rhythm guitarist for keeping things going like a metronome on the "Tennessee Waltz". Flatt & Scruggs' bluegrass tunes come next. When the bandleader starts calling up a list of armatures from the audience to sing, Joe demands to know what-the-riff-raff is happening. I explain that it is open mic night. Someone pulls out a washtub to plunk bass.

"Which one's Hodge-Podge-Mike?" he says with a concentrated expression.

The bandleader calls his own wife to the stage chortling, "Come alive, Nancy, come alive!" Well, Pauly, who is holding my hand across the table, starts hootin' as Nancy makes her way to the microphone. But he's hollering at *me* to come alive like I'll never hear the end of this new phrase he's appropriated. We are all slapping the table for rhythms to "El Paso City" and other tunes from the '20s and then to Pete Seeger and Woody Guthrie.

My father's eyes shine as he sings the words with his wife, heads bobbing. The music is much like their Gospel jamborees back home. He leans forward and expresses disappointment that he didn't know about signing up on the list. We've sadly missed out on him singing a chocolate ice cream cone ditty. (He sings it to us at break anyway, so we know what we've missed).

Joe just sits there with his fingers woven together, an overwhelmed smile on his face, which runs between politely amused to surprise and then stunned. Checking him out makes us laugh, clap, and holler all the more. He leans forward and whispers in my ear, "I'll never understand you."

Later, at home, he walks into the hall, stops in place and announces, "Maudie and I lived what you might call a subdued life. Boy, have things changed in the past nine months! What a hoot!"

Paul shouts from upstairs, "As Pete Seeger said, 'A good song can only do good…'"

Joe searches around him for the voice. "What? What'd he say?"

July 9, 2014

I'm lying on top of the bedspread, my hair soaking my pillow after a fresh shower when Paul comes home from work. "How did it go today?" It's a routine question from him. He is really more interested in sorting the mail.

"How did it go today? Humph. Well, Paul," I begin to hear a regular diva rant tumbling out of my mouth. "You know the sticking of the front door that irks your dad so bad, right? For years! So guess what? When I walk in from grocery shopping today, I find him attempting to take the pins out of the hinges." Sitting up, I prop my back against the headboard to command Paul's full attention. "I hadn't tackled the sticky door, yet, because hinges are always more complicated than expected, and because I have been looking for a new front door anyway."

Paul stares hard at me. I know he only hears clanging dollar signs, so I raise my grumbling timbre a couple of decibels to help him understand better.

"Your dad's determination to fix things, at his age, is exasperating! I tried shutting out the thought of that door falling on him, squishing him like a frog, but I couldn't do it. So, I set down the groceries and hurried to the garage to get a hammer. He'd sprung my patience as soon as I walked in on him, and I hadn't even begun to help yet!"

I stand up. Paul sits down. Reenacting the drama is gonna take a scene "So 45 minutes later, sweating like a pig, I finally maneuver the door around your dad and lay it flat. He calmly examines the weather stripping on the bottom edge".

."Of course, he measures it every which way, and after another half hour, he gives me his measurements. He wants me to go buy a new weather tack strip. But guess what? Getting new weather stripping *Dear*, is harder than it would seem. Jester was barking *nonstop* in the back yard the whole time the front door was off its *hinges*! Your dad apparently couldn't hear him... "

"Then at the store, I find the only available weather strips are thicker, or wider than the one we presently have. It seems doors have *evolved* in forty years, as have building codes and manufacturers. So, at both stores, I rush through the aisles and bring him back the only three options suggested by the pros, but by the time I make it home, your dad has already removed the old tack strip. It's lying like a crumpled ribbon beside the door. He's disappointed that none of my three weather strips are thin enough, and your dad doesn't believe me that there are no other choices!" I've ramped up my act to the hilt. "He tries to *jerry-rig* one of them, and thinks he's got it, so we lift up the door and balance it on one of your decks of cards to get the angle right to get the hinges back on, but then the door won't shut!"

"Of course." Paul nods agreeably, his merry eyes making me seethe.

"How do you know that?"

"Because you just told me." He ducks his head and chortles.

"Do you know how heavy a solid core door is, Hon? Your dad couldn't handle it, so I had to be the one to keep walking it back and forth, lifting it, hammering in the pins, and taking it all out again!"

"I'm so sorry, my little candlelight."

His newest endearment makes me turn a jiggly circle. "You obviously don't get it. Jester ran away twice, the ice-cream melted into the green beans in the bag in the kitchen, and I had to throw away one of the weather strips, return the other two unused ones, while your dad chiseled off the edge of the door and replaced the crumpled strip he had taken off. "This'll save your electric bills next winter," he says…all in good cheer of course.

"Well," Paul shrugs. "You obviously got the door back on its hinges. It swung open to let me into the house."

"Errrgh! Just! Like fifteen minutes ago, with sweat pouring down my shirt, I finally got the door back together."

He raises his eyebrows and grins. "Oh, so that's why you are all clean and shiny for me?"

"You! Stay away from me. Don't even think about it."

July 11, 2014

"I haven't been to Kiowa in 70 years!" Mr. B exclaims watching the pine trees through the passenger's side window. "It smells so good to be in the country again!" His exclamation draws me out of my thoughts today.

I frown at the stranger in the passenger's seat. "What? How long?"

"Yeah, it's been seventy years. Whew! That's a long time!"

"But you only moved to Colorado forty-four years ago."

"Oh." Meekly. "Maybe so, Miss." Joe stares forward without expression.

When we arrive at my friend's home to see the new landscaping, he says, "Eddy and I used to roll lawns in the springtime, sometimes with a concrete roller, sometimes with a barrel of water. You know water weighs 62.5 pounds per cubic foot? So, that's a lot of weight, and it would just roll out the bumps in the wet lawn so nicely! If we had salt water, it weighs 65 pounds for the same space." He's back to himself, I sigh. Yet, he tires quickly, and sits down often during the afternoon. I've been noticing him doing that this summer when he mows. He took three breaks while mowing the back yard this last week. I chop down the hours of our day's visit to two hours, and on the way home Mr. B exclaims what a nice surprise this day has been.

Later, I explain to Paul what happened. He tells me that his father had also forgotten the silver dollars he used to save for him, and finding one in his dresser, he had brought it downstairs this week and declared, "Look Pauly! I've *neveh* seen one like this before!" When Paul reminded him about the collection he had given him, he said, "Oh. I musta forgot."

July 12, 2014
We sit in my car, overlooking the waterlogged banks of the sparking lake nearby our home. How many times has a short meander around this lake put the spring back into my step this year? Mister B grasps the back of my hand and squeezes. "This is just what I needed. You have some good ideas, Miss, like comin' here! See how it sparkles, really sparkles, with the sun and the wind?" I look at him and nod. "Those are some fierce elements of nature, and yet here they are making the water sparkle!"

After a while, I turn the ignition in my car and start to reverse out of the parking space. He says, "You know, thinking about the velocity of the wind, I remembered how much I admire Michael Faraday, the British physicist."

"Why's that?"

"Oh, because he developed four mathematical equations by doing some electrical experiments over and over, and he came up with the beginning of the modern motor. Imagine experimenting with what cannot be seen, and developing something that the world uses every day! He coulda made a lot of money on that, but he gave it away! Anyway, as much as I read about it, I still don't understand electricity."

The Hebrew saying, "faith is the substance of things hoped for, the evidence of things unseen," bores into my mind. I've never been so inspired by the application of science to the pictures of faith as I have lately been stirred up by my companion's musings.

Thinking that Michael Faraday's tenacious experiments in electricity are similar to what it means to walk in faith, I look up the man for more information as soon as we arrive home. I find that he was a devout Bible-believing Christian and substitute pastor for his congregation as well as having developed four renowned scientific theories for the benefit of the world. God gave Faraday four treasures in secret places that were hidden to most people and throughout the ages. Apparently the man liked to delight his Christian friends with his adventures in science and the spiritual parallels. Of course, I have to tell Joe that his physics hero was a committed Christian. Joe turns his lip down. All he says is, "Hmph," shrugging. "So was Dr. von Braun!" And he pulls the toothpick out of his mouth, turns and shuffles to his blue velvet chair.

July 13, 2014

Paul passes over a theater coupon for the newest Marvel Comics movie to his father. "Wanna see the Avengers with us tonight, Chief?"

"Pee-you." Joe snorts. "Noooo way, José!"

"What?" Paul exclaims. "Don't you know that's Captain America, the Hulk, Thor, and Iron Man?"

"Yes, I know that, but really, they make me feel deflated!"

July 14, 2014

Paul whispers, "My friend told me this place was great. Don't tell Dad. We'll just find him something to eat."

With all three of us in the car, Joe starts the questions. "Where are we going? How far is it? If I don't like your little prank, I'll just walk home. It's less than a mile. I can make it in a pinch, don't you worry."

"Well, Chief, why don't we try that when the next blizzard snows us in?" Paul suggests agreeably.

"Oh, you are mean. But, really. Where are we going?"

Our car turns into a small shopping area, practically parks itself, and we hop out. Joe not so much. He wrangles out of the seatbelt and rocks back and forward to fling himself out of his seat. Once on the pavement, he weaves in his tennis shoes and then takes my arm, waving off Paul's hand. "I'd rather take a gal's arm than yours, sorry to say."

Paul leads the way, opening the doors.

Joe hobbles at my side then stands in the entry with wide blinking eyes at the white linen and black décor. "Wow!" He shouts.

A diminutive Asian waitress seats us in lounge chairs with our menus propped on the table.

"I'll take soup." Joe declares.

"You'll like their soup too, Chief. It's full of fresh things."

"Well, I'm not very hungry tonight."

Paul places our orders. We try to distract Joe with talk of the day, good references for the restaurant, and the weather.

"It's a very clean place." Joe decides aloud. "Clean was always important to Maudie."

His large bowl of sizzling rice soup arrives, along with a small fire grill and a plate with strips of marinated beef on skewers. He seems pleased with the fire grill and picks up a skewer of meat. We watch a smile begin to spread across his face.

Then our meals arrive. Not a word is mentioned about fried shrimp or sauces. "Mr. B, Chinese food is generally shared, so let me put a piece of this on your plate to see if you like it, okay?"

"Well okay, but just one piece."

Paul also slides a piece from his heaping plate onto his father's nearly empty plate. I add a couple pieces of steamed green peppers, carrots, and onion. Joe spears a breaded piece of pork and smacks his lips after he downs it. "Eh. Szynka. Pretty good!" He bites into a grilled marinated beef strip. "How long has this place been here?" He slurps up his soup from a shovel of a spoon. "Ummm. Different, but good. Why haven't I ever seen it before?" Then we watch as he pierces the shrimp with his fork and sweeps it into his mouth.

Paul side-bumps my leg under the table. Cha-ching! Our risky gamble has opened up a dinner option for us! He pours me a cup of green tea, and we toast to success.

July 15, 2014
I'm wearing a purple Mardi Gras circle of beads that Joe threw over my head an hour ago upon arriving at, Lucile's, the neighborhood creole restaurant. Upping the grace of his successful lasso, he declares, "Put that in that journal you are writing!" He says this with all the joyful swagger of Fred Astaire.

We always try to pick a seat where he can watch the antics of a child at breakfast. Today, however, there is no cutie pie to entertain Mr. B.

Over the table, he regretfully declares he doesn't remember the taste of the strong cinnamon tea, though he seems delighted with it as usual; neither does he recall that sugar-dusted beignets are like donuts, which he decidedly likes especially with strawberry jam on top. But, after he cut into one and downs a couple of bites, he begins to discuss, in depth, the German Teutonic Order of Knights and crusaders, Catholics, and mercenaries. He reaches his hand into the air and points at an imaginary map where Estonia is at the top, then Latvia, Prussia, and Lithuania.

"The Polish government was stupid! You know? In 1938, we had the largest cavalry in the world, the world, mind you! But what is that against machine guns and airplanes?" His eyes water and he looks away as he recites the awful fact of German forces descending into Poland from the Baltic triangle, making a beeline to Warsaw, and their slaughter of the unprepared Polish army boys arriving at the train depot for battle training on the same day the Germans arrived to show them who was boss. "Oh, our guys did do battle. They killed about a thousand Germans, but most of their guns were still lying in boxes when the Germans published their newspaper photos of the slaughter for propaganda."

Joe recites how they herded 50,000 of the Pole professionals, teachers, doctors, lawyers, and politicians into the Katyn forest, forcing them to chop down the trees, and then incinerating the best of Poland together with the lumber. "My mothea hated the Germans, and poor Paul, when he jumped ship, he was just trying to escape the same thing as Mothea hated, but she pinned it all on him and never forgave him. I guess that's all of us. If we lose someone in a terrible way, we tend to resent it forever." Mr. B shrugs and wipes his nose with a cloth napkin. I can taste his bitterness as he spits out, "Russians hated the Poles as much as the Germans did, and who can stand against a people the size of Russia?" He pauses. "It was discovered soon enough that Russia's adamant denial of involvement in the slaughter was a ruse. Even today, every year, the Poles make a big deal about Russia's cowardly collusion with the Germans in the Katyn affair."

Joe is anxious to tromp about in nature, so to speak, so fortified with a happy-go-lucky breakfast, we baby step our way to the river path named after he and Maudie's deceased poker pal, Mary Carter. Immediately, he asks to take the shorter jaunt around a pond saying, "I don't think I can walk very far, Miss." He will be 99 in just six months.

"Okay, Joe, that's fine by me."

His tennis shoes step carefully. "I don't know how to say, Joe, my own name in Polish. I know *Józef,* (the J is pronounced like a Y) but not how to say Joe!"

"Woudn't it be 'Yo?'" Then I start ribbing him. "Hey, Yo! You'd fit right in with the younger crowd, Mr. B, I mean, 'Yo'!"

He has a chuckle at that, trying it on for size. "Yo? You think that's what it would be? Heh, heh, well, I guess that's all right."

He mentions again that his father had a specimen of pampas grass, as tall as two men, situated in the middle of Mr. Kimbal's backyard. I offer to get another couple ornamental grasses to complete the crescent edge of our patio, and he grins with approval. Nearing the end of the pond's circle, my companion sighs. "Why do they have all the seating so far away from the pond? I'm not tired;" he insists, "it's just curious." He and I have made good conversation about a variety of dipping ducks, the frog prince, some early geese awaiting their winter flock, marsh reeds, algae and exploding silky seed pods, but there is no bench at the edge of the pond. Mr. B may not want us to spend money on funeral arrangements, but as he and I are walking, and lingering at the water's edge this morning, I remember how much Mr. B has always loved walking in nature, mushroom hunting, gathering seedpods and cattails to varnish and arrange in a vase. A memorial bench for Joseph Byk here seems appropriate.

In my personal time this afternoon, something jumped out at me: specifically, Numbers 16:46-48. "Then Aaron ran and did what Moses commanded. He put on the incense and made atonement for the people in the midst of them. He took his stand between the dead and the living, so that the plague was checked." It occurs to me that "standing between the living and the dead" for me means catching Mr. B whenever he turns around without his feet under him, or whenever I hold out his cane to take to the library or whenever I play chauffeur for his needs, I am making physical atonement for him, standing between life and death. Now, Mr. B could leave this earth another way, but I see there is a definitive value in my personal sacrifice in running around to meet my father-in-law's needs.

July 16, 2014

Mr. B and I are splitting a giant strawberry shortcake at Ted's Montana Grill. He keeps drawing the line across the platter, teasingly, making sure I know whose half is whose. With shining eyes, he looks up at me. "You know, it was awful last night. I just couldn't sleep. I just kept thinking about how big the universe is, how the Halley's Comet comes around only once every 75 years, and how far out it must go to cycle back only once in a human life! I kept putting the zeros on, but no matter how many I added, I couldn't accept it. Then, I just couldn't understand that the light we are seeing from out in the universe is arriving after traveling, how many light years?" He huffs and forgets his strawberry sauce leaking off of his leaning spoon.

"Then, I thought of the random shooting stars. Why are they falling out of the universe, but still all the planets in our solar system, and all the other stars, are suspended in their rotations perfectly? I remember that there was a science teacher who asked our class to find the amount of displacement of the water in a bathtub with a certain equation, and one of the students' smart answers was to 'take a bath.' That was the best he could come up with. Well, my teacher worked and worked wid me to try to teach me mathematics, but I just kept asking 'why? Why? WHY?'

"She just stood there and told me she didn't know why. I just had to *accept* it." He shakes his head, holding a near-empty spoon. "Finally, I did accept it. I just relied on the equations and did the problems, and after the final test, she came two steps into the room and shouted, 'Byk got a 96!' She was really congratulating herself, you know." He looks down and scoops up another melted delicious bite, then slurps up the red syrup and melted cream.

"She'd worked hard to teach you something that my teachers could never make me understand, Mr. B. Knowledge is one thing, but understanding the facts and figures and the meaning of all that is another." Having paid the bill, we are now walking slowly towards the car.

"Yes, but it's terrible that at my age, I am still unable to accept some things. Like, how is it the guys make all these planets suspend themselves in space?"

I pull out of the parking lot. "Oh, Joe," My heart goes out to him. "What 'guys' are you talking about?"

"The guys who started this creation thing! They can only explain so much! I listened to a guy lecturing on how big the universe was, and that guy didn't know beans! It's terrible." He looks at the river flowing under the bridge and covers his eyes against the setting sun.

I jump head in. "All I know is Colossians 1:17 in the Bible says that it is Jesus who holds all things together. Apparently, that's part of His job as God. And, someday, I am going to skip all over the universe asking Him these questions that you and I are talking about: 'How's this? Why is that?'"

"Well, I guess you have your religion to comfort you." He puts his hand up and lays it along the side of his head. "I hope you can tell me all about it."

"It's not religion, Mr. B. It's the person of God who comforts me, His Word, His Holy Spirit. You could ask Him too."

"I could never ask. I'd be too embarrassed."

"It's like you have to accept that He loves you just like you have to accept math for it to work. You can line up all the numbers to explain all the universe you want, but those numbers are just a symbol of the reality. They cannot begin to explain the majesty of the universe or of the Creator."

"I'm supposed to be the practical guy."

"You just have to accept that God loves you so much that He forgives you, no matter what. It's the same thing as working your math problems. Mr. B, it's great to be practical, but different kinds of math apply to different kinds of questions. You can be really generous and moral and good, but that only applies to one realm of study. It helps you, it helps the people around you, but it doesn't get you into heaven. That's a whole different equation with Jesus as the key and His love for you."

We have turned into our driveway. "Well, here we are, Miss. I'm not going to argue wid you. But, it was a good argument anyway." He hands me his house key. "I noticed you didn't bring your purse to dinner."

I lift up my set of keys to show him. "You're right. I left my wallet and all my money at home, but I still have the key to the house."

Mr. B points down at a grasshopper crouched on the threshold and poised for a single hop into the house with the big kids as soon as the door opens, but my father-in-law sweeps it away with his foot. As the hinges open, Jester pokes out his nose and neck. He greets us with a whine and circles the hallway excitedly.

My keys find their way to the top of the hall commode. "Thank you for a wonderful discussion tonight, Mr. B, and thank you for chowder and strawberry shortcake, too."

"Oh sure, sure, Sweet Pea." He pats me on the back agreeably.

July 17, 2014

"Maybe that dog will clean up this plate for me." It's the end of dinner, and Mr. B is licking his lips from the tasty trout, sautéed on the grill with dill and a pad of butter inside. Paul went fishing today and brought back a catch for me to clean and prep. It's hard to believe Paul's turning 60 this year, with his brown silky hair and sparkly blue eyes, but his joints say otherwise. His fishing days are coming to a close. At least to a pause.

"That was good, maybe the best fish I've had!" Joe pushes

away his empty plate of trout skin and aluminum foil, with a mowed corncob beside it. "How did you make that fish, Miss?"

I admit to the salt and pepper and dill, never to the butter. "There's a little mystery to it, Mr. B. A cook has to have her secrets, you know."

"I'm sorry that Paul had to eat my fried green tomatoes. I just couldn't do it. You know some people eat *any*thing," Joe's eyebrows arch. "Some Asians and Africans eat worms!"

"No worms in there. I promise. But Americans are eating seaweed these days. I saw a girl at the summer beach party the other day pushing square sheets of seaweed into her mouth. She declared it was her favorite treat. They were packed like crackers in the box. Seaweed is pretty good in salad."

"Seaweed? In salad?!" Mr. B. demands. "That's stupido. We used to see it float by like trash in the ocean current. Crazy." Joe shakes his head. "I've read books about mountain men who knew how to skin a skunk, avoiding the scent pouch, to eat the meat."

"Starving troops have eaten rats and the French eat horse," Paul offers.

"Yah, yah, Maudie's fathea, Dr. Brownlee, used to say horse was a cleaner meat than much of the meat we eat. America ships horses to the French. I know that."

"Nah," growls Paul. "I couldn't eat it."
Joe makes us some miniature greenhouses.

"Well, it's not cleaner than our trout. I cleaned those fish very well, thank you." Fanning my dripping face then, "I seem to have steamed myself up today. The sheets were washed by midmorning, and I cleaned before the thermostat hit 90 degrees outside, but..."

"I see you've vacuumed and cleaned house today too, honey."

"Yeah. Just look at my hair. I sat on the patio under the fan trying to cool off too, but..."

"You're hot stuff any way you slice the day!" Paul pulls a long

 curl in my hair. "Look! It springs back, just like you."

("This is repayment for helping me fix the front door," he says.)

spent a lot of years trying to outrun or outsmart vulnerability by making things certain and definite, black and white, good and bad. My inability to lean into the discomfort of vulnerability limited the fullness of those important experiences that are wrought with uncertainty: Love, belonging, trust, joy, and creativity to name a few.
–Brene Brown

The first flight simulator at Lockheed Martin Company. Astronaut, Ed White, practiced sitting and standing on this bucket seat, with a rod between his knees, designed by Joseph Byk. On June 3, 1965, during the flight of the Gemini 4, Ed White became the first man to successfully "walk" in space tethered to the Gemini spacecraft.

IN RETROSPECT

We moved into Joe's house in August, a year ago. I can't help but consider the life maxims of King Solomon:

For everything there is a season, and a time for every matter under heaven: a time to be born, and a time to die; a time to plant, and a time to pluck up what is planted; A time to give birth and a time to die; a time to kill, and a time to heal; a time to break down, and a time to build up; a time to weep, and a time to laugh; a time to mourn, and a time to dance, a time to cast away stones, and a time to gather stones together; a time to embrace, and a time to refrain from embracing; a time to seek, and a time to lose; a time to keep, and a time to cast away; a time to tear, and a time to sew; a time to keep silence, and a time to speak; a time to love, and a time to hate; a time for war, and a time for peace. What gain has the worker from his toil? I have seen the business that God has given to the children of man to be busy with. He has made everything beautiful in its time. Also, he has put eternity into man's heart, yet so that he cannot find out what God has done from the beginning to the end. I perceive that there is nothing better for them than to be joyful and to do good as long as they live. (Ecclesiastes 3:1-12) ESV

I will never regret this year's decision to help Mr. B live at home. He could have lived independently, almost, but for the loneliness. Would he remember to take his meds at breakfast without me? And, who would bring the stubborn summer worker, Mr. B, hydrating juices in the afternoon? Who would call on him to tell his stories and drive him around?

Since we've now sold both of our houses in the City-Which-Shall-Not-Be-Mentioned, I no longer have title to any house at all. Yet, I know what circumspect living looks like.

A man from the Greatest Generation, born in 1916, the WWI era, Mr. B accepts his limitations in a practical manner. Things move on. The Great War generation grew up from the poverty of the Great Depression followed by wartime, mostly annihilating innocence and idealism. Their primary aim was to beat the odds to secure some stability for themselves. In achieving great practical things, they felt grateful for the physical security these things brought them, which is why Mr. B wept to recount his penniless job search in California, having survived his childhood living under the roof of immigrant parents. The immediate fear of coming to naught after all his personal diligence must have been psychological torture. This generation remains proud of what they have honestly earned in life. They don't throw things attached to these memories and values away just because fads come and go, or because the new thing is more convenient. They do not value debt because debt removes autonomy and leads to a desperate path.

Fads are social foolishness. If things aren't broken, Mr. B won't upgrade or replace them. If they are broken, he uses his ingenuity to devise the least expensive fix. He was on his knees in the grass yesterday, wire brush in hand, cleaning the bottom of our patio table.

When I entertain my book club again this month, I will share our humble home with them in contentment and good humor. After all, we are the advantaged ones. We, who are out of debt.

There is also Joe's value of saving more money than he spends. This is another passion born from the angst of poverty and hunger.

Saving money is not an option, even on lean wages. Joe keeps his head down and works hard to earn his way, even now he feels strongly about this.

He sympathizes with my bucking of injustice and is even proud of me for trying to make a change, but he has proven to me that a meek life is a happier life. After working for the government through the wars, he knows that little can be done to change the plight of a human life when its value is hedged against the budget.

Having survived, on his feet, debt free, with a house and a small savings account is like a bird in the hand to Mr. B. He takes care of himself, trusting no one else to do it the way he likes. Not all, but part of his generosity toward his own children is generated for the sake of investment security. Family is all. Family takes care of family. This is a lesson in kingdom ethics for me as a Christian. Feed the family first. Stop judging them for not living up to my standard. Help them thrive while mentoring them. We cannot save all those falling to the right and to the left, but we can surely help those who find their way into our homes and community.

On the way to the hospital for a routine visit today, the radio announces yet another car manufacturer recall on automobiles. I have to explain to Joe what the radio announcer is talking about. I wonder aloud how an automobile company survives the losses when they admit a piece of their design or implementation was faulty?

"Your life and mine was worth fifty-seven cents to them," gripes Joe. "That was the choice they made by installing the inferior part. Now they have to pay for it out the back end."

Joe would have made a formidable judge.

"Do they budget for these recalls since the law requires they fess up? Do they slow down all production or return to the start, make new evaluations, and just take a setback on the chin?"

"Aw, setbacks are part of life. They help us do better next

time," Mr. B returns as pleasantly as the shady catalpa trees in white bloom we are passing by.

Wisdom has been kind in granting me new eyes to see. Remembering our own setback, and how intensely I feared moving into Joe's house, thinking it was the worst day of my life, worse than all the punishment our neighbors had put to us, I now smile at that loathing. All of us have thrived. I have thrived serving this ol' man in the passenger seat beside me. The bitterness has leaked out.

"What are you laughing about now?" He chuckles.

"Oh, nothing. Just myself."

"'Bout time. It's your turn," he says.

Mr. B's good will and humor, with my husband's, turns my head. I don't need to control events, power mongers, contractors, or quarrelsome people to make something good or right happen. I'm letting them go each their own way. They belong to the sovereign LORD. I don't like those raw edges of me being exposed responding to politics, house renovations, or family drama; neither do I relish being defined by anger, so I choose to withdraw from most conflicts. Having an oasis to reconsider the angles in life has helped guide my passions to better resolutions.

The hospital's courtyard is full of blooming, fragrant, red roses and Mr. B asks, "Won't you go and bite one off for me?" At first, I'm alarmed that he would utter such a request, and suddenly I remember his story about his own father smelling every beautiful flower he came across. If he liked it, he would bite off a sprig, hide the sprig in his pocket, and take it home to grow one for himself.

Our new vegetable garden in the raised beds is abundant in happy production, and the ornamental grasses planted in new beds where his sprinkler system drenches them on a regular basis are stretching and waving their new feathers. We are responsible for hand watering the exotic lily and rose gardens. On the other hand, we practically ignore his good drought-tolerant, long-lasting perennials which has had no detrimental impact. The Johnny jump-ups, sweet lavender verbena, and multicolored snapdragons that Mr. B had flourishing in his sun-drenched, hard-packed, rocky ground like their homes there. I agree with Joe: why pay for more water when we can be just as happy in our garden without emptying our pockets? Clever guy.

We must broach the subject of new flooring, however, sooner than later. Paul came home from work one May afternoon, while I was in the kitchen dishing up food and announced, "Dad, I read an article today that said people bring in an average of 40 pounds of dirt a year that settles into the carpet."

"Uh, uh. You're joking, right?"

"No! It was a real piece of research I read. Do the math: 40 times 44 years."

"I have no comment to that," says Mr. B. "Except that we should maybe vacuum more."

I shout from the kitchen, "Why vacuum when we can just live in a mud hut with a mud floor? Lotsa people do it!"

Joe squints around the corner. "What'd she say in there?"

One day I explain to my father-in-law that I would pay for new carpet throughout the entire house, for yes, I am *just that desperate*. I hold out some swatches to him and ask him to walk around the house with me looking at the light in the rooms to decide *together* which carpet we agree on. "Well, alright," he murmurs. "If the carpet is acrylic, but only if!"

I explain to him that there is a holiday special at the carpet store, and we could use my decorator-sister's discount. After criticizing my hard-sell tactic, asserting that there will always be another *sale*, he grasps my arm with his pinchy fingers and admits he likes the idea! "I enjoyed walking around the house with you, Miss, and I admit that I could actually see the way the shades turn different colors in the light of different rooms." We easily agree on a lighter color upon which he can see his own feet moving better. We file into the store and agree with the sales chap that the cheaper pad is better for older people because it is not so plush that it trips them.

Back at home, Joe suddenly admits that he should have updated the house a long time ago, but he was too cheap. "You two have added so much to this place. I really didn't think I would like that big flagstone patio, but boy! I was wrong!" His look of surprise makes me grin. "Every time I look at the patio floor, it is a surprise, a real nice-looking surprise. I'm not going to fight you on the carpet, Miss. I just want to make sure you spend your money wisely. That's all. And, if there's one thing I've learned, it's that you are an aggressive young lady in negotiations, just like Maudie was, and that's a good thing." He smacks his lips, shakes his head looking at his tennis shoes, and removes the toothpick from between his lips.

"Thank you, Mister B." I ignore the choice of his term, 'aggressive.'

Suddenly he sucks in his cheeks, then bugles, "Some people worry too much about other people's approval. If someone gets too excited about compliments too much, I don't approve. That's not a sign of a strong person. Sometimes you gotta fight for what really matters to you, and ignore the rest."

Yet, this year I've found there is a difference between the experience of self-direction and the human rich story experience God grants while we are making plans - just to embellish on the Beatles' lyrical theme. Both may be full of adventure, but the second instance is accepted in surprise, as a gift. These surprise stories are cautiously inked with a listening hand in the curling paths of my new suburban wonderland. I've been feeling so happy and grateful lately, that I have to remind myself to return thanks to the Giver, and not just drink the ink. I'm not journaling accomplishments here, from a seat of authority or office. I'm journaling gifts of relationships, the meaning of life, really. I do not know the full ending, only that I am watching with a child's eye, blinking after awakening.

Gratitude was something Paul brought back into my life when we met many years ago. Today, I know gratitude is what continues to extend a blessing. This weekend, Paul, Joe, and I were quietly waking up, sitting on the back porch drinking our coffees, when Joe exclaimed, "I was sitting on that chair over there on the flagstone enjoying the bees on those huge dahlias yesterday and thinking that I *neveh* woulda had the gumption to change the backyard, *neveh*! But you did, and I *like* it!" He paused with a smile plastered over his face then added, "I saw a picture of you, Miss, when you were a child, back at your house on Pearl. Sometimes I think of you as one of the kids walking with Paul and Victoria along the beach, and seeing those sand sharks in shallow water swimming around, or finding wooden containers of ammo washed up on the Maryland shore after the war, and buying iced lobsters for a buck at lobster shacks there. You woulda liked it."

"I remember that, Chief." Paul adds. "You took a picture of me next to a big shark, though. I think it was six feet long, Dad! 'Cuz, they used to kill the sharks that came too close to shore and drag 'em up there to die."

Feeling both delight and revolt, I accept this. "Well, you both describe it so well, I feel like I was there with you."

Placing a small glass of sweet peas in water on the windowsill later in the day, I recall there was a time I felt so desperate to share in real community with others that I made all kinds of concessions to invite perfect strangers into my home, all to be ministers in hospitality.

After years of struggle and disillusionment, I was plopped kicking and hissing into Joe's place. The wild cat that I had become was meant to be a companion to the head of the family in his old age. Here, with time, I've placed Mr. B first because I've learned how important and practical the *common* things of life are. Habits of being kind and considerate, listening, and laughing can build up community and character over time. Here, there is no place for teaching, preaching, or running nonprofit organizations "for" God as if he needed anything.

Mr. B needs me. But he also out-gives me in his meekness and thoughtfulness, to say nothing of his generosity. I know he wouldn't appreciate the comparison, but it reminds me of my relationship with a certain heavenly Father. I've never been able to out-give Him either.

Joe has taught me how important it is for older people to share their history with the young, and the things that matter to them, the facts of life that we often build upon, not understanding the tensile strength of the foundation. Because he delights in me preparing his plain meals, I have found delight in my new kitchen challenges.

Every time I reflect on how much I love and respect Mr. B, I wonder what he would have done if, in our youthful power and impatience, we had reduced him to a room in an old folk's home? And really, what would I do without all his help and advice? It's been so important for Joe to have his choices, his dressers in his house where things are filed as he remembers them, and the garden work as he can do to lure him into this day's purpose.

Is Mr. B an angel? He has certainly been an honest tutor in the importance of human kindness and speaking difficult truth carefully. Mr. B's thoughtful meanderings are a rowboat carrying us along through history, and through our own transition to the future. I'm learning from things that don't make sense in the first instance. While it's said that time heals all wounds, I think healing must require a few other ingredients, too. I have some new reflections on my own aging process now, and Joe is helping me turn that page with an important perspective.

Is Mr. B a devil? Walking with Mr. B is an exercise in patience. I remind myself, "What's the hurry? Where's the deadline?" I also have hours of feeling jilted, disappointed with my life, and worried. The emphasis I have put on the importance of *things* collides with the preciousness of an, albeit rascally, soul, and I get confused. The other day in the doctor's office, however, I chose to pick up a magazine with an interesting photo of a human being instead of the home design magazine beside it. Baby steps.

Paul and I bought a new washer and dryer this summer, and we are delighted by what it handles. I don't have to clean the lint from the filter out in the yard anymore, and it does bulky blankets! Joe, on the other hand, thinks we've wasted our money since the old appliances weren't broken. Plus, there's the-old-dog-learning-new-tricks problem. Since we are doing his laundry now, it becomes apparent that this is one more chore we've taken off his plate of responsibilities, one less thing engaging his mind.

I still get frustrated with how slowly reality moves, but it is moving in a quality direction. The last time I filled in a doctor's questionnaire, I circled 2 for my stress level. That's got to be *good for my health*. I've lost more than a few pounds walking and cycling the neighborhood and eating the same food that I prepare for Joe.

Tonight, Paul grills the lean pork chops that are sure to please his papa. I make a salad with tomato wedges, also Mr. B's favorite rabbit food. Sure enough, he picks up each tomato, carrot, pepper, and piece of lettuce with his fingers slogging them down with his warm crescent roll. "A surprise!" He shouts when he sees the watermelon on his plate. Then, while he's attacking it, I serve him a small bowl of caramel toffee ice cream. He looks at it sideways like he can't gulp in the watermelon fast enough to get to his final bowl. The greedy glance has Paul and I snickering. "What? Did I miss something?" demands the ol' man.

"I don't think you've missed anything tonight, Chief," Paul teases.

"I'm relieved your appetite has caught up!" Happiness is unanimous.

△ ෆ ☙

Have I overly simplified my life? Shouldn't I be working harder?

Our abundance comes not by way of money, but by way of mutuality, tenderness, and good humor.

Jesus came to bring life in abundance, and Jesus is the "constant". We've now been to the edge of our resources and back. He hasn't failed us. Part of that security was the Lord's orchestration of Paul's father's life in ours.

So, Paul and I have turned a corner. Stewardship has become a secret thrill. Beyond maintaining the necessities of housing, we've found that trying to keep up with the Joneses is a darned sure way to liquidate emergency funds. The Jones aren't gonna be there when I fall onto bad times. Fads are hard to maintain because new styles in décor and technical gadgets will abound from one day to the next. There's something to the brave Tiny House idea, or to inheriting a parent's home and making the best of it.

I think my fundamental error in building the hospitality lodge was trying to materially spoil the missionaries and seminary students with all the best I could give them. Yet, Paul and I were only able to provide them this lifestyle because of credit cards and a high mortgage! The wind had to topple over our stance on the edge of the world's values in order to create real faith and trust in God. He will spoil us in His own way and timing, and His spoiling doesn't have much to do with the Jones' luxury.

"Too much! Too much!!" That's Mr. B's main distress these days. Too much food, too much commotion, too many choices and activities. There is, yes, a time to feast, and indulge in things, but it isn't every day! How difficult would it have been to peel off that pride of life if it hadn't have been for Mr. B's example of modest living and partnership? So now Mr. B's investment and patience with us is being paid back at a time when he is needy. That's only right. When he forgets that he drinks Gatorade or Ovaltine regularly, and tells me what a nice surprise this is, I know I'm serving the right person at the right time.

Family partnership is a good and rich life. We presently have new budget choices to make with the funds we earned from our real estate investments. Shall we save rolls of paper dollars under a mattress? Or should we spend them on better investments including heavenly returns? Maybe we'll finish the basement for an apartment for someone to live with us again, but we are taking our time deciding about lifestyles, investments, and trying to listen to God better. Self-control is making me happy! It's the new ability to self-edit and tell myself "no" even against uncanny urges for more.

There are a few ways of looking at the same situation, I guess. Like, I was looking at the equation all wrong when I disparaged the money we made on Pearl as a loss far below the appraised value. Then I came to realize we had also made tens of thousands on that investment, more money than what I would have been able to *save* had I had been working elsewhere for those six years. The Lord is very kind. He patiently waited for me to come around to notice His blessings. Our houses in the City-Which-Shall-Not-Be-Mentioned proved to be a wonderful financial investment even if the ministry aspect didn't pan out. Recently, someone told me that if we second-guessed whether we had really heard and followed God, dependent solely on the outcome, we would have to say that

Jesus himself misunderstood his calling!

Certainly, I no longer feel my house renovation efforts were an epic fail. We are able to reinvest and also replenish a savings account, replace drafty aluminum windows with new windows, and paint our new home with Mr. B's approval. In two weeks, the painters are due, and the body of the house will be painted in shades of antique silver, touches of linen trim to match the brick and cedar, and weathered seaside gray shutters with linen pillars to please all the lovers of color in this household. It's fun to reinvent tired architecture. But, I don't have to have the latest exterior fad to find happiness in the inside rooms with Paul and Mr. B.

For Paul's sixtieth birthday, we planned the vacation we've been putting off. Joe's granddaughters and my sisters offered to spend time with Mr. B to let us run away. In anticipation of the event, I stuck a green piece of tape on the microwave "minute" button so that he could use it to heat up soup for dinner. Otherwise, his memory and eyesight prevent him from using it. Yet today, Mr. B brought the telephone to me and asked me how it worked, "It's been so long," he says, "I've forgotten!" This is a game changer. In my heart I know we'll be taking Mr. B with us wherever we choose to go.

None of the shame that I feared to face in my husband's repudiation or in Joe's judgment came to be. My design work did pay off well. They defer to my experience now so long as we have the budget for it. But I defer to Joseph Byk's ownership of this house. So, it's mostly hands off. I'm happy with that limitation at this stage in my life, and I have never been loved better.

I know Joe has made a lot of adjustments of his own. He could have made my life very difficult here with him, but he's maintained an air of hospitality throughout. He's rarely critical unless he can speak his mind with the questions of an engineer, or with humor or by example.

Even if, of late he has mentioned that everything I prepare for dinner tastes new, asking repeatedly during any given meal, "Have I eaten this before? What is that flavor? The food seems to be multiplying on the plate, or I can't finish all of this, Miss. It's just too much… " so that I want to toss the plates in the air and go out to eat…(ah, but I digress). Even this is to be taken in stride. He's grieved the loss of driving and the sight in his eye, but he continues to take interest in life, pushing himself and letting me live happily, without nagging. He self-edits, which makes things easy on us all.

Like any situation, these living conditions are comprised of benefit and sacrifice. Happiness often comes through the back door. Most certainly, now we know where the assurance of our security lies: God can make a new community out of family members estranged. He is full of good humor in our weakness. What a gift to understand true belonging, and I more often than not would rather stay at home than do anything else.

First Space Shuttle Launch

Endnotes

October, 2013 Chapter Endnote 1.
Clifton Kern's YouTube video on Mushroom Identification for Beginners recommends the *National Audubon Society Field Guide* for identification of mushrooms. But, there is no key, except online.
http://www.chowhound.com/food-news/54811/know-your-mushrooms/

December 4, 2013 Chapter Endnote 1.
The presentation of the three tributaries to joy, being streams from the past, the present and the future, was made by Dr. Darrell Ferguson

February, 2014 Chapter Endnotes:
Pg. 188 [1] http://www.wmof.com/bt-13.html
Pg. 189 [2] http://www.wmof.com/bt-13vultee.htm

April, 2014 Chapter Endnotes:
1.1 Samuel 2:34
2.1 Samuel 4:17

ACKNOWLEDGMENTS

I owe a great debt to my father-in-law for his veritable storytelling. What comes first to mind is this: I had no comprehension of the stress a person undergoes who is involved in the development of aeronautics, or that the single focus of accuracy is the engineer's task over every other human temptation. Accuracy was Joseph Byk's lifelong career aim. Joe's aerospace stories made me realize, as no teacher has ever been able to convey, the importance of math in the application of science to safety. My father-in-law taught me that numbers are, much like truth, self-evident. Mr. B's personal integrity in his stress engineering career during war times, and after, saved lives and often the industry's wallet.

The Polish family's traditional pastime of mushroom hunting is only one of the many topics that ignited a heightened education from Mr. B's stories. The earliest movies, his past times, his adult understanding of the value of good work and war's tragic strategies, his poor family's menial service relationship to the ironically wealthy but childless Kimbal couple, and the superhuman personality of his mother prior to women's liberation provided me with hours of entertaining education.

There is a second thing, though, topping what I've gained from my friendship with Mr. B. The gift was learning to serve. Forming a meaningful relationship with my parents presented a cultural mission that I had carefully meted and measured out until I turned 53. Though Jesus himself taught that caring for elderly parents is more honorable to God than giving alms to strangers in His name, I couldn't see my parents' special needs living far off. I also thought I had already committed myself to meaningful human service in other ways. When I learned that the commandment to honor one's parents did not primarily mean having feelings of respect or voicing compliments about them — but rather, the verb to "honor" is rooted in action toward the welfare of another, it still didn't change my involvement much. In fact, it was only through a series of personally tragic circumstances that my upwardly mobile lifestyle was catapulted into the service of my father-in-law in a significant way.

While parents can be difficult to serve because of our history with them, the same personal history can also make this experience *more rewarding*. Deeply rooted relationships sometimes seek new sources of nourishment as life passes. With an attitude of respect and hospitality, it is possible that each family member can experience a great benefit and personal reward.

Our relationship is a unique one. In no way do I mean to put comparisons of our companionship against any other parent/child or elder/caregiver relationship.

My graphic artist friend, Kathryn Swezy, is to be credited for her cover design, which is probably the reason why you considered reading this book.

There are not enough words to explain the awe I have for the feat of my Publisher, Capture Books, and particularly for Laura Bartnick regarding her passion, logistics corralling, editorial work, proofing, formatting, consistent communication and handholding to bring me into this lucid land of authorship.

Many thanks belong to my writing pals: Tonya Blessing, M. B. Drake, and Kathy Spackman, who coached the best of Joe's stories from me vicariously. To those who read my first hideous pages of description, (Cher Smith) and those helped me edit to the end: Susan Carter, Sue Lockwood Summers; the Queen of Commas. I am grateful to Amy Hoppes and Victoria Pless who each proofread Mister B, and saved me from humiliating errors, and to my friend indeed, Charm Hafen, for tenaciously re-reading, offering insightful suggestions, and helping me turn a personal journal into a Greatest Generation memoir. They declared this was a story needing lungs to breathe in the world. Their thinking minds, red lips, and pens of blood dripped with enthusiastic editing and gave my flow of consciousness structural bones with skin-like detail for wings. Their skills propped and welded together my most lacking attention to detail like Mr. B's steel L-brackets did to tie rocket domes to man-rated chambers.

Finally, I thank my husband for his buoyant vision and loving support through my compulsive and drug-like obsession to journal his father's conversations, spinning history like cotton candy. I highlight my gratitude for his care to bolster both his father and me during the writing of this book.

ABOUT THE AUTHOR
Lynn Byk continues to live with her three boys, Mr. B, Pauly, and their dog, Jester, in the front range foothills of Colorado. If you liked this book, please give the author a good review. "LIKE" <u>Lynn Byk Author</u>, on Facebook to join the community or on Twitter get updates.

Living with a 98-Year-Old Rocket Scientist

Book Club Questions

1. In Joe's youth, he admired and envied Mr. Kimbal, the self-proclaimed, "self-made man." Do you think he was also able to become a self-made man? If so, do you think the stress he endured was worth it?

2. How much difference do you think the "bones" or decor of a house makes in the happiness or unhappiness of a home? Why?

3. Youth are conscripted into the army because they are at the optimal physical age to serve a national purpose. What do you think the purpose of Joe's life is? Are you awaiting a greater purpose to be realized in your own life or do you think your time has passed?

4. What kind of sacrifices did each person in this household have to make to gain belonging with each other and a loving community?

5. Considering the phrase, "familiarity breeds contempt," why do you think the relationship between Lynn and Mr. B worked so well?

6. What is the value of the gift Mr. B's children gave him by helping him to stay in his own home in his later years?

7. What do you think about the amnesty given to the German aerospace engineers in America?

8. "I told Polish jokes in elementary school, Mr. B. I never meant anything by them. Everyone was doing it. I didn't even know any Poles until sixth grade."

   "Well, that's the thing about communication. You might not intend any harm when you are speaking, but other people who hear your words may experience terror or pride or laughter depending upon their perspective. Communication is a funny thing. It's got to be thoughtful. If it's not, then an awful lot of forgiveness or alienation takes place."

Did Joe and Lynn's discussion regarding intentional communication have any effect on you?

9. Which of Mr. B's characteristics do you find most important in life: Exploration, Integrity, Dependency on fact and evidence, Humor, Hard Work, Bettering Oneself, Generosity or Meekness?

10. Can you name some of the risks described in this story that Mr. B experienced? What kinds of things did you learn from Joe about his needs?

11. How do you think being married to Maudie, an educated doctor's child, with a family title and privilege, affected Mr. B?

12. Do you think the elderly Byks' determination to help their children throughout adulthood was beneficial or detrimental to their relationship?

13. Can you name some ways Lynn changes in her year living with Mr. B?

14. What do you think the author meant by asserting 1 Timothy 5:4 at the end of January, saying she is "practicing"?

15. What kinds of treasures did each character find by sharing a home together in a cross-generational, cross-cultural situation?

Go to: http://www.CaptureBookstore.com
for our other Honest-To-Goodness book selections

A Personal Note:
I appreciate you taking the time to read my story. Readers buy books based on other readers' endorsements. I could use yours!

Please tell your friends about Mister B and rate my book if you enjoyed it. Also, I'd love to connect with you personally if you have some thoughts you would like to share with me on social media.

On Goodreads

Barnes & Noble ① ② ③ ④ ⑤ ⑥ ⑦ ⑧ ⑨ +

On Amazon:

I LOVE IT!

www.ingramcontent.com/pod-product-compliance
Lightning Source LLC
Chambersburg PA
CBHW080404300426
44113CB00015B/2402